"Of all the immortal geniuses of literature, none is personally s⟨⟩ is exasperating, and almost incredible, that he should be so. After all, he lived in the full daylight of the English Renaissance, in the well-documented reigns of Queen Elizabeth and King James I. He wrote thirty-six plays and [154] highly personal sonnets. He was connected with some of the best-known figures in the most conspicuous court in English history. Since his death, and particularly in the last century, he has been subjected to the greatest battery of organised research that has ever been directed upon a single person. And yet the greatest of all Englishmen, after this tremendous inquisition, still remains so close a mystery that even his identity can still be doubted." (1962)

– Hugh Trevor-Roper, Regius Professor of History at Oxford University; the British intelligence officer who tracked Hitler during WWII

"Perhaps we should despair of ever bridging the vertiginous expanse between the sublimity of the subject [Shakespeare] and the mundane inconsequence of the documentary record [of Shakspere of Stratford]." (1991)

– Samuel Schoenbaum, Distinguished Professor of Renaissance Studies, University of Maryland; president, Shakespeare Association of America

"It is plain . . . that the bard of our imagination was unknown to the men of that age." (1874)

– C. M. Ingleby, Founder Trustee of the Shakespeare Birthplace Trust

"I have never seen the slightest reason to doubt his [Mr. Shakspere's] authorship." (September 2007)

– Stanley Wells, CBE, Chairman, Shakespeare Birthplace Trust

"Why, in the face of so much evidence for reasonable doubt, do Birthplace Trust people refuse to consider the alternatives, and only reply with worn out clichés, cheap insults, pop psychoanalysis and *ad hominem* arguments? The answer is that they are defending both a quasi-religious orthodoxy and a fat living. If they allowed themselves any kind of doubt, whatever the evidence, it would threaten both their incomes and the beliefs in which they have invested their identities. If they can so glibly accuse doubters of snobbery and parricidal tendencies, we can in turn accuse them of being authoritarian personalities and/or hypocrites. The truth is they are afraid of the scholarship of the doubters, rarely read it, and continue to think that poking fun at Delia Bacon's infirmity... is a substitute for honesty and scholarly integrity. To ask the Shakespeare Birthplace Trust to openly research the question of doubt is like asking the College of Cardinals to honestly research the Resurrection. The issue for them is settled and like all good authoritarians they prefer to keep it that way." (November 2011)

– Robin Fox, University Professor of Social Theory, Rutgers University; Author, *Shakespeare's Education* (Laugwitz Verlag, 2012)

"The lack of any reasoned, evidence-based and impartial response from Stratfordian scholars to the suggestion that there is 'reasonable doubt' that the man from Stratford wrote the plays attributed to William Shakespeare surely blows an enormous hole in the orthodox argument. Instead, not only the credibility but the sanity of doubters is called into question. Academics' partiality and self-interest makes rational debate almost impossible. A healthy 'imagination' plus an alleged propensity to talk to strangers cannot explain the contents of the First Folio."

– Sir Derek Jacobi

"It is good that there is a book and place where people can learn why some of us doubt the attribution of the Shakespeare canon to William Shakspere of Stratford-upon-Avon. The Declaration of Reasonable Doubt, and now this book, may help to dispel some of the negative impressions and untruths being spread about authorship skeptics by the Shakespeare Birthplace Trust of Stratford-upon-Avon."

– Mark Rylance, Artistic Director (1995-2005), Shakespeare's Globe Theatre

"Stratfordians have long been wrong about Shakespeare, obstinately wrong since Delia Bacon, and absurdly wrong since the Declaration of Reasonable Doubt. They seem determined to be the last to recognize that 'the Emperor' is woefully under-clad. Every chapter in this powerful book is devastating to the orthodox case. One that stands out is Alexander Waugh's scathing critique of Stratfordian academics for their failure to recognize that the author must have been someone who traveled extensively in Italy and returned to tell us his story. This is a bombshell of a book!"

– Michael York, M.A., Oxford; Actor/Author

"Authorities tell us there is no doubt that Shakespeare wrote Shakespeare. Should we trust them? This book comes at a critical time, with defenders of orthodoxy deceiving the public about how weak their case really is. Their vulnerability leads them to slander the 'heretics,' comparing authorship doubters to Holocaust deniers and creationists. It is time to replace the *ad hominem* attacks with a serious re-examination of the evidence. This book does just that."

– Richard Waugaman, M.D., Clinical Professor of Psychiatry and Faculty Expert on Shakespeare for Media Contacts, Georgetown University, Washington, D.C.

"Shakespeare scholars should take the authorship debate much more seriously. Too often absurdities in the traditional attribution are dismissed with hand-waving references to the presumed power of 'genius.' After studying geniuses for more than three decades, I can say with confidence that even geniuses do not possess such supposed mysterious powers. The real author was a genuine human being deeply rooted in a biographical past. We will never understand his genius until we know the experiences that shaped his development."

– Dean Keith Simonton, Distinguished Professor of Psychology, University of California at Davis; Francis Galton Award for Outstanding Contributions to the Study of Creativity; author of 153 articles, 12 books, incl. *Origins of Genius*, and editor, *Handbook of Genius*

"Students from grade school to grad school delight in challenging long-held assumptions. There has never been a better time to re-examine the question of Shakespeare's identity. Shahan and Waugh's book makes the case for doubt about Shakspere easily accessible. The plays themselves provide details of geography, history, music, law, language, and literature that point to an author other than Shakspere. It is unreasonable not to doubt!"

– Ren Draya, Chair, Dept. of English & Communications, Blackburn College

"I have doubted that Shakspere of Stratford was Shakespeare the playwright for forty years— not because I am a snob, not because I am a conspiracy theorist, not because I scorn the idea of unprivileged genius but because I passionately love this playwright and want to know everything about the real man behind the plays. Now we have a book that assembles historical facts and rational arguments which should raise reasonable doubt in the minds of Stratfordian academics and shake their fanatical belief in the Stratford myth."

– Kristin Linklater, Professor of Theatre, Columbia University

"Academics have a responsibility to be rigorous and objective in questioning assumptions. Nothing is totally 'beyond doubt.' Shakespeare scholars need to consider *all* of the evidence, not just what supports our own views. That is what these authors do so ably, without pushing any personal agenda about the real author. The focus of this book is entirely on the evidence."

– Felicia Hardison Londré, Curators' Professor of Theatre, University of Missouri-Kansas City; Dean, College of Fellows of the American Theatre

"Scholars and students finally have a book that enables them to understand the hotly-contested Shakespearean Authorship Controversy without prejudice. The core arguments are clearly and persuasively made. The Italian plays emerge as a key to the issue, as do the author's multiple levels of education. We also come to understand why the author would have used a pseudonym. The layers of fantasy obscuring this greatest of all theatrical mysteries are finally lifting. Bravo!"

– Don Rubin, Professor of Theatre Studies and Former Chair, Department of Theatre, York University, Toronto; Editor, *World Encyclopedia of Contemporary Theatre*

"This book is a reasoned, well-informed response to a concerted effort by Stratfordian academics to bury the many good reasons to doubt that Mr. Shakspere was the author. For example, there is no other case, then or since, of a full-time working actor also being a prolific playwright. It is too exhausting. Such considerations are swept under the rug."

– William Rubinstein, Professor of History, University of Wales, Aberystwyth

"Students deserve to hear both sides of a controversy, and a professor worth his or her salt should be able and willing to present both sides. Let us hope that, at some universities, students of English literature will be encouraged to study the Shakespeare Authorship Question with open minds, and encouraged to draw their own conclusions."

– Peter A. Sturrock, Emeritus Professor of Applied Physics, Stanford University; author of *AKA Shakespeare: A Scientific Approach to the Authorship Question*

Shakespeare

Beyond Doubt?

Exposing an Industry in Denial

EDITED BY

**John M. Shahan
& Alexander Waugh**

FOR

The Shakespeare Authorship Coalition

Llumina
Press

Organized and Published by

The Shakespeare Authorship Coalition

John M. Shahan, Chairman and CEO

ISBN: 978-1-62550-033-5
     978-1-62550-034-2

Printed in the United States of America by Llumina Press

Library of Congress Control Number: 2013937770

**To students of Shakespeare at
colleges and universities everywhere**

Terminology and Spellings

This book makes a distinction between William Shakespeare, the author of the works that have come down to us under that name, whoever he was, and William Shakspere of Stratford-upon-Avon, the man traditionally said to have been the author of the works. Authorship doubters think the name "William Shakespeare" was a pseudonym, so the crux of the controversy is whether Shakespeare and Shakspere were the same person. In this book we use the following conventions:

William Shakespeare – refers to the author of the poems and plays and assumes the name is a pseudonym. The hyphenated form "Shake-speare" is also occasionally used.

William Shakspere – refers to the Stratford man whose role as an author is disputed. Also "Mr. Shakspere," "the Stratford man," "William of Stratford," etc.

Authorship doubter or skeptic – generic terms for those who doubt that Shakspere wrote the works of William Shakespeare; also "non-Stratfordian," "anti-Stratfordian."

Stratfordian – refers to those who attribute the works of William Shakespeare to Shakspere of Stratford-upon-Avon; also "orthodox," "traditional," "traditionalist."

Also, since the words in the main title of this book are the same as those in the book *Shakespeare Beyond Doubt* (SBD), edited by Paul Edmondson and Professor Stanley Wells (Cambridge University Press, 2013), we will refer to the two different books as:

The Stratfordian book, or the Birthplace Trust book – *Shakespeare Beyond Doubt*, Paul Edmondson and Stanley Wells, eds. (Cambridge University Press, 2013).

The Doubter book *Shakespeare Beyond Doubt?* (SBD?) – This book: *Shakespeare Beyond Doubt?*, John M. Shahan and Alexander Waugh, eds. (Llumina Press, 2013).

Birthplace Trust – The Shakespeare Birthplace Trust in Stratford-on-Avon, sponsoring organization of the Stratfordian book *Shakespeare Beyond Doubt.*

Coalition – The Shakespeare Authorship Coalition, sponsoring organization of this book.

Shakespeare Beyond Doubt? – Exposing an Industry in Denial
Edited by John M. Shahan and Alexander Waugh

CONTENTS

General Introduction and Challenge to the Shakespeare Birthplace Trust   i
    – John M. Shahan, Chairman, Shakespeare Authorship Coalition

Twenty-one Good Reasons to Doubt that Shakspere was "Shakespeare"   xi

Part I: Shakespeare Beyond Doubt?   1
Introduction to Part I: Overview of reasons to doubt – John M. Shahan   2

A. Who was Shakspere of Stratford?   13

1. The Man Who Was Never Shakespeare – A. J. Pointon, Ph.D.   14
2. Shakspere's Six Accepted Signatures: A comparison – Frank Davis, M.D.   29
3. The Missing Literary Paper Trail – from the landmark book by Diana Price   41
4. Shakspere in Stratford and London: Ten Eyewitnesses – Ramon Jiménez   46
5. Shakspere's Will: Missing the Mind of Shakespeare – Bonner Miller Cutting   58
6. The Rest is Silence: The absence of tributes to the author – A. J. Pointon, Ph.D.   69

B. Shakespeare's Vast Knowledge   71

7. Keeping Shakespeare Out of Italy – Alexander Waugh   72
8. Could Shakespeare Think Like a Lawyer? – Thomas Regnier, J.D., LL.M.   86
9. How did Shakespeare Learn the Art of Medicine? – Earl Showerman, M.D.   99

C. The First Folio and Stratford Monument   112

10. Shakespeare's Impossible Doublet – John M. Rollett, M.A., Ph.D.   113
11. The Ambiguous Ben Jonson – Richard F. Whalen   126
12. The Stratford Bust: A Monumental Fraud – Richard F. Whalen   136

Part II: Exposing an Industry in Denial: The Coalition responds to   152
    the Shakespeare Birthplace Trust's "60 Minutes With Shakespeare"

Conclusion and request to read and sign the Declaration of Reasonable Doubt   224

Appendices
A. Shakspere's Last Will and Testament – Bonner Miller Cutting   225
B. Stylometrics: How Reliable is it Really? – Ramon Jiménez   228
C. Social Network Theory and Shakespeare – Donald P. Hayes, Ph.D.   237
D. Heminge and Condell Letters in First Folio   249

Recommended reading   251
Acknowledgments and Contributors   252

General Introduction and Challenge
To the Shakespeare Birthplace Trust

By John M. Shahan

"First they ignore you, then they ridicule you, then they fight you, and then you win."

– Mahatma Gandhi

The Shakespeare Birthplace Trust in Stratford-upon-Avon claims in its book *Shakespeare Beyond Doubt* that there is no doubt that William Shakspere of Stratford wrote the works of William Shakespeare. This book questions that claim, so we have given it the nearly identical title *Shakespeare Beyond Doubt?* Since our two books present diametrically opposed views of the same subject, both should be read before reaching a conclusion.

This book is about evidence and arguments that contradict claims that there is "no room for doubt" that Mr. Shakspere of Stratford wrote the works of William Shakespeare. It is not about who we think the real author was, or what motivated him to remain hidden. It has nothing to do with the alternative scenario presented in the feature film *Anonymous.* Those looking for alternative candidates and sensational scenarios should look elsewhere. Our aim is a scholarly presentation of the case for "reasonable doubt" about Shakspere to make it understandable to the public and to the students to whom this book is dedicated. The only alternative we offer is that the name "William Shakespeare" was the pen name of some other person who chose to conceal his identity.

The threshold question in the authorship controversy is whether there is room for doubt about the traditional author from Stratford. If not, then there is no authorship issue. If there is reasonable doubt about him, then the issue should be regarded as legitimate in academia and in our public discourse, and scholars should be free to pursue it and students free to inquire, study and discuss it without being attacked and vilified as they are today. Answering this question is a necessary first step toward the ultimate goal of identifying and gaining recognition for the true author. It might seem like a step backward to those who are familiar with the evidence and think they already know Shakspere was not the author, but most people do not know that. To succeed, the public must be brought along.

The Birthplace Trust will not want you to read this book. They want to present their side of the issue as if it were the only side worth considering in this complex debate. In claiming that it is "beyond doubt" that Shakspere wrote the works of Shakespeare, they use legal language derived from our system of adversarial judicial proceedings. What is missing is the normal opportunity for the other side to present its case on an equal footing. By having twenty-two orthodox Shakespeare scholars present their view, and calling the resulting book *Shakespeare Beyond Doubt*, the Birthplace Trust assumes a quasi-judicial role—judge, prosecutor and jury—and renders a "verdict" that the issue has been resolved "beyond doubt." They want the field to themselves so they can argue from their perceived authority in order to suppress the issue without ever acknowledging the contrary evidence. Anyone who has served on a jury knows that if you hear only one side in a case it is easy to get a false impression. As a party to the dispute, the Birthplace Trust is in no position to adjudicate it. We, as another party to the dispute, demand our right to be heard.

One indication that the Birthplace Trust has a bias is how it frames the question: "Did Shakespeare write Shakespeare?" It's a trick question. Of course Shakespeare wrote Shakespeare. If that was the name on the title pages of the works, then by definition the author was Shakespeare, just as "Mark Twain" on a work means the author was Mark Twain. But who was Mark Twain? A man of that name, or a man using it as a pen name? In the case of Twain we know that the name was really the pen name of Samuel Clemens. Did Mark Twain write Mark Twain? Of course he did. That is a tautology, not a question.

John M. Shahan

Who *was* Mark Twain is a real question; and that is the correct way to frame the Shakespeare authorship question: Who *was* William Shakespeare? The Birthplace Trust claims that the names Shakspere and Shakespeare refer to a single person—William Shakspere of Stratford. The names are similar, but not the same; and even if they were the same, it still would not follow that they refer to the same person: that requires evidence. The Birthplace Trust book never addresses the possibility of a pseudonym, an omission that shows its authors had no intention of taking the question seriously.

There are important facts the Shakespeare Birthplace Trust never tells you about in its book: for example, (1) William Shakspere of Stratford-upon-Avon never used the name "Shakespeare" in his life, even when it would have been to his advantage to do so; (2) the only *alleged* writings in Shakspere's hand are signatures that are poorly executed; (3) Shakspere alone, of twenty-five top writers of the period, left no evidence of a writing career in ten categories of evidence still extant for other writers; (4) ten people who knew of both Shakspere and Shakespeare never connected the two; (5) not one thing in Shakspere's detailed will suggests he had been any sort of writer; (6) when Shakspere died in 1616, no fellow actor or writer paid any tribute to him or to "Shakespeare."

The above facts are not mentioned in the Birthplace Trust book, though it claims to be about the evidence. They are the subject matter of the first six chapters of this book, on the question "Who Was Shakspere of Stratford?" They are followed by three chapters on "Shakespeare's Vast Knowledge," focusing on knowledge of Italy, law and medicine found in the plays. The Birthplace Trust book simply ignores the problem that the vast knowledge found in the works, including in these specialized areas, poses for their claim.

The final three chapters in Part I of this book address the problems posed by the First Folio publication of Shakespeare's plays and the monument in the Stratford church. Thus Part I of this book has evidence and arguments the Birthplace Trust largely ignores, even though they are well known, and some of them have been known for centuries.

In addition to omitting evidence and arguments, what is included in the Birthplace Trust book is often distorted, misleading or even false. Let's take, for example, Chapter 7: "Allusions to Shakespeare to 1642," by Stanley Wells, Honorary President of the Birthplace Trust and co-editor of *Shakespeare Beyond Doubt*. Of mentions and allusions to Shakespeare up to Shakspere's death in 1616, Wells writes:

> despite the mass of evidence that the works were written by a man named William Shakespeare, there is none that explicitly and incontrovertibly identifies him with Stratford-upon-Avon.... (81)

Here Wells concedes that none of the allusions to "Shakespeare" up to 1616 explicitly identifies the author as a man from Stratford. Yet he says they show the works were written by "a man named Shakespeare." They do not; they show the works were *published* under that name, and so people referred to the author by that name, just as people talked about Mark Twain. None of the many allusions Wells cites proves that anyone knew the author personally. Wells simply assumes that every allusion to the author Shakespeare is a reference to Shakspere. He never mentions the possibility of a pen name, even though that is what the argument is all about. If Shakespeare were a pen name, it would help explain why no one seems to have known him.

Wells also writes:

> The death of 'William Shakespeare gent.' recorded in the Stratford registers for 1616 is memorialized in the monument and epitaphs which clearly identify the Stratford man as a great writer.... On a literary level, the death was mourned in an elegy first printed in a collection of John Donne's poems in 1633, but certainly written by 1623, if not earlier. (81)

First, the name in the burial register is not "William Shakespeare," it is "Will Shakspere." This is seen in the Stratford church records at the end of Chapter 1 of this book: "The Man Who Was Never Shakespeare," by A.J. Pointon (p. 27). Here is the image of the actual burial record:

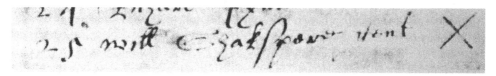

Stratford parish burial register showing "Will Shakspere gent.," April 25, 1616

It is one thing to argue (doubtfully) that the two names are the same in spite of the different spellings, but quite another to falsify the name and put it in quotation marks.*

Second, Wells says Shakspere's death was mourned in an elegy first printed "in 1633, but certainly written by 1623, if not earlier." It is not at all clear that the elegy was written as early as 1623; more importantly, however, 1623 was more than seven years after Shakspere's death, and it is the *only* example he provides of an elegy, other than in the First Folio. Seen in that context, the elegy looks more like part of a cover up that took place in 1623 than someone mourning a death that occurred seven years earlier in 1616. Wells pays no heed to the significant fact—the incredible anomaly—that there were no tributes to the author Shakespeare at the time of Shakspere's death in 1616.

Wells also writes:

> Opposite the title-page engraving by Martin Droeshout is placed a short poem by "B.I." —in context, clearly Ben Jonson—praising it as a likeness. (84)

It is also not clear that the short poem by Ben Jonson opposite the Droeshout engraving praises it as a "likeness." It ends with "Reader, looke/ Not on his Picture, but his Booke." In other words, the poem tells readers to ignore the engraving (see Chapters 10 and 11 of this book.)

Wells continues:

> No one expressed doubt that [William Shakspere of Stratford] wrote the works attributed to him—give or take a few suggestions that some of the plays might have been written in collaboration with other professional writers, as was extremely common at the time—until the middle of the nineteenth century. We know more about him than we know about many of his contemporaries, such as John Lyly, Thomas Kyd, John Webster or John Ford. (87)

No one expressed doubt that Shakspere wrote the works during his lifetime because no one ever suggested he did in the first place. Wells never shows that anyone ever said he did. One does not bother to deny something unless there is reason to think it in the first place. Does the fact that no one has expressed doubt that I am a king mean that I am one?

People did express doubt about the identity of the author Shakespeare at the time, and after Shakspere's death. See the seven examples cited in our answer to "Question 40: When did people start to question Shakespeare's authorship. . ." in Part II of this book.

---

* This is not the only example of the falsification of the spelling of the name in the records in the Stratfordian book *Shakespeare Beyond Doubt*. See the introduction to Part I, Section A (page 13).

It is true that collaboration among writers was common at the time, but no document shows that Shakespeare ever collaborated in person with anyone. There are only inferences based on stylometrics—a problematic discipline discussed further below.

Yes, we do know a lot about Shakspere. The problem is not *how much* we know, but *what* we know. Some seventy documents relate to him, but all are non-literary. How is it that Wells fails to mention that none of these documents supports the point of his book?

As for knowing more about him than we do about Lyly, Kyd, Webster and Ford, that would hardly be significant, even if it were true. They were all much less important. Yet there is enough literary evidence to show that each of them was a writer, writing in his own name. There is nothing similar for Shakspere or Shakespeare. Where are all of the literary documents one would expect to find for the leading court dramatist of the "King's Men?" Given his alleged prominence over a long period, and all of the research focusing on him, it is no wonder Professor Trevor-Roper found his elusiveness "exasperating and almost incredible."

Wells again:

> There are certainly gaps in the records of Shakespeare's life, but there is nothing unusual about them. (87)

This is false. Shakspere's supposed literary career is all one giant gap. He is unique in this regard (see Chapter 3 in this book: "The Missing Literary Paper Trail").

The Birthplace Trust book makes much of the idea that Shakespeare collaborated with other writers, a claim based entirely on stylometric evidence. The point of this claim is that "collaboration" means they worked together, which means his collaborators would have known who he was, and so he must have been Shakspere of Stratford or someone would have said something. We point out repeatedly in this book that the more orthodox scholars claim direct collaboration between Shakespeare and other writers the odder it is that (1) there is no documentary evidence of the alleged collaboration—not even so much as a letter exchanged between Shakespeare and any fellow writer, (2) none of the alleged collaborators wrote tributes to Shakespeare when Shakspere died in 1616, and (3) none of the alleged collaborators who were living in 1623 was among those who wrote elegies to Shakespeare in the First Folio. The silence of the putative collaborators speaks volumes.

This book does not include a chapter on stylometrics—a complex and difficult subject for most readers. But it does include an appendix for those who are interested—Appendix B: "Stylometrics: How Reliable is it Really?" It makes the point that if different stylometricians find different collaborators on the same play their findings are unreliable. In Part II, we also include our rebuttals to the answers of Gary Taylor, Eric Rasmussen, Peter Kirwan and MacDonald P. Jackson to questions 24, 25, 26 and 27 in the Birthplace Trust's "60 Minutes with Shakespeare" (September 2011, described below), all dealing with collaboration and stylometrics. Jackson and Rasmussen also have chapters in the Birthplace Trust book. The points we made in our four rebuttals are our reply to them.

For the general reader, we would say that Stylometrics involves comparing the style of one person's writing in a piece known to have been written by him with the style of another piece to see if he was the author. In statistical terms the mismatch between the writing styles of Shakspere and Shakespeare is infinite, because we have nothing known to have been written by Shakspere.

I'd like to say something about my own involvement with stylometric research, since I've put much time and effort over the past decade into refuting claims that every alternative authorship candidate has now been eliminated by the results of stylometrics. My conviction that they are wrong helps to explain why I feel so strongly about the issue.

I am a scientist. I first trained in the natural sciences and mathematics, then in the social and behavioral sciences, and then in health planning, policy analysis and research. In each of these disciplines, I focused on research methods, research design and statistics. Once one learns research methods and statistics as well as I did, one doesn't easily forget. The first time I read an article on stylometrics, back in 2001, it was clear to me that there were imperfections in the research design, any one of which could invalidate the study's conclusion. I wrote an article which appeared as a letter to the editor in the next issue.

One of the two authors of the article I had critiqued, Professor Ward E.Y. Elliott, wrote a nice reply agreeing with some of my points, but not entirely agreeing with others. In the years since, he and I have gone back and forth in a series of letters and contentious articles, now totaling nine, I believe, in the annual journal of an authorship organization. In some of them we fight like cats and dogs over issues key to the validity of his results.

In 2009, I challenged him to a debate at the Shakespeare Authorship Roundtable of Los Angeles, the original sponsor of his study, and he graciously agreed to participate. The contest was held at the Beverly Hills Library, with some forty people in attendance. A narrow majority thought I won, but the same people had favored my position going in, so nobody's mind was changed. In that sense the outcome was a not-so-surprising draw.

If nothing else, it should at least be clear that this authorship doubter is not at all intimidated by Stratfordian stylometricians with computers. If the Birthplace Trust wants to fight this issue out on that ground, it will be fine with me.

As luck would have it, Professor Elliott and I both live in the same community, and we see each other occasionally. Despite our sharp differences, we are on good terms. I do not believe he would deny that I have been a worthy, at times formidable, opponent. One does not write many articles in reply to, or bother to debate, an unworthy opponent. [Nor does one write a book in response to one.]

What I've said so far is probably enough of an introduction to this book for most readers. Most general introductions would end here, but because this issue is so contentious I have decided to use this book to issue a challenge that I've long planned to issue at some point. What is the challenge and what makes me think I have standing to issue such a challenge? For those who are interested, the rest of this general introduction answers those questions.

The Coalition and the Declaration of Reasonable Doubt

Why did the Shakespeare Birthplace Trust feel compelled to write a book at this time, claiming that it is "beyond doubt" that William Shakspere of Stratford wrote the works? The modern authorship controversy has lasted for more than one hundred and fifty years. The Birthplace Trust and its allies have already had ample opportunity to make their case. The answer is that the evidence is not nearly as clear as they say, and increasing numbers of very credible and even prominent people are questioning it, and speaking up about it.

But doubters have always included such people. The list of notable past doubters is long and distinguished. The Birthplace Trust never wrote a book in response to them. What is different now?

What's different is that doubters are becoming increasingly organized around a strategy of focusing first on the weakness of the case for Shakspere in order to *legitimize* the authorship issue, rather than trying to solve it outright by advancing another candidate. Doubters increasingly recognize that Stratfordian academics have a strong vested interest in the *status quo*, and that they are much better at spotting specks in the eyes of doubters than logs in their own eyes that blind them

John M. Shahan

to the huge problems with their own candidate. In such a climate it is futile to try to promote any alternative candidate in the absence of incontrovertible evidence. Lacking that, solving the authorship controversy is a two-step process, and the first step is to legitimize it in academia so scholars feel free to pursue it. How does one legitimize the issue? By greatly increasing public awareness that, despite what Stratfordians claim, there are good reasons to doubt that Shakspere was the author.

This is the strategy of the still relatively new Shakespeare Authorship Coalition, incorporated as a private, non-profit educational charity in the State of California in 2006, and of which I am founder, chairman and CEO. The Coalition is best known as the issuer of the *Declaration of Reasonable Doubt About the Identity of William Shakespeare*—a 3000-word statement that can be read and signed at our website at: DoubtAboutWill.org. The press release announcing the Stratfordian book *Shakespeare Beyond Doubt* refers to the "renowned" Declaration of Reasonable Doubt, and features a chapter on it in its table of contents. So it is clear that their book is, at least in part, in response to the Declaration.

Another manifestation of the increasing doubts about the identity of the author is the Roland Emmerich film *Anonymous*, released in the fall of 2011. The Birthplace Trust initiated its current campaign against doubters with a new website on September 1, 2011, two months prior to the release of *Anonymous*. The campaign featured an audio website, "60 Minutes with Shakespeare," with 60 actors, writers and scholars each addressing one of 60 questions in 60 seconds each. Although the immediate impetus for the new website was the approaching launch of the film, and uncertainty about how it might be perceived, it was clear that "60 Minutes with Shakespeare" targeted the entire authorship movement. Roland Emmerich got one of the "60 Minutes," but none of the others dealt with the film, and all except Emmerich were supporters of the orthodox view that Shakspere was Shakespeare.

Recognizing the threat, but also the opportunity to expose their poor scholarship, I initiated a collaborative effort to write rebuttals to the "60 Minutes." In just ten weeks, thirty-seven of the best scholars in the authorship movement, including several notable academics, wrote rebuttals to each of the Birthplace Trust's "60 Minutes." The resulting report, entitled *Exposing an Industry in Denial* ("*Exposing*") presents the rebuttals that resulted from this effort. The original version of *Exposing* is available as a pdf download at the Coalition website at DoubtAboutWill. org/exposing. A slightly abbreviated version** is included as Part II of this book.

Did the Coalition take a position on *Anonymous*? No, we did not, since the film is about an alternative candidate. To the extent that *Anonymous* increased awareness of the controversy, we are pleased it was made. Speaking for myself, however, I wish the film had not included so many historical inaccuracies. Of course any filmmaker must exercise a certain amount of artistic license, but in such a contentious environment the inaccuracies rendered *Anonymous* vulnerable to attack.*** Even many supporters of Roland Emmerich's alternative candidate disagreed with the scenario he presented, dividing that community of doubters.

** The main difference is that six questions relating to three alternative candidates are not included in this book. As a coalition of organizations and individuals backing various alternative candidates, or none, we take no position on alternative candidates. Supporters of the three candidates attacked in "60 Minutes" were allowed to reply, but this book deals only with the Stratford man.

*** A funny thing happened as a result of one attack on *Anonymous*—a Stratfordian organization inadvertently acknowledged the excellence of the scholarship of a doubter organization. How so? The *Shakespeare Gesellschaft*, a scholarly organization devoted to the Stratford man, sponsored a competition to identify errors of historical fact in *Anonymous*, with the winning entry to be posted on its website. Unbeknownst to them, the *Neue Shake-speare Gesellschaft*, a doubter organization, submitted an entry and won first prize! The winning entry identified forty-nine inaccuracies and is posted in English at the NSG website at: http://shake-speare-today.de/front_content.php?idart=691.

Perhaps the most important contribution of *Anonymous* was that it elicited a response from the Birthplace Trust. Rather than ignoring and ridiculing, they attacked. One does not attack an opponent who poses no threat. In attacking doubters, they have legitimized us, and the authorship controversy, and given us an opportunity to respond. We put "60 Minutes with Shakespeare" to shame with *Exposing an Industry in Denial*, and we think we've done the same here with our response to *Shakespeare Beyond Doubt*.

The Declaration of Reasonable Doubt was launched in April of 2007 in same-day signing ceremonies at the Geffen Playhouse in Los Angeles, and at Concordia University's Shakespeare Authorship Studies Conference in Portland, Oregon. Signers at the Los Angeles event were ten founding members of the Shakespeare Authorship Roundtable. The signers in Portland were ten Concordia University faculty members and executives.

Five months later it was launched in the U.K. in Chichester, West Sussex, in a signing event featuring Coalition patrons Derek Jacobi and Mark Rylance immediately after a performance of Rylance's play about the authorship question, "I Am Shakespeare." The event coincided with the advent of Brunel University's master's degree program in Authorship Studies under Dr. William Leahy, then Head of English at Brunel University. That combination gained coverage throughout the U.K. and the English-speaking world.

Birthplace Trust Chairman Stanley Wells wrote to *The Stage* magazine attacking the Declaration and warning Jacobi and Rylance that they risked insanity, like Delia Bacon. Rylance replied in a letter in *The Stage* and in a rebuttal on the Coalition website.

In 2009, the *Wall Street Journal* published an article on Supreme Court Justices' views on the authorship issue, focusing on then-Justice John Paul Stevens. In addition to Stevens, Justice Antonin Scalia and former Justice Sandra Day O'Connor were doubters. Stevens and O'Connor signed the Declaration.

In April 2010, we were mentioned favorably in James Shapiro's *Contested Will* (218-19). He said good things about the Declaration and offered no direct rebuttal, but it was clearly a warning to his colleagues about the dangers of ignoring an organization like ours in the age of the Internet.

In October 2010, there was a signing event at the Oregon Shakespeare Festival in Ashland, Oregon, featuring OSF Executive Director Paul Nicholson, long-time OSF actor James Newcomb, and several other actors and directors and prominent theater professors.

Later in 2010 actor Keir Cutler produced a YouTube video about the Declaration, viewed over 16,000 times. In 2011 we added an audio recording of Michael York reading the Declaration. That brings us up to the 2011 response to *Anonymous* already discussed.

Why is the Birthplace Trust so concerned about the Declaration of Reasonable Doubt? Because it is a major threat to their ability to continue suppressing the authorship issue. The Birthplace Trust and its allies have long pursued a deliberate strategy to stigmatize and suppress it. First, they claim there is "no doubt" that Mr. Shakpere wrote the works. So there must be another reason why authorship doubters continue to promote heresies. They launch into *ad hominem* attacks, alleging that authorship doubters are all defective, either in our mental capabilities (intelligence, rationality, sanity, etc.) or in our character, e.g., that we're all class snobs who can't accept that a commoner could be a great writer.

None of this is true, of course, but the strategy has largely succeeded. The authorship issue is now effectively delegitimized and stigmatized. In much of academia it has become a taboo subject. If there is no room for doubt about Will Shakspere, then considering alternatives is inherently irrational, and authorship doubters of all persuasions can be summarily dismissed. Rather than deal with contrary evidence, they can intimidate and marginalize authorship doubters with ridicule. The fact that there is a great deal of evidence contradicting their claims about Shakspere, and *no* empirical evidence supporting their allegations about doubters, is simply ignored. The Birthplace Trust and its allies have been able to argue from authority with impunity. Understandably, those in the media often feel just as intimidated as academic dissenters.

The Declaration of Reasonable Doubt challenges head-on the claim that there is no doubt. To continue suppressing the authorship issue, the Birthplace Trust must distract attention from (1) the evidence, and (2) the fact that highly credible people are doubters. The Declaration calls great attention to both in a way that had not been done before.

The Declaration was written to (1) make the issue accessible to a wider audience by providing a concise, definitive presentation of the evidence for and against Shakspere, (2) call increased attention to the many prominent doubters of the past, and (3) provide a way for present-day doubters, especially prominent ones, to put themselves on the record. In effect, the Declaration first counters the false negative stereotype by naming the twenty prominent past doubters, then presents the evidence and arguments that made them doubt, and then invites present-day doubters to take their stand with the prominent past doubters.

The Declaration is factual in content and moderate in tone and in its conclusions. It was written to be objective and eminently reasonable to belie the negative Stratfordian stereotype of doubters and maximize the number of people who would be willing to sign. It was also written to unite doubters behind something we agree on: "reasonable doubt." Its narrative format accommodates an enormous amount of factual information. Some three dozen scholars spent four years writing it, and it still holds up well after six years.

I want to respond to characterizations of the Declaration as an online "petition." The Declaration is not a petition. A petition is addressed to and recognizes the authority of some body to decide a question, and it requests that they decide it in a particular way. The American colonies did not "petition" King George III, asking him to give them their independence; they *declared* their independence from England, whether he liked it or not. Our Declaration is exactly what its title says it is—a declaration—a statement, issued on the authority of signatories, and, as stated in its opening line, addressed to "Shakespeare lovers everywhere, as well as to those who are encountering him for the first time." It is emphatically *not* addressed to the orthodox Shakespeare academic establishment, which has abdicated its responsibility to deal with the authorship issue in a fair, objective way.

The Declaration is not a document that many people sign casually, nor should it be. Unlike most petitions, it contains much information that will be new to most people, since its main purpose is to educate. Most signatories appear to be knowledgeable about the issue by the time they sign it. They are taking a stand—a highly visible public stand. Some do so in spite of significant risks involved; the guardians of orthodoxy are vigilant. The remarkable thing is the number and quality of Declaration signatories in spite of this. We have signatories from almost every field. But the largest single category, both among all college graduates and among current and former college/university faculty members, is those in English Literature—this in spite of efforts to indoctrinate and/or intimidate them.

To those who belittle our 2,600 signatories, over 2,000 of them college graduates, 950 with advanced degrees, 36 notables (including two U.S. Supreme Court Justices) and academics from every field—many outstanding in their field—and including our very best Shakespearean actors, I would ask where are your signatories? Where is your declaration? I have asked for one repeatedly. Now you respond with a book that argues from authority. Like James Shapiro in

Contested Will, you offer no direct rebuttal to our Declaration—not even in your chapter on it. As near as I can tell, you have twenty-two scholars ready to sign on to your point of view. Why are so many English professors unable to write a declaration to compete with ours? Just fifty-six people signed the Declaration of Independence, pledging their Lives, their Fortunes and their sacred Honor. We have enough to challenge you to prove your claim.

Challenge to the Shakespeare Birthplace Trust

Since the Birthplace Trust is so enamored of stylometrics, I begin this section with a quote from Harold Love's landmark book on the subject: *Attributing Authorship: An Introduction* (Cambridge University Press, 2002):

> evidence gained from quantitative analysis has to submit itself to a broader, rhetorically conducted system of assessment. Its influence within this process . . . is not a substitute for the adjudicatory process but a contributor to it, and is ultimately bound by its rules. The stylometrist is an expert witness—not a learned judge. (210)

We agree, and more generally, as we said earlier, the Birthplace Trust, as a party to the authorship dispute, is in no position to adjudicate it. We are happy to have their representatives as expert witnesses, provided we also have an opportunity to be heard and a chance to cross examine them. We hereby challenge the Birthplace Trust to prove its claim that it is beyond doubt that William Shakspere of Stratford-upon-Avon wrote the works of William Shakespeare.

We challenge them to do this in a quasi-judicial proceeding—a mock trial before an impartial panel of judges and jurors. There have been previous trials and debates, but none that addresses this specific question. As the party claiming that the matter is beyond doubt, the Birthplace Trust should bear the burden of proving its claim and should prove it "beyond a reasonable doubt."****

Indeed, the Birthplace Trust asserts not just that the matter is beyond doubt, but that it is so clear and incontrovertible that "Shakspere wrote Shakespeare" that anyone who disagrees should be regarded as unfit to serve on the faculty of any English department at an institution of higher learning, or to teach Shakespeare in any high school English class. If it is really so clear, the Birthplace Trust should welcome the opportunity to expose us, once and for all, in order to finally put the Shakespeare authorship issue behind them.

The Birthplace Trust and its allies compare doubters to Holocaust deniers and to creationists who advocate teaching so-called "intelligent design" alongside evolution in biology classes. The contest over intelligent design versus evolution provides a model for the sort of trial we have in mind. In 2004, the Dover, Pennsylvania, school board ordered its science teachers to tell students that intelligent design was an alternative to evolution. Parents filed a lawsuit accusing the board of violating the separation of church and state.

The trial that followed, *Kitzmiller v. Dover*, was the first legal test of intelligent design as a scientific theory, with the plaintiffs arguing that it is thinly veiled creationism. At the trial, lawyers for the plaintiffs showed that evolution is one of the best-tested, most thoroughly confirmed theories in the history of science, and that its unresolved questions are normal research problems—the type that will arise in any flourishing scientific field.

The U.S. Public Broadcasting Service science program *NOVA* filmed parts of it, did interviews, and made the documentary "Judgment Day: Intelligent Design on Trial." It has "a

---

**** This challenge will also be communicated in a letter to Peter Kyle, OBE, Chairman of the Shakespeare Birthplace Trust, along with a copy of this book prior to its date of publication.

powerful scientific message at its core," said executive producer Paula Apsell. "Evolution is one of the most essential yet least understood of all scientific theories.... We felt it was important ... to heighten public understanding of what constitutes science and what does not, and ... what is acceptable for inclusion in the science curriculum...."

We would welcome the opportunity to have our proposed mock trial filmed and made into a documentary to educate students and the public if anyone is willing to do so. We believe that if the Birthplace Trust is sincere in its claims, they will welcome it too.

The Coalition will solicit proposals from organizations interested in hosting the proposed trial. We will post a request for proposals (RFP) on our website, but interested parties should send an initial expression of interest to the email address at the Coalition website by September 1, 2013, and then plan to submit a final proposal by November 1, with a copy to the Shakespeare Birthplace Trust. Examples of organizations from which we would like to receive proposals are the four Inns of Court (law schools) in London—Gray's Inn, the Inner Temple, Lincoln's Inn and the Middle Temple; the Literary and Continuing Education Committee of the Association of the Bar of the City of New York; and American University in Washington, D.C., host of the moot court trial before three U.S. Supreme Court Justices in 1987, in cooperation with the U.S. Supreme Court Bar. We would also welcome the suggestions and participation of PBS and the BBC.

Proposals should include provisions for guaranteeing the impartiality of judges and jurors and for sufficient time to explore complex issues and cross-examine witnesses. They should also include a statement of the specific question to be adjudicated and of the rules that would apply. An example of an approach would be to place it in the context of a hypothetical criminal trial, with all of the rules that normally apply in such trials in effect. Specific question: "If writing the works were a crime, would there be enough evidence to convict Mr. Shakspere of having committed that crime beyond a reasonable doubt?" The Birthplace Trust would prosecute Mr. Shakspere, while the Coalition would defend him. It would be billed as "The Trial of William Shakspere." There are probably other formats and other ways to frame the question to achieve a valid test of the Birthplace Trust claim.

An ideal scenario might involve a one-week trial (during a summer break so well-qualified attorneys and judges would be able to participate) with presentations of opening arguments on a Sunday so members of the public could attend; then two 2-hour sessions per day Monday and Tuesday with the prosecution presenting its case the first hour and cross-examination by the defense the second hour; then two 2-hour sessions per day Wednesday and Thursday with the defense presenting its case the first hour then cross-examined by the prosecution the second hour; then Friday off so both sides could prepare strong final arguments for presentation on Saturday, again with some members of the public present. We would envision a panel of three impartial judges—one chosen by each side, with the two of them selecting a third judge to preside—and twelve neutral law students as jurors, both groups rendering verdicts.

For examples of what might be included in the Coalition's legal brief, read the next section: "Twenty-one Good Reasons to Doubt that Shakspere was 'Shakespeare.'"

— John M. Shahan, Chairman, Shakespeare Authorship Coalition

Works Cited

Edmondson, Paul, and Stanley Wells, eds.: *Shakespeare Beyond Doubt: Evidence, Argument, Controversy* (Cambridge University Press, 2013).
Love, Harold: *Attributing Authorship: An Introduction* (Cambridge University Press, 2002).
Shapiro, James: *Contested Will: Who Wrote Shakespeare?* (New York: Simon & Schuster, 2010).

Twenty-one Good Reasons to Doubt that Shakspere was "Shakespeare"

1. People often think Shakspere *claimed* to have written the works. No such record exists. Nor did any family member or descendant ever claim that he was the author Shakespeare. (Not that either of his daughters would have left such a record, since neither could write.) No contemporary indicated that they thought of him as the author until long after he died. At least ten people who knew of both Shakspere and the author never connected the two.

2. During the lifetime of William of Stratford (1564-1616), nobody ever claimed to have met the poet-dramatist Shakespeare. A few people indicated at the time that they thought the name was a pseudonym. Orthodox scholars ignore the possibility of a pen name and treat every occurrence of the name Shakespeare as a reference to Mr. Shakspere, but no reference to the author specifically identified Shakspere of Stratford during his lifetime.

3. Contrary to the popular perception that Shakespeare became a prominent public figure, no record shows that he ever addressed the public directly (after his first two dedications) and none shows that either Elizabeth I, or James I, ever met him, or mentioned his name. As a professional actor, we do not know any role he ever played in any play on any date. Nor does any contemporary record say that anyone ever saw him act in any of his plays.

4. Not one play, not one poem, not even a letter in Shakspere's hand has ever been found. Very few authorial manuscripts of plays or poems from the period survive, but no letters? Mr. Shakspere divided his time between London and Stratford—a situation conducive to correspondence. We have letters for most other major writers of the period, and even for some lesser ones. How is it that *not one* survived for the most prolific writer of them all?

5. William Shakspere of Stratford-upon-Avon never spelled his name "Shakespeare" in his life, and his name also was probably not pronounced the same as the author's name. There is a clear, consistent difference between the spelling of the author's name on the works and the spellings of Mr. Shakspere's family name in the Stratford church records. Even the orthodox used to make the distinction, but now pretend the names are the same.

6. The only writings said to be in Shakspere's hand are six shaky, inconsistent signatures on legal documents. If these signatures are his, they reveal that he experienced difficulty signing his name. Some experts doubt they are his and say they were done by law clerks. No two are spelled the same way, and some say no two letters are formed the same way. His signatures compare badly with those of known writers and most actors at the period.

7. Nobody knows how Mr. Shakspere acquired the vast knowledge found in the works. The range would be remarkable for any man, let alone someone who never traveled or went to university. Not that a commoner, even in the rigid caste system of Elizabethan England, could not have managed to do it somehow, but how could it have happened without leaving a single trace? All we get from traditional biographers is speculation.

8. Orthodox scholars, unable to account for how the author acquired his knowledge, fall back on the idea that he was a "genius," and attribute it to his exceptional "imagination." But even a genius must *acquire* knowledge and cannot do it by simply imagining things. Academic experts on geniuses see little reason to think that Mr. Shakspere was a genius.

9. The orthodox claim that we know more about Shakspere than other writers of his time. The problem is not *how much* we know, but *what* we know. Over 70 documents relate to him, but all are non-literary—church records, business dealings, lawsuits. It is incredible to think all of these records survived, but all relating to his alleged literary career are lost.

10. The orthodox claim that the plays and poems prove Shakespeare was from Stratford. If he was born and raised in Stratford until he was well over twenty-one, he would have had a Warwickshire accent and dialect. Yet these are both totally absent from the works. The works use neither the language, nor the history, nor the geography of Warwickshire.

11. Mr. Shakspere was a money-conscious businessman who repeatedly sued over small amounts of money. Yet he never sued over any pirated edition of his alleged plays, and nothing shows that the author was ever paid to write, or that he ever published any play.

12. Mr. Shakspere had a hard time getting approval for his application for a coat of arms. This makes little sense if he was the celebrated poet, author of *Venus and Adonis* and *Lucrece,* and had a noble patron. Warwickshire poet Michael Drayton, for example, had no trouble getting a coat of arms.

13. Shakespeare, the poet, wrote no commendatory verse to anyone, and no one wrote any to him until long after Mr. Shakspere died in 1616. The mutual silence is very odd, especially for a playwright who is said to have actively collaborated with other writers.

14. Allegedly a prominent playwright under James I, Shakspere was seldom present in London. Never in his career did he own a home in London or move his family there. Early in the reign of James I, records place him in Stratford while the plays were being performed at court.

15. Mr. Shakspere's detailed will contains *nothing* that suggests he was any sort of writer—no books, plays, poems, letters, writing materials, or intellectual property of any kind. Nothing about it suggests in any way that this was a man who lived an intellectual life.

16. When Will Shakspere died in 1616, no one seemed to notice. Not so much as a letter refers to the author's passing. If he were Shakespeare, he would have been memorialized by his literary peers. Even the fellow actors mentioned in his will had no known reaction.

17. The First Folio edition of Shakespeare's plays, published seven years after Shakspere died, and the monument erected in the Stratford church, appear to be part of a deception to give the impression that Shakspere had been the author of the plays. Supporting evidence for this claim is provided in Chapters 10-12 of this book.

18. Mr. Shakspere was supposedly a full-time actor, performing in different plays several times a week, outdoors in English weather and on annual extended tours to the provinces. He was

a theater shareholder, responsible for the business. He maintained two households three days' journey apart, commuting over bad Elizabethan roads. Yet he is also supposed to have written thirty-seven plays, nearly all of them requiring extensive research often in foreign languages. There is no other example, then or since, of a still-working actor writing plays.

19. If the evidence were really as clear as orthodox scholars claim, they would just *make* it clear. Instead they engage in personal attacks against anyone who disagrees with them. They promote a false stereotype of doubters, and this calls their credibility into question. These tactics of traditional scholars, and especially of the Shakespeare Birthplace Trust, are intended to stigmatize and suppress the authorship issue and make it a taboo subject. The SBT has a clear conflict of interest and no basis to claim to be neutral and objective.

20. By claiming that it is "beyond doubt" that Shakspere of Stratford wrote the works of Shakespeare, the SBT implies that the issue has now been adjudicated and resolved; but if they had to prove their case beyond doubt in an impartial forum, they could not do so. No impartial body has ever ruled "beyond doubt" that Will Shakspere was Shakespeare.

21. A petition from Cuthbert Burbage to the Lord Chamberlain, Philip Herbert, provides strong evidence that William of Stratford was known as a player, but not as a playwright.

This requires some explanation. In 1635, Cuthbert Burbage, brother of the famous actor Richard Burbage, had to prepare a petition to the Lord Chamberlain, then Philip Herbert, Earl of Pembroke and Montgomery, in a legal case. Richard and Cuthbert Burbage were the founder-investors in the Globe Theatre in 1599, and William Shakspere was a sharer. So Cuthbert knew Shakspere, and surely knew the role he played in the acting company. In the petition, Cuthbert names those who risked their money by investing in the Globe, referring to "Shakspere," and "Shakspeare," as one of several "deserving men" and also as one of several "men players." These terms don't make it sound like Cuthbert thought of him as the poet-playwright Shakespeare, but rather just another member of the acting company.

Perhaps most important is the two spellings of the name, both without a medial "e." By 1635, after the publication of the first two Folios, the name "Shakespeare" was well known, and would always have been spelled that way in print, as Burbage surely knew. Furthermore, the man to whom he was writing—the Lord Chamberlain, Philip Herbert—was one of the two dedicatees, with his brother William, of the First and Second Folios. If Burbage knew that the "deserving man" and "man player" was also their playwright, one would expect that he would have (1) spelled his name "Shakespeare," and (2) made some reference to this Shakespeare being the one whose plays had been published in the First Folio (1623), and the Second Folio (1632), both dedicated to Philip and his brother. This would have greatly strengthened the force of his petition. The fact that he did not do so suggests that he knew his fellow actor-sharer was not the author William Shakespeare.

For all of these reasons, most of which are not addressed in *Shakespeare Beyond Doubt*, the Shakespeare authorship controversy should be regarded as legitimate. We hope you agree after considering the evidence and arguments presented in this book.

Part I:

Shakespeare Beyond Doubt?

Introduction to Part I: Shakespeare Beyond Doubt? – Overview of reasons to doubt Shakspere's authorship

By John M. Shahan*

> "Perhaps a few apparent incongruities could be explained away, if taken in isolation; but there are so many!"
>
> – Shakespeare Authorship Coalition, Declaration of Reasonable Doubt

A full presentation of the reasons to doubt that William Shakspere of Stratford-upon-Avon was the author William Shakespeare is beyond the scope of this book. Here we provide an overview of the more important reasons that are addressed in the twelve chapters in Part I. We also recommend reading *The Man Who Was Never Shakespeare*, by Professor A.J. Pointon (Parapress, 2011); *Shakespeare's Unorthodox Biography*, by Diana Price (revised paperback edition: shakespeare-authorship.com, 2012); and *The Shakespeare Guide To Italy: Retracing the Bard's Unknown Travels*, by Richard Paul Roe (HarperPerennial, 2011). All three are recent, and all are neutral about the true identity of the author of the Shakespeare canon, as is this book, except we all agree that there are good reasons to doubt Shakspere.

As a rule, an author's name correctly identifies the author—i.e., the name on the title page is that of the real author. There really was an author named Charles Dickens; there really is an author named Danielle Steel. The use of an authorial name on a book is evidence, even strong evidence, of that person's authorship. But it is not conclusive proof of authorship; if it were, we would have to believe that there existed real persons named Mark Twain, George Eliot and Currer Bell. Those names, of course, are the pseudonyms used by Samuel Clemens, Mary Ann Evans and Charlotte Brontë, respectively. Many more literary works have been published anonymously, with no author named. Anonymous or pseudonymous publication was far more prevalent from the sixteenth through the nineteenth centuries than today.[1] During particularly dangerous times, like Shakespeare's, most plays were published anonymously, or not at all.

Most pseudonyms are made-up names created by the real author,[2] but there is another subset of pseudonyms—the use of the name of another real person as that of the author. Though it is less common, the practice dates to antiquity and famously recurred in America in the 1950s.[3]

If we cannot be certain of authorship from an author's name, how else might we determine whether the author is correctly identified? Taking the name on published works as the first "test" of the author's identity, there are these additional tests we can use:

2. Is the biography of the named author consistent with (a) the biography of a writer, and (b) the particular works that carry his name?

3. Did the named author take credit for the works, or in any way acknowledge them?

4. Did the author himself, whoever he was, have anything to say about his identity anywhere in the works? Did he mention a possible motive for using a pseudonym?

---

* With thanks to Alex McNeil for the first draft of this introduction and for helping to edit the book.

5. Did others in a position to know the truth of the matter attribute the works to the named author, and is there any reason to doubt whether they were telling the truth?

6. Did others in a position to know the truth of the matter express doubt about the author's identity in his own time, and do their expressions of doubt seem credible?

7. Have doubts been raised in later times, including our own, by persons qualified to judge the truth of the matter, and, if so, do their expressions of doubt seem credible?

In this book, these tests will be applied, along with an examination of the similarities and differences between the names of the author William Shakespeare and William Shakspere of Stratford. Here we provide an overview of these seven areas, which, taken together, are key elements of what is known as the Shakespeare Authorship Question: did Mr. William Shakspere of Stratford-upon-Avon really write the works of William Shakespeare?

1. The Name

There is no doubt that a man named William "Shakspere" was born and baptized in Stratford-upon-Avon in 1564, and died there in 1616. But his name was usually not spelled the same as the author's name, and it was never spelled like the author's name in Stratford church records. There the name is consistently spelled "Shakspere," or close variants like "Shaksper." Likewise, the name on the plays and poems was almost always spelled the same way—either "Shakespeare," or "Shake-speare" with a hyphen. So there is a consistent difference between the spelling of the author's name on published plays and poems, and the spelling "Shakspere." The issue is whether these two very similar names are the same, referring to one and the same person, or different names, referring to two different persons. Additional issues are whether the names would have been pronounced the same, whether the appearance of a hyphen in "Shake-speare" implies a pen name, and whether it would have been understood as such.

Traditionalists claim that Shakspere and Shakespeare are different spellings of the same name. Spellings were not standardized at the time; but while there was great variation in how people who were unfamiliar with a name might spell it, there was much less variation in how people spelled their own names. Nothing shows that Shakspere *ever* spelled his name "Shakespeare." This suggests that Shakspere and the author Shakespeare were different people, or at least that there is room for doubt. Even orthodox scholars once regarded them as different names, but now pretend that there is only one name and change all instances of Shakspere to Shakespeare, as if the name Shakspere had never existed. All of these questions are examined in Chapter 1, "The Man Who Was Never Shakespeare," based on the book with that title by Professor A.J. Pointon of Portsmouth University.

2. The Biography

Many facts about the life of William Shakspere of Stratford-upon-Avon can be stated with certainty. We know that he was baptized there in April 1564; that he was married and had children there; that he spent parts of his adult life in London; that he was a shareholder in a London theatrical company; that he became an actor (although no record shows any role he ever played on any date); and that he spent the last part of his life in Stratford-upon-Avon, where he made out a detailed will before his death in April 1616. We know that he became wealthy. As early as 1597, he was able to buy New Place, the second largest house in Stratford, and in 1605 he purchased income-producing tithes in Stratford for a large sum. We also know that in 1597, and again in 1598, London tax authorities couldn't find him; that a man who felt threatened by him sought "sureties of the peace against William Shakspere;" that in 1598 the town of Stratford paid him for a load of stone; that in 1598 he was cited in Stratford for hoarding grain during a time of famine; that he sued two townsmen over debts in 1604 and 1609; that in 1612 he gave a deposition in London concerning a legal matter related to events that occurred eight years earlier, but he couldn't remember much; and that in 1613 he purchased a house in London and promptly mortgaged it back to the previous owner.

Beyond that, little is known, and nothing that is known connects him to the literary world. This gulf between what is known about Shakspere and what one would expect to find if he were Shakespeare is what first fueled the authorship controversy. The breadth and depth of knowledge found in the works is enormous. In the section in this book on "Shakespeare's Vast Knowledge," chapters 7-9 focus on three areas to illustrate the point—knowledge of Italy, knowledge of the law, and knowledge of medicine—by author Alexander Waugh, attorney Tom Regnier, and Dr. Earl Showerman, respectively. In each case we find a level of knowledge far beyond what one would expect in any writings, unless the author had studied the subject intensely, and also had extensive personal experience. Nothing known about Shakspere explains his supposed knowledge in any of these areas.

That such a gulf exists is seldom admitted by traditional biographers (Schoenbaum was an exception). They would have it that Shakspere attended the Stratford grammar school and received a first-rate education. In fact, no record shows that Shakspere ever attended school. He may have attended the Stratford grammar school, but the records from that time are lost. They speculate widely about his "lost years"—the period between 1585 and 1592, when his whereabouts are unknown; they speculate that he became a lawyer's clerk, or a schoolmaster, or had some other opportunity to acquire the vast knowledge displayed throughout the works. In fact, nothing is known, except that he had a wife, child and two infants in Stratford in 1585. They tell you he went to London sometime in the late 1580s, where he became first an actor, then a writer. In fact, no one knows when he first arrived in London; it could have been any time between the late 1580s and about 1594. They tell you that by 1594 he had a patron, Henry Wriothesley, 3rd Earl of Southampton. Although "William Shakespeare" dedicated his first two published poems to Southampton (*Venus and Adonis* in 1593, and *Lucrece* in 1594), no record shows that Southampton was his patron, or that the two ever met or corresponded. They tell you they know when Shakespeare was active as a playwright, and that they have a good idea of the chronology of his plays. In fact, no one knows for sure when any of the plays was written, or in exactly what order. And they tell you that in 1611 Shakspere retired from the theater, went home to Stratford-upon-Avon, and wrote nothing the last years of his life. In fact, no one knows how Shakspere split his time between London and Stratford, or exactly when he decided to return permanently to his home town. Some think it was as early as 1604.

Traditional biographies are classic examples of faulty reasoning—reasoning backward from the conclusion, circular reasoning, treating speculation and inference as fact and ignoring or dismissing contrary evidence. The conclusion, of course, is that Shakspere was Shakespeare. It goes something like this: "We know Shakspere wrote the works of Shakespeare. The name on the works and the First Folio and Stratford monument say so—there is no room for doubt.

We know Shakspere lived from 1564 to 1616. Based on those dates, and dates of published plays and poems, he must have begun his writing career in his mid-twenties (c. 1588-1590) and continued into his late forties (c. 1611-1612)." With that as a framework, they confidently claim that Shakspere *must* have gone to school, *must* have learned Latin (and French, Italian, Spanish and Greek), *must* have had access to an enormous library (where he read works not yet translated into English), and *must* have acquired the vast range of knowledge found in the works, including law, medicine, botany, music, history, equestrian sports, and even falconry.

How Shakspere did all of this without leaving any *evidence* of it is never explained. Stratfordians accuse doubters of snobbery, claiming that we say people who come from humble origins cannot achieve greatness. That is *not* our position. In all fields of human endeavor, history offers examples of persons who came from humble origins and achieved greatness. As we say in the Declaration of Reasonable Doubt, "not that a commoner, even in the rigid, hierarchical social structure of Elizabethan England, could not have managed to do it ..., but how could it have happened without leaving a single trace?" That's the issue, not that it *couldn't* have happened, but that *no evidence shows it did.*

In Chapter 3, "The Missing Paper Trail," we show Diana Price's analysis of the records biographers normally cite as evidence that a named author had a literary career. Comparing Shakspere with two dozen writers of the period, she found that he is the only one for whom no evidence could be found in any of the ten categories she developed. This enormous gap between Shakspere and his contemporaries is significant for three reasons: (1) records for writers of the period *do* exist, and we would expect to find them for Shakspere if he were the author; (2) Shakspere allegedly wrote for twenty years—far longer than most of his contemporaries, so there should be *more* evidence for his career than theirs, not less; and (3) as Professor William Rubinstein notes, "Shakespeare has been more intensively studied by researchers, by a factor of many orders of magnitude, than any of his contemporaries. If an equivalent 'paper trail' exists for Shakespeare even remotely similar to that of his fellow authors, it should clearly have been discovered long ago and become common knowledge."[4]

In addition to the absence of documentary evidence cited in Chapter 3, many other oddities about the known life of Shakspere are inconsistent with his having been a literary man. Some will be discussed in later chapters. Briefly, they include the following:

2a. Evidence of Literacy

(1) Handwriting—the only alleged examples of Shakspere's handwriting are six signatures on four legal documents executed between 1612 and 1616. They are inconsistent with each other, and their crudeness suggests they are by a man unskilled at writing. Dr. Frank Davis compares Shakspere's signatures to those of contemporary actors and writers in Chapter 2.

(2) Letters—no letter in Shakspere's hand has yet been found, nor even a reference to one. One letter addressed *to* Shakspere exists; it was from a Stratford neighbor, Richard Quiney. It requested a loan and had nothing to do with literary matters. The plays are full of letters. If Shakspere were the author, dividing his time between literary activities in London and tending to business and his family in Stratford, some of his letters should have survived.

(3) Books—no record shows that Shakspere ever owned, borrowed, or possessed any book. Lending libraries did not exist at the time. Yet we know that the author used a vast number of

books in writing the works, and books are featured prominently in several of them. That there is no known connection between Mr. Shakspere and books is strange, to say the least.

2b. Shakspere's Descendants

Shakspere died in Stratford-upon-Avon in 1616, and was survived by daughters Susanna (bapt. 1583) and Judith (bapt. 1585). Neither could write. To many doubters, this fact is among the most damaging to his claim. While schools were only for boys, educated people often provided for the schooling of daughters and other female relatives, as Bonner Miller Cutting notes in Chapter 5. Note also that the plays feature many well-educated women. Stephen Greenblatt noted that, "It is striking how many of Shakespeare's women are shown reading."[5] Again, there is a gap between the author Shakespeare and Shakspere.

It is worth noting that nothing shows any of his descendants ever mentioned him. Daughter Susanna lived until 1649, Judith until 1662 and granddaughter Elizabeth until 1670. Yet nothing shows any family tradition that they descended from Shakespeare.

2c. Record of Travel

Nothing shows that Mr. Shakspere ever traveled in England, except between Stratford and London, and nothing shows that he ever left England. Most scholars do not believe he did. Yet it appears that the author traveled widely. Most of the comedies and several tragedies are set on the Continent. The number of plays set in Italy, in particular, is striking.

Stratfordians claim that there is nothing in the Italian plays that he could not have learned from books or from talking to others who had traveled there. They say the Italian plays contain errors which indicate that the author didn't have firsthand knowledge. These claims are not true. Alexander Waugh shows in Chapter 7, "Keeping Shakespeare out of Italy," that his knowledge of the settings of the Italian plays is so detailed, and so accurate, that it must have been acquired firsthand.[6] Even minor details are almost always correct.

Time and again, Shakespeare is shown to have gotten it right and academics wrong. Why would a playwright who had never been to Italy, and whose audience had never been there, go to the trouble to get so many details right? It makes no sense if Shakespeare was a commercial playwright motivated by profit. Why didn't he set more plays in his own time and place so his audiences could more easily relate to them? Why did he never mention the town of Stratford, or set a play there? It would have been easier than setting plays in Italy, if, in fact, he were the author and had spent all his formative years there, into his twenties.

2d. Who Knew Shakespeare?

Contrary to impressions that the author was well known, he was evidently an elusive figure. No one seems to have known him personally; there is not even a hint of it, until 1623. Although some contemporaries made references to the author Shakespeare, or to his works, during Shakspere's lifetime, no one claimed to have met, or seen, the author. At a time when writers often dedicated works to one another, no one dedicated any literary work to Shakespeare; nor did Shakespeare dedicate anything to any fellow writer. Further, Shakespeare wrote no commendatory verse to anyone, and no one wrote any to him. These strange silences are also addressed in Chapter 3: "The Missing Literary Paper Trail."

Only two extant records reflect anyone speaking with Shakspere—in 1612 two deponents in the Bellott-Mountjoy lawsuit recalled discussing the matter with him[7] and in 1614 the Stratford town clerk wrote that Shakspere had spoken to him about a land matter. Neither record is about literary matters. Not until the publication of the First Folio in 1623, over seven years after he died, did anyone suggest that Shakspere of Stratford had been a writer. This is not to say that no one knew Shakspere. Clearly some did, both in Stratford and in London. Strangely, however, no one associated him with the author Shakespeare. In Chapter 4, Ramon Jiménez provides evidence of "Ten Eyewitnesses Who Saw Nothing."

2e. Shakspere's Will

Executed within months of his death in 1616, Shakspere's last will and testament is a detailed three-page document, evidently in the hand of a law clerk, listing many items of property and making many specific bequests. But what it doesn't contain is as interesting as what it does. There is no mention of books, poems, manuscripts, musical instruments, costumes, shares in any theater, or any other property that would suggest a writer or man of the theater. Everything about it is consistent with all of the other documents that suggest a businessman. There is no bequest to that Stratford grammar school where he supposedly got his education. Nor is there any provision for the education of his young granddaughter.

It does contain bequests of money for rings for three actors, "John Hemynge[,] Richard Burbage & Henry Cundell." Curiously, however, the bequest is an interlineation added later. There is no reason to think it was made posthumously—interlineations are common in wills of the time. What seems odd is that it apparently did not occur to Mr. Shakspere to leave anything to these supposed close associates when he first drafted the will. Rather, it appears to have been an afterthought, or perhaps someone reminded him.

What is more difficult to explain is why he failed to remember any fellow writers. The actors tie him to the theater, but *nothing* suggests a literary career. Why no bequests to any of the still-living "collaborators" who, we are told, knew him in person? Why did he leave no bequest to his alleged patron, the Earl of Southampton, or to Richard Field, the printer of the poems that made "Shakespeare" famous, and who supposedly also grew up in Stratford? All of these omissions raise serious doubts about whether he was the author. Bonner Miller Cutting compares Shakspere's will to other wills of the period in Chapter 5.

2f. Absence of Tributes

Of all the oddities in Shakspere's biography that undermine his claim, none is more damaging than the absence of tributes to "Shakespeare" following his death in 1616. Not only was he not eulogized and buried with honors in the Poets' Corner in Westminster Abbey (as one would expect for the great "Soul of the Age!"), there was total silence. For over seven years, not so much as a letter refers to the death of the author Shakespeare. Even his fellow actors, Heminges, Condell and Richard Burbage, all named in his will, had no recorded reaction. Nor did the printers who owned rights to published plays and poems rush new editions into print. This wasn't normal. Francis Beaumont was much less important, yet when he died the previous month he was buried in Westminster Abbey.

Professor Pointon elaborates on this problem in Chapter 6, "The Rest is Silence: The absence of tributes to the author Shakespeare at the time of Shakspere's death." We also include, in Appendix C, an article by Cornell University sociologist Donald P. Hayes on "Social Network Theory" and the claim that Mr. Shakspere was the famous dramatist. Hayes explains why this is the biggest threat to Stratfordianism: the more Stratfordians suggest that the author's collaborators must have known him, the odder the silence.

3. Did Shakspere Take Credit?

Authors usually prefer to take credit for their works. It is true today, when name recognition and marketing are seen as key to commercial success. It was true in the 19th century when Dickens toured to promote his works, including two trips to America. William Thackeray toured.[8] Writers in Shakespeare's time didn't do book tours, but they took credit for their work in various ways—mentioning it in correspondence, or, in Ben Jonson's case, supervising publication of his collected works. Those who acknowledged literary works in their correspondence include Jonson, Thomas Nashe, Philip Massinger, Gabriel Harvey, Edmund Spenser, Samuel Daniel, George Peele, Michael Drayton, George Chapman, William Drummond, Thomas Lodge, Thomas Dekker and Thomas Kyd.[9]

Notably absent from this list is Shakspere. No record shows that he ever claimed to have written anything. As we have noted, none of his descendants is known to have mentioned his name, much less claimed that he was the author Shakespeare. Nor did anyone in Stratford ever refer to him as a literary man. If he had been, he would have been the most famous man in town. His townsmen would have been proud of the connection.

Nothing shows that he ever put on a play in Stratford, or that any resident saw him as a poet. These silences suggest that Shakspere did *not* take credit for writing the works. If he had, surely some family member or townsperson would have left a record of it. There is the monument, but nothing shows that anyone in Stratford was involved with it. Its inscription is ambiguous, as we shall see, and it does not actually say that Shakspere was Shakespeare.

4. The Author's Own Words

One would think that Shakespeare biographies would emphasize *"Shake-speares Sonnets,"* published in 1609. They are, after all, his only openly self-revelatory works. The problem is that they do not support the traditional attribution, so they get ignored, and downplayed. None of the Shakespeare Birthplace Trust's "60 Minutes with Shakespeare" deals openly with them. Nor are they mentioned in the table of contents of *Shakespeare Beyond Doubt*. People should ask why the Shakespeare Birthplace Trust avoids this important evidence.

The Sonnets—154 highly personal, private communications to close intimates—depict an older, reclusive man in some sort of disgrace. They are no match for Shakspere. The orthodox admit as much when they say they are fictional, but they don't treat them as fictional when they attempt to identify the characters addressed and referred to in them—the Fair Youth, Dark Lady and Rival Poet. If the Sonnets were fictional, we would expect the author to have given names to his characters, but he did not. The author seems to have harbored secrets, and even traditionalists have said that he did not want us to know him. If, as commonly thought, they depict a scandalous bisexual love triangle, this isn't surprising.

Did the author say anything about his identity in the Sonnets? Yes, he wrote that he did not *want* his name to be remembered (No. 72: "My name be buried where my body is") and that he did not *expect* it to be remembered (No. 81: "Your name from hence immortal life shall have,/

Though I, once gone, to all the world must die"). Neither statement makes sense, unless his real name wasn't known at the time. This suggests he used a pseudonym. Both sonnets appear in their entirety in Part II: Exposing an Industry in Denial in our answer to Question 5: "Five key questions the SBT did not ask, and cannot answer." The author says that he is in disgrace. Is it hard to imagine that such a man might not have wanted his name associated with his works? Read them and see for yourself why the author may have wished to conceal his identity.

5. The Attributions of Others

The best evidence for Shakspere is the testimony of Ben Jonson, plus a few friends, in the First Folio collection of the plays, published in 1623. The Declaration says this explicitly. But the First Folio is problematic, as orthodox scholars discovered long ago. One problem is that it appeared late. Another is that it is uncorroborated by contemporaneous evidence. Absent the Folio, it is hard to imagine that anyone would ever have thought that Shakspere was the author. His case rests on the credibility of the Folio, and especially on Ben Jonson. Did others in a position to know the truth attribute the works to the named author? Yes. Is there reason to doubt whether they were telling the truth? Yes, there are several reasons.

A few problems with the First Folio testimony are mentioned in the Declaration. Two problems that have since come to our attention are (1) the absence of the Shakspere coat of arms, and (2) the absence of tributes from notable writers other than Ben Jonson. The absent coat of arms is relevant because one would expect it to provide confirmation. The absence of tributes from his fellow writers is relevant because some were still alive. Jonson's 1616 folio of his own collected works contained many more tributes. Why, for example, was John Fletcher (yet living)—one of Shakespeare's alleged collaborators—not included? None of the other three persons who wrote tributes for the First Folio was a noted literary figure, then or now. Rather, they seem to have been people Jonson knew he could rely on.

In response to Question 33 about the credibility of the First Folio in "60 Minutes," David Bevington, Professor of English at the University of Chicago, says, in part: "That Ben Jonson, and so many others, would have consented to a widespread conspiracy to perpetuate a lie . . . is simply inconceivable." Was it really "so many," or only a few—a bare minimum, given the author? Were they "perpetuating a lie," or honoring his wishes, stated in the Sonnets? Richard Whalen replied as follows (complete exchange in Part II):

> There is no evidence of a 'widespread conspiracy to perpetuate a lie.' Doubters make no such claim, and no 'widespread' conspiracy would have been required. This is an assumption that Stratfordians impose on doubters for the sake of argument. If a writer uses a pseudonym, does this mean that he, his family, friends and publisher are part of a 'widespread conspiracy' to conceal his identity? What is 'widespread'? There is little evidence that people knew who the author Shakespeare was in the first place.

And:

> . . . the claim that actors Heminges and Condell wrote [their epistles] in the First Folio, or edited the plays, was shown to be false by George Steevens in 1770. His conclusion has been accepted by most Shakespeare scholars ever since. Would they and Ben Jonson have helped to perpetuate a myth for some good reason? Probably yes. We know this claim is false. Why assume everything else is true?

Whalen's position on the topic is shown in its entirety in Chapter 11. He points out that Jonson was a master of ambiguity—a fact known to his biographers but ignored by Stratfordian academics who prefer to perpetuate the myth of Honest Ben Jonson.

The most obvious problem with the First Folio, and perhaps the most damaging, is the frontispiece, ostensibly depicting the author, created by the engraver Martin Droeshout. It has many odd features, and Jonson advised readers, on the page opposite the engraving, to "looke/ Not on his picture, but his Booke." Ignoring the advice, Dr. John Rollett studied it closely and concluded that the oddities are deliberate—an implicit warning not to believe what follows. His article on "Shakespeare's Impossible Doublet" is shown in its entirety as Chapter 10. His analysis by itself is good evidence that the Folio front matter is a fraud.

Was the Stratford monument, first mentioned in the First Folio, part of the fraud? Richard Whalen suggests that Jonson may have written the cryptic inscription and cites one study that supports this. But the main issue Whalen addresses is whether the monument has been altered. He makes a case that the original effigy, depicting a man holding a sack, was altered in the nineteenth century to depict the writer shown in today's effigy. Records show that it was "repaired" and "beautified" several times. Even a prominent Stratfordian scholar agrees that the effigy was changed to depict a writer. Since the original did not depict a writer, townsfolk who knew Shakspere, and knew he was not a writer, would not have found it odd. Whalen describes the evidence in detail in Chapter 12.

Taken together, these three chapters destroy the two main pillars of the traditional attribution. At the very least, they strongly support our view that there is room for doubt.

6. Doubts of Others at the Time

Is there room for doubt about whether the Stratford man wrote the works of Shakespeare? With few exceptions, scholars assert that there is *no* doubt and that the case for Shakspere rests on the unshakable foundation of over two centuries of scholarship. Stratfordians who even recognize that anyone doubts Shakspere's authorship routinely denigrate doubters.

If they consider them at all, Stratfordians claim the doubts are a recent phenomenon.[10] They claim the controversy began long after Shakspere died, as if there were some statute of limitations and time has expired. They ignore the fact that doubts were expressed soon after the name Shakespeare appeared beneath the dedication to *Venus and Adonis* in 1593. In other words, some of his *contemporaries* thought that "Shakespeare" was a pseudonym. This is addressed in our answer to Question 40 in Exposing an Industry in Denial (Part II). There we cite seven instances of doubts expressed during the Elizabethan-Jacobean period. Were doubts raised by those in a position to know the truth of the matter at the time? Yes.

7. Doubts of Later Generations

Stratfordians ignore early expressions of doubt, saying none was expressed until the 1850s, when Delia Bacon published a book on the subject, claiming Shakspere was not the author. She is often called a Baconian—one who thinks that Francis Bacon (no relation) wrote the works. In fact, she proposed that the plays were the creations of a group of writers, including Bacon, Sir Walter Raleigh and other notable intellectuals of the period.

Over the next half century, the issue attracted the attention of many notable people, including Lord Palmerston, Nathaniel Hawthorne, Ralph Waldo Emerson, Walt Whitman, Henry James, William James, John Galsworthy, Sir George Greenwood and Mark Twain. Early in the 20th century, the issue gained traction with the arrival of some interesting new candidates, and Sigmund Freud, Orson Welles, Charlie Chaplin, Tyrone Guthrie, Malcolm X, scholar Mortimer Adler and actor John Gielgud took positions on the side of the doubters.

They were joined by actors Mark Rylance, Derek Jacobi and Michael York; statesmen like Ambassador Paul H. Nitze, and Harvard Professor William Y. Elliott; and academics like Robin Fox, University Professor of Social Theory at Rutgers University, and Professor Dean Keith Simonton at the University of California at Davis. At least five U.S. Supreme Court Justices—Harry A. Blackmun, Lewis F. Powell, Jr., John Paul Stevens, Sandra Day O'Connor, and Antonin Scalia—have openly expressed doubts. Have doubts been expressed by "persons qualified to judge the truth of the matter?" Yes.

Are we arguing from authority by pointing this out? No, merely refuting the false Stratfordian stereotype of doubters so people will take the issue seriously and examine it. Stratfordians say *they* are the only ones qualified to judge. They are not. *They* are the ones who argue from authority, who say there is nothing to consider, and who attack dissenters. Doubters are the ones who focus on evidence and invite you to look and see for yourself.

Over 2,600 people have signed the Declaration of Reasonable Doubt since 2007—over 2,000 college graduates, over 950 with advanced degrees, and more than 440 current or former college/university faculty members. The largest category by academic discipline, for both current and former faculty and all college graduates, is those in English literature. Given so many doubters, how can anyone say there is no room for doubt? There clearly is doubt, as a matter of empirical fact—*reasonable* doubt, expressed by very credible people.

The Birthplace Trust says these people do not matter (or even that they are insane) because, among other reasons, (1) the controversy only began in the 1850s, (2) it began with Delia Bacon, who died in an asylum, and (3) there are many alternative candidates. That any of these arguments is taken seriously by any Stratfordian is an embarrassment. It ignores that the theater tradition was lost in the mid-1600s, during the English Civil War, when the theaters were closed for a generation. Knowledge of secrets no longer relevant and not stated was lost. Once intergenerational transmission was interrupted, it is hardly surprising that it took time to notice all of the contradictions in the case for Shakspere.

How, where and when Delia Bacon died is irrelevant to the validity of her claim. Has no Stratfordian ever had a breakdown? If so, does it invalidate their authorship views? The number of alternative candidates reflects the level of skepticism about Mr. Shakspere. Most have only a small following, but many are more viable than Shakspere. These arguments are red herrings intended to distract attention from what really matters—the evidence. That is the focus of the Declaration of Reasonable Doubt, and of this book. Any theory should be evaluated based on the best arguments of its strongest proponents, not based on the misrepresentations and false stereotypes of a self-interested industry.

If Shakspere did not write the works, how did he come to be identified as the author? Many important details remain unknown. Was Shakspere involved from the start? Did the true author know him before the pseudonym first appeared in 1593, and decide to use him as a front man because he was suited to the task? Or did the author choose the pen name "Shakespeare" first and only later discover Shakspere? Or was Shakspere selected to play his role much later, perhaps long after the real author died? Was he an "active" front man, passing himself off as the author, or did he keep a low profile? Since *no one* seems to have thought of him as the author during his lifetime, the latter seems most likely. But in any case, we hope you agree that there is enough room for doubt to continue reading this book.

John M. Shahan

Endnotes

1   Mullan, John: *Anonymity: A Secret History of English Literature* (Princeton University Press, 2007, pp. 4-6, 286-287, 296).

2   Noting that "Often it is difficult to distinguish between an anonymous and a pseudonymous work" (p. 6), Mullan discusses both in *Anonymity*.

3   The Roman playwright Terence was accused of being a front for the playwrights Scipio and Laelius. During the "Red Scare" of the 1950s, some screenwriters who were blacklisted, and could not submit scripts to producers or receive writing credit under their own names, were able to continue working by using "front men" – other persons who would put their names on the blacklisted writers' submissions. Some front men were fellow writers, others were not.

4   Rubinstein, William D.: *Who Wrote Shakespeare's Plays?* (Amberley Publishing, 2012, 24).

5   Greenblatt, Stephen, general ed.: *The Norton Shakespeare* (W.W. Norton & Co., 1997; Greenblatt, "General Introduction," p. 11).

6   See esp. Roe, Richard Paul: *The Shakespeare Guide to Italy: Retracing the Bard's Unknown Travels* (HarperPerennial, 2011).

7   Nicholl, Charles: *The Lodger Shakespeare: His Life on Silver Street* (Viking, 2007, 12-13).

8   Mullan, 287.

9   Price, Diana: *Shakespeare's Unorthodox Biography: New Evidence of an Authorship Problem* (Greenwood Press, 2001, pp. 114-125, 302-313).

10 Shapiro, James: *Contested Will: Who Wrote Shakespeare?* (Simon & Schuster, 2010).

Part I, Section A:
Who was Shakspere of Stratford?

This section deals with key evidence relating to the identity of the Stratford man. In six chapters we examine (1) the spelling of his name—whether it was in fact "Shakespeare," as traditionalists claim; (2) how his alleged signatures compare with those of other actors and writers of the period; (3) how the evidence for his supposed literary career compares with that for other writers of the period; (4) the ten people who knew the Stratford man, or knew who he was, and also knew of the author Shakespeare, but never connected the two; (5) how his will compares with other wills of the time; and (6) the fact that nobody lamented the passing of the author Shakespeare at the time of Shakspere's death in 1616. This evidence is all of a piece and totally refutes the idea that there is no room for doubt.

In the opening chapter, which closely examines the spelling of the two names, Professor A. J. Pointon accuses Stratfordian academics of airbrushing the name "Shakspere" out of existence and replacing all occurrences of that name with "Shakespeare" in their writings. He first pointed this out in his book, *The Man Who Was Never Shakespeare,* published in 2011, but Stratfordian academics still persist in the error. One example is Stanley Wells' false claim (*Shakespeare Beyond Doubt*, page 81), mentioned in the General Introduction above, that Shakspere's name was spelled "Shakespeare" in the burial record in Stratford. Another example is this by David Kathman in Chapter 11[*] of *Shakespeare Beyond Doubt*:

> Quiney's son Thomas eventually married Shakespeare's daughter Judith,
> and they named their first son, born in 1617, 'Shakespeare.' (125)

This is incorrect on three counts. First, the Stratford church records show that the son of Thomas Quiney was born in November of 1616, not in "1617." He *died* in May of 1617. Second, the entry in the record of his christening in 1616 shows the name as "Shakspere." Third, the entry in the record for his burial in 1617 shows the name spelled "Shakspere." So regardless of which of the records he was looking at, Kathman misspelled the name! It's hard for us to imagine that Kathman misspelled it "Shakespeare" purely by accident since he has an article on the spelling debate on his website and is supposedly an expert. So here is another blatant example of the "airbrushing" to which Professor Pointon refers.

---

[*] David Kathman, in the same Chapter 11 (entitled "Shakespeare and Warwickshire") in the book *Shakespeare Beyond Doubt,* also claims that Shakespeare's plays and poems "are peppered with dialect words from Warwickshire and the West Midlands" (129). He made this same claim in his answer to Question 7 in the Birthplace Trust's "60 Minutes with Shakespeare" (Part II below). In his rebuttal (also below), Michael Egan wrote: "David Kathman is wrong; the plays are not 'peppered' with Warwickshire dialect words. In point of fact, Warwickshire and West Midlands references and dialect words form a distinct minority among the places and people Shakespeare refers to and in the speech forms he uses." Egan also notes that *The Oxford Companion to Shakespeare* (Dobson & Wells) has this to say: "It is somewhat strange that Shakespeare did not... exploit his Warwickshire accent, since he was happy enough to represent, in phonetic spelling, the non-standard English of French and Welsh speakers, and the national dialects of Scotland and Ireland."

Chapter 1:
The Man Who Was Never Shakespeare[*]:
The spelling of William Shakspere's name

By A. J. Pointon, Ph.D.

"It is not certain from the title pages that the name printed on them necessarily refers to Mr. Shakspere. Shakspere's last name was spelled numerous ways, even after many of the works had been published. The name on the works was virtually always spelled one way, 'Shakespeare;' but it was often hyphenated—a rarity for English names at the time. Scholars have no definitive explanation for the hyphenated name. Mr. Shakspere's name was *never* hyphenated in other contexts, such as his business dealings in Stratford. On his baptismal record, even on his monument [his] name was spelled with no 'e' after the 'k.' The same is true of its three appearances in his will, twice spelled 'Shackspeare,' and once 'Shakspeare.' Some think it may have been pronounced with a short 'a,' like 'Shack,' as it was quite often spelled."

– Shakespeare Authorship Coalition, Declaration of Reasonable Doubt

It is not surprising that it takes most people a long time to realize that the name William Shakespeare, invented for himself in 1593 by the writer of the poem *Venus and Adonis*, was a pseudonym—and some may never get it. All pseudonyms can be difficult to penetrate, even when the real writers take only the simplest precautions; however, in this case it was made far worse. When this writer's collected plays were published thirty years later, in 1623, someone had the idea, not entirely original, of setting up a decoy for him, with hints that the pseudonym hid some other known real person. This strategy cleverly used as decoy an actor-businessman from Stratford-upon-Avon with a name similar to "Shakespeare"— William Shakspere—who, being dead, could not object.

Their aim was to continue to protect the identity of the real author at a time when writing dramatic fiction was thought unbecoming for some (as it was until the twentieth century) and possibly dangerous. Writers who touched on political, religious or personal issues could be at risk—as when Ben Jonson and others went to prison for poking fun at Scotsmen who had come to London with James I—and so might their families.

Today, the Shakespeare substitution, based on the theft of an innocent man's identity and helped along by generations of scholars, has led to the widespread myth that Stratford's William Shakspere was actually named "Shakespeare," which he was not; and that he wrote magnificent plays and poems, when he was not writing at all. Now, after many centuries spent bolstering this "orthodox" view of Shakespeare, people find it hard to accept that they might have fallen victim to a clever confidence trick.

The orthodox position can be expressed by a quote from R. C. Churchill (1959):

That William Shakespeare of Stratford wrote the plays and poems attributed to him is not a theory at the present time, it is a fact at the present time—and will continue to be a fact until it is definitely proved wrong.

---

[*] This chapter is based on chapters 1-3 of A.J. Pointon's book of the same title, *The Man Who Was Never Shakespeare: The Theft of Shakespeare's Identity* (Parapress, Tunbridge Wells, U.K., 2011).

Here we take up that challenge—a good starting point, even if an unscholarly assertion. We will show Churchill's supposed "fact" is a misapprehension, just as there never was a William Shakespeare of Stratford. This may seem to imply there has been complicity among orthodox scholars in sustaining the Shakspere myth, but if readers look in books and articles on "Shakespeare" and note how many of them hide, overlook or disregard the fact that William Shakspere and his brothers and sisters and children were all baptized as Shakspere, and that—as Bill Bryson (1990) has pointed out—he never used the name Shakespeare in his life, they may start to wonder about it for themselves. Oddly, one will often hear it asked whether it matters how Shakspere spelt his name: it certainly does, or orthodox scholars would not be so keen to change it. The myth about this name is strong: generations have been brought up on it and fortunes and reputations built on it.

How the Theft Began

When he died in 1616, the actor-businessman William Shakspere of Stratford was one of the richest men in his home town, if not the richest. In spite of that, he would never have thought of being long remembered after his death, and certainly not of being remembered four hundred years later as one of the most famous and important men in all of history. He made no arrangements for a memorial in his will. He left no personal written records of himself or his life, nor did his family. Yet more records have been uncovered for him than for any of his contemporaries of similar standing. This is not a tribute to Shakspere himself, for the records are of no intrinsic interest; it is rather a tribute to the researchers who have directed their prodigious efforts—always unsuccessfully—to the discovery of any record that might show this William Shakspere was the writer Shakespeare.

Shakspere held no public offices in his home town and none in London where he worked on and off for perhaps ten or fifteen years. He left no great bequests or great works that would have moved his fellow citizens to honor him, nor any mementoes that would recall him to their minds. It is actually not known, in spite of what might be claimed, whether his real grave lies inside or outside Holy Trinity Church, his parish church in Stratford where his burial was recorded on 25th April 1616. For over seven years after Shakspere's death, there was no indication he would be remembered at all.

Then, in 1623, the deafening silence ended. A magnificent book of thirty-six plays was published with clever but ambiguous hints that Shakspere had all the time been a playwright. Not just any playwright, mind you, but the writer of plays published as by "William Shakespeare," a pseudonym first made famous with the appearance of the best-selling erotic poem *Venus and Adonis* in 1593. That name, Shakespeare, belonging to no known writer, was printed beneath the dedication of that poem to the nineteen-year-old third Earl of Southampton. It was identified as a pseudonym within a year when the poem was parodied by an equally erotic one, *Oenone and Paris*, by a "T.H.," with its dedication parodied by a dedication pointing to a "hiding" and a "lurking" author. The hints given in 1623 suggested (ambiguously) that Shakspere had been the writer behind the pseudonym Shakespeare, many of whose masterpieces had been presented in performances and in books called "quartos."

That 1623 book, with its 900-plus pages and thirty-six plays, was impressive. It is now known as the Shakespeare First Folio; "Folio" because of its large folio-sized pages and "First" because it ran to second, third and fourth full-sized editions. Its actual title was *Mr. William Shakespeares Comedies, Histories, and Tragedies*, and the world had seen nothing to compare with it.

15

The hints in the introduction to the First Folio suggesting that Mr. Shakspere was its author were backed by the erection of a monument in Stratford's Holy Trinity Church. This complex memorial to Shakspere, erected by persons who themselves remained anonymous, contained additional ambiguous hints about him. They suggested he had been something very different from what people who had known him had thought him to be, though these hints did not make clear what that difference actually was.

It is perhaps not surprising that the hints in the First Folio, and on the monument, that William Shakspere of Stratford was the writer Shakespeare did not immediately take root with the townsfolk of Stratford. Yet, by the end of the eighteenth century, dozens of invented "facts" had been created, designed to reinforce those hints, or even replace them. For example, locations in Shakespeare's plays were "discovered" to be near Stratford, though they were not. Friends and relatives were discovered for him whom he would never have known, but who were chosen because they might be of use, with a little sleight of hand, to help his identification as Shakespeare. Denizens of Stratford were dubiously put forward as models for characters in the plays. Real people whom Shakspere might actually have known had their relationships to him exaggerated; and, if there was any chance the relationship might be used in an anecdote that suggested he was a writer, it would be firmed up by assertion and invention into an intimate friendship.

Scholars who believed Shakspere was Shakespeare often took delight in using circular arguments to "prove" he was educated enough to write the plays and poems of Shakespeare. One example is that readers would be told that they knew Shakspere must have gone to the Stratford grammar school because, if he had not, he could never have become the great Shakespeare. Another is that Shakespeare was only able to refer to schools, schoolboys, schoolmasters, and boys going to school in his plays because, as Shakspere, he had gone to Stratford grammar school. Of course, such circular arguments tell us only that some people have been sufficiently desperate to believe that Shakspere was or could have been Shakespeare to overlook or ignore the fallacy in their reasoning. All they are saying is that, if Shakspere was Shakespeare, he must have gone to school. Totally missing from their arguments is any evidence that Shakspere ever did so at all.

Now these assertions are used in a sort of game in which anyone who doubts Shakspere wrote the plays is called a snob, because, it is claimed, they are denying that a grammar school boy could have written them. However, orthodox scholars have never been able to prove Shakspere was even literate, let alone went to grammar school.

The most effective deception—the change to his name—took hold around 1916, the tercentenary of Shakspere's death. It was then that orthodox scholars, individuals and organizations involved in what had become the lucrative "Shakespeare business" began airbrushing the name "Shakspere" out of existence. In all new publications it would be replaced by Shakespeare, while every Shakspere family tree published became the Shakespeare family tree. By this technique, people would eventually believe the Shaksperes of Stratford were really called Shakespeare and doubts about it would be met with astonishment and incomprehension. With this bold approach, anyone who ever had a name vaguely like Shakspere would eventually be converted by orthodox scholars to a "Shakespeare," and our William Shakspere would disappear as a man in his own right.

This airbrushing of Shakspere's name was a good trick. It allowed students and the public to be told there was no doubt that "Shakespeare" wrote the plays of "Shakespeare," and it allowed anybody who raised a doubt about the authorship of Shakespeare's plays, however reputable a scholar he or she might be, to be treated like a moron who thought that "Shakespeare" did not write his own plays. Such is the power of brainwashing.

This deliberate changing of Shakspere's name was, and is, total disinformation. Today, if one types "Shakspere" into a computer, it will be shown as a spelling mistake or "corrected" to Shakespeare. Yet, the name Shakspere seems to have been a well-loved family name. The assertion some make that few people in Elizabethan times, including Shakespeare and other learned writers, could not spell their own names consistently is an exaggeration used to bolster claims that Shakespeare was the true name of our Shakspere, when it was not. No, spelling was not as well codified then as it is today, but readers who have believed such claims may be amazed by what they find in the next section. Both the spellings of the author's name, and those of the Shaksperes, are actually quite consistent.

Shakspere – A Well-Loved Family Name

Separated by fifty-two years almost to the day, two related entries appeared in the registers of Holy Trinity Church, Stratford. The first was on 26th April 1564, when the baptismal register recorded the arrival of the subject of this book as

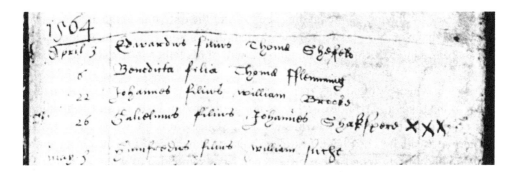

Fig. 1: Gulielmus filius Johannes Shakspere

or, translated from the Latin, William son of John Shakspere. Here was the first son and third child of John and Mary Shakspere.

Much less cheerfully, there was an entry in the burial register on 25th April 1616, possibly written by a less educated clerk than the one at the baptism, for it announced in plain English that our subject had departed this life as Will. Shakspere, gent. The title or dignity of "gent." added to his name was short for Gentleman and indicated our William Shakspere had bought a family coat of arms and with it higher social status. More importantly, this entry shows that those close to our William Shakspere used his father's family name for him faithfully, right up to his death (as he did himself).

Some biographers will tell their readers that those entries both called him "Shakespeare," which they did not. Dr. Germaine Greer, for example, stated in the many editions of her popular book, *Shakespeare*, that the baptismal entry was "Gulielmus filius Johannes Shakespeare." Given that the main argument for Shakspere being Shakespeare is that this was his name, it may have been thought best not to confuse readers by printing what was actually written.

As noted above, spelling in Elizabethan times was not fixed as it is today. A person's name was likely to be spelled in many different ways by other people, especially when someone, a clerk for instance, wrote down a name phonetically: it happens frequently enough today, especially over the telephone, while the semi-literate might sometimes misspell their own names. But that is really no excuse for scholars and biographers to pretend that this is what happened in the records of the Shakspere family. Some people have claimed to have found twenty spellings of the name Shakspere around Stratford, with as many as eighty-three being claimed by going further afield—and one joker actually published a list of four thousand variants of the name Shakspere, finishing up with the French "Jacques père." For some reason, this is supposed to make it easier to give the Shakspere family the name "Shakespeare," when in fact we will see the opposite is the case. A list of the family Shakspere entries in the records, with references, is given at the end of this chapter, and the conclusion is obvious: Shakspere was Shakspere. Some may query how an illiterate family might keep their name consistently spelt, but it is well known that people who can read almost nothing else can recognize their own names when they are written down for them.

We begin, though, by considering an outline history of William's immediate family and the way the name Shakspere runs through it. To start with, it seems John Shakspere must have been born around 1530, though we have no record of his baptism. This educated guess would mean that when his first son, William, was born in 1564, John would have been about thirty-four. We can arrive at this estimate of his age because he must have been at least twenty-one in 1552 when, as a tenant or (less likely) owner of a house in Henley Street, he was fined as "John Shakspere" for having an illegal dung-heap—not the only one in the area—outside it. It appears he must have married his wife, Mary Arden, in or about 1557 because their first child, a girl, was baptized in 1558, and, according to the will of his father-in-law Robert Arden, Mary was still single in 1556.

The house in which William was born is not known, nor is it known where John and Mary were living at the time. Today, however, so as not to disappoint visitors, an Elizabethan house has been reconstructed on one of several sites John Shakspere is known to have owned later, and it is cheerfully called "The Shakespeare Birthplace." It has been furnished in an appropriate Elizabethan country-town style so that visitors can have some idea of what the writer William Shakespeare's early life would have been like, if only he had been William Shakspere.

By the time of William's birth, John and his wife Mary had already had two daughters, Joan in 1558 and Margaret in 1562, both of whom were baptized as Shakspere. Both died in infancy. That was not such a rare thing then, and, as parents often did in such cases, John and Mary were to name another child in memory of their first. The second Joan, born in 1569 (also baptized as Shakspere), kept the memory of the deceased Joan alive. Indeed, she survived to be the longest lived of all John and Mary's children, outliving her eldest brother, William, by thirty years. Their other daughter who survived beyond infancy was baptized as Anne Shakspere but lived only seven and a half years from her birth in 1571. Besides his two surviving sisters, William had three younger brothers who were all baptized as Shakspere, and who all predeceased him: Gilbert (1566–1612), Richard (1574–1613) and Edmund (1580–1607).

William was the only Shakspere son to get married and to attempt to carry on the family name, at least legitimately, but, before he married, a period of eighteen years was to elapse after his baptism during which nothing was heard of him. This gap would be the first and longest of his "lost years."

Then, in November 1582, there was a flurry of activity. Urgent preparations were made for William to be married before the start of the Christmas season on 3rd December, which that year was the date after which weddings—and even the reading of the banns that had to precede weddings—would not be allowed.

William's bride, Anne Hathwey, a young woman from nearby Shottery was already four months pregnant. Anne was twenty-five, and her family would have been desperate to establish both her security and her respectability. William, being eighteen, was still a minor. In a period of fifty years, he was the only Stratford man who married under the age of twenty and out of necessity. Moreover, because he was a minor, Anne's family was required to lodge a bond with the Bishop of Worcester as a guarantee in case any complaint of irregularity might come to light later. The bond was for £40 (around £24,000 in today's money), a sum so large that it certainly must have been refundable in the event of there being no later problems—and the plain evidence is that there were not.

There was some confusion over the marriage or over its registration, or both. William's name may have been misheard, for it appeared as "Shagspere" on the certificate that was issued by a clerk at Worcester on 28th November 1582 giving permission for him to marry Anne Hathwey of Shottery. Yet this is a trivial problem for the biographer compared with what had happened only the day before, on 27th November. On that day another certificate had been issued at Worcester for William to marry an Anne Whateley of Temple Grafton, and this time his name was spelt "Shaxper." Of course, both those spellings of his family name are consistent with it being told to the clerks uniformly as "Shakspere," and not "Shakespeare;" we discuss the difference in pronunciation below.

Because so little is known about the persons involved in this confusion, the speculations that can be made about William Shakspere and the two Annes are unlimited. There has also been no limit on the speculation about where the marriage took place. Stratford, Shottery, Luddington and Temple Grafton have all been proposed, all being within three miles of Stratford, but there is simply no surviving record. One thing is certain, however: the marriage did take place and Anne Hathwey became Anne Shakspere. Another is that, contrary to what is sometimes said, she was not at all old for marrying at that time: it was William who was unusually young. Anne was obviously sexually attractive to the teenager and she was to outlive him by over seven years.

The outcome of the premarital liaison that must have occurred between William and Anne in the summer of 1582 and precipitated their marriage was a little girl who was baptized as Susanna Shakspere, daughter of William Shakspere, on 26th May 1583. For some reason her baptism record has been specially picked out by some and claimed to be in the name "Shakespeare," yet the entry clearly reads Shakspere with no medial "e" and no "a" in the last syllable. This girl was to be her father's favorite; she would certainly have done him proud when, in 1607, and in spite of her rich father giving her no education, she married Dr. John Hall, the local physician. Although the bridegroom was well known as a Puritan, the marriage certificate shows the wedding took place in the parish church—there was no real alternative—with the bride as Susanna Shaxspere, another obvious phonetic spelling of "Shakspere."

In May 1584, a year after the birth of Susanna, Anne was pregnant again, this time with different-sex twins. On 2nd February 1585, in the parish church, the boy would be baptized as Hamnet Shakspere and the girl as Judith Shakspere. It appears they were named after Hamnet and Judith Sadler who were the Shakspere's neighbors and, if that was so, it implies that these two probably stood at the font in Stratford's Holy Trinity Church as joint godparents for both infants in a standard Protestant baptism. Hamnet Sadler's name would appear thus thirty-one years later as witness (as well as legatee) to Shakspere's will.

The adherence of Shakspere to his family name was amazingly consistent. When William's only son died aged a mere eleven and a half years, he was buried on 11th August 1596 as "*Hamnet filius William Shakspere*." The boy had been the hope of both his grandfather John

Shakspere and father William Shakspere to carry on the family name in direct line from his great-grandfather Richard Shakspere who had lived at nearby Snitterfield. The death must have been a bitter blow for both John and William. It occurred when the family fortunes were improving after difficult times, and William was about to revive an application for a coat of arms which his father had first made twenty years previously. Responsibility for the continuance of the family name passed to the three younger Shakspere brothers—Gilbert, Richard and Edmund—but all were to predecease their elder brother and die leaving no descendants. Anne was only twenty-seven or twenty-eight when she had the twins, but, as appears to have been fairly common at the time, the birth of twins may have ended her ability to have children, as she had no more.

William's daughter Judith did try to keep the family name going when she was married (and quickly got pregnant) just before her father's death in 1616. Her first child, a boy, was baptized with the name spelled Shaksper Quiney (though he was buried as Shakspere Quiney). Judith's wedding (as Shakspere) to Thomas Quiney of Stratford on 10th February 1616 had been hurried. It took place during Lent, the time of fasting, a circumstance that required the bridegroom to obtain a special license, and he did not. As a result, Thomas Quiney was temporarily excommunicated from the Anglican Church.

William Shakspere's parents did not live to see the birth of Shakspere Quiney. His father had been buried in 1601 as simple "*John Shakspeare*." He sadly could not be entered in the burial register as "Gent.," the title he had so long coveted, because the coat of arms he had first applied for twenty-five years previously had not quite been granted. William's mother was buried as "*Mayry Shaxspere*" in September 1608, and she had lived to see the birth of her first grandchild, Elizabeth Hall, who was baptized in the February of the same year.

The second member of William Shakspere's family who could have been buried as Shakspere but was not—that is if we accept his mother's "Shaxs" stood for "Shaks"—was his brother Edmund. His burial was registered on 31st December 1607 in London as "Shakespeare," being given the better known spelling of the name with the medial "e"; and this London burial was the only time in the context of family matters that the spelling Shakespeare was used. Incidentally, Edmund's burial is the only one in the family of which we have some details. He is recorded as being buried as a player and with the main bell tolling, at a cost of 20 shillings, in the parish church that is now Southwark Cathedral. It is naturally assumed, though without evidence, that the arrangements were made by his brother William. Edmund's name has been put on a stone in the Cathedral choir, but it is of late date and the location is too grand for a player.

Edmund did have a baby son, but he died in infancy and was buried in London with his name recorded as Edward "Shackspeere" on 12th August 1607. However, the child was illegitimate and would have had no right to carry on the Shakspere arms.

The Stratford burial of the last of William's brothers, Richard, occurred in February 1613 and was recorded as "Shakspeare."

Though William Shakspere used his family name to the end of his life, it was in the face of great difficulties. When he got to London and began his rise in the theater world, mainly as a manager and shareholder but also as a player, the first time his name was written into any record it was as "Shakespeare." The occasion, on 15th March 1595, was when £20 was paid for a Christmas (or rather St. Stephen's Day) performance before Queen Elizabeth at Greenwich in 1594. The payment was made to three managers of the Lord Chamberlain's Men, our Shakspere, Richard Burbage and William Kempe. Some scholars, puzzled to find there were two performances that could have involved the Lord Chamberlain's Men on the same day, one at Greenwich and one at the Inns of Court, have suggested this record was a rogue entry in the ledger, possibly inserted by someone trying to pocket cash by making a fraudulent claim. Yet, whether that was so or not, it seems it was the Stratford man to whom the ledger entry referred. It would, of course, have been made in the absence of the parties and at a time when the person making the entry would have been familiar with the name "Shakespeare," now famous from its appearance on two erotic poems much read by young literate males, *Venus and Adonis* and *The Rape of Lucrece*.

On a few occasions (perhaps six), people around Stratford wrote the Shaksperes' name as "Shakespeare," but not when the family was represented, and nothing like the number of times it was written that way in London by literate clerks who would have known those poems. William Shakspere suffered the fate of all those of us whose names have a better known alternative spelling. In 1612, when he made a witness statement in what is known as the Bellott–Mountjoy case, the lawyer or clerk who took down his deposition wrote his name five times in the body of the document with the famous spelling "Shakespeare"; yet, when Shakspere gave his oath to his name when it was written on the document in the place where his signature would have been, the name was nothing like Shakespeare. It was badly written, but it clearly looks as though it was intended for "Shakspere," being normally read as just "Shakp" or "Shaxp."

There are actually six instances we know of when there was a requirement for Shakspere's name to be written on legal documents to signify his assent to them, and in no case did he affirm to Shakespeare. There were three on his last will and testament where, even though his name was written differently in the body of the document—twice as Shackspeare and once as Shackspere—it reads as a badly made Shakspere for each of the three so-called "signatures." It seems William Shakspere had a proprietary interest if not a pride in his name and wished to use no other. Even when he was having problems getting his coat of arms because he was only a player, and it would have helped his case if he had identified himself as the poet William Shakespeare, he did not do so.

Speaking of the will, notice that in three appearances of the name in the body of the will, and three signatures on the three pages, not once in six appearances is it spelled "Shakespeare." This when the poet Shakespeare was at the peak of his fame, with many works in print and much praise for him as William "Shakespeare," and the Stratford man signed his name "Shakspere" three times in his will? It boggles the mind. Then, later that year, presumably in his honor, and to perpetuate the family's name, his daughter and son-in-law gave their first-born (Shakspere's grandson) the name "Shaksper Quiney."

Fig. 2: "Shaksper" Quiney birth record, left. "Shakspere" Quiney burial record, right.

Is it any wonder that Stratfordian David Kathman decided he had to change that spelling, and that the Birthplace Trust feels they have to change the spelling of all the family's names?

The move by orthodox scholars to take Shakspere's name from him and his family, either deliberately or through sloppy scholarship, even changing Shaksper Quiney's name to Shakespeare, seems to have started seriously after 1916. Up to then, many orthodox scholars acknowledged their candidate for the authorship was named Shakspere. This spelling was used in the text of books and in their titles, showing that Shakspere was thought to have done the writing but not under his real name. Charles Knight used it in his famous and oft reprinted *Pictorial Shakspere* (1839) and in two other books in 1843 and 1849. Ingleby wrote his *Shakspere Allusion Books* in 1874, Coleridge his *Lectures and Notes on Shakspere* in 1883, and Boas his *Shakspere and his Predecessors* in 1895. The "New Shakspere Society" was founded by orthodox scholars in 1873, but their use of the proper spelling for Shakspere of Stratford had to give way to twentieth-century pressure: its name was changed to "New Shakespeare Society." A *Shakspere Concordance* appeared in 1875. The *Shakspere Quarto Facsimiles* (reproductions of the small-sized copies of the Shakespeare plays) were published in 1891. But the name had begun to vanish. One major publication did use the Stratford man's name in 1923 (*The Bibliographical Study of Shakspere*), and *Shakspere's Small Latin and Less Greek* by Baldwin, possibly the last, came in 1944. Thus Shakspere's name was taken from him, along with his true identity, by those holding the center, so-called orthodox ground of Shakespeare scholarship.

The trigger for killing off Shakspere's true name seems to have been the three-pronged attack on the orthodox theory of Shakespeare that occurred around the tercentenary of Shakspere's death in 1916. The first prong was a growth of support among senior legal and literary figures for the old theory that Francis Bacon was Shakespeare. The second was the growth of skepticism about the idea that William Shakspere had ever been Shakespeare, encouraged by the publication of Mark Twain's *Is Shakespeare Dead?* in 1909. The third prong of the attack came from the publication around 1920 of two forceful claims, one for William Stanley, 6th Earl of Derby, the other for Edward de Vere, 17th Earl of Oxford, that each was the writer Shakespeare, adding to claims already made for Marlowe and Bacon.

To be generous to orthodox scholars who thought Shakespeare was Shakspere, one might suppose they thought it best to use the same name for both to avoid confusion. But that still would not excuse them denying that two different names had existed, one for the writer and one for the Shakspere family, and using that denial to argue that they were the same man.

As pointed out earlier, it was of great advantage to the orthodox theory to pretend William Shakspere's name had really been "Shakespeare" as it made possible arguments such as "Nobody ever doubted William Shakespeare wrote the plays that were published under his name." The mistreatment of Shakspere's name is now so well embedded that most new biographies of "Shakespeare"—and that includes the 30,000-word article about "William Shakespeare" in the prestigious 2004 *Oxford Dictionary of National Biography*—will nowhere alert their readers to the most basic fact regarding the Stratford man about whom they think they are reading: that he used the name Shakspere, his baptismal, burial and family name, and never used "Shakespeare." It is like omitting the information that George Eliot was, in fact, a woman.

It seems that the only British reference book still to use the proper family name of Shakspere for the actor-businessman from Stratford is the Oxford English Dictionary. Yet it does so under pressure. The OED's use of Shakspere has been said to be its *"greatest idiosyncrasy."* What is idiosyncratic, of course, is how orthodox Shakespeare scholars have managed to mislead the public for so long about Shakspere's name. Actually, Bill Bryson, the writer who made the above comment about the OED, drew attention in his book *Shakespeare* to the fact that Shakspere of Stratford never used the name "Shakespeare."

There is, however, something else that this unilateral changing of someone's name doesn't take into account: it ignores the fact that, however many ways other people may spell a man's name, it does not stop the man himself from knowing how he prefers it spelt. This is very important because whoever wrote under the name "Shakespeare" was remarkably consistent with the spelling of that pseudonym and never spelt it as "Shakspere." That fact alone in any ordinary investigation would be highly indicative that here were two different persons using two apparently similar but actually different names. If William Shakspere had been the brilliant, intelligent writer he has been claimed to be, it is hard to believe he would have wasted his time and risked confusion by writing his name one way at home, so to speak, and in a similar—but clearly different—way for a writing career in London.

Orthodox scholars may pour scorn on the idea that people like Bacon or the Earl of Oxford might have used a pen name so different from their own. But they take it for granted that it would not be odd for Shakspere to have taken a pen name so similar to his own as Shakespeare. A trawl through hundreds of authors who used pseudonyms shows almost all of them took names totally different from their own. The odd ones were Addison who used the name "Atticus," Ben Jonson who deliberately and publicly dropped the "h" from his family name to distinguish himself from the hundreds of other "Johnsons," Quincey who raised himself in status to "De Quincey," and Harold Rubin who deliberately anglicized his name to "Harold Robbins." Nobody went for the sort of accidental change that it is claimed happened with Shakespeare. As will become clear, there was somebody who deliberately chose the pseudonym "Shakespeare" and used it rigorously.

When the poem *Venus and Adonis* was published in 1593, its dedication had the name "Shakespeare" spelt the same in all five quarto editions and all eight octavo (half-quarto size) editions. For *The Rape of Lucrece* it was uniformly "Shakespeare" in the one quarto and five octavo editions. Nineteen of Shakespeare's plays were published in various quarto editions before the First Folio appeared in 1623. Of these editions, which numbered fifty-two in total, sixteen had no author's name. For the other thirty-six Quartos, all dated between 1598 and 1622, the author's name appeared thirty-nine times, three of which were in the announcements of the registration of particular quartos. On nineteen of those thirty-nine occasions, the name was given as "Shakespeare" and on fifteen it was "Shake-speare" with a hyphen. Of the remaining five, "Shak-speare" occurred twice and "Shakespere" three times. The Sonnets' author's name was given as "Shake-speare," as was the author of the odd (and originally untitled) *The Phoenix and Turtle*. With this consistency—the playwright-poet's name being spelt Shakespeare or Shake-speare 92 percent of the time, and never Shakspere—it is nonsense to suppose the writer was someone who did not know how to spell his name, or that the consistency of its spelling on the plays was some enormous statistical aberration. It is also nonsense for one to think the writer was a William Shakspere, who never used the name Shakespeare in his life, even when others were using it in writing about him, and it would have been advantageous for him to do the same.

Some scholars, perhaps realizing Abraham Lincoln's famous maxim that you can't fool all the people all of the time also applies to them, have tried a bold bluff to explain how William Shakspere's name got changed to Shakespeare. They (including some senior scholars) assert that it had to be changed because of a printing problem. They tell us that when typesetters first came to put the letters "k" and "s" in Shakspere's name next to each other in an Italianate form of italic type, they found that the forward tail or curlicue on the "k" would break the backward tail that occurs on the "s"; to avoid that problem, they say, the printers had to put an "e" between those two letters, thus creating the central "kes" of "Shakespeare" instead of the "ks" of "Shakspere." Unfortunately, as any Shakespeare scholar may observe, the first printings of the name "Shakespeare" appeared on the *Venus and Adonis* and *The Rape of Lucrece* dedications, and neither used Italianate script. They used a Roman typeface which had no tails or curlicues and in which the "k" and "s" could not possibly overlap (see Figure 3). This invented explanation indicates the problem orthodox scholars have with the differences in spelling and their need to distract readers from their problem. Figures 4a-d show how Shakespeare's name was typeset on various quarto editions, and it is obvious that typefaces could have been chosen so that the "k" and "s" would never overlap.

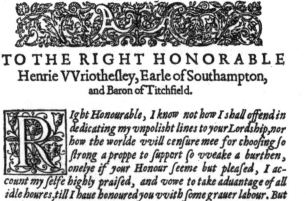

TO THE RIGHT HONORABLE
Henrie VVriothesley, Earle of Southampton,
and Baron of Titchfield.

Right Honourable, I know not how I shall offend in dedicating my vnpolisht lines to your Lordship, nor how the worlde vvill censure mee for choosing so strong a proppe to support so vveake a burthen, onelye if your Honour seeme but pleased, I account my selfe highly praised, and vowe to take aduantage of all idle houres, till I haue honoured you vvith some grauer labour. But if the first heire of my inuention proue deformed, I shall be sorie it had so noble a god-father : and neuer after eare so barren a land, for feare it yeeld me still so bad a haruest, I leaue it to your Honourable suruey, and your Honor to your hearts content, vvhich I wish may alvvaies ansvvere your ovvne vvish, and the vvorlds hopefull expectation.

Your Honors in all dutie,

William Shakespeare.

Fig. 3: Dedication from *Venus and Adonis,* 1593,
the earliest example of Shakespeare's name in print.

Fig. 4a: Detail from the title page of the 1603 Quarto of *Hamlet*.

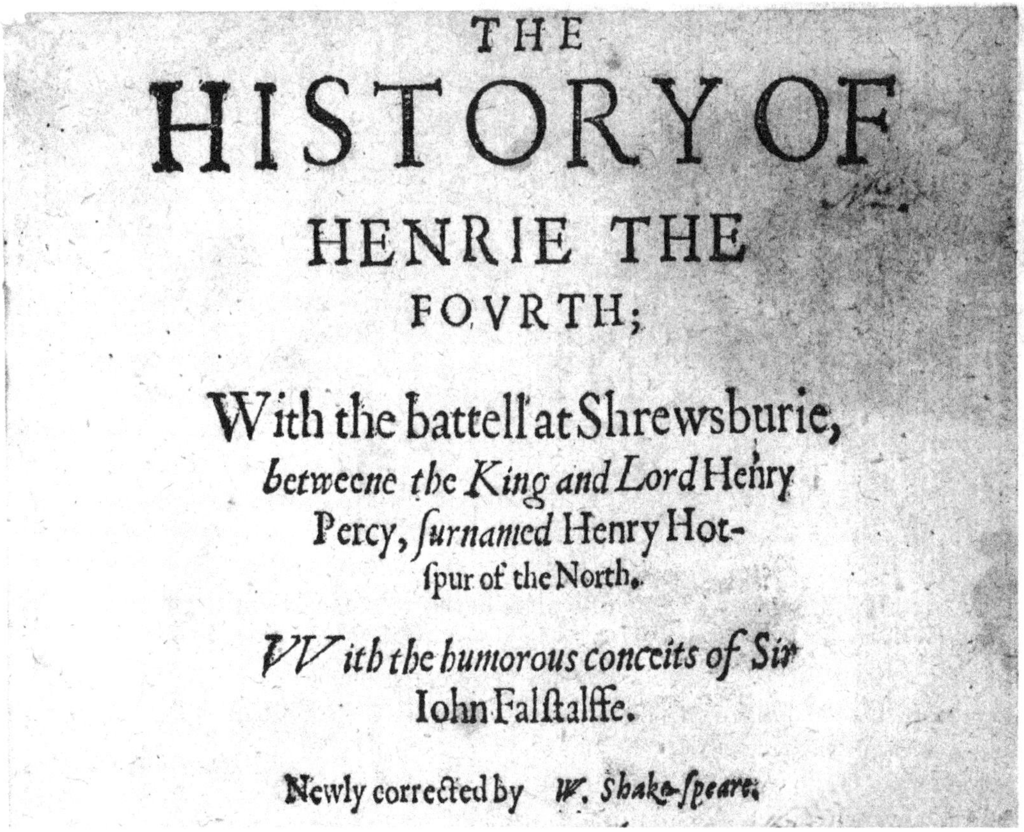

THE
HISTORY OF
HENRIE THE
FOVRTH;

With the battell at Shrewsburie,
betweene the *King and Lord* Henry
Percy, *surnamed* Henry Hot-
spur of the North.

VVith the humorous conceits of Sir
Iohn Falstalffe.

Newly corrected by *W. Shake-speare.*

Fig. 4b: Detail from the title page of the 1599 Quarto of *Henry IV Pt 1*.

Written by William Shakespeare.

Fig. 4c: Detail from the title page of the 1600 Quarto of *Henry IV Pt II*.

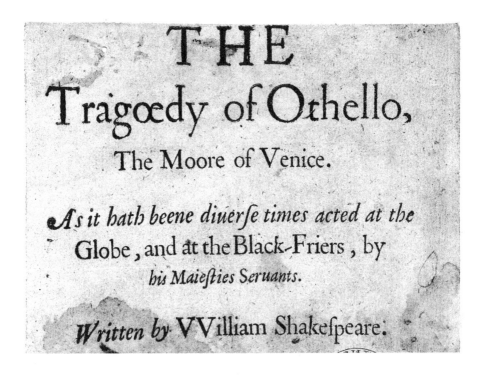

Fig. 4d: Detail from the title page of the 1622 Quarto of *Othello*.

A minor point in this discussion is the different pronunciations of "Shakspere" and "Shakespeare." Some orthodox scholars argue that they must have sounded the same, possibly hoping to explain why those who did not know how Shakspere spelt his name might have preferred to use the form Shakespeare. Such an argument is counter-productive, as it would accentuate how determined the Stratford man and the poet-playwright must have been, one to use Shakspere, the other Shakespeare. From what is known of Midlands pronunciation in the nineteenth century, and the way it carried through from Anglo-Saxon, the short flat "a" of, say, "hat" and the drawn out "a" of, say, "date" (sounding almost like "dirt") were quite different. It seems impossible "Shak" and "Shake" ever sounded the same. We can still usefully distinguish the two names and the two men by using the modern different pronunciations.

The orthodox theory about Shakspere being Shakespeare or Shake-speare faces another major problem in having to explain why Shakspere, who never had his name hyphenated, might, if he had been the writer, have hyphenated "Shake-speare" on so many of the quartos, as well as on the Sonnets. Some have tried to get around this problem by saying that the printers or publishers would have inserted hyphens in names on their own whims. Yet that has to assume the gritty Shakspere—as the great writer—would not know what was happening or was happy for his name to be messed about on a regular basis; it did not happen for others. It is far more convincing to say that printers might have preferred the form Shake-speare if they knew it was a pseudonym.

During what is known as the Martin Marprelate or Mar-Prelate controversy around 1589, hyphenated pseudonyms were thick on the ground. The name was the pseudonym of a still-unidentified pamphleteer who wrote scathing criticisms exposing corrupt practices and cynical behavior by officials in the church hierarchy. In addition to Marprelate itself, other pseudonyms that were so treated were Mar-Martin, Mar-ton, Mar-tother, Trouble-knave, Signior Some-body,

Tom Tell-truth and—this one being known to have hidden Thomas Nashe—Cuthbert Curry-knave. Shake-speare looks to fit into that pseudonymous class very well. Moreover, Pallas Athena, warrior goddess of the arts, praised as the tenth muse in Shakespeare's Sonnet 38, was a spear-shaker, and William was a standard nickname for a poet—used, for example, for Philip Sidney. So the name William Shake-speare adopted by a poet who was noted by Jonson to *"shake a lance ... at ignorance"* looks too good to be coincidental. In a period when the use of pseudonyms as an alternative to straight anonymity was common, this would have been a good one for a poet-playwright. The hyphenation of the name alone would not prove "Shake-speare" was a pseudonym, but it is entirely consistent with all the other evidence that it was.

The truth is that, whatever protests orthodox scholars may make, there would be nothing odd about an Elizabethan writer hiding behind a pseudonym. As the research of Taylor and Mosher[**] showed, the sixteenth and seventeenth centuries were the golden age for pseudonyms.

A discussion of the different names used by the Stratford man and the writer is very important. The false claim that those names were the same is used as the main, sometimes the only argument for William Shakspere being the great poet-playwright. In effect, the argument goes full circle. It is claimed Shakspere's name was really Shakespeare and then claimed that that is enough to prove he was the writer Shakespeare. But even if Shakspere had been baptized as Shakespeare that would not prove he was the writer. There were lots of Robert Greenes around in Elizabethan times but they were not all the playwright of that name. To prove a given man named Robert Greene was the writer Robert Greene would need rather more evidence than the similarity of name.

Here, by way of redress for the way William Shakspere's family name has been effectively airbrushed out of history, is a list of official entries for the Shakspere family.

Shakspere family records with sources.

C = Christening, B = Burial, M = Marriage.

C	**Joan (1st):**	*"Jone Shakspere daughter of John Shakspere"*; 15 September 1558	
C	**Margaret:**	*"Margareta filia Johannis Shakspere"*; 2 December 1562	
B	"	*"Margareta filia Johannes Shakspere"*; 30 April 1563	
C	**William:**	*"Gulielmus filius Johannes Shakspere"*; 26 April 1564	
B	"	*"Will. Shakspere, gent."*; 25 April 1616	
C	**Gilbert:**	*"Gilbertus Filius Johannis Shakspere"*; 13 October 1566	
B	"	*"Gilbert Shakspere adolescens"*; 3 December 1612 (1)	
C	**Joan (2nd):**	*"Jone the daughter of John Shakspere"*; 15 April 1569	
C	**Anne:**	*"Anna filia magistri Shakspere"*; 28 September 1571	
B	"	*"Anne daughter of Mr John Shakspere"*; 4 April 1579	
C	**Richard:**	*"Richard Sonne to Mr John Shakspere"*; 4 April 1574	
B	"	*"Rich. Shakspeare"*; 4 February 1613	
C	**Edmund:**	*"Edmund Sonne to John Shakspere"*; 3 August 1580	
B	"	*"Edmund Shakespeare a player"*; 31 December 1607 (2)	

[**] Taylor, A. and Mosher, F.J., *The Bibliographical History of Anonmya and Pseudonmya* (Univeristy of Chicago Press, 1951).

M	**William:**	License entry for *"Willellmum Shaxpere and Annam Whately"*; 27 November 1582
M	"	Bond of Sureties Entry for *"William Shagspere on thone partie and Anne Hathwey"*; 28 November 1582
C	**Susanna:**	*"Susanna daughter to William Shakspere"*; 26 May 1583 (3)
C	**Twins:**	*"Hamnet and Judeth sonne and daughter to William Shakspere"*; 2 February 1585
B	**Hamnet:**	*"Hamnet filius William Shakspere"*; 11 August 1596
B	**Father:**	*"Mr Johannes Shakspeare"*; 8 September 1601
M	**Susanna:**	*"M. Hall gentleman & Susanna Shaxspere"*; 5 June 1607
B	**Edward:**	*"Edward, sonne of Edward* [mistake for Edmund] *Shackspeere player, base-borne"*; 12 August 1607 (4)
B	**Mother:**	*"Mayry Shaxspere, wydowe"*; 9 July 1608
M	**Judith:**	*"Tho Queeny tow Judith Shakspere"*; 20 February 1616
C	**Shaksper:**	*"Shaksper fillius Thomas Quyny"*; 23 November 1616
B	"	*"Shakspere fillius Tho. Quyny"*; 8 May 1617

(1) *adolecens* = unmarried; (2) Registered in London; (3) Chambers and many others give Susanna as "Shakespear", but the register is clearly "Shakspere"; (4) Registered in London: father should be Edmund.

Sources: these details are all given in E.K. Chambers, *a Study of Facts and Problems* (1930), in plain type, and all but one spelt as in the records (note (3) above). They are in Schoenbaum, *Shakespeare: A Documentary Life* (1975), in facsimile, with eleven of the twenty-six in his more accessible *Shakespeare: A Compact Documentary Life* (1987), including Susanna.

Chapter 2:
Shakspere's Six Accepted Signatures: A comparison to signatures of other actors and writers of the period

By Frank Davis, M.D.

"Not one play, not one poem, not one letter in Shakspere's own hand has ever been found. He divided his time between London and Stratford, a situation conducive to correspondence. Early scholars . . . expected that at least some of his correspondence would have survived. Yet the only writings said to be in his own hand are six shaky, inconsistent signatures on legal documents . . . If, in fact, these signatures are his, they reveal that Shakspere experienced difficulty signing his name. Some document experts doubt that even these signatures are his and suggest they were done by law clerks."

– Shakespeare Authorship Coalition, Declaration of Reasonable Doubt

Alleged signatures of William Shakspere of Stratford-upon-Avon have been discussed and debated at length over the past 200 years by "experts" in paleography and graphology, often disagreeing on the signatures' authenticity. Today we are left with six signatures that are widely accepted as authentic in academia, although they, too, are not without question.* Some of these questions will be explored, but for the purpose of this paper the six signatures will be treated as authentic to allow their comparison to signatures of players and writers who were Shakspere's contemporaries in order to test whether they support the view that he was a professional writer *even if one assumes they are his*.

The idea for this paper developed out of a yearlong study of Henslowe's Diary. This collection of documents is a treasure trove of information about the activities and operation of the Elizabethan theater. It contains many autographs of actors, writers and others who signed receipts for payments and loans by Henslowe. Often the receipt itself was written by the receiver or borrower, at other times by Henslowe. These documents are reproduced in part in two works: one by R.A. Foakes and another by W.W. Greg. The latter includes many autographs in addition to those found in the Henslowe documents. More recently, the entire Henslowe and Alleyn diary and papers are now available online by the Dulwich College digitalization program, which is of monumental help.

A striking feature of the signatures of the actors and writers in these documents is that all of the writers, and many of the actors, signed their names using the Italian script, although some used a mixture of Italic and English script, which was not unusual at the time. The signatures on more important documents characteristically were more carefully written. The signatures of the writers and actors (shown below) contrast starkly with Shakspere's six signatures (also shown below).

---

* Per the epigraph above, the Shakespeare Authorship Coalition, sponsor of this book, does not believe that the six signatures discussed in this paper are necessarily in the hand of Shakspere.

Frank Davis, M.D.

Italian Script vs. English Secretary Hand

It is often said, correctly, that William Shakspere *may* have attended the Free Grammar School in Stratford where he would have learned the "English hand." This is indeed the script attempted in his six accepted signatures. The English secretary hand was derived from the German Gothic form brought over with William the Conqueror. In the sixteenth century the older English hand was giving way to the more modern Italian (Italic) hand, and the Italic hand was considered indicative of better education. In 1899 Sylvanus Urban called attention to this when he said:

> Educated men who had been to the Universities or had travelled abroad were capable of employing with equal facility both the English and the Italian character, and though they employed the former in their ordinary correspondence, they signed their names in the Italian hand (206).

Furthermore, Urban reports:

> Nowhere have I found a signature [i.e. Shakespeare's] so distinctly "English" (207).

Sir George Greenwood found it "extraordinary" that Mr. Shakspere, as author of the plays and poems of Shakespeare, should not have learned to write the Italian script (*Shakespeare's Handwriting*, 22). Greenwood goes on to admonish Sidney Lee for his statement that Shakspere "should not have taken the trouble to do so" [write in the Italian hand]. Greenwood points out that Shakespeare certainly knew the value of the art of good handwriting, quoting from *Hamlet*:

> I sat me down;
> Devised a new commission; wrote it fair
> I once did hold it, as our statists do,
> A baseness to write fair, and labour'd much
> How to forget that learning: But, sir, now
> It did me yeoman's service.
>
> (V.ii.32-37)

And from *Twelfth Night*, where Malvolio speaks of the forged Olivia letter:

> I think we do know the sweet Roman hand.   (III.iv.26)

Non-authentic Signatures

Before proceeding to the six accepted signatures, the following are some examples of "non-authentic" signatures. The British Library owns a copy of John Florio's translation of *Montaigne's Essays* (1603) which contains an alleged autograph, "Willm Shakspere." Sir Fredrick Madden, the Keeper of the Manuscripts for the British Museum, purchased the book in 1837 for £140. He was allegedly the "greatest authority" on handwriting of his day, and he vouched for the authenticity of the annotation. This was confirmed by Charles Knight, who called it an "undoubted signature" of William Shakspere (Greenwood: *Shakespeare's Handwriting,* 28). However, Professor Charles Wallace (discoverer of the Mountjoy signature) said that it was "still an open question," and Sir Edward Maunde Thompson, Director and Principal Librarian of the British Museum (1888-1909), pronounced it an "undoubted forgery" (Greenwood: *Shakespeare's Handwriting* 10).

But there is more: Thompson, after dismissing the signature in Florio's translation, then claimed that the abbreviated autograph ("Wm. Sh") in the Aldine *Ovid's Metamorphoses* (1502) is a "higher character" of forgery. Sidney Lee had said that it was "a genuine autograph of the poet" (Greenwood: *Shakespeare's Handwriting* 21), but then said "the genuineness of that signature is disputable" (Lee 296).

The point of these examples (and there are many more) is that there is no certainty as to the authenticity of alleged Shakspere signatures except in the mind of each "expert." It is therefore curious that present-day Stratfordian David Kathman claims that forgeries (e.g., those of Ireland and Collier) "are easy to spot for a modern scholar with knowledge of Elizabethan paleography" (2). If this is the case, one wonders why there is still so much disagreement among knowledgeable scholars over the authenticity of various signatures. For this study it would serve little purpose to discuss in detail the numerous signatures that have been discounted as forgeries.

Shakspere's Six Widely-accepted Signatures

The issue of Shakespeare's signatures became increasingly important as the authorship issue gained momentum in the late nineteenth and early twentieth centuries. Something had to be done to counter questions of literacy raised by Shakspere's alleged signatures, and also by the fact that no play, poem or even a letter in his hand had ever been found. Looking at the available autographs, could it be that these scraggly signatures actually belonged to the greatest, and one of the more prolific, writers in the English language?

The six Shakspere autographs that Tannenbaum called "unquestioned" (vii) in 1927, and which are still generally accepted by most Shakespeare scholars to this day, include two on documents relating to the purchase of the Blackfriar's gatehouse (March 10, 1613), three on Shakspere's will (1616), and one on the deposition in the Bellott vs. Mountjoy lawsuit (May 11, 1612). The latter document was discovered in 1909 by Dr. and Mrs. Charles Wallace, American scholars who spent many years in England searching for Shakespeare-related documents.

It is important to remember that questions of authenticity remain even for these six signatures. Most telling is the opinion of Jane Cox, then Custodian of Wills at the Public Records Office:

> It is obvious at a glance that these signatures, with the exception of the last two [on the last two pages of the will] are not the signatures of the same man. Almost every letter is formed in a different way in each. Literate men in the sixteenth and seventeenth centuries developed personalized signatures much as people do today and it is unthinkable that Shakespeare did not. Which of the signatures reproduced here is the genuine article is anybody's guess (33).

31

 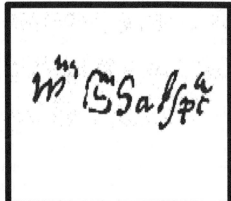

Fig. 1a and 1b: The Blackfriars Signatures

The two documents related to the purchase of the Blackfriars gatehouse consist of a deed (now in the Guildhall Library) for conveying the house, dated March 10, 1613, and a mortgage deed (now in the British Library) dated March 11, 1613. These documents are described in detail by Greenwood, Thompson, Halliwell-Phillipps and others. Regarding the dates, Greenwood says he has "no doubts" that the transactions were actually carried out on the same day (14).

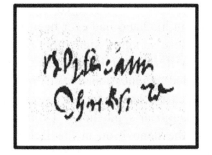 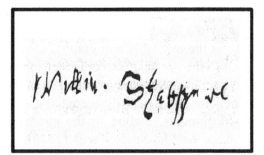

Fig. 2 a, b, c: Signatures on Shakspere's Will

The three signatures on Shakspere's will include one each at the bottom of pages one and two, and a third in the middle of page three (Fig. 2 a, b, c). It is especially important to notice the third signature (c). The first part of the signature, "By Me William," is clearly in another hand than that which wrote "Shaksper." Even some Stratfordians have noticed this. C.C. Stopes suggested that the words "By me" may have been written by the lawyer (Tannenbaum 153). Edward Thompson postulated that Shakspere suffered from "writer's cramps" and that "It was only when he came to the capital S… that his hand gave way" (64-5). The question of "writer's cramps" was investigated by Ralph W. Leftwich, M.D. He studied the signatures and compared them with twenty "recognized signs" of writer's cramp, finding "unimpeachable" evidence with nineteen present:

> Thus every one of the nineteen signs collected by me is present and I submit that a diagnosis of writer's cramp is unimpeachable. Every condition precedent, whether of age, of occupation, of chronicity, or of freedom from bodily or mental disease is fulfilled in the history of the case and every objective sign in the handwriting has been demonstrated. It should be a source of satisfaction to us that any misgivings as to Shakespeare's illiteracy have been set at rest by these investigations, for Baconians and others have been hard to argue with. (37)

On the other hand, Tannenbaum, also a physician, said that he had completely disproved the notion of "writer's cramps" (131-158). Tannenbaum says:

> As a result of these [his own] studies I have, it seems to me, disproved the more or less current notion that Shakespeare suffered from "writer's cramp" during the last years of his life, and I have been able to show that his handwriting presents no indications of chronic alcoholism or any form of acute or chronic disease of the nervous system; that he wrote both the old English ("Gothic") and the new Roman scripts neatly, fluently, clearly and with average speed; that his retirement to his native town and rural activities was in all probability due to chronic disease of the heart; and that the indications are that he died from an attack of angina pectoris, a painful disease of the heart, brought on, possibly, by distress about his younger daughter's unfortunate marriage and her threatened excommunication. (ix)

Here Tannenbaum claims to recognize not only the superb character of Shakespeare's writing ability, but also diagnoses his terminal medical problem and even the cause of Shakepeare's presumed angina pectoris. It is hoped that his paleographic expertise exceeds his medical acumen because his medical diagnosis is baseless despite the fact that he was a physician. His prejudice is obvious—a prejudice seen all too often in matters relating to the issue of Shakspere's authorship. More likely Shakspere's poor handwriting is due to his lack of writing skill or to his being too sick, as has sometimes been suggested. However, illness doesn't explain the similarity with the other signatures attributed to him, some years before the signatures of his will, when his health was not in question.

Fig. 3: Signature on Mountjoy Deposition

Frank Davis, M.D.

The signature on the Bellott-Mountjoy deposition is the only writing sample of the alleged Bard that is universally accepted in academia. There seems to be no difference of opinion that this was the signature of the man, Shakspere, not that of a scribe or attorney. Yet it is still a poorly contrived autograph, despite the accolades some orthodox scholars attempt to give it.

Despite more than a century of scrutiny, experts still cannot agree on the spellings of Shakspere's name in his six signatures. Their illegibility makes it difficult to tell, but no two of them appear to be spelled exactly the same way. Either Shakspere was an exception to Jane Cox's comment (supra) that "Literate men in the sixteenth and seventeenth centuries developed personalized signatures… and it is unthinkable that Shakespeare did not," or Shakspere was not, in fact, a literate man and not the author Shakespeare. The problem is even more apparent when his signatures are compared with those of his contemporaries.

Signatures of Contemporaries

Shown below are examples of signatures of both writers (Fig. 4) and actors (Fig. 5) who were contemporaries of Shakspere. Whether in the English secretary or Italian hand, they are all quite clear and legible. Almost without exception, the signers seem to make an effort to sign with clarity and decisiveness—something not found in Shakspere's six signatures. This should be sufficient to show there is reason to question Shakspere's writing ability.

Those not trained in reading the English secretary hand may find it difficult to compare signatures written in this hand, whereas reading and comparing with the Italic hand is not difficult as our present handwriting is based on the Italic. It is important to note that with the signatures in the English secretary hand invariably each letter can be distinguished in the comparison signatures, whereas this is not the case with Shakspere's six alleged signatures.

Assuming the alleged signatures are by Shakspere, it is difficult to justify the obvious discrepancy between his ability to sign his name relative to other actors, let alone his contemporary writers.

Fig. 4: Writers' Signatures

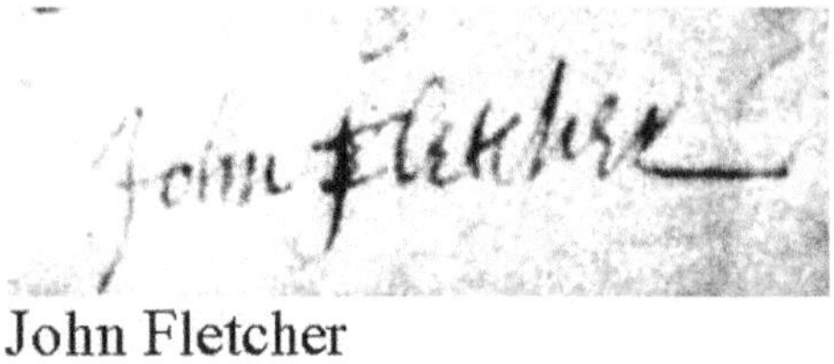

John Fletcher 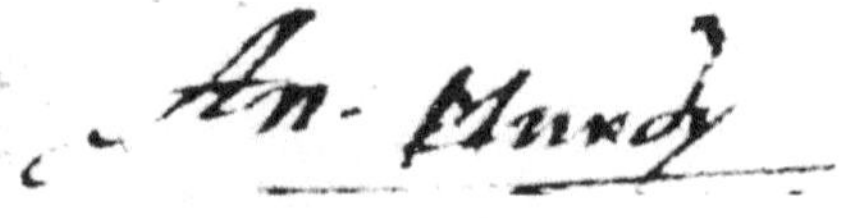   Anthony Mundy

Michael Drayton

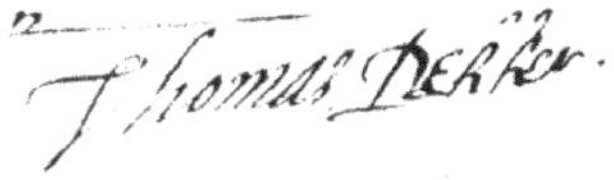

Thomas Middleton

Thomas Dekker

Robert Duborne

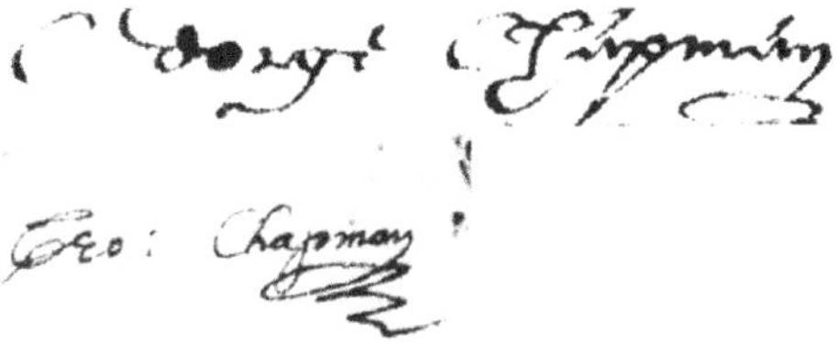

George Chapman
(both Italic and English secretarial hands)

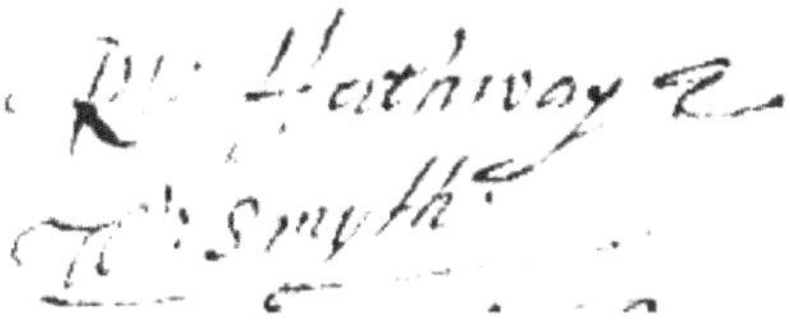

George Turbervyle

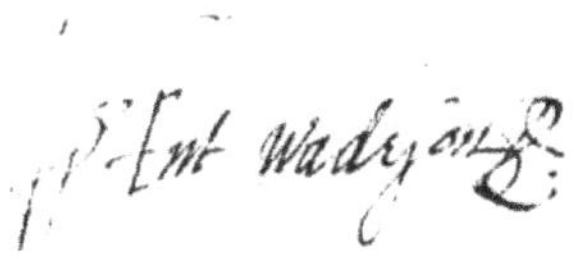

Thomas Heywood

Richard Hathway & William Smyth

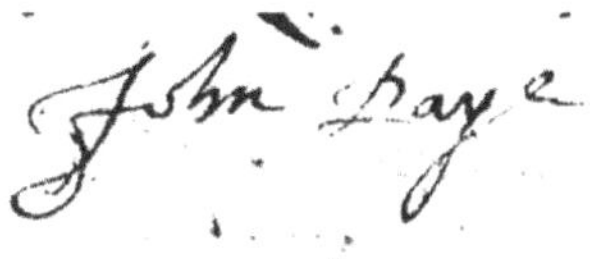

Robert Wilson

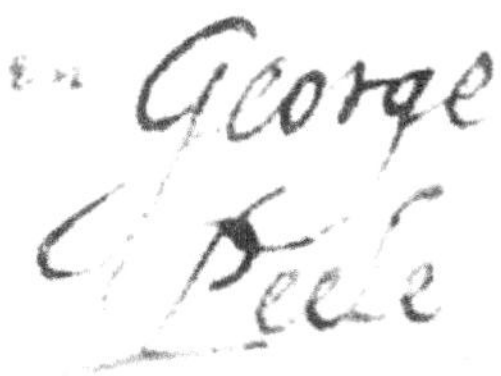

John Daye

George Peele

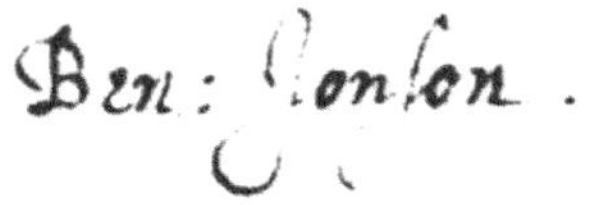

Ben Jonson

Anthony Wadeson

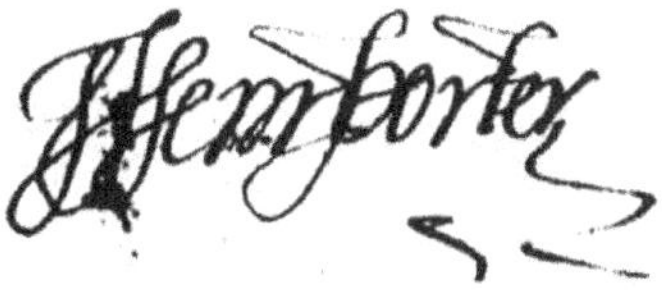

Henry Porter

Nathan Field

Thomas Kydd

Jhon Lyly

Thomas Lodge

John Marston

Philip Massinger

Henry Cheek

Edward Dyer

Samuel Danyel

Gabriel Harvey (Latin signature)

Edmund Spenser

Jhon Phillips
(secretarial signature distinctively showing each letter)

Fig. 5: Actors' Signatures

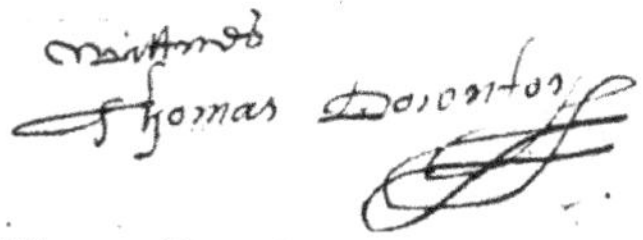

Thomas Downton

Richard Jones

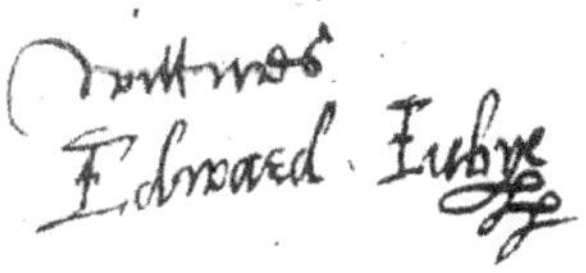

Edward Jubye

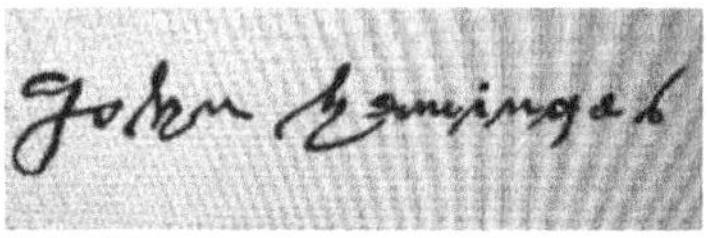

John Heminges

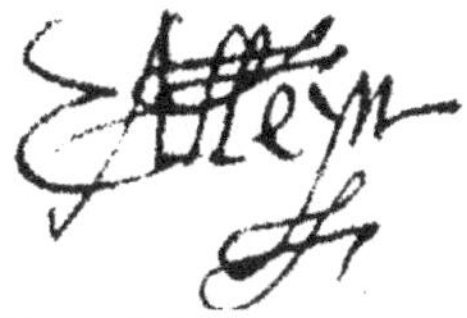

E lward Alleyn

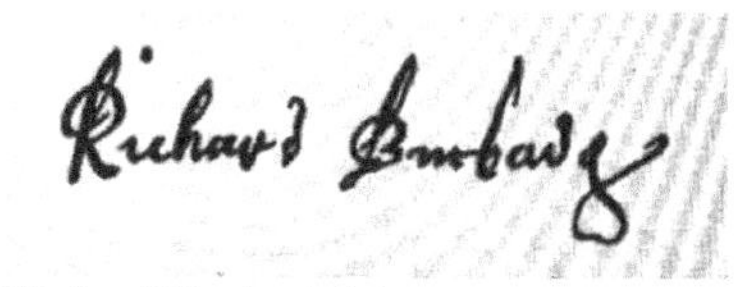

Richard Burbadg(e)

Robert Shaa & Thomas Towne

William Birde & Gabriell Spenser

William Birde

Frank Davis, M.D.

Many more examples can be found in Henslowe's diary and papers, and W.W. Greg's books on autographs and manuscripts. Curiously, Greg omitted Shakspere's signatures from his great work, *English Literary Autographs*. His explanation for not including Shakspere's six accepted signatures is given in the introduction to his book:

> Of course, it will be understood that of many authors I should have liked to include no autograph was available, beyond, in some cases, a bare signature, which I had decided was of no use for my purpose.

It seems possible that Greg was concerned about the effect of a side-by-side comparison of Shakspere's penmanship to that of his contemporaries, as has been done in this paper.

Shakspere's Literacy

Was William Shakspere, the actor, literate? The surprising answer is, not necessarily; but first we must examine what is meant by "literacy." In 1984 Laura Stevenson demonstrated that "Writing skills don't necessarily reflect one's ability to read" (53). Thomas Corns echoes this: "…social historians have often argued that the ability to read may have been enjoyed by some who were not able to write" (2). According to John Brewer (1997), literacy today means "the ability to read *and* write." He adds:

> Throughout history, reading has been more common than writing, partly because writing materials were so expensive… It's generally believed that the reading rate was substantially higher than what would be indicated by the number of people who could write (155).

THE
ENGLISH SCHOOLE-
MAISTER,

Teaching all his Scholers, of what age
foeuer, the most easie, short, and perfect order of
distinct reading, and true writing our English tongue
that hath euer yet been knowne and
published by any.

And further also teacheth a direct course, how any vnskilful
person may easily both vnderstand any hard english words, which the
shall in the Scriptures, Sermons, or elsewhere heare or reade: and also be
made able to vse the same aptly themselues. And generally whatsoeuer is necel
sary to be knowne for English speech: so that he which hath this booke only, needeth buy no other to make him fit, from his letters, vnto the
Grammar schoole, for an apprentice, or any other his owne pri-
nate vse, so farre as concerneth English. And therefore
is made not onely for children, (though therfit
booke be meere childish for them) but
also for all other especially that
are ignorant in the La-
tine toogue.

In the next page the Schoole-maister hangeth forth his table, to the
view of all beholders, setting forth some of the chiefe
commodities of his profession.

Deuised far chy faire that wanteth any part of this skill, by Edmund Coote
Maister of the Free-schoole in Bury S. Edmund.

Perused and approved by publike authoritie.

AT LONDON
Printed by the Widow Orwin, for Ralph Iackson and
Robert Dexter, 1596.

A clear example of the ability to read but not write is found in a work contemporary with Shakespeare. Edmund Coote's *The English Schoole-maister*, published in 1596, contains this revealing exchange:

John: How do you write people?
Robert: I cannot write.
John: I mean not so, but when I say write I mean spell, for in my meaning they are both one.
Robert: Then I answer you p,e,o,p,l,e.

(Cressy 21)

Also, according to James Daybell (2005), "The ability to perform a rudimentary signature rather than making a mark, an act that could be learned as a trick, does not provide a qualitative indication of the extent of individuals' literary skills" (695).

Most players were undoubtedly literate in the full sense. Henslowe's Diary and other documents noted by Honigmann & Brock in *Playhouse Wills* provide evidence that most actors could read and sign their names legibly. There are, however, documented exceptions, e.g., William Sly who, as reported by Honigmann, signed his will with an "X."

Conclusion

Evidence from Henslowe's Diary, Greg's *English Literary Autographs* and other documents show that during William Shakspere's time, virtually all writers and many actors signed their name with the newer Italic hand generally indicative of a higher degree of education. These documents show no signature of a writer so poorly executed as Shakspere's generally accepted autographs, calling into question whether he would have chosen to become a writer as his profession to earn a living.

Most actors were certainly literate, or at least capable of signing their own name legibly. The ability to write was not, however, a requirement for being an actor as it was common at the time to be able to read, yet not able to write. The anomalous case of Mr. Shakspere, actor and entrepreneur, is easily resolved if he was not the author of the plays attributed to him. The plays and poems are certainly beyond the scope of someone who, at best, could barely write his own name.

Works Cited:

Collier, J. Payne. *Lives Of The Original Actors In Shakespeare's Plays*. London: Shakespeare Society. 1853.

Collins, Churton. *Studies in Shakespeare*. New York: E.P.Dutton, 1904.

Corns, Thomas N. *A History of Seventeenth-Century English Literature*. Malden: Blackwell, 2007.

Cox, Jane. *Shakespeare in the Public Records* (Section on the Will and Signatures). London: Her Majesty's Stationery Office, 1985.

Cressy, David. *Literacy & the Social Order*. New York: Cambridge University Press. 1980.

Dawson, Giles and Kennedy-Skipton, Laetitia. *Elizabethan Handwriting* 1500-1650. New York: W.W. Norton, 1966.

Daybell, James. Interpreting Letter and Reading Script:Evidence for Female Education and Literacy in Tudor England. *History of Education*, Vol. 34 no.6, pp. 695-715, Nov. 2005.

Foakes, R.A. *Henslowe Diary and Papers*. Cambridge: CUP, 1977.

Greenwood, George. *Is There a Shakespeare Problem?* London: John Lane, 1916.

————*In Re Shakespeare Beeching v. Greenwood.* London: John Lane, 1909.

————*Shakspere's Handwriting*. London: John Lane, 1920.

————*The Shakspere Signatures and "Sir Thomas More"*. London: Wyman & Sons, Ltd., 1924.

Greg, W.W. *English Literary Autographs*. Oxford: OUP, 1932.

Halliwell-Phillipps, James O. *Outline of the Life of Shakespeare*. London:Longman's, 6th ed. Vol. 1, 1886.

Honigmann, E.A. & Brock, Susan. *Playhouse Wills, 1558-1642*. Manchester Univeristy Press, 1993.

Kathman, David. *Shakespeare's Will*. http://shakespeareauthorship.com/shaxwill.html.

Frank Davis, M.D.

Lee, Sidney. *A Life of William Shakespeare.*New York: Macmillan & Co. 1898.

Stevenson, Laura. *Praise and Paradox: Merchants and Craftsmen in Elizabethan Popular Literature.* Cambridge University Press, 1984.

Tannenbaum, Samuel. *Problems in Shakespeare's Penmanship.* New York: Century, 1927.

Thompson, E. Maunde. *Shakespeare's Handwriting.* London: OUP, 1916.

Urban, Sylvanus. *Gentleman's Magazine*, Vol. 287. London: Chatto & Windus, 1899.

Chapter 3:
The Missing Literary Paper Trail

Based on *Shakespeare's Unorthodox Biography*, by Diana Price

> "It is not that there are no documents for Mr. Shakspere; there are close to seventy, but all are non-literary. They reveal a businessman of Stratford, plus a theater entrepreneur and sometime minor actor in London . . . The orthodox see nothing unusual in the lack of documentation for Mr. Shakspere's ostensible career, but he is the only presumed writer of his time for whom there is no contemporary evidence of a writing career."
>
> – Shakespeare Authorship Coalition, Declaration of Reasonable Doubt

In *Shakespeare's Unorthodox Biography: New Evidence of an Authorship Problem*, scholar Diana Price compared existing evidence for the writing careers of twenty-four of Shakspere's contemporaries with the evidence (or lack thereof) for Shakspere's supposed writing career. The comparison group included Ben Jonson, Edmund Spenser, Gabriel Harvey, Thomas Nashe, Robert Greene, George Chapman, Thomas Dekker, Thomas Heywood, John Marston, Francis Beaumont, John Fletcher, Samuel Daniel, George Peele, John Lyly, Thomas Watson, Christopher Marlowe, Thomas Kyd and others. Price's findings, organized into ten categories, are revealing. Here is a summary:

1. Evidence of Education—exists for 18 of 24 of Shakspere's contemporaries

Shakspere: none. No record shows he ever attended any school. He may have attended the Stratford grammar school, at least for a time; but all records for the period are lost. Records survive for Oxford and Cambridge universities, but none places him at either. Outstanding grammar school boys, like Marlowe, could win scholarships to the colleges. Nothing shows that anyone thought Shakspere was a good student, or any sort of student.

His success as a businessman and actor with the Lord Chamberlain's Men and King's Men suggests he could probably read, but his alleged signatures suggest he could barely write. The absence of any surviving letters in his hand suggests he probably did *not* write. His detailed will, containing no bequest for education, suggests he didn't value education.

2. Record of correspondence, especially concerning literary matters—exists for 14 of 24 contemporaries

Shakspere: none. Not one letter in his hand has ever been found. One letter addressed *to* him survives. It requested a loan, and it was unopened and undelivered. It did not relate to literary matters. Price notes that "Nearly every play mentions letters, so we know the dramatist considered correspondence part of everyday life. . . . Shakspere divided his time between London and Stratford, a situation particularly conducive to letter-writing, so this gap in his records is doubly suspicious" (128). There is no record of correspondence between Shakespeare and any of his "collaborators."

3. Evidence of having been paid to write—exists for 13 of 24 contemporaries

Shakspere: none. No record shows that any William Shakespeare was ever paid to write.

4. Evidence of a direct relationship with a patron—exists for 15 of 24 contemporaries

Shakspere: none. *Venus and Adonis* (1593) and *The Rape of Lucrece* (1594) were dedicated to Henry Wriothesley, 3rd Earl of Southampton. Orthodox scholars say the dedications show that Shakespeare sought patronage from Southampton, and received it. In fact, no record shows that Shakespeare ever had a patron—not Southampton or anyone else (other than King James I, patron of the King's Men, not of Shakespeare personally). Orthodox scholars spent years searching records relating to Southampton, hoping to find something to document their relationship; they found nothing. The two dedications by themselves do not constitute evidence that the men ever met. Price interprets the line that some cite as evidence that they did meet as follows:

> In the dedication to *Lucrece*, Shakespeare wrote that 'the warrant I have of your Honourable disposition' made his poem 'assured of acceptance.' In other words, Shakespeare had heard reports of Southampton's presumably generous disposition. Writers often made overtures to potential patrons by professing that they had been assured of this lordship's disposition or that ladyship's generosity. (142)

In contrast, she gives this example by a man who *did* have Southampton as a patron:

> John Florio dedicated his Italian-English Dictionary, *A Worlde of Wordes*, to the 'most Honourable Earl of Southampton, in whose pay and patronage I have lived for some years.' (143)

She notes that even orthodox scholar Gary Taylor "thought that 'one might as reasonably say that the dedications express a desire/hope/expectation that the chosen patron' . . . would take note of the poems" (144).

5. Original manuscript—exists for 10 of 24 contemporaries

Shakspere: none; nor is any poem or play manuscript mentioned in his will.

6. Handwritten inscriptions, receipts, letters, etc., touching on literary matters—exists for 14 of 24 contemporaries

Shakspere: none.

7. Commendatory verses, epistles, epigrams contributed or received—exist for 20 of 24 contemporaries

Shakspere: none. Shakespeare wrote no commendatory verse and dedicated no play to anyone—not to Elizabeth I, nor to James I, patron of the King's Men acting company. No other writer wrote commendatory verses or dedicated works to Shakespeare.

Almost uniquely among Elizabethan poets, Shakespeare remained silent following the death of Elizabeth and wrote no verse commemorating the accession of King James I. Nor did he write a eulogy on the death of Prince Henry, the popular heir to the throne.

8. Miscellaneous records (e.g., referred to personally as a writer)—exist for all 24 contemporaries

Shakspere: none.

9. Evidence of books owned, written in, borrowed, or given—exist for 10 of 24 contemporaries

Shakspere: none. Traditionalists *assume* that Shakspere's books, never mentioned in his will, were listed in an inventory, now lost. This is unlikely (see Chapter 5). No book that Shakspere owned, or that is known to have been in his possession, has ever been found.

10. Notice at death as a writer—exists for 10 of 24 contemporaries

Shakspere: none. Price included evidence up to twelve months following death. The fact that the record is silent for over seven years following Shakspere's death suggests that his fellow actors, shareholders, and the writers of his day knew that he was not Shakespeare. If he was Shakespeare, he should have been eulogized and buried in Westminster Abbey. (see Chapter 6.)

This evidence is summarized in the Chart of Literary Paper Trails below. Documentation of the information in the Chart is in the revised edition of Price's book (see Works Cited).

Conclusion

Diana Price found evidence for the literary careers of twenty-four contemporary writers, but no comparable evidence for Shakspere's alleged literary career *relative to his peers*. Her criteria derive from *what exists for them*, not on *a priori* criteria she created herself. There is no denying this fact, and Stratfordian academics and the Shakespeare industry, based in Stratford, have given no rational explanation as to why this should be the case.

Works Cited

Price, Diana: *Shakespeare's Unorthodox Biography: New Evidence of an Authorship Problem* (Greenwood Press, 2001)

Price, Diana: *Shakespeare's Unorthodox Biography: New Evidence of an Authorship Problem* (paperback edition with corrections and additions, shakespeare-authorship.com, 2012)

Chart of Literary Paper Trails

	Evidence of Education	Record of correspondence, especially concerning literary matters	Evidence of having been paid to write	Evidence of a direct relationship with a patron
Ben Jonson	✓	✓	✓	✓
Thomas Nashe	✓	✓	✓	✓
Samuel Daniel	✓	✓	✓	✓
Edmund Spenser	✓	✓	—	✓
Philip Massinger	✓	✓	✓	✓
George Peele	✓	✓	✓	✓
Gabriel Harvey	✓	✓	—	✓
Michael Drayton	—	✓	✓	✓
George Chapman	—	✓	✓	✓
William Drummond	✓	✓	—	—
John Marston	✓	✓	✓	—
Anthony Munday	—	—	✓	✓
Robert Greene	✓	—	✓	✓
John Lyly	✓	✓	—	✓
Thomas Heywood	—	—	✓	—
Thomas Lodge	✓	✓	—	✓
Thomas Middleton	✓	—	✓	—
Thomas Dekker	—	✓	✓	—
Thomas Watson	✓	—	—	✓
Francis Beaumont	✓	—	—	—
John Fletcher	✓	—	—	—
Thomas Kyd	✓	✓	—	✓
John Webster	—	—	✓	—
Christopher Marlowe	✓	—	—	—
William Shakespere	—	—	—	—

*Price, Diana: *Shakespeare's Unorthodox Biography: New Evidence of an Authorship Problem*

Chart of Literary Paper Trails

Original manuscript extant	Handwritten inscriptions, reciepts, letters, etc. touching on literary matters	Commendatory verses, epistles, or epigrams contributed or received	Personally referred to as a wirter; misc. records	Evidence of books owned, borrowed, or given	Notice at death as a writer
✓	✓	✓	✓	✓	✓
✓	✓	✓	✓	✓	—
✓	✓	✓	✓	—	✓
—	✓	✓	✓	✓	✓
✓	✓	✓	✓	—	—
✓	✓	—	✓	—	—
✓	✓	✓	✓	✓	—
—	✓	✓	✓	—	✓
✓	✓	✓	✓	✓	—
—	✓	✓	✓	✓	—
✓	✓	✓	✓	—	✓
—	✓	✓	✓	—	✓
—	✓	✓	✓	—	—
✓	✓	✓	✓	—	✓
—	—	✓	✓	✓	—
✓	✓	—	✓	—	—
—	✓	✓	✓	—	—
—	—	✓	✓	—	✓
—	—	✓	✓	—	✓
—	—	✓	✓	✓	—
—	—	—	✓	—	—
—	—	✓	✓	—	—
—	—	—	✓	—	✓
—	—	—	—	—	—

(paperback edition with corrections and additions, shakespeare-authorship.com, 2012)

Chapter 4:
Shakspere in Stratford and London:
Ten Eyewitnesses Who Saw Nothing

By Ramon Jiménez

> "Several people who knew the man [Shakspere], or knew who he was, seem not to have associated him with the author [Shakespeare], including his son-in-law, Dr. John Hall, poet Michael Drayton and prominent historian William Camden."
>
> – Shakespeare Authorship Coalition, Declaration of Reasonable Doubt

It is well-known that the first references in print that seemed to connect William Shakspere of Stratford-upon-Avon to the plays of the playwright William Shakespeare were made in a collection—the First Folio, seven years after Shakspere's death. On the other hand, we can identify at least ten people who personally knew the William Shakspere of this Warwickshire town, or met his daughter, Susanna. At least six of them, and possibly all of them, were aware of plays and poems published under the name of one of the country's leading playwrights, William Shakespeare. All ten left us published books, poems, letters, notebooks, or diaries, some of which referred directly to events or people in Stratford. Yet *none* of these nine men and one woman—it is fair to call them "eyewitnesses"—left any hint that they connected the playwright with the person with the same, or similar, name in Stratford-upon-Avon.

William Camden

William Camden was the most eminent historian and antiquary of the Elizabethan age, and was deeply involved in the literary and intellectual world of his time. He knew Philip Sidney, was a valued friend of Michael Drayton, and was Ben Jonson's Headmaster at Westminster School. His most famous work was *Britannia*, a history of England first published in Latin in 1586. It was translated, and frequently reprinted, and he revised it several times before his death in 1623.

Another of Camden's books was *Remaines Concerning Britain*, a series of essays on English history, English names and the English language that he published in 1605. Camden wrote poetry himself, and in the section on poetry, he referred to poets as "God's own creatures." He listed eleven English poets and playwrights who he thought would be admired by future generations—in other words, the best writers of his time (*Remaines* 287, 294). Among the eleven were six playwrights, including Jonson, Chapman, Drayton, Daniel, Marston, and William Shakespeare.

Two years later, in 1607, Camden published the sixth edition of his *Britannia*, which by then had doubled in size because of his extensive revisions and additions. He arranged the book by shire or county, with his description of each beginning in the pre-Roman period and extending to contemporary people and events. With Camden's interests and previous work in mind, it is surprising to find that in this 1607 edition, and in his subsequent editions, in the section on Stratford-upon-Avon, he described this "small market-town" as owing "all its consequence to two natives of it. They are John de Stratford, later Archbishop of Canterbury, who built the church, and Hugh Clopton, later mayor of London, who built the Clopton bridge across the Avon" (*Britannia* 2, 445). In the same paragraph, Camden called attention to George Carew, Baron Clopton, who lived nearby and was active in the town's affairs.

There is no mention of the well-known poet and playwright, William Shakespeare, who had supposedly been born and raised in Stratford-upon-Avon, whose family supposedly still lived there, and who by this date had supposedly returned there to live in one of the grandest houses in town. Elsewhere in *Britannia*, Camden noted that the poet Philip Sidney had a home in Kent. We know he was familiar with literary and theatrical affairs because he was a friend of the poet and playwright Michael Drayton (Newdigate 95), and he noted in his diary the deaths of the actor Richard Burbage and the poet and playwright Samuel Daniel in 1619.[1] He made no such note on the death of William Shakspere of Stratford-upon-Avon in April 1616.

It might be suggested that Camden was unfamiliar with the Warwickshire area, and wasn't aware that one of the leading playwrights of the day lived in Stratford-upon-Avon. But could this be true? In 1597 Queen Elizabeth appointed Camden to the post of Clarenceaux King of Arms, one of the two officials in the College of Arms who approved applications for coats of arms. Two years later, John Shakspere, William's father, applied to the College to have his existing coat of arms impaled, or joined, with the arms of his wife's family, the Ardens of Wilmcote (Chambers 2:18-32). Some writers have asserted that William Shakspere himself made this application for his father, but there is no evidence of that. What is likely is that William paid the substantial fee that accompanied the application.

The record shows that Camden and his colleague William Dethick approved the modification that John Shakspere sought. However, in 1602 another official in the College brought a complaint against Camden and Dethick that they had granted coats of arms improperly to twenty-three men, one of whom was John Shakspere. Camden and Dethick defended their actions, but there is no record of the outcome of the matter, and the Shakspere coat of arms, minus the Arden impalement, later appeared on the monument in Holy Trinity Church. Because of this unusual complaint, Camden had good reason to remember John Shakspere's application, and it is very probable that he had met both father and son. At the least, he knew who they were and where they lived.

William Camden had another occasion to come in contact with the Shaksperes. In the summer of 1600, when the famous Sir Thomas Lucy died, Camden bore Lucy's coat of arms in the procession and conducted the funeral at Charlecote, only a few miles from Stratford-upon-Avon (Malone 2:556). Thomas Lucy knew the Shaksperes also. When he was justice of the peace in Stratford-upon-Avon, John Shakspere was brought up before him more than once.

So, even though William Camden revered poets, had several poet friends, and wrote poetry himself; even though he knew the Shaksperes, father and son, and even though he mentioned playwrights and poets in his books and in his diary, he never connected the Shakspere he knew in Stratford-upon-Avon with the one on his list of the best English poets.

Michael Drayton

Another eyewitness is the poet and dramatist Michael Drayton, who was born and raised in Warwickshire, only about twenty-five miles from Stratford-upon-Avon. It is hard to imagine that Michael Drayton was unaware of William Shakespeare. The two were almost exact contemporaries. They both wrote sonnets, and many critics have even found the influence of Shakespeare in Drayton's poetry (Campbell 190-1). Also, they both wrote plays that appeared about the same time on the London stage in the late 1590s. In 1599 Drayton, along with Anthony Munday, Robert Wilson, and Richard Hathaway, wrote a play—*Sir John Oldcastle*—that was supposed to be a response to Shakespeare's plays about Falstaff (Chambers 1:134).

In 1612 Drayton published the first part of *Poly-Olbion,* a poetical description of England, and a county-by-county history that included well-known men of every kind. In it were many references to Chaucer, to Spenser, and to other English poets. But in his section on Warwickshire, Drayton never mentioned Stratford-upon-Avon or Shakespeare, even though by 1612 Shakespeare was a well-known playwright. It seems that Drayton never connected the writer to the William Shakspere he must have known in Stratford-upon-Avon.

How do we know he knew him? Many supporters of the Stratford theory think so. Samuel Schoenbaum wrote that it is "not implausible" that Drayton and Shakespeare, and Ben Jonson as well, had that "merry meeting" reported in the 1660s by John Ward, the vicar of Stratford-upon-Avon (Schoenbaum 296). In fact, more than one scholar has found evidence that Michael Drayton was the "Rival Poet" of the sonnets. But we have better evidence than that.

Drayton's life is well-documented. He had a connection to the wealthy Rainsford family, who lived at Clifford Chambers, less than three miles from Stratford-upon-Avon. Drayton had been in love with Lady Rainsford from the time she was Ann Goodere, a girl in the household in which he was in service in the 1580s. She was the subject of his series of love sonnets, *Ideas Mirrour*, published in 1594. Although she rejected him and married Henry Rainsford in 1595, Drayton hung around their household and made himself a friend of the family. He apparently never stopped loving her, and from the early 1600s until his death in 1631 he made frequent visits to their home at Clifford Chambers, sometimes staying all summer.

The Shakespearean scholar Charlotte Stopes was certain that Shakespeare would have been "an honored guest" at the Rainsford home because of the family's literary interests, but there is no record of such a visit (Stopes 1907, 206). But even if Shakspere may never have visited the Rainsfords, Dr. John Hall, the man who married his daughter, certainly did. Hall was the Rainsfords' family doctor and once treated Drayton for a fever, probably at the Rainsford home. The doctor made a record of it in his case book, and even noted that Drayton was an excellent poet (Lane 40-1). His treatment for Drayton's fever was a spoonful of "syrup of violets," but he did recover.

Another reason that Drayton must have been aware of a playwright named Shakespeare was that in 1619 *Sir John Oldcastle,* the play Drayton had written with three others, was printed by William Jaggard and Thomas Pavier with Shakespeare's name on the title page (Chambers 1:533-4). This is something an author would notice.

It is very probable that if Drayton thought that Dr. Hall's father-in-law was the famous playwright and poet, he would have written or told someone about him. But there is no mention of Shakspere anywhere in his substantial correspondence. In all his writings—the collected edition is in five volumes—despite his mention of more than a dozen contemporary poets and playwrights, Drayton never referred to William Shakespeare at all until more than ten years after Shakspere's death in 1616. When he finally did, he wrote four lines about what a good comedian he was. It is unclear whether he was referring to him as a playwright, an actor, or in some other capacity.

Thomas Greene

Our third eyewitness connects Michael Drayton and William Shakspere of Stratford-upon-Avon even more closely. In the 1603 edition of one of Drayton's major poems, *The Barons' Wars*, there appeared a commendatory sonnet—a Shakespearean sonnet—by one Thomas Greene.[2] Also in 1603, the bookseller and printer William Leake published a poem by this same Thomas Greene titled *A Poet's Vision and a Princes Glorie.* In seventeen pages of forgettable verse, Greene predicted a renaissance of poetry under the new King, James I. (For more than twenty years, beginning in 1596, William Leake was the holder of the publishing rights to *Venus and Adonis* [Chambers 1:544].)

Orthodox scholars agree that this Thomas Greene was none other than the London solicitor for the Stratford Corporation, and the Town Clerk of Stratford-upon-Avon for more than ten years (Dobson and Wells 173). He had such a close relationship with the Shaksperes that he named two of his children William and Anne. He and his wife and children lived in the Shakspere household at New Place for many months during 1609 and 1610 (Schoenbaum 282). He was also the only Stratfordian contemporary of Shakspere to mention him in his diary. This was in connection with the Welcombe land enclosure matter, where he referred to him as his "cosen" (Campbell 272).

Thomas Greene was also a friend of the dramatist John Marston, and they were both resident students at the Middle Temple during the mid-1590s. Yet nowhere in his diary or in his surviving letters does Thomas Greene—apparently the author of a Shakespearean sonnet himself—even hint that the Shakspere he knew was a poet. Greene made no comment in his diary about a book called *Shake-speare's Sonnets*, with its strange dedication to "our ever-living poet," that was published in London in 1609, about the time he was living in the Shakspere household. Nor does he mention in his diary the death of the supposedly famous playwright in the spring of 1616. Stopes wrote that "It has always been a matter of surprise to me that Thomas Greene, who mentioned the death of Mr. Barber, did not mention the death of Shakespeare." For this she offered the astounding explanation—"Perhaps there was no need for him to make a memorandum of an event so important to the town and himself" (Stopes 1907, 89). Thomas Greene's failure to make any note of his friend's supposed dramatic genius is especially unusual because he knew him so well, and because he was a published poet himself.

John Hall

Our fourth eyewitness is that same Dr. John Hall who came to Stratford-upon-Avon from Bedfordshire in the early 1600s, and married Susanna Shakspere in 1607. During his more than thirty years of practice in Warwickshire, Dr. Hall was considered one of the best physicians in the county, and was called often to the homes of noblemen throughout the area. As a leading citizen of the town, he was elected a Burgess to the City Council three times before he finally accepted the office. On the death of his father-in-law in 1616, Dr. Hall, his wife Susanna, and their eight-year-old daughter Elizabeth moved into New Place with William Shakspere's widow Anne.

A few years after Dr. Hall's death in 1635, it transpired that he had kept hundreds of anecdotal records about his patients and their ailments—records that have excited the curiosity of both literary and medical scholars. Two notebooks were recovered, and one containing about 170 cases was translated from Latin and published by one of his fellow physicians. The other, possibly once in the possession of the Shakespearean scholar Edmond Malone, has, unfortunately, disappeared. In the single surviving manuscript are descriptions of dozens of Dr. Hall's patients and their illnesses, as well as his wife Susanna, and their daughter Elizabeth. Also mentioned are the Vicar of Stratford-upon-Avon and various noblemen and their families, as well as Michael Drayton's friends the Rainsfords, and of course Drayton himself. In his notes about one patient, Thomas Holyoak, Dr. Hall mentioned that his father Francis Holyoak had compiled a Latin-English dictionary. John Trapp, a minister and the schoolmaster of the Stratford Grammar School, he described as being noted "for his remarkable piety and learning, second to none" (Joseph 47, 94).

But nowhere in the notebook that has survived is there any mention of Hall's father-in-law William Shakspere. This, of course, has vexed and puzzled scholars. Dr. Hall surely treated his wife's father during the ten years they lived within minutes of each other. Why wouldn't he record any treatment of William Shakspere and mention his literary achievements as he had Michael Drayton's and Francis Holyoak's? The accepted explanation has always been that of the few cases in Dr. Hall's notebook that he dated, none bears a date earlier than 1617, the year after Shakspere's death. For decades scholars have assumed that any mention of Shakespeare was probably in the lost notebook.

But recently this assumption was proved false when a scholar found that at least four, and as many as eight, of the cases Hall recorded can be dated before Shakspere died, even though the doctor didn't supply the dates himself. Because Dr. Hall nearly always noted the age and residence of his patients, most of them have been identified and their birth dates found in other sources. The earliest case in the existing manuscript can thus be dated to 1611, others to 1613, 1614 and 1615, and another four to 1616, the very year of Shakspere's death (Lane 351).

It appears that Dr. Hall made his notes shortly after treating his patients, but didn't prepare them for publication until near the end of his life. Hall was obviously aware and admiring of his patients' status and achievements, especially their scholarly and literary achievements, as his comments about Drayton, Holyoak, and others reveal. By 1611 William Shakespeare was well-known as an outstanding, if mysterious, playwright. By then more than a dozen of his plays had been issued in quarto, and there had been several printed tributes. Thus, there is good reason to expect that Dr. John Hall would have noted his treatment of William Shakspere of Stratford-upon-Avon during the ten years he knew him—if he thought he were someone worthy of mention. It is indeed strange that in the early 1630s, as he was collecting the cases he wished to publish, he should neglect to include any record of his treating his supposedly famous father-in-law. Stopes called it "the one great failure of his life" (Stopes 1901, 82).

James Cooke

Our fifth eyewitness is Dr. James Cooke, a surgeon from Warwick who was responsible for the publication of John Hall's casebook. Although he was about twenty years younger than Hall, Cooke was acquainted with him from the time they had both attended the Earl of Warwick and his family. In the 1640s a Parliamentary army was contending with the army of Charles I in a civil war that would end with Charles' defeat, and eventual beheading in 1649. Both royalists and rebels occupied Stratford-upon-Avon on different occasions. In 1644 Dr. Cooke was attached to a Parliamentary army unit assigned to guard the famous Clopton Bridge at Stratford-upon-Avon. At this date, when Dr. John Hall had been dead nine years, James Cooke and a friend decided to visit Hall's widow Susanna "to see the books left by Mr. Hall" (Joseph 105).

When they arrived at New Place and met Susanna, Cooke asked if her husband had left any books or papers that he might see. When she brought them out, Cooke noticed two manuscript notebooks written in a Latin script that he recognized as Dr. Hall's. Susanna was confident that it wasn't her husband's handwriting, but when Dr. Cooke insisted, she agreed to sell him the manuscripts, and he carried them away with great satisfaction.

He eventually translated one of the notebooks, added some cases of his own, and published it in 1657 under a long title that is commonly shortened to *Select Observations on English Bodies*. On the title page John Hall is described as a "Physician, living at Stratford upon Avon, in Warwickshire, where he was very famous" (Joseph 104). In his introduction to the book, Cooke described his visit with Susanna, during which neither of them referred to her supposedly famous father, nor to any books or manuscripts that might have belonged to him. In fact, from Dr. Cooke's report of the meeting, neither Shakspere's daughter Susanna nor the doctor himself was aware of any literary activity by the William Shakspere who had lived in the very house they were standing in.

As is well known, William Shakspere of Stratford-upon-Avon mentioned no books, papers, or manuscripts in his will. After certain specific bequests, he left the rest of his goods and "household stuffe" to his daughter and her husband, John Hall. In contrast, Dr. Hall referred in his will to "my study of books" and "my manuscripts," and left them to his own son-in-law Thomas Nash (Lane 350).

Sir Fulke Greville

A sixth eyewitness is Sir Fulke Greville, later Lord Brooke, whose family had lived near Stratford for more than 200 years, and who must have known the Shakspere family. He was born in 1554 at Beauchamp Court less than ten miles from Stratford-upon-Avon, in the vicinity of Snitterfield, the home of Richard Shakspere, grandfather of William. Fulke Greville was a man of importance in Warwickshire. In 1592 he, Sir Thomas Lucy, and five others were appointed to a Commission to report on those who refused to attend church. In September of that year, the Commission reported to the Privy Council that nine men in the parish of Stratford-upon-Avon had not attended church at least once a month. Among the nine was John Shakspere, father of William (M. Eccles 33). Throughout his life Fulke Greville sought preferment at court, and eventually became Chancellor of the Exchequer and Treasurer of the Navy. On the death of his father in 1606, Fulke Greville was appointed to the office his father had held—Recorder of Warwick and Stratford-upon-Avon, and remained in it until his death in 1628. In this position he could hardly have been unaware of the Shakspere family.

Fulke Greville was also a serious poet and dramatist. During the late 1570s he composed a cycle of 109 poems, forty-one of which were sonnets, and two decades later wrote three history plays. But he was one of those noblemen who disdained appearance in print, and in fact refused to allow any publication of his work while he was alive. The only work of his that appeared during his lifetime was an unauthorized printing of his play *Mustapha* in 1609. This was the same year that a book called *Shake-speare's Sonnets* was published—probably without the permission of its author, supposedly his neighbor down the road.

Greville preferred the company of poets and philosophers, and his closest friends were the poets Edward Dyer and Philip Sidney. Greville was also acquainted with John Florio, Edmund Spenser, and Ben Jonson. Another poet and playwright, William Davenant, who claimed to be a godson, or maybe a son, of William Shakespeare, entered Greville's household as a page when he was eighteen (*ODNB*). Greville corresponded with the poet and playwright George Chapman (Crundell 137), who was mentioned by Francis Meres in 1598, as was William Shakespeare, as one of the best English playwrights. Greville was a patron of Samuel Daniel, the poet and playwright from nearby Somerset who dedicated "Musophilus," probably his finest poem, to him in 1599. Both Chapman and Daniel were about the same age and from the same social class as William Shakspere of Stratford-upon-Avon.

Greville's plays have never been performed, and he is best known today for his biography of Philip Sidney, in which he wrote about both himself and Sidney, and their twenty-year friendship. A number of letters to and from Fulke Greville have survived. Yet nowhere in any of Fulke Greville's reminiscences, or in the letters he wrote or received, is there any mention of the well-known poet and playwright, William Shakespeare, who supposedly only lived a few miles away.[3] Even Charlotte Stopes, who thought Shakspere wrote the Shakespeare plays, wrote: "It is always considered strange that such a man should not have mentioned Shakespeare" (1907, 171). Fulke Greville has been described as "one of the leaders of the movement for the introduction of Renaissance Culture into England" (Whitfield 366). Yet so far as we know, Greville never made any connection between the resident of the nearby town and the dramatist who bore a similar name and who, more than any other, used Renaissance literary sources for his plays—William Shakespeare.

Edward Pudsey

Another eyewitness who must have known William Shakspere of Stratford was an obscure theatergoer named Edward Pudsey, who was perhaps only the second individual we know of to write out passages from a Shakespeare play. Although Edward Pudsey came from a large family, many of whom lived in Warwickshire in the 1590s, biographical details about him are scarce (Savage vi-viii). It is known that he married in 1605 and settled at Tewkesbury, about twenty-five miles from Stratford-upon-Avon (*ODNB*).

In 1888 scholars were fortunate to discover a ninety-page manuscript that was inscribed "Edward Pudsey's Book." In it Pudsey had copied passages from several literary works in the fields of history, philosophy and current events—as well as from contemporary plays. The dates entered in the manuscript range from 1600 to 1612, the year before Pudsey died. Besides passages from Machiavelli, Thomas More, Francis Bacon, and others, Pudsey transcribed selections from 22 contemporary plays—four by Ben Jonson, three by Marston, seven by Dekker, Lyly, Nashe, Chapman, and Heywood. And eight by William Shakespeare.

The extracts from *Hamlet* and *Othello* are especially interesting because of their variations from the printed versions. The quotation from *Hamlet* is slightly different from both the 1604 Quarto and the 1623 Folio. The quotation from *Othello* contains lines that do not appear in the Quarto, which was not published until 1622. After the *Othello* quotation, Pudsey wrote the letters "sh," a reasonably clear indication that he knew that the play was by William Shakespeare. The English scholar who examined the manuscript asserted that the quotations from *Othello* and *Hamlet* were written in a section that she dated no later than 1600 (Rees 331). Thus, it appears that the performances of these plays that Edward Pudsey saw differed from what was later printed, or that he simply wrote out the dialogue incorrectly. But nowhere in the hundreds of entries in Edward Pudsey's Book is there any indication that he was aware that the playwright whose words he copied in it lived in nearby Stratford-upon-Avon.

Queen Henrietta Maria

Our eighth eyewitness is Henrietta Maria, the fifteen-year-old daughter of King Henry IV of France and Marie de' Medici, who, by arrangement, became the wife and Queen of Charles I soon after his coronation as King of England in 1625. The new American colony of Maryland, founded in 1632, was given its name in honor of Henrietta Maria.

Both King Charles and Queen Henrietta were theater buffs and enthusiastic patrons of the drama. King Charles even collaborated on a play with James Shirley in the 1630s, and was so fond of Shakespeare that he kept a copy of the Second Folio by his bedside. In this copy are found the alternative titles he assigned to several of the plays, such as "*Pyramus and Thisbe*" for *A Midsummer Night's Dream* and "*Malvolio*" for *Twelfth Night* (Birrell 45). To the Puritans, who executed Charles in 1649, his dissolute character was exemplified by his love of plays. One Puritan pamphlet asserted that he would have succeeded as king "had he studied scripture half so much as he did Ben Jonson or Shakespeare" (Campbell 107).

Queen Henrietta was also an amateur playwright, and even more enamored of the stage than her husband. She was the first English monarch to attend a performance in a public playhouse, and enjoyed performing the leading roles in her own masques at Court —behavior that shocked the English public (Campbell 312). According to Michael Dobson and Stanley Wells, the word "actress" was first used in reference to her (187). In her 1632 masque *Tempe Restored*, professional women singers took the stage for the first time in England.

In 1642 Charles and his Parliament reached an impasse over taxes, and when he attempted to arrest five members, Parliament authorized an army, and a civil war broke out. The Queen was in Holland at the time, but she quickly began rounding up support for the Royalist cause. Early the next year she landed in Yorkshire with a large supply of ammunition she had solicited on the continent. From there she journeyed south to relieve her husband who was in the field with his army near Oxford. Traveling on horseback, the "Generalissima," as she called herself, reached Warwickshire in early July 1643, and on the 11th arrived in Stratford-upon-Avon at the head of an army of 3000 foot, thirty companies of horse and dragoons, six pieces of artillery, and 150 wagons (Plowden 186).

The records of the Stratford Corporation document the visit of Queen Henrietta Maria and the substantial expense it incurred to provide a banquet for her (Fox 24). Although specific records of it are lacking, scholars accept a tradition that the Queen stayed two nights at New Place, then the home of William Shakspere's daughter Susanna, her daughter Elizabeth and son-in-law Thomas Nash (Lee 509; Schoenbaum 305).

Queen Henrietta was an exceptional letter-writer. Hundreds of her letters to her husband, her nephew Prince Rupert, and others have been collected and printed. But none of the letters she wrote before or after her visit to Stratford-upon-Avon contains any mention of her stay at New Place, or any indication that she had met the daughter and granddaughter of the famous playwright whom she emulated and whom her husband venerated.

What could be the explanation for this? By 1643 there had been several visitors to the Holy Trinity Church, where the statue of William Shakspere had been installed more than twenty years earlier (Chambers 2:239, 242-3). But if Queen Henrietta thought she was staying in the home of the famous playwright, or had walked over to the church to see his memorial, she never wrote about it. One explanation might be that she knew that the Stratford Shakspere was a myth. She was acquainted with Ben Jonson, who had written two masques in which she performed in 1631 (Riggs 321-3). He could have told her that the name William Shakespeare was a pseudonym. He could have told her that she would find nothing about the playwright Shakespeare in Stratford-upon-Avon.

Further evidence suggests that plays and playwrights were not welcome in Stratford-upon-Avon. It is well known that during the thirty years between 1568 and 1597 numerous playing companies visited and performed there. But by the end of this period the Puritan officeholders in the town finally attained their objective of banning all performances of plays and interludes. In 1602 the Corporation of Stratford ordered that a fine of ten shillings be imposed on any official who gave permission for any type of play to be performed in any city building, or in any inn or house in the borough. This in a year that three or four plays by Shakespeare, their alleged townsman, were being performed in London.[4]

In 1612, just four years before their neighbor's death, this fine was increased to ten pounds. In 1622, when work on the great First Folio was in progress, the Stratford Corporation paid the King's Players the sum of six shillings not to play in the Town Hall (Fox 143-4). Surely by 1622, some 30 years after his name had first appeared in print, the people of Stratford would have been aware that one of England's greatest poets and playwrights had been born, raised, and then retired in their own town. That is, if such a thing were actually true.

Philip Henslowe

Our ninth eyewitness was a London businessman who decided to build a playhouse, and then became a successful theatrical entrepreneur. Philip Henslowe and his partner had operated the Rose theater for about four years before he began, in 1592, making entries in an old notebook about his theater and the companies that played in it, primarily the Admiral's Men (Foakes xv). The surviving 242-page manuscript, now called Henslowe's Diary, is a gold mine of references to plays, playhouses, and playing companies in London, and mentions the name of just about everybody who was anybody in the Elizabethan theater in the 1590s.

Although Henslowe kept his Diary on and off for less than ten years, we can find in it, or in other Henslowe manuscripts, the names of 280 different plays, about 240 of which have entirely disappeared. The names of fully 170 of these plays would be totally unknown today, except for their mention in Henslowe's accounts (Bentley 15). The Diary contains reports of performances at the Rose by all the major playing companies of the time. There are also dozens of actors named, and no less than twenty-seven playwrights.

In his Diary Henslowe kept records of the loans he made to playwrights, and of the amounts he paid them for manuscripts. Among the playwrights mentioned are the familiar names of Chapman, Dekker, Drayton, Jonson, Marston, and Webster. There are also some unfamiliar names, such as William Bird, Robert Daborne, and Wentworth Smith, the other "W.S." But there is one familiar name that is missing. Nowhere in the list of dozens of actors and twenty-seven playwrights in Henslowe's Diary do we find the name of William Shakespeare or William Shakspere.

It might be objected that Henslowe also failed to mention several other familiar playwrights, such as Beaumont, Fletcher, Ford, Lyly, Kyd, Marlowe, Greene, and Peele. But there are good reasons for these omissions. Beaumont, Fletcher, and Ford didn't begin writing plays until after the period of Henslowe's Diary. Marlowe and Greene died within a year of the first entry in the Diary; Kyd died a year later, and Lyly and Peele wrote their last plays in 1593 and 1594.

Admittedly, William Shakespeare is supposed to have been an actor, playwright, and sharer in the Chamberlain's Men company, which performed at the Globe theater, the principal competitor of Henslowe's Rose theater. But the Globe and the Rose were situated very near each other, and Henslowe had to walk past the Globe every day on his way to work (C. Eccles 69). His Diary contains many transactions with actors and playwrights associated with the Chamberlain's Men, and his entries for June 1594 record that the Chamberlain's Men and the Admiral's Men performed more than a dozen plays during that month at his Newington Butts theater about a mile away (Campbell 583). This is the period during which most scholars claim that William Shakespeare was acting with the Chamberlain's Men.

If Shakespeare really were the busy actor and playwright we are told he was, then Henslowe would surely have known him, and mentioned him somewhere in his Diary. But although Henslowe mentioned several Shakespeare plays that were performed in his theater, he never mentioned the name of the man who wrote them, and had an attachment to a theater just a hundred yards away.

Edward Alleyn

Our last eyewitness is Edward Alleyn, the most distinguished actor on the Elizabethan stage. He was also a musician, a book and playbook collector, a philanthropist, and a playwright (Wraight 211-19). He was born about two years after William Shakspere and came from the same social class. His father was an innkeeper, and Alleyn was still in his teens when he began acting on the stage. He was most famous for his roles in Marlowe's plays, but he also must have acted in several of the Shakespeare plays performed at the Rose, such as *Titus Andronicus* and *Henry VI* (Carson 68). In 1592 he married Philip Henslowe's stepdaughter and entered the theater business with his father-in-law.

Edward Alleyn also kept a diary that survives, along with many of his letters and papers. They reveal that he had a large circle of acquaintances throughout and beyond the theater world, including aristocrats, clergymen, and businessmen, as well as men in his own profession, such as John Heminges, one of the alleged editors of the First Folio. In his two-volume edition of Edward Allen's *Memoirs* (1841), John Payne Collier printed several references that Alleyn made to Shakespeare and to his plays, but they have all been judged forgeries (Chambers 2:386-90). The alleged reference by Alleyn to Shakespeare that has puzzled scholars the most is one that Collier claimed he found on the back of a letter written to Alleyn in June 1609. There, Alleyn supposedly recorded a list of purchases under the heading "Howshowld stuff,"—at the end of which are the words "a book. Shaksper sonetts 5d." Although this letter has been lost, the entry has been accepted as genuine by some scholars (Rollins 2:54; Freeman 2:1142), but rejected as a forgery by others (Race 113; Duncan-Jones 7). But forgery or genuine, it fails to suggest a connection with William Shakspere of Stratford-upon-Avon.

Except for this one questionable reference, nowhere in Alleyn's diary or letters does the name William Shakespeare appear. It is impossible to believe that Edward Alleyn, who was at the center of the Elizabethan stage community for more than thirty-five years, would not have met the alleged actor and leading playwright William Shakespeare, and made some allusion to him in his letters or diary.

To sum up: we have the literary remains of ten different eyewitnesses, eight of whom must have come into contact with William Shakspere of Stratford-upon-Avon—or should have if he were the actor and playwright we are told he was—and two who met his daughter Susanna. If two or three of these ten eyewitnesses had failed to associate the well-known playwright with the man bearing the same name in Stratford-upon-Avon, it would not be worth mentioning. But

Ramon Jiménez

none of these ten, all of whom left extensive written records, apparently connected the man they knew, or his daughter, with the well-known playwright.

We can be sure that if any one of these ten people had, just once, referred to William Shakspere of Stratford as a playwright, or if his name had, just once, appeared in Henslowe's Diary as having being paid for a play, then there would be little reason to reject the Stratford theory. But, in fact, there is no record of anyone associating Shakspere of Stratford-upon-Avon with playwriting or any other kind of writing until the questionable front matter in the First Folio seven years after his death. Instead, the facts support the argument that the name William Shakespeare was the pseudonym of a concealed author who did not write for money, did not sell his plays to playing companies or publishers, and was indifferent to their appearance in print.

Endnotes

1. Camden's Diary appeared in *Camdeni Vitae*, a life of Camden published in 1691 by Thomas Smith. The Diary is online at *http://e3.uci.edu/~papyri/diary/*, where the entries can be seen in the months of March and October under the year 1619.
2. The text of the sonnet appears in v. 2 of *Michael Drayton: Complete Works,* J. W. Hebel, et al, eds.
3. In *Statesmen and Favourites of England since the Reformation* (1665, p. 504), David Lloyd asserted that Greville wished to be "known to posterity" as "Shakespear's and Ben Johnson's Master" [sic]. But he cited no evidence to support the claim, and it is generally considered to be a fabrication. See Chambers 2, 250.
4. *Hamlet, Twelfth Night, The Merry Wives of Windsor, All's Well that Ends Well.*

Works Cited

Bentley, Gerald E.: *The Profession of Dramatist in Shakespeare's Time 1590-1642* (Princeton University Press, 1986).

Birrell, T. A.: *English Monarchs and their Books: From Henry II to Charles II* (British Library, 1986).

Camden, William: *Remains Concerning Britain* (1605) (University of Toronto Press, 1984).

_____: R. D. Dunn, ed.: *Britannia* (6th ed. 1607) Tr. Richard Gough (John Stockdale, 1806).

Campbell, Oscar and E. G. Quinn, eds. *The Reader's Encyclopedia of Shakespeare* (MJF Books, 1966).

Carson, Neil: *A Companion to Henslowe's Diary* (Cambridge University Press, 1988).

Chambers, E. K.: *William Shakespeare, A Study of Facts and Problems* 2 v. (Clarendon Press, 1930).

Crundell, H. W.: "George Chapman and the Grevilles" (*Notes and Queries*, v. 185, 1943, p. 137).

Dobson, Michael and Stanley Wells: *The Oxford Companion to Shakespeare* (Oxford University Press, 2001).

Duncan-Jones, Katherine: *Shakespeare's Sonnets* (Thomson Learning, 1998).

Eccles, Christine: *The Rose Theatre* (Routledge/Theater Arts Books, 1990).

Eccles, Mark: *Shakespeare in Warwickshire* (University of Wisconsin Press, 1963).

Foakes, R. A., ed.: *Henslowe's Diary* (Cambridge University Press, 2nd ed. 2002).

Fox, Levi: *The Borough Town of Stratford-upon-Avon* (Stratford-upon-Avon Corp., 1953).

Freeman, Arthur and Janet Ing Freeman: *John Payne Collier: scholarship and forgery in the nineteenth century* (Yale University Press, 2004).

Hebel, J. W., K. Tillotson and B. H. Newdigate, eds.: *Michael Drayton: Complete Works* (Blackwell, 1961).

Joseph, Harriet: *Shakespeare's Son-in-Law: John Hall, Man and Physician* (Archon Books, 1964).

Lane, Joan: *John Hall and his Patients* (The Shakespeare Birthplace Trust, 1996).

Lee, Sidney: *A Life of William Shakespeare* (Dover Publications, 14th ed., 1968).

Lloyd, David: *Statesmen and Favourites of England since the Reformation* (Samuel Speed, 1665).

Malone, Edmond: *The Plays and Poems of William Shakspeare* 2 v. James Boswell, ed. (R. C. & J. Rivington, 1821).

Newdigate, B. H.: *Michael Drayton and his Circle* (Basil Blackwell and Mott, Corrected Edition, 1961). *Oxford Dictionary of National Biography* (Oxford University Press).

Plowden, Alison: *Henrietta Maria: Charles I's Indomitable Queen* (Sutton, 2001).

Race, Sydney: "J. P. Collier and the Dulwich Papers" (*Notes and Queries* v. 195, 1950, pp. 112-14).

Rees, J.: "Shakespeare and 'Edward Pudsey's Booke', 1600" (*Notes and Queries* v. 237, 1992, pp. 330-1).

Riggs, David: *Ben Jonson, A Life* (Harvard University Press, 1989)

Rollins, Hyder H., ed.: *A New Variorum Edition of Shakespeare: The Sonnets* 2 v. (Lippincott, 1944).

Savage, Richard, ed.: *Shakespearean extracts from "Edward Pudsey's booke" temp. Q. Elizabeth & K. James I* (Simpkin and Marshall, 1888).

Schoenbaum, Samuel: *William Shakespeare, A Compact Documentary Life* (Oxford University Press, 1977).

Stopes, Charlotte C.: *Shakespeare's Family* (Elliot Stock, 1901).

_____: *Shakespeare's Environment* (G. Bell, 1907).

Whitfield, Christopher: "Some of Shakespeare's Contemporaries in the Middle Temple--III" (*Notes and Queries* v. 211, 1966, pp. 363-69).

Wraight, A. C.: *Christopher Marlowe and Edward Alleyn* (Adam Hart, 1993).

Chapter 5:
Shakspere's Will: Missing the Mind of Shakespeare

By Bonner Miller Cutting

"His detailed will, in which he famously left his wife my second best bed with the furniture, contains no clearly Shakespearean turn of phrase and mentions no books, plays, poems, or literary effects of any kind. Nor does it mention any musical instruments, despite extensive evidence of the author's musical expertise. He did leave token bequests to three fellow actors (an interlineation …), but nothing to any writers. The actors' names connect him to the theater, but nothing implies a writing career."

– Shakespeare Authorship Coalition, Declaration of Reasonable Doubt

"To deny Shakespeare's authorship is to deny the primary sources, above all his will."[*]

– Michael Wood, Life Trustee, Shakespeare Birthplace Trust
(From his answer to Question 7 in *Exposing* in Part II below)

"As 'primary sources' go, the Stratford man's will is actually the one document that's most damaging to claims that he was the author of the Shakespeare canon."[*]

– Ramon Jiménez, Author, Independent Shakespeare Scholar
(From his response to Wood's answer above to Question 7)

Traditional scholars and biographers of William Shakspere of Stratford-upon-Avon vacillate between two conflicting positions concerning his documented life. Some claim that his life as a writer is well documented; others accept that it is not well documented, but claim that this does not matter. In either case they usually either ignore, or downplay, the most important document from his life: his Last Will and Testament. Rarely does any biographer devote more than two or three pages to this key document. A.L. Rowse spent only three laconic paragraphs discussing it in *Shakespeare The Man*. Might there be more that posterity can learn from the three detailed pages of Mr. Shakspere's Will?

It was Reverend Joseph Greene who first found the original of the will in 1747.[1] Greene immediately recognized problems inherent in his discovery, and wrote to his friend, the Honorable James West, that the will "appears to me so dull and irregular, so absolutely void of the least particle of that Spirit which Animated Our great Poet, that it must lessen his Character as a Writer, to imagine the least Sentence of it his production."

Greene's comment is apt. Once the contents of the will are understood, it is hard to believe that the testator was a writer at all, much less the poet-playwright Shakespeare. The Prerogative Court of Canterbury, perhaps recognizing the magnitude of the problem, forbade reproduction

---

[*] **Editor's note**: as you read this chapter, think about which of these two opposed claims is correct. If Wood were correct, one would expect the will to be featured prominently in the Birthplace Trust book *Shakespeare Beyond Doubt*. We predict that it will not be discussed, and not shown. We show a verbatim transcript of it in Appendix A to this book. Read it and see if you think it is Shakespeare's will.

of the original will with the canceled passages and interlineations. The PCC relented in 1851, allowing James Halliwell to publish a limited edition of 100 books in which the will was displayed for the first time in its original form, as best it could be set in type.[2] In this chapter, it will become clear why the authorities were in no rush to publish the will with its original alterations, as it appeared upon its inception over two centuries earlier.[3]

E.A.J. Honigmann recognized that this will "stands out as different." Looking at the document, the first thing that stands out is how messy it is. The will is full of interlineations and cancellations, leading Honigmann to say that it is "a more heavily revised will than any I have seen." Samuel Tannenbaum struggled to rationalize why this "slovenly looking document [was] made to do duty for the final will." The usual excuse is that Shakspere was dying, so we should cut him some slack. But wills were often drawn up in testators' last days, and other testators, often with the help of scribes, managed to do a better job.

So who is responsible for this messy piece of work? After much academic debate, the consensus favors the idea that a clerk or scrivener in the office of Francis Collins, a Warwickshire solicitor, wrote out Shakspere's will. This may well be correct, though it ignores the fact that the author of Shakespeare's works had legal knowledge far surpassing that of a country lawyer and his clerk. If the attribution were correct, would this individual have left it to a lowly clerk to determine the appearance of the final document of his life?

In fact, lawyers rarely wrote wills at that time. In small market towns like Stratford, wills were usually written by a townsperson—just a literate neighbor—who took it upon himself to write wills for the inhabitants.[4] And even if a scribe wrote it out, Shakspere was still expected, as the testator, to dictate his own will. Whoever put the words on paper was expected to write down what the testator said in as close to the exact words as possible. It is clear from wills of the time that people said what was on their minds. Their voices are authentic. Moreover, in the event that a will was challenged in court, the scribe could be called to testify that the testator had been in control of the will-making process.[5] Wills reflected what the testator said, and, by extension, what he thought. That expectation carries huge implications for the Stratford Will. Clearly, Shakspere did not write the will himself, as his three scrawled signatures do not match the handwriting of the will. But even if he was too ill to write, as some have proposed, he could still talk—otherwise he would have been unable to execute a will in the first place.

The will is no work of art. It was written without punctuation or paragraphs, although these are often added by modern editors to give it a semblance of structure. Each of its three pages bears a signature, allegedly Shakspere's. In a final oddity at the end of the will, the preparer, whoever he was, originally wrote that the testator would put his "seal" to the document. The use of the single word "seal" strongly suggests that the testator would subscribe the will with only his seal, not an actual signature. Most wills call for "hand and seal," but in this case, the word "seal" was struck out and "hand" written above it. Evidently the scribe did not expect Shakspere to sign the will, and the signatures were an afterthought.[6] It is hard to imagine that he would have thought this if the testator had been a writer.

What's missing?

Studies of the Stratford Will usually focus on items *not* found in the will, and the absence of books is a serious omission. No one has ever argued that the Stratford man, their "Shakespeare," simply did not own any books. Archives and records have been searched for centuries for even a mention of his name, yet no book that he ever owned has been found.

But the absence of any mention of books in the will is just part of the problem. Other absences are consistent with the idea that Shakspere wasn't a man of letters. There is no mention of furniture that would hold books, or would be used for writing purposes. Literate people often mentioned cupboards, hampers, cases, boxes, presses or chests that might hold books. There is no mention of a desk, or of pens or ink with which to write.[7] John Florio bequeathed three desks replete with inkhorns. Francis Bacon instructed his executors "to take into their hands all of my papers whatsoever, which are either in cabinets, boxes or presses, and then to seal up until they may at their leisure peruse them." Such items were not limited to the erudite. A clothier of Gosfield left a great chest to stow his books in and "one little chest which I lay my writings in." A yeoman of Broomfield listed "the chest at my bed's feet wherein my evidences and writings lie."[8]

Some propose that the books were included in the category of "household stuffe." When the use of the term is examined in other wills—and nearly all include this standard verbiage—it is clearly a catchall phrase for miscellaneous articles too inconsequential to itemize. It is usually found in a list along with bedding, plate, jewels, kitchen equipment, farm implements, farm animals and foodstuffs. In the Stratford Will, "all the rest of my goods chattels Leases plate Jewels and household stuffe whatsoer" are left to his daughter Susanna. The language is merely formulaic. Nothing suggests that books were included.

A more careful testator is John Bentley, a servant to a knight, who left his son an impressive list of books—music books, Dictionaries of Cowper's, Barrett's, and Thomasin's, dictionaries in Greek, Latin and "other languages whatsoever," *Tully's Offices*, books "pertaining to divinity," "all other my books in English written or printed whatsoever," statute books, law books, a Livius and "my maps." To his "singular good master," he bequeathed "my new bible in Latin, imprinted in Venice," and to his Lady, a "very pleasant book called the *Instruction of a Christian Woman* made by Ludovicus Vives." Sir Thomas Smith left his Latin and Greek books to Queen's College, Cambridge, directing that the Fellows "send carts to fetch them away within 10 to 12 days" and that they "chain them up in their library." Such was the care he took that his books be preserved for future generations.

Stanley Wells of the Shakespeare Birthplace Trust argues that the missing books were listed in a separate inventory, now lost. That idea is worth considering. Unfortunately, it comes up short. Roughly two million wills and one million inventories survive from early modern England.[9] Of the surviving inventories, very few include books. According to historian F. G. Emmison, "wills yield far more details than some inventories in which only valuation totals of items are given," and he notes that wills themselves often functioned as "quasi-inventories" with detailed bequests of movables, furnishings, and, as we have seen, books. An interesting example can be found in the will and inventory of the Reverend John Bretchgirdle, the minister who baptized Shakspere. He made detailed bequests of books to his friends in the body of his will, but the inventory simply stated that the books were valued at ten pounds.[10]

The inventory excuse overlooks that testators, then as now, wanted their most precious possessions to go to beneficiaries who would appreciate them. People wanted their important items to be well bestowed.[11] It was one of the primary purposes of a will. Inventories were made by "indifferent" men after the testator's death; the testator himself had no hand in the inventory. The lack of mention of books in the Stratford Will indicates that, even if this testator owned books, they were not meaningful enough to him to merit inclusion in the body of his will. In addition, books were valuable intellectual property, which is why they made excellent gifts to important people. William Camden willed most of his books to Robert Cotton. John Florio left

340 books to the Earl of Pembroke. Viscount John Scudamore "thought the present of a book the best way to reward a scholar who despised the material wealth which most men prized."[12] It strains credulity to think that no book would have been carefully directed to any special beneficiary in "Shakespeare's" will. Surely he had a friend who would value a book that he owned, such as his alleged patron the Earl of Southampton?

Not only did Shakspere leave *nothing* to Southampton, he left nothing to *any* of the people he supposedly knew at court. Nor did he leave anything to any fellow writer—not even to those with whom he allegedly collaborated on some of the plays. Nor did he mention any apprentices he may have had, or even the printer Richard Field, publisher of the two narrative poems that first made Shakespeare famous, who was still living at the time and supposedly also from Stratford. Some Stratfordians propose that he read the books in Field's print shop, and that this is how he had access to certain books. Apart from the fact that there is no evidence for this claim, it is odd that Shakspere did not return the favor by leaving Field a few books, or anything else for that matter.

What else is missing from the will? Music and musical instruments are part and parcel of Shakespeare's imagery, as well as accoutrements of an actor's vocation. Musical instruments were valuable. It is curious that a playwright who used so many musical terms and metaphors, and included so much music in his works—far more than other writers—would have owned no musical instruments, or regarded them as not worth mentioning. By contrast, Shakspere's fellow actor Augustine Phillips left his apprentice a bass viol, a citterne, a bandore and a lute. Even ordinary gentlemen and yeomen bequeathed a fair number of lutes, viols, and virginals.[13] The absence of musical instruments in the Stratford Will is almost as odd as the absence of books.

Surprisingly, no item in the will suggests his life as an actor, other than a bequest of money for three fellow actors to buy rings, added between the lines, suggesting it was an afterthought. This links him to the theater, but nothing suggests a writing career. There is no mention of any shares in an acting company, or of theatrical apparel, memorabilia or playbooks. Actors Augustine Phillips, Thomas Pope, John Heminges, John Shank, and Henry Condell bequeathed shares in the premises and proceeds from their theater holdings. Why didn't Shakspere, if, indeed, he owned such valuable property?[14]

He left no maps, odd for a dramatist who set plays in foreign lands he evidently knew in minute detail, but to which he never traveled. There are no pictures, wall hangings, tapestries or art works of any kind. Such items were prized heirlooms. The poet John Donne bequeathed many paintings (called "pictures") to beneficiaries in his will. If Shakspere's will is any indication, he lived without physical trappings of culture. This is puzzling for someone whose life was supposedly one of great cultural achievement.

There is no mention in the Stratford Will of education of any kind, for anyone. In wills of the time, bequests to minor children almost always include instructions for their education. For someone who supposedly received an excellent education at the Stratford grammar school, launching him on a career of unparalleled success, it is odd that he did not provide for the education of his grandchild, Elizabeth Hall, or any future grandchildren (though it is consistent with the fact that his daughters were illiterate). His granddaughter is named three times: first with a reversionary interest of £100 if his younger daughter Judith dies; second with "all my plate"; and third as residuary legatee for all the "premises" that remain after the default of the heirs male enumerated up through seven sons. How hard would it have been to add "for her education," or "to be brought up in learning," if, in fact, he was a man of learning who valued education?

This neglect of education is in stark contrast to many other testators at the time. Even ordinary folk made the connection between education and quality of life for their family and people in their community. A yeoman of Rochford left an annuity to keep his son at "grammar school until 15 and afterwards in one of the universities and after that in one of the inns of Chancery or Court for his better preferment and advancement." Although females were not provided for as often as males, some did receive educational bequests. Tomas Collte, a gentleman of Waltham, left a hearty £50 annuity "toward the education and bringing up of my two daughters during their minority," and if they died without issue, this money was to go to the "setting up of a free school for ever for the teaching of poor men's children." Jacob Meade provided for the education of his granddaughter. In a short will of less than a page, a clothier of Dedham included a bequest "to the maintenance of poor students at Cambridge that…sincerely seek God's glory." Shakspere left his godson 20 shillings in gold. A widow of Chingford left the same amount to her godson, but specified that it was "to buy him books." Had William Shakspere merely added those four little words, "to buy him books," it would have given the orthodox something to hang their hat on. As it is, they have nothing. How credible is it that ordinary people provided for the education of children, but "Shakespeare" did not?

It was not unusual for testators to leave endowments to schools and universities. A yeoman of Wivenhoe left money to St. John's College, Cambridge, "for the maintenance of poor scholars there and especially such as shall come out of the Grammar School of Colchester." An esquire left an annuity to the Free School of Chelmsford so that the school "may be better maintained and the youth and children may be the better attended and instructed in learning and virtue." A clothier willed that after the death of his sister, "the tenement given to her [will go] to the Governors of the public Grammar School in Dedham and their successors for ever, to be employed for a dwelling house for a school master to teach children to read and write." Schoolmaster John Harte of Saffron Walden left a large bequest to pay "a discreet, honest and learned schoolmaster" to teach poor children of Great and Little Chesterfield "freely and without reward."[15] Finally, Edward Alleyn, whose life paralleled Shakspere's in that he was born poor, had a successful stage career, and became a wealthy businessman, founded Dulwich College and provided for its perpetuation in his will.

According to Robin Fox of Rutgers University, "A mark of a man's success in business was that he should endow a school in his birthplace." Traditionalists propose that Shakspere was successful as both a writer and a businessman. But he left nothing to the Stratford grammar school—the source of the putative education that allegedly set him on the path to success, and was the main institution of learning in the town in which future generations of his family would be educated.

Shakespeare the writer understood this, giving eloquent voice to Lord Saye for his beneficence to education:

> Large gifts have I bestow'd on learned clerks,
> Because my book preffer'd me to the King,
> And seeming ignorance is the curse of God,
> Knowledge the wing wherewith we fly to heaven. (*2 Henry VI*, IV.vii.71-74)

Shakespeare the writer praises Cardinal Wolsey for his contributions to the Ipswich Grammar School and Oxford University:

He was most princely. Ever witness for him
Those twins of learning that he raised in you,
Ipswich and Oxford! One of which fell with him,
Unwilling to outlive the good that did it: (*Henry VIII*, IV.ii.45-47)

How credible is it that, with all his good fortune, Shakspere of Stratford took no interest in the school to which he presumably owed so much? As Fox states, "it was something almost required of a local boy made good."

The Stratford Will was composed at a time when charitable giving reached its zenith in early modern England. In ten counties, a total of £3.1 million was left to charitable causes, reaching a peak of "incredible generosity" from 1611 to 1640.[16] Bequests for repairs of roads and bridges were common, and might have been expected of a man who traveled often between London and Stratford. Shakspere's will contains none. Then as now, churches were frequent beneficiaries, and one might have expected that Shakspere would leave something to Holy Trinity Church where he was to be buried. He left nothing to the church. Nor did he give to any hospital, almshouse, or prison.

Testators often forgave debts owed to them. Shakspere forgave none, and this is not surprising for a man who sued over small amounts. He did leave a tersely worded bequest of ten pounds to the poor of Stratford, fulfilling a duty of testators for charitable deeds required by custom.[17] In contrast, many testators showed genuine compassion, with elaborate provisions for the poor. A yeoman of Harlow set out legacies to the poor in eleven towns, as well as to the poor prisoners of Colchester, Newgate, the Marshalsea, the King's Bench, Ludgate and all London, and Stortford [Hertfordshire]. This example is not unusual, even among ordinary testators.

What's included?

So what *is* in his will? Quite a lot—it is three pages, and most wills of the time could fit on just one page. Like most, Shakspere's will opened with a religious preamble.[18] Surprisingly, the greatest poet in England took his statement of faith right from a standard handbook. B. Roland Lewis was the first to note that it was a common formula from William West's popular *Symbolaeographia*. Seemingly embarrassed at saying such a thing, Lewis added that "One would think that William Shakespeare virtually copied his *Notificatio* and its exordium from William West's *Simboleographie* (1605), a volume of typical legal forms widely used in his day."[19] In reading the following, this is exactly what one would think.

West's *Symbolaeographia*	William Shakspere
Sick in body but of	in perfect health[20]
good and perfect memory	& memory
God be praised	god be praised
do make and ordaine	doe make & ordayne
this my Last wyll and testament	this my last will & testament
In manner and forme following	in manner and forme following
that is to say	That is to saye
first I Commend my soule	ffirst I commend my soule

unto the hands of God	into the handes of god
my maker	my creator
hoping assuredly	hoping & assuredly beleeving
through the only merits	through thonelie merittes of
of Jesus Chryst my saviour	of Jesus Christe my savior
to be made partaker	to be made partaker
of life everlasting	of life everlasting
And I commend my bodie	And my bodye
To the earth	to the Earth
whereof it is made	whereof yt ys made

If Shakspere was Shakespeare, why did he not take the opportunity to write, or dictate, a personalized preamble? Why use a banal formula derived from an almanac?

After the religious preamble, testators usually devised their real estate holdings. Shakspere instead spends most of the first page making complex financial arrangements for his younger daughter Judith. He apparently does not like her new husband and wants to get the income from £300 to Judith while keeping it out of the hands of her husband, his newly acquired son-in-law. These good intentions would be the high point of the will, were it not for the problem that his garbled verbiage left his son-in-law grounds to challenge it. Scholars have wondered why a reasonably competent attorney (assuming Shakspere had legal advice) did not improve upon these conflicting instructions.[21]

The language itself is curious. Not one word or phrase seems Shakespearean. For example, the lump sums to Judith are called "stock," and before she receives these payouts she is to get what is termed "consideration" to be paid according to a rate of "two shillings in the pound." The words "stock" for principal and "consideration" for interest are terms from money-lending. A check in the *Harvard Concordance* reveals that these words are never used in a financial context anywhere in the Shakespeare canon[22] (in spite of the extensive use of legal and accounting terms in the works—see Chapter 8).

After the "Judith Page," the second page might be called the "Property Page." Here he devised all his real estate, including five houses, to daughter Susanna and her husband John Hall, bestowed his personal property, and made monetary gifts to family and friends. With the exception of the interlineation naming the London actors, all of his friends were from the Stratford community. After these bequests, he launched into a long and curious entail for his estate, going through seven heirs male "lawfully issuing" from Susanna's body. It is an odd feature for two reasons: first, the seven sons were not yet born, and given Susanna's age it is unlikely that she would have that many children. As it turned out, her daughter Elizabeth Hall was her only child. Second, this repetitious entail takes up eighteen lines, almost a fifth of the will. He could have accomplished the same thing in a line or two. Couldn't a lyric poet have made better use of the space?

The third and final page contains, in another interlineation, that notorious bequest to his wife, "my second best bed with the furniture." It is the only thing he left her, and he didn't even specify her name. In summing up the problems engendered by this bequest, Harvard English Professor Stephen Greenblatt notes: "Writers have made a strenuous effort to give these words a positive spin."[23] Thereafter, Mr. Shakspere closed his will with the standard verbiage, appointing his executors and residuary legatees, again turning to his daughter Susanna and her husband John Hall, instructing them to discharge his financial obligations and pay his funeral expenses.

Was he wealthy?

In light of his real estate holdings and the monetary legacies in his will, was Shakspere wealthy? The lack of bequests for education and philanthropy are more significant if Shakspere was wealthy, so orthodox scholars often avoid that question. Honigmann says, "we cannot tell from his will how rich he was." Perhaps not precisely, but we can learn a great deal about his wealth from the will. His primary residence, New Place, was a mansion. It was a three-story rectangular structure with ten chimneys and five bay windows, a courtyard, orchards, gardens, barns and stables.[24] It is estimated to have had twenty to thirty bedrooms. Halliwell-Phillips examined the footings and found it to be 60 feet across and 70 feet deep.[25] The math is simple: 60' x 70' x 3 stories means it was over 12,000 square feet. Few people today live in houses that large. A.J. Pointon estimates that Shakspere's estate was worth over £2,000, or well over £1 million today.[26] Historians categorized people as "middling rich" if their estate was worth £200 to £500.[27] Mr. Shakspere was indeed one of the wealthiest men in Stratford when he died.

Conclusion

Nothing in the Stratford Will indicates that the testator had ever been any sort of writer, or that he had led a cultured life or possessed a cultivated intellect. There are no books, papers, writings, manuscripts or related furniture; no musical instruments, art, tapestries, maps, or intellectual property of any kind. There are no shares in a theatrical company, theatrical attire or memorabilia. He makes no provision for the education of his heirs, or anyone else. Nothing suggests a philanthropic spirit: no bequests to schools, colleges, almshouses, hospitals or churches; nothing for public projects such as the repair of roads and bridges, despite the fact that he accumulated a large estate and died wealthy.

No wonder Reverend Greene was shocked when he discovered the will in 1747. No wonder the Prerogative Court of Canterbury prevented a full printing of it until 1851. No wonder traditional biographers tend to downplay or ignore it. Nothing can redeem it. It is full of oddities and oversights, and in places is downright silly—not what one would expect from the great-spirited man of enormous intellect who was William Shakespeare.

In 1590 Henry Swinburne published a monumental treatise that remains the most important compendium on wills of the era. He concluded with this thoughtful comment: Even when all the legalities are observed and formal language is in place, it is still "the mind, not the words, that giveth life to the testament."[28] Reading through Mr. Shakspere's Last Will and Testament, it seems inescapable that the mind that gave life to the greatest literary works in the English language is not to be found in this document.

Editor's note: Looking again at the opposing claims of Michael Wood and Ramon Jiménez at the beginning of this chapter, and after having read it, *now* which of the two do you think is correct? If there is any doubt left in your mind, read the will, shown in Appendix A, and see for yourself.

Endnotes

1 Samuel Schoenbaum,: *A Documentary Life* (New York: Oxford University Press, 1975, 242). Schoenbaum calls the will a copy, but a copy is not the same as the original will. According to Schoenbaum, "The copy mentioned by Vertue is very likely the one independently discovered by the Rev. Joseph Greene in Stratford a decade later. His transcript, with a covering letter (dated 17 September 1747) to the Hon. James West, is in the British Library (MS Lansdowne 721, ff.2-6). The copy found by Greene, which belongs to the first half of the seventeenth century and which was probably made after Dr. Hall's death in 1635, is now in the Shakespeare Birthplace Trust records Office." Schoenbaum then directs the reader to the article by Levi Fox, "An Early copy of Shakespeare's Will," *Shakespeare Survey 4* (Cambridge, 1951, pp 69-77.) Not all authorities follow Schoenbaum's timeline, but a full exploration of the provenance of the original will, the various transcripts and copies is beyond the scope of this chapter.

2 J. O. Halliwell, *Shakespeare's Will Copied from the Original in the Prerogative Court* (London: John Russell Smith, 1851. Rpt, New York: AMS Press, 1974), pp. iii, iv. Halliwell wrote in the Preface: "The authorities of the Prerogative Court steadfastly refused to allow a facsimile of the Will to be made, and the only course which remained was to print it as nearly in its original form as was practicable in modern type."

3 Samuel Schoenbaum, *Shakespeare's Lives* (Oxford: Clarendon Press, 1991), p. 232. Schoenbaum offers that "the first complete text of Shakespeare's will, with the notorious misreading of the brown best bed," appeared in the *Biographia Britanica* in 1763. He does not point out that the substantial revisions in the will were not included at the time.

4 Margaret Spufford, *Contrasting Communities: English Villages in the Sixteenth and Seventeenth Centuries* (Great Britain: Cambridge University Press, 1974), pp. 320-34. In the chapter "Wills and Their Writers," the scribes under discussion are predominantly ordinary citizens, though Spufford notes that village scribes could "range from the lord or lessee of the manor to the vicar, curate, church clerk or churchwarden to the schoolmaster, a shopkeeper, or any one of the literate yeoman or even husbandmen in a village who could be called in to perform this last neighborly office for a dying man." J. D. Alsop concurs: "It appears that a large number of wills in early modern England were written by professional notaries, scribes, clergy, family, friends and neighbors for both literate and non-literate testators." p. 20. Harvard's eminent Professor Greenblatt acknowledges that testators dictated their wills. Stephen Greenblatt, *Will in the World* (New York: W. W. Norton, 2004), p. 385. E. A. J. Honigmann states that draft wills "probably give us the testators words as spoken." *Playhouse Wills*, E.A.J. Honigmann and Susan Brock, eds. (Manchester: Manchester University Press, 1993), p. 11.

5 J. D. Alsop, "Religious Preambles in Early Modern English Wills as Formulae" *Journal of Ecclesiastical History* (vol. 40, no. 1, 1989) pp. 19-27. Edmund Winstanley, a gentleman of Lancashire, died the day after his will was prepared. His will was subsequently contested and the scrivener called to testify. The court ruled that despite the "somewhat confused behavior of the testator," he was nonetheless "in control of the procedure." Thus the will passed probate.

6 Charlton Ogburn, Jr. *The Mysterious William Shakespeare* (New York: Dodd, Mead & Company, 1984), pp. 36-37. Ogburn points out the troubling logic in the orthodox "illness" theory. "Are we to believe that the solicitor, being unaccustomed to having Mr. Shaksper sign papers, prepares the will for his seal, then, upon discovering him to be too ill to control his hand, elects to have him sign the three pages of the will after all? Or that Mr. Shaksper himself decides to reverse his practice now that signing has become almost impossible?"

7 Diana Price, *Shakespeare's Unorthodox Biography* (Connecticut: Greenwood Press, 2001), pp. 146- 47.

8   F. G. Emmison, *Elizabethan Life: Wills of Essex Gentry and Yeomen* (Chelmsford: Essex County Council, 1978 and 1980). Quotes from wills are taken from Emmison's transcripts.

9   Tom Arkell, Nesta Evans, Nigel Goose, eds., *When Death Do Us Part: Understanding and Interpreting the Probate Records of Early Modern England* (Oxford: Leopard's Head Press Limited, 2000), pp. 103-04.

10 Edgar Fripp, *Shakespeare Studies: Biographical and Literary* (London: Humphrey Milford, 1930), pp. 23-31.

11 D. G. Vaisey, "Probate inventories and Provincial Retailers," *Probate Records and the Local Community*, ed. Phillip Riden (Gloucester: Alan Sutton, 1985), p. 97.

12 Kevin Sharpe, *Sir Robert Cotton 1586-1631* (Oxford: Oxford University Press, 1979, rpt., 2002), p. 59. Wills provide information on the peregrinations of books from hand to hand. Sharpe notes that "The Antiquaries were clearly liberal in their donations of books to Cotton, Walter Cope, and George Carew, among a list of notables, and "some manuscripts came as gifts from noblemen…" p. 58.

13 Tom Arkell, "Interpreting Probate Inventories," *When Death Do Us Part,* eds. Arkell, et al., p. 94.

14 E. K. Chambers, *William Shakespeare, A Study of Facts and Problems vol. ii.* (Oxford: Clarendon Press, 1930, pp. 52-71). Chambers discusses the substantial value of these shares and acknowledges that no shares of the Globe or the Blackfriars are mentioned in the Stratford Will. He postulates several theories to account for the lack of a paper trail.

15 F. G. Emmison, *Essex Wills: The Archdeaconry Courts 1591-1597* (Essex: Essex Record Office, 1991), pp. 117-18.

16 Nigel Goose and Nesta Evans, "Wills as an Historical Source," *When Death Do Us Part*, eds. Arkell, et al., pp. 50-51.

17 Jeff and Nancy Cox, "Probate 1500-1800: A System in Transition" *When Death Do Us Part*, eds. Arkell, et al., p. 24.

18 Ralph Houlbrooke, *Death, Religion & the Family in England, 1480-1750* (Oxford: Clarendon Press, 1998), p. 123.

19 B. Roland Lewis, *The Shakespeare Documents, vol. ii* (California: Stanford University Press, 1940), p. 482.

20 Regarding the testator's health, most willmakers follow West's formula, adhering to the phrase "sick in body." The only divergence from the formula in the Stratford Will is the testator's claim to "perfect health," an ironic touch when the deficiencies of the will are blamed on his supposed ill health.

21 Samuel Tannenbaum, *Problems in Shakspere's Penmanship Including a Study of the Poet's Will* (New York: Kraus Reprint Corporation, 1966), pp. 98-102.

22 Martin Spevack, *The Harvard Concordance to Shakespeare* (USA: Georg Olms Verlag, 1973). The word "consideration" appears in the canon eight times, and is clearly meant to indicate reflection or judgment, as in *Henry V*, I.i. 28: "Yea, at that very moment/ **Consideration** like an angel came/ and whipt th'offending Adam out of him." The word appears in other variants a total of 79 times, and none of them deal with interest on money. Likewise, the word "stock" does not occur anywhere in the canon in a financial context. The word appears twenty-six times, occasionally as a shortened form for "stockings," but more often as an indicator of quality descent, as in *Henry V*, I ii, 70-71: "Of Charles the Duke of Lorraine, sole heir make / Of the true line and **stock** of Charles the Great." In other variants, "stockings" are always socks, and "stocks" are a holding device for punishment.

23 Greenblatt, p. 145.

24 Park Honan, *Shakespeare A Life* (New York: Oxford University Press, 1999), pp. 236-37.

25 Chambers, ii, pp. 95-99.

26 A. J. Pointon, *The Man Who Was Never Shakespeare: The Theft of William Shakspere's Identity* (UK: Parapress, 2011) p. 94.

27 Christine North, "Merchants and Retailers in Seventeenth Century Cornwall," *When Death Do Us Part*, Arkell, et al., eds. p. 300.

28 Henry Swinburne, *A brief treatise of Testaments and last Wills., Part VII* (London: John Windet, 1590), p. 520.

Chapter 6:
The Rest is Silence: The absence of tributes to Shakespeare at the time of Mr. Shakspere's death

By A. J. Pointon, Ph.D.

"Nobody, including literary contemporaries, ever recognized Mr. Shakspere as a writer during his lifetime; and when he died in 1616, no one seemed to notice. Not so much as a letter refers to the author's passing. If Mr. Shakspere was Shakespeare, surely *something* dating from 1616 should mention the author's death. Even Heminges, Condell and Richard Burbage, whom he mentioned in his will, had no recorded reaction."

– Shakespeare Authorship Coalition, Declaration of Reasonable Doubt

A major problem for the theory that Shakspere of Stratford was the author Shakespeare is the huge hole bang in the middle of it—when Shakspere died in 1616, no one appeared to notice. Shakspere, if he were Shakespeare, would have been known to many groups of people: those who bought the various editions of his works, or saw him acting in his plays and wrote about him in diaries or in letters to friends or relatives; his fellow actors and poet-playwrights, who would have followed him in both of those roles with envy and admiration, and who, according to some, had collaborated with or disputed with him personally. He would have been known to courtiers, including James I, patron of the King's Men, who saw more performances of his plays at court than anyone else's, and the Earl of Southampton, to whom he had dedicated his first two poems, *Venus and Adonis* and *Lucrece*. There were colleagues, players and shareholders, with whom he had worked at the Globe and elsewhere, and people with whom he had lived, worked, and traded in and around London and Stratford, including the Heralds who had worked on the Shakspere coat of arms. And there were those who met his son-in-law, Dr. John Hall, or his patients, like Michael Drayton, and the Town Clerk of Stratford, Thomas Greene, who had lodged with him for some years, and so on.

With such a wide circle of admirers and acquaintants, one would expect that there would have been notes made of that important death in 1616, immediately after it occurred, such as letters of sorrow at Shakespeare's passing, as occurred later for Richard Burbage, the fellow player and theater shareholder and close associate of Shakspere's in the King's Men. But the only extant contemporary record of his passing is that of the clerk who recorded the interment of "Will. Shakspere, gent" in the burial register of Stratford's Holy Trinity Church.

One would expect to have seen this great writer interred with honors in Westminster Abbey in 1616, as his inferior, Francis Beaumont, had been just one month earlier alongside Spenser and Chaucer, as Michael Drayton, his supposed fellow Warwickshire native, would be in 1631, and as Ben Jonson was in 1637. Others honored with burial in the Abbey include historian Isaac Casaubon (1614), poet Robert Ayton (1638), authors William Camden (1623) and Henry Spelman (1641). Charles Dickens, Shakespeare's chief rival as the greatest English author, was buried in the "Poets' Corner" at the Abbey (though he had not wished it). But in 1616 Shakspere was buried in his home town without his name carved on any gravestone.

One would expect publishers to issue new editions of his poems and plays. It did not happen. On the occasion of the death of a Shakespeare, elegies would be expected to appear:

from fellow writers, from amateur and academic poets seeking to show off their talents, and from those who simply wished to make public their sense of bereavement. There were none.

The significance of the lack of tributes from Shakespeare's literary peers is analyzed in Appendix C by Donald P. Hayes, Professor of Sociology at Cornell University (deceased), who treated it as a quantifiable social phenomenon. But it is also interesting to see *here* what conclusions might be drawn by comparison with the elegies written for other great writers.

When Ben Jonson, a writer close in stature to Shakespeare, died in 1637, there was an immediate outpouring of elegies. Of these, thirty-three were chosen for publication in a book, *Jonsonus Virbius*. We can estimate the number of people who might have been expected to have written publishable elegies for Jonson in 1637 at a hundred, so one-third actually wrote. Assuming the same number of expected publishable elegists for Shakespeare, and assuming they were as likely to write for him as for Jonson, the probability that *none* of them wrote an elegy in 1616 is less than one in a trillion. Even if there were only fifty expected publishable elegists for Shakespeare, and they were only half as enthusiastic as Jonson's, the odds are still less than one in ten thousand that there would be no elegy for him, and we have ignored all of the incompetent elegists who might have written for him. The situation would be even worse had we used the death of Francis Bacon in 1626 as the basis of comparison: 52 elegies appeared in *Manes Veruliami*, and many more were omitted.

Stratfordians make desperate attempts to explain away the lack of elegies, saying that Shakespeare was no longer in high regard, that Shakspere had been retired for so long that he had been forgotten, that he had died of a disease his son-in-law did not want people to know about, or that news of his death simply did not reach London. None of it works. Shakespeare's plays were often performed at court and in the theaters after 1610. There was a regular carrier between Stratford and London, and patients of Dr. Hall, such as Michael Drayton and the Earl and Countess of Northampton, could easily have gotten their messages to London. Shakspere remembered fellow actors John Heminges, Henry Condell and Richard Burbage in his will; they would have been informed, and would have received the money he left them to buy rings. The idea that Shakspere had contracted some horrendous disease was *made up* to explain away his inability to write, and the fact that no one wrote a single tribute for him.

Stratfordians claim that the elegies for Shakspere arrived with the First Folio in 1623; but that is seven years too late, and it was hardly a spontaneous expression of grief or praise. It was orchestrated by Ben Jonson, using a handful of nonentities. Lacking anything genuine, those who want Shakspere to be Shakespeare desperately grasp at a poem that first appeared in print in 1633. The heading of that poem betrays the fact that it is a late fabrication:

On Wm Shakespeare/He died in April 1616

An elegist does not explain who the subject of an elegy is by telling when he died if he is famous and the elegy is written at the time. This poem is often attributed to a William Basse, but for years it was only circulated in manuscript. The earliest known copy is dated after 1620 and is in the handwriting of poet William Brown, who worked closely with Ben Jonson. As Richard Whalen says in his answer to Question 37 in Part II, "Three dozen manuscript copies of the poem have turned up, but only eight have titles mentioning Stratford or death in 1616. None indicates who added these references to Stratford, or to his burial in Stratford in 1616. They were likely added to the eight copies after 1633, almost two decades after he died."

The fact that no elegies to the author Shakespeare appeared at the time of the death of Mr. Shakspere is one more piece of unimpeachable evidence that they were two different men.

Part I, Section B:
Shakespeare's Vast Knowledge

This is a very large topic—too large to cover adequately even in a book-length treatment. The approach we have taken here is to focus on three areas that are very much in dispute as to whether the author had any specialized knowledge unavailable to the Stratford man. These are (1) whether the evident knowledge of Italy found in the works could have been acquired without having been there, (2) whether the knowledge of law found in the works suggests an author with sophisticated legal training, not merely a writer using legal terms, and (3) whether the knowledge of medicine evident in the works suggests the playwright had considerable medical training.

Addressing these topics in the three chapters in this section are three outstanding scholars, each with first-hand knowledge and expertise in the areas under consideration: (1) Alexander Waugh, the noted author and scholar, who traveled to Italy to verify claims about specialized knowledge in the plays that was unavailable in England, (2) Thomas Regnier, J.D., LL.M., who has taught courses and written extensively about Shakespeare's knowledge of law, and (3) Earl Showerman, M.D., educated at Harvard and the University of Michigan, and former head of an emergency services department. All three are experts not only in their own field, but in Shakespeare Authorship Studies.

It is important, however, to keep in mind that the poet-dramatist's knowledge in these specialized areas is the tip of a large iceberg, most of it hidden beneath the surface. Orthodox Shakespeare scholars deny that the author had specialized knowledge beyond that of a grammar school boy who had finished his schooling (if schooled at all) by the age of thirteen, who was forced to marry an older pregnant woman at age eighteen and had three children by twenty-one, who never went to university and never left England. We respectfully disagree, and cite the following summary statement of the author's vast knowledge—all of it well documented from information found in the works themselves:

> "Some say that the Stratford grammar school would have provided all the formal education Mr. Shakspere would have needed to launch him on a trajectory consistent with the author's literary output. We disagree. The works show extensive knowledge of law, philosophy, classical literature, ancient and modern history, mathematics, astronomy, art, music, medicine, horticulture, heraldry, military and naval terminology and tactics; etiquette and manners of the nobility; English, French and Italian court life; Italy; and aristocratic pastimes such as falconry, equestrian sports and royal tennis. Nothing we know about Shakspere accounts for this. Much of the knowledge [found] in the works was the exclusive province of the upper classes, yet no record places Mr. Shakspere among them for any length of time. The works are based on myriad ancient and modern sources, including works in French, Italian, Spanish, Latin and Greek not translated into English. How Shakspere . . . acquired knowledge of these sources is a mystery."

> – Shakespeare Authorship Coalition, Declaration of Reasonable Doubt

Chapter 7:
Keeping Shakespeare Out of Italy

By Alexander Waugh

"Scholars have found few, mostly dubious connections between the life of the alleged author and the works . . . Why is only one play set in Mr. Shakspere's Elizabethan or Jacobean England? Why are so many in Italy? How did he become so familiar with all things Italian that even obscure details in these plays are accurate?"

– Shakespeare Authorship Coalition, Declaration of Reasonable Doubt

"The anti-Stratfordians express astonishment that a man from Stratford could write plays set in Italy as if there were no books to read, no one to talk with, and as if the power of the imagination did not exist."

– Professor Stanley Wells, CBE (*The Stage*, 27 September 2007)

There was a time when many prominent Stratfordians supported the idea that Shakespeare's plays were written by a person with first-hand knowledge of Italy. In 1883 the German scholar, Karl Elze, noted that even "English Shakespearean scholars do not regard it with unfavourable eyes." He was referring (among others) to Charles Knight, who considered it "the most natural supposition," and to C. A. Brown who wrote that "nothing can uproot my belief of his having been there." Elze himself showed how precise allusions to Italian places and things in the ten plays that Shakespeare set in Italy attest to his having traveled there in person, and as late as 1932, a leading Stratfordian, Professor Arthur Cooper-Pritchard, confirmed how "the milieu of the time and place with regard to Italy is so intimate that it is difficult to avoid the belief that Shakespeare himself actually visited and lived for some time in that country." Even that great doyen of Stratfordian scholarship, Edmund K. Chambers, conceded that in certain scenes Shakespeare was "remarkably successful in giving a local colouring and atmosphere," appearing to demonstrate a "familiarity with some minute points of local topography."[1]

All that has now changed. While the man from Stratford cannot be placed with any certainty outside the narrow bounds of Warwickshire and London, several of the so-called "alternative authorship candidates" have, more recently, been shown to have visited those very cities—Florence, Venice, Verona, Padua, Milan, Mantua, Messina—that served for Shakespeare's Italian settings. Those who actively speak on behalf of the Stratfordian movement—mainly academics of literary criticism—are now banded together and of one accord. Appalled by the swelling and threatening tide of anti-Stratfordianism, and fearful lest the slightest agreement on Italy be seen as a concession in the wider authorship debate, they chant together a triple versed anthem that goes something like this:

Verse 1: Shakespeare plucked his ideas about Italy from out of his imagination, inventing as he went along or injecting errant English detail into his Italian settings.

Verse 2:   Shakespeare consulted expatriate Italians living in London, or travelers recently returned from abroad, to find out what Italy was really like.

Verse 3:   Shakespeare gained his knowledge of Italy by reading lots of books about it.

Each of these arguments is vulnerable and, taken together, they amount to an absurd and contradictory explanation of the playwright's working method—one which assumes both a rigorous, painstaking and precious desire for accuracy while simultaneously admitting of the exact opposite—a reckless disregard for correctness of detail. Over the course of this debate, which now sharply divides literary academics from their non-Stratfordian adversaries, it has become increasingly clear that the standard of scholarship displayed by the former is of a far lower grade than that of the latter, and nowhere is this more obvious than in the Stratfordian insistence upon Verse 1—the argument which proposes an English playwright imagining his Italian settings, or mischievously decking them in English garb. Let us take, for example, the seeming trifle of St. Peter's in Verona, a church mentioned three times by Shakespeare in *Romeo and Juliet.* Stratfordian John Doherty has this to say about it:

> There has never been a Saint Peter's Church in Verona. There is a San Tomaso's, a San Stefano's, a Santa Anastasia's etc… There is also a San Bernadino's church with an attached Franciscan monastery. This would have been a suitable location for Friar Laurence's cell… However, Saint Peter's was as good a name for a church as any for Shakespeare.[2]

The difference between this and the method used by non-Stratfordian scholars is both considerable and typical, for where the Stratfordian is content to affect the carefree pose of an armchair pundit, the non-Stratfordian rolls up his sleeves, gets himself to Verona, trawls the streets and minutely examines the local archives—not in order to discover if there is a church in Verona called St. Peters, but to establish which of the *four* churches of that name—San Pietro in Castello, San Pietro in Archivolto, San Pietro Martine or San Pietro Incarnario—might have been the one that Shakespeare had in mind. By a process of steady elimination—the text requires a building that was used as a parish church and held under Franciscan control in the 14th century—American scholar Richard Paul Roe was able to confirm Shakespeare's precise eye for Italian detail by identifying the place of Juliet's proposed marriage to Paris as *San Pietro Incarnario* in the Via San Pietro Incarnario.[3]

Doherty may not have known that "Peter" translates into Italian as "Pietro," but that is not the point. His lapse cannot be considered unique. In *The Merchant of Venice,* where Shylock asks his friend Tubal to "meet me at our synagogue," Stratfordian academic Benedikt Höttemann objects, "but there surely was no Synagogue in Venice."[4] Again it is left to the non-Stratfordian scholar to ascertain which of the five synagogues built in Venice between 1529 and 1584 Shakespeare intended as the meeting place of Shylock and Tubal.[5]

Insisting that Shakespeare filled his Italian plays with imaginary detail is a risky business as it can often and easily be shown that he didn't. If Stratfordians wish to progress the debate they will need in future to turn away from the key texts they are currently using and find some better examples to fit their claim. A survey of recent literature on Shakespeare and Italy reveals consistent reliance on just two Stratfordian texts—an essay by Professor Mario Praz and a short book by Professor Murray Levith.[6] Praz, late of Rome University, published his article called "Shakespeare's Italy" in 1954, and reprinted it with some minor amendments in the influential *Shakespeare Encyclopaedia* of 1966. Levith, a professor at Skidmore College, New York, amplifying most of Praz's remarks, added a few of his own to a treatise entitled *Shakespeare's Italian Settings and Plays,* published in booklet form in 1989. Together Praz and Levith have succeeded in providing the main source for almost everything subsequently penned by Stratfordian academics on this topic. That so many have drawn uncritically (and sometimes verbatim) from these two works is, as we shall see, a matter for considerable vexation and regret.

Often cited by Stratfordian academics as the single most important proof of Shakespeare's ignorance of Italy is the suggestion that he transformed the inland cities of Milan and Verona (to which some add Padua and Mantua) into seaports. This, according to the great architect of modern Stratfordian scholarship, Sir Sidney Lee, "renders it almost impossible that he could have gathered his knowledge of northern Italy from personal observation."[7] Lee's point was seized upon by Praz, and has since been passed like a relay baton to Levith, Bate, Schoenbaum, Höttemann, McCrea, Doherty, Foakes, Matus and countless others.[8] You only have to Google the phrase "Verona to Milan by Sea" to discover how far the infection has spread. But Shakespeare never described any of those cities as seaports. In *Two Gentlemen of Verona* he sent Valentine from Verona to Milan *by boat*, that is all, but in support of their claim, the academics seize upon the word "road" (meaning a place where a boat may lie safely at anchor) and Panthino's lines: "Launce, away, away, aboard! thy master is shipped, and thou art to post after with oars… Away ass! You'll lose the tide if you tarry any longer." One has only to check the definitions of "road," "tide" and "shipped" in the *Oxford English Dictionary* to see that none of them applies exclusively to the sea. Shakespeare, moreover, signals to his audience that Valentine's journey is not to be taken by sea, but by river and, just in case of any lingering doubt, he has Panthino explain that by *lose the tide*…"I mean thou'lt lose the flood, and in losing the flood, lose thy voyage." The "flood" thereby refers to the timed rising of the water in the locks, which in the case of boats traveling from Verona to Milan, were located on the *fossi* that linked the rivers Adige, Tartaro and Po. It is now known precisely where those canal links were situated. Some of them are still in use today. All are well documented. Only in the rarefied world of Stratfordian academia is their existence still petulantly denied.

Could the playwright himself have traveled the river-canal route from Verona to Milan? That is what we should be asking ourselves, but the academics can't catch up and are still stuck with their claim that there is no such route. This is peculiar because over one hundred years ago the literary scholar Sir Edward Sullivan published a whole raft of quotations from the pens of Strabo and Pliny to the public histories and private letters of Renaissance merchants and travelers, all confirming the common and frequent use of the rivers and interconnecting canals of Northern Italy for travel, commerce and even naval warfare.[9] The vast river Po, running 400 miles from west to east, served as the main artery, and the Milanese had not just one, but two navigable canals linking their city to it. The first, called Naviglio Grande, was fully operational by 1258, and the second, Naviglio Martesana, was inaugurated in 1465, a century before Shakespeare. As to Verona, there are paintings and prints showing the boats that sailed to and from that city. In 1581 Montaigne wrote of Verona's "huge quay beside the Adige" being, evidently, the same quay from which the English Ambassador, Sir Henry Wotton, sailed on his way from Verona to Venice via Legnano in 1607. Sullivan's references established, beyond question, that the rivers Po and Adige were connected by navigable canals at least as early as 1506, if not before, and that the journey by river, though slower, was often regarded by Renaissance travelers as more comfortable, more secure and more convenient than the over-land alternative. As French traveler Seigneur de Villamont wrote in 1598, "One can, if one wishes, go by coach to Padua but the journey by river is nicer due to the beautiful palaces built along its banks."[10]

The academics have responded to Sullivan's findings either by ignoring them completely or by peremptorily dismissing them. Praz, for example, states "so far as Shakespeare is concerned it seems wide of the mark," and Levith that "Sullivan's findings have always seemed strained and unconvincing to all but the most willing to believe." Höttemann, while conceding that a river journey from Verona to Milan "might have well been possible in Shakespeare's lifetime," mysteriously leaps to the conclusion that "Sullivan is clearly wrong." None of them presents any reason for rejecting his evidence. Professor Scott McCrea, a Stratfordian academic from Purchase College, State University of New York, in a book claiming to end the authorship question once and for all, bullishly assesses Sullivan's essay thus:

> He claimed to discover waterways that connected the cities during the 1500s. Probably he was looking at German maps of the period that view Italy from the Alps and inaccurately show a maze of rivers… There is no archaeological evidence these waterways existed. Surely after only 400 years there would be some trace of them…such canals are absurd.[11]

While adverting (unintentionally) to the international importance of 16th century Northern Italian waterways, McCrea lets slip that he has not actually read the article upon which he is commenting, for Sullivan made no such claim and the phrase, "probably looking at German maps," would not have been necessary if he had known precisely what he was talking about. Nor, on his previous page, would McCrea have seen fit to counter Prospero's line from *The Tempest*— "[at Milan] they hurried us aboard a bark,"—with "But Milan is not near any river that can carry a bark"—if he had really read Sullivan, and seen quoted there a line from Montaigne's *Travels in Italy* of 1581: "We crossed the river Naviglio, which was narrow, but still deep enough to carry great barks to Milan."

As to there being no archaeological evidence that these canals ever existed, this is so wide of the mark that it need not be dignified with a response: but if Professor McCrea and his fellow academics are really determined not to read any of the multitude of serious books and studies on this matter, perhaps they can at least check out "Google Earth," an online resource, where most of these "absurd canals" can be still viewed on recently taken satellite photographs.

It is a poor show when a fellow picks up his cudgels to thump a book he hasn't read, but Stratfordians are not ashamed of doing this. Oliver Kamm, a British commentator who believes non-Stratfordianism to be some sort of conspiracy of democracy-hating anti-Semites, wrote that although he had not read Richard Roe's *Shakespeare Guide to Italy*:

> I will make an educated guess that [he] will nowhere in his research deal with the conundrum that Old Gobbo, in *The Merchant of Venice*, has a horse—in Venice—and that Milan is described in *The Two Gentlemen of Verona* as a port city.[12]

It was foolhardy of Kamm to vaunt his "educated guess" from a standing position of ignorance, and, needless to say, he was wrong. Roe, referencing old maps, Italian books and his own on-site research, provided ample proof of horses in Venice and was able to identify the precise river and canal links that would have taken Valentine by boat from Verona to Milan in the late 16th Century.

In 1918, a decade after publication of his first essay, Sullivan produced another in which he wrote: "It is comforting to think that the old stream of misrepresentation is beginning to dry up, and that the worn out insistence on Shakespeare's having made seaport towns of Milan and Verona and other cities is breaking down."[13] How ridiculous he would have found Kamm, Bate, Doherty and their Stratfordian allies harping on about Veronese and Milanese seaports a hundred years on!

The same absurd remonstrance returns in relation to Shakspeare's *Taming of the Shrew*. Here Lucentio and Biondello are represented as traveling by boat to Padua and, once again, Levith, Praz, Höttemann, Schoenbaum, Doherty, McCrea and others appeal: "But Shakespeare must have imagined this because Padua is not a seaport!" Their evidence is taken from Lucentio's line in Act I, scene 1: "If, Biondello, thou wert come ashore, we could at once put us in readiness." Professor McCrea tells his readers that "these lines make no sense unless the author envisions inland Padua with a seacoast." But why? Are we to suppose that Shakespeare—with the richest vocabulary of any writer dead or alive—understood the word "shore" only to mean a "sea-shore"? Is that it? Never mind that *The Oxford English Dictionary* defines "shore" as "the land bordering on the sea or a large lake or river;" or that old maps clearly label and display a river port at Padua; or that in 1511 Sir Richard Guylforde "wente by water to Padua by river of Brente;" or that Fynes Moryson, in 1594, wrote of "taking boate at the east gate of Paduoa;" or that Coryat, in 1611, described the "Barkes that go forth and backe betwixt Padua and Venice"—only the Stratfordian academic is prepared to ignore all this, so desperate is he to keep Shakespeare out of Italy.

Not satisfied that "Padua the seaport" is quite enough of itself to confirm Shakespeare's total ignorance of Italy, many go on to assert that he mistakenly placed the city within the Duchy of Lombardy. Evidence in support of this claim is drawn from a speech delivered by Lucentio in *Taming of the Shrew*:

> Tranio, since for the great desire I had
> To see fair Padua, nursery of arts,
> I am arrived for fruitful Lombardy,
> The pleasant garden of great Italy.[14]

Here many footnoted editions take issue, some stating that Shakespeare wrongly supposed Padua to be in Lombardy, others that he mistakenly believed Lombardy to cover the whole of Northern Italy, but look carefully at the text. Lucentio says he has arrived "*for* Lombardy" (whatever that is supposed to mean) and not *in* Lombardy. Some 350 typographical errors have been identified in the First Folio edition of *Taming of the Shrew*—more than any other play in that folio. Several modern editions change "for" to "in," thus canonizing the error, but clearly the line should read: "I am arrived *from* fruitful Lombardy." We know this, not just because "*for* Lombardy" makes no sense and "*from* Lombardy" does, but because Lucentio has journeyed by road from Pisa and arrived by boat at Padua. This means that his journey must have taken him through Lucca, Pavullo and Modena, arriving at Revere in Lombardy where he would have boarded a boat on the Po to Ostiglia and thence (by rivers Adige and Brenta) to Padua. But then Padua, we are told, is to Shakespeare a seaport, so how would he have known all that?

With the same captious half-think that accuses the playwright of imagining coastal ports at Verona and Milan, we are asked to believe that he took a reckless guess about Bergamo too.[15] "Shakespeare cannot have visited Italy," they say, "because, if he had, he would not have mentioned a sail maker from Bergamo, since Bergamo is nowhere near the sea." How difficult would it have been for any one of these academics to check this out before blindly copying from Levith and Praz? In less than half an hour (using only books—not the internet) I was able to establish that Bergamo was a leading city of textile manufacture in the 16th century, that silk, hemp, flax, linen, bergamot (note the name—"a tapestry fabric made of ox and goats' hair woven with cotton or hemp"), as well as wax-cloth (out of which sails have been made since the 14th century), were all produced there. A few minutes of extra research brought me a list of towns situated far from the sea where sails have been historically manufactured. Bologna, for instance, supplied sails to the Arsenale in Venice, there was Retford in England, Anhalt in landlocked Silesia and the city of Arzamas, right in the middle of Russia, which for centuries was the principal manufactory of sails for St. Petersburg, 750 miles away on the Baltic.[16]

With Shakespeare's Bergamo, we find an apparently insignificant detail about a Lombard city revealing a precise topographical knowledge of Italy. Shakespeare was right, the academics are once again wrong. Shakespeare uses this technique time and again. Consider, for instance, the following few lines from a scene set in Florence from Act III of *All's Well that Ends Well*:

> WIDOW: God save you, pilgrim! Whither are you bound?
> HELENA: To Saint Jacques le Grand.
>   Where do the palmers lodge, I do beseech you?
> WIDOW: At the Saint Francis here beside the port.[17]

Shakespeare gives three distinct references here—one to a pilgrimage site called Saint Jacques le Grand, one to a lodging house called Saint Francis that caters to "palmers" (pilgrims), and one to a nearby port. Great efforts have been made by Stratfordians to convince their readers that he invented all three while sitting at his desk in England, that Florence has no port, that "Saint Jacques le Grand" is a muddled allusion to Santiago de Compostella in Spain, and that there is no Saint Francis lodging house for pilgrims in Florence. Doherty, who complains of Helena's using the French name Saint Jacques when in Italy, states that Shakespeare was confusing Italy with Spain and insists that "lack of precision regarding this shrine points to a writer who had heard the name but was unsure of the shrine's location…as he had often done, he took the name without regard to any precise detail."[18]

Professor Praz, however, disagrees, reluctantly conceding that Shakespeare *did* have a precise location in mind, and that was a church called *San Giacomo d'Altopasco* just outside Florence, which Shakespeare might have learned about from expatriate Italians in London or from some now lost manuscript source. Needless to say both Praz and Doherty were wrong. Again, if either had taken the trouble to investigate Florence past and present he would have soon discovered that there was once a Florentine port on the Arno, which flourished from Roman times until the mid-18th century, and beside it, on the Piazza Ognissanti, may be found, to this day, the St. Francis pilgrim's hostel with its original stone-carved sign of the crossed hands of Christ and St. Francis still projecting proud above the door. Just across the river, in plain view and bold to the skyline, is the church of San Jacopo Sopr'Arno, dedicated to, and named after, the apostle San Giacomo Maggiore (French: *Saint Jacques le Grand*), whom the Florentines believed to have been the first prior there. Since the 13th century this shrine has featured on the pilgrim route to Spain. Its windows are in the shape of the *coquilles St. Jacques,* the scallop shell symbol of St. James. The reason Helena called it "Saint Jacques le Grand," instead of "San Giacomo Maggiore," is because she was a French woman, recently arrived from Rousillon.

In *Taming of the Shrew,* which is set in Padua, the playwright's *mise en scène* requires a rich man's house to be situated next to a quay where boats may be moored. The house and the quay must be located in a parish of St. Luke's and in sight of a large lodging house where Lucentio can stay while he takes courses in rhetoric, music, poesy and metaphysics at a nearby university. Shakespeare is correct in describing the city as "nursery of the arts." Padua's *Universitas Artistarum,* founded in 1373, was at that time one of the best universities for the arts in Europe. He was also correct in placing the lodging house, the merchants' houses and the parish church of St. Luke's near to one another by the port.[19] This precise alignment of topographical detail cannot be found in any Renaissance city other than Padua. In London there was no church of St. Luke's until 1733, nor any university until 1826. Undeterred, Stratfordian Benedikt Höttemann, writing of Shakespeare's Padua, declares that "England is never out of sight… Shakespeare was thinking of London when he composed the play."[20]

Very rarely will the modern academic cede to any fact of Shakespeare's accuracy about Italy. Professor Praz was "puzzled" in 1954, Professor Levith "surprised" in 1989 and Benedikt Höttemann "astonished" in 2010, to learn that Shakespeare appeared to know of a St. Gregory's Well in Milan.[21] Only Professor McCrea held against the tide, insisting that "Milan's St Gregory's Well was regularly mentioned by other Elizabethan writers."[22] Nonsense! No single "other Elizabethan writer" has ever mentioned it, and McCrea knows this perfectly well. Levith and Höttemann believed that Shakespeare "might have found out about this well" from a famous 1582 map of Milan by Braun, but they did not go to the length of checking it out themselves; nor did J. Madison Davis or Daniel Frankforter, who stated in their *Shakespeare Name and Place Dictionary* (1995) that "a print of the city showing the well appeared in Braun's *Civitates Orbis Terrarum* (1582)." No, it did not. If any of them had stirred themselves to look at this map, they would have noticed that St. Gregory's Well is not depicted upon it.[23] By the way, as Shakespeare seems to have known (and the academics have not realized) St. Gregory's Well was not a well at all, but a burial pit for corpses of the plague.

The superficiality of Stratfordian scholarship is nowhere more in evidence than when it is considering the question of Shakespeare and Venice. Höttemann admits that in *Othello* and *Merchant of Venice* Shakespeare incorporates "extraordinarily accurate details of Venice," but then goes on to insist that the plays were "composed in London, far away from Venice." The most frequent reason given for this "fact" is that the playwright failed to mention the city's most famous sites—the Grand Canal, the Doge's Palace, the Piazza San Marco, the Arsenale etc. A more fatuous argument can hardly be imagined. That Dickens' London does not mention Trafalgar Square and Buckingham Palace, or that Tom Wolfe's New York does not incorporate the Statue of Liberty and the Empire State Building, tells us nothing about those writers' relationships to those cities. Shakespeare was not a travel writer in the manner of his contemporaries, Coryat and Fynes Morrison, nor, like Ben Jonson (who set *Volpone* in Venice without ever having been there), did he need to overstate his claim by listing all the most obvious and celebrated features of those places where he set his plays. Shakespeare's method, which we see repeated time and again, was to pepper his plays with frequent, minor and precise touches of local color. In both of his Venetian plays he presents many little facts about the city that can be traced neither to the original sources from which he drew his plots, nor to any known travel books of the time. In Othello, for instance, he mentions the "Sagittary," a dark, narrow street where the arrow makers lived (now called the Frezzaria); he mentions the "penthouse" in the *Ghetto Nuovo* (still standing on the square today); the Venetian clogs, or *zoccoli*; the "tranect" at Liza Fusina[24]; he shows knowledge of the "common ferry," (the *traghetti* which brought passengers from the "tranect" to Venice); he is precise in his measurement of distance between his Belmont (The Villa Foscari), Liza Fusina and Venice; he refers to the gondola and the gondolier, to Magnificos and Signiors, to the merchants' Rialto district, and the Venetian custom of presenting "a dish of doves" as a gift or peace offering.

Before passing from the argument of "imagination" to that based upon the books Shakespeare may or may not have read, and the people he may or may not have met, I should like to give brief consideration to that related contention (incorporated into Verse 1 of the Stratfordian anthem)—that he took details from England and placed them willy-nilly into his Italian scenes. Here again one can fairly say that the modern Stratfordian performance has been lackluster. A few points have been raised, most of them, as we have come to expect, lifted directly from Levith and Praz. It was Praz, for instance, who first promoted the idea that Shakespeare was thinking of Staffordshire when he described the Italian custom of begging for soul-cakes at Hallowmas.[25] But when informed by his Italian friends and cousins that begging for soul-cakes (known in Italy as *pani dei morti*) was a well-known Italian custom dating back to the 9th Century, Professor Praz cut this observation from the 1966 and 1978 reprints of his essay.[26] Professor Levith, however, failing to notice the correction, copied the inaccuracy from Praz's 1954 draft into his booklet of 1989.

It is also from the Levith-Praz stable that we learn how Shakespeare was thinking of England when he mentioned an Italian "ale-house" in *Two Gentleman of Verona*. "Italy," they point out, "is primarily a nation of wine drinkers." That may be so, but neither acknowledges that in Shakespeare's day ale was the most popular alcoholic drink among the poorer classes throughout Europe; that the first Italian alehouse was opened in the days of Agricola in the 1st century AD; that the world's first abbey brewery was at the Benedictine monastery of Monte Cassino, near Rome, and that John Florio gave two perfectly good Italian words for "alehouse" (*hostaria* and *hosterietta*) in his *Italian Dictionary* of 1598. It is most unlikely that Shakespeare's characters Speed and Lance would have been unable to find any place serving beer in a Renaissance city of the size and international importance of Milan.

Professor Levith similarly opines that the Venetian Gobbo would be more likely to dream of "a plate of pasta than a 'rasher on the coals.'" Once again he takes his idea from Praz, who had earlier maintained that Shakespeare's "'rasher on the coals' alludes to that peculiarly English dish, a fried slice of bacon." It does not. A rasher could be a thin cut of any meat, and besides Renaissance Italians *did* eat bacon, which they called *porciuto*. A popular Northern Italian dish of Shakespeare's day was called *carbonata*. This word may be found in Florio's *Italian Dictionary* of 1598 where it is defined as "meate broiled upon the coles, a rasher."

Doherty briefly departs from the Levith-Praz script to pick a few of his own examples of Shakespeare's Englishing. In response to a detail from *Romeo & Juliet* about flint streets in Verona, he argues that "flint paving was common in England at least since Roman times… and can still be seen in places as far apart as Lewes in Sussex and Stirling in Scotland." To reinforce his point Doherty cites three modern pamphlets about conservation of flint walls in Hertford, Sussex and Scotland. Of what relevance are these? The debate is not about Hertford, Sussex or Scotland, it is about Verona and whether or not Shakespeare ever went there. Needless to say, he ignores the highly relevant fact of Veronese flint (recently in the news for turning blue), which has been mined at Verona since prehistoric times, was exported as flintlocks in the 17th and 18th centuries and may still be bought as paving slabs in Verona today.[27] Is it not more likely that Shakespeare was thinking of Verona's flint paving when he wrote about it in *Romeo and Juliet* than of some random flint walls in Hertford, Sussex and Scotland?

Moving from mineral to vegetable, Doherty proposes that Shakespeare only mentioned a sycamore grove in Verona because this tree was "introduced into England toward the end of the sixteenth century." Here again he misses the point. With a little more research he might have discovered that in Shakespeare's day the name "sycomore" (note, with two *o*'s) properly applied to a species of fig tree from the Middle East that could not grow as far north as England or Verona. The tree that was introduced into the gardens and parks of the English nobility in the 1580s was in fact the "Great Maple"—which English noblemen (and the playwright) wrongly called "sycomore."[28] Now we need some explanation as to why Shakespeare placed this specific type of maple, mistakenly labeling it "sycamore," along Verona's western wall precisely where a grove of that same species may still be found today.[29]

Each and every example of Shakespeare's imagining or Englishing his Italian settings has been thoroughly refuted by scholars Sullivan, Grillo, Jeffery, Magri, Roe and others, using hard evidence to the contrary, so that it is no longer possible for the Stratfordian to sing the first verse if his anthem without knowing that it is wrong. Let us then pass to Verse 2—that which envisages a playwright gleaning facts about the geography, topography, language and literature of Italy from Italians resident in London.

Professor of English at Columbia University, James Shapiro, in a derisive history of the non-Stratfordian movement, writes that "a curious Shakespeare could have learned everything he needed to know about the Italian settings of his plays from a few choice conversations."[30] Could he? Shakespeare set 106 scenes in Italy in which may be found over 800 references to Italy in general; 400 references to Rome; 52 to Venice; 34 to Naples; 25 to Milan; 23 to Florence; 22 to Padua and 20 to Verona. Beyond these may be found incidental but precise references to Genoa, Mantua, Pisa, Ferrara, Liza Fusina, Villafranca di Verona, Messina in Sicily and many others.[31] In light of this, Shapiro's "few choice conversations" seem grossly inadequate. If all these details were really gleaned in such a casual way, with whom, we may ask, did Shakespeare have these conversations? It is in answer to this question that the academics show themselves, once again, to be thoroughly inexpert and corrupted. To support their claim they have sought names of Italians—any Italians—who might have lived in or near London during Will Shakspere's lifetime and who could have taught him all he needed to know about Italy. Professor McCrea produces a directory of Italian names that includes a restaurateur called Paolo Lucchese; a bookseller, Acanio de Renialme; a merchant, Nicolo De Gozi, and a physician Theodore Diodati; but with no evidence that Will Shakspere ever met any of them, let alone drew from their unlikely topographical knowledge of fifteen Northern Italian cities and interconnecting waterways, his proposition immediately collapses upon itself in a gross exhibition of teenage fatigue. So he changes tack: Robert Armin (the actor-clown who replaced William Kempe around 1600 as an important figure in Shakspere's acting troupe) "was, believe it or not, a good Italian scholar."[32] It was generous of McCrea to offer the "believe-it-or-not" get-out clause, for as he well knows, anyone investigating his claim will go, without hesitation, straight for the "not" option. McCrea took the idea from Levith, who had previously stated it like this: "Another likely source for detail may have been Shakespeare's fellow actor Robert Armin who was, by all reports, a good Italian scholar." By what reports? Can he name one? The closest Robert Armin came to being an Italian scholar was when he himself suggested that a naïve English ballad he had written was a translation of an Italian fairy-tale. This is now known to be false.[33] There is no other evidence that Armin learned Italian, read or spoke it, visited Italy, or was a scholar of any sort.

Professor Bate (among others) speculates that John Florio (the above mentioned dictionary compiler, Italian scholar and mentor to Queen Anne) was "the obvious person" to have introduced Shakespeare to his Italian sources, but realizing that Florio's known connections to the Earl of Southampton and to Ben Jonson are insufficient of themselves to link him in any way to the man from Stratford, Bate further urges his readers to suppose that Shakspere took Florio's wife for a mistress. This follows the method of Professor A. L. Rowse who, several years earlier, had proposed an Italian lover for Shakspere in the shape of Emilia Bassano-Lanier. Knowing there to be no foundation to any of these assertions, the majority of Stratfordians settle for a more generalized explanation involving a helpful crowd of unknown, unnamed Italians squished into a pub near the Globe Theatre on Bankside. Of the many who have repeated this improbable claim I shall quote one as typical of them all:

> [Shakespeare] might have acquired all the geography necessary for his "Italian" plays in his own back yard. The Oliphant, a Bankside inn, sat close by the Globe and largely catered to Italian customers. Shakespeare must have passed it every day on his way to work and perhaps he knew it well.[34]

So let us look carefully at the origin of this yarn and try to establish how much genuine scholarship has gone into formulating it. All that is known about the "Oliphant" pub on Bankside is contained in the vestry records of the Parish of St. Saviour, Southwark. There it is confirmed that by late 1598 there was an inn at this location "sometime called the Red Harte and now called the Oliphant." Nothing about Italians there. Skip forward to 1923 when an Italian writer named G. S. Gargano publishes, in Florence, a book containing a partial quotation from a letter of 1591. This letter was written in Italian, by a merchant from Dubrovnik (who happened to be staying in London), addressed to his business partner in Italy. The merchant writes (concerning an acquaintance called Vanni), that "he [Vanni] may be found either in his *Piero del Giardino,* or in the house of the Elefante."[35] It is not entirely clear what this means as Gargano denies his readers the luxury of full context. However, one thing is certain—that the Dubrovnik merchant was not referring to a pub in London, which was anyway at that time called the "Red Harte." His original Italian gives *casa dell' Elefante*—back to Florio's 1598 Italian Dictionary where *casa* is defined as "a house, a mannor or dwelling place. Also a family, a blood name, or stocke. Also a mans owne home or native country." *Casa* does *not* mean an inn, a pub, a tavern, or an alehouse. "Elefante" is the surname of an old and well-respected mercantile family from Barletta (the nearest Italian port to Dubrovnik) where there is both a Casa Elefante and a church of St. Peter.[36] It was Gargano who first tried to link the "house of Elefante" to Shakspere's Globe, Praz who mischievously fueled the flames among gullible Stratfordians by suggesting that one man, Vanni, constituted an "Italian clientele," and Levith who finally transformed the Red Harte/ Oliphant into "*The Elephant*, a bankside London inn near the Globe Theatre frequented by Italians."

With no evidence to support the Stratford man's connection to a single Italian, or to any traveler willing or able to teach him about the byways of Florence or the "sycomore" groves of Verona, those who insist that he was the playwright and that he never went to Italy, need to look for other ways to puff the sails of their claim.

Let us turn then to Verse 3 in which Shakespeare gains his knowledge of Italy by reading lots of books about it:

In the Stratfordian book *Shakespeare Beyond Doubt* the whole subject of Shakespeare's remarkable Italian knowledge is blithely glossed in a single sentence:

> There was plenty he got from books, not from experience: travel in Italy, the geography and customs of Venice; Mediterranean shipwrecks; Cleopatra's arrival at Cydnus; fratricide; witchcraft; men turned into asses.[37]

So what are these books from which the playwright is supposed to have drawn all of his precise details of Italian routes, cities and customs? Since none has so far come to light, the beleaguered Stratfordian is forced to rely on attenuating reiterations of the unfortunate phrase "he may have found it in some now lost source." If it were known that Stratford Shakspere had owned a single book or manuscript, that might help; but the absence of any bibliographic or literary bequest in his will suggests otherwise. An Italian proverb from *Love's Labours Lost* (*Venechia, Venechia, Che non te vede, che non te prechia*) is said to have been lifted from John Florio's book *First Fruites*, but since Shakespeare's two versions differ significantly from Florio's, the link must be ruled out.[38] Elsewhere Shakespeare refers to the nasal accents of the Neopolitans, the gravity of the Pisans, and uses Italian proverbs with no connection to Florio or to any other written source.[39]

There is not unfortunately enough space here to itemize every example of Stratfordian error. My intention is simply to provide an introduction to the poor standard of scholarship among "professional academics" and to encourage them, where possible, toward a less emotional and more rigorous reaction to the many outstanding questions. They need to answer, for instance, how Shakespeare came to know about the churches of Florence, Padua and Verona, about the streets of Venice, the distances between unmapped Italian sites, Venetian customs, Italian monasteries and country estates, and the navigable canals and river routes of northern Italy? Where did he find copies of books in Italian by Giovanni Fiorentino, Cinthio, Ariosto and Luigi da Porto? How did he learn to read and write the language? How was he able to describe specific works of art by Luca Penni, Correggio and Titian that had never left Italy? How did he gain his detailed knowledge of spoken Italian dramatic forms—*Commedia dell'Arte* and *Commedia Erudita*? How was it possible, in 1965, to publish a 100-page glossary of Shakespeare's seafaring and naval terms (not otherwise defined in print until Mainwaring's nautical dictionary of 1644) if the playwright never boarded a ship or sailed out of England?[40]

These are the sorts of questions that Stratfordians need to think about, but so long as they continue to evade the central issues and to prop themselves against the faltering scaffolds of Levith and Praz we shall have to submit—over and over—to the same stuck record with all its familiar moans and concomitant insistencies: to be told that the Mantuans and Veronese had no ships; that departing from Milan by the north gate and along the Alpine foothills would be the wrong way to Mantua; that Gobbo could not have had a horse in Venice; that Florence had no port; that the Bentivoglii were from Bologna, not from Florence or Pisa; that Giulio Romano was not a sculptor; and that Shakespeare wrongly called the Venetian "Doge" a "Duke," and wrongly believed him to preside over civil cases. In all these points Shakespeare has now been conclusively vindicated and the Stratfordian academics shown to be in error, but that will not stop them from repeating these points again and again, in the hope perhaps that their readers, bored to death, might not seek to check the veracity of their claims.[41]

Shakespeare's knowledge of Italy is a fascinating and rewarding subject worthy of serious attention, but one, sadly, with which the modern literary academic is reluctant to engage—not (as he would have us believe) because he is a "professional" whose unique "methodology" allows him to know best about Shakespeare, but because he is bounded and compromised by the internal politics of his profession. Academics draw their salaries from the public purse, but their advancement is dependent not upon the good opinion of governments or taxpayers, but on mutual approval according to the system of peer review. As I have explained, the Italian question touches a raw nerve in the authorship debate, and so long as this remains the case, no ambitious Shakespearean academic should expect to advance his career by submitting authorship doubt to the scrutiny of his colleagues.

If the literary academics are really so barren of ideas, we should ask them to leave the stage to make way for the more considered presentations of historians, paleographers, scholarly "amateurs" and those with greater knowledge of Italian custom, language and topography than they themselves possess. If they cannot do this, but insist on hogging the limelight with their same flawed and feeble "methodologies," then they must learn to accept, with some grace, all the eggs and rotten tomatoes that are showered upon them.

In the meantime, let us look forward to the day when some plucky Stratfordian mainstreamer breaks from the citadel, stiffens the sinew, and signals to his colleagues that the time is come at last to do some proper work, to lay aside his prejudice, to examine the facts, and in calm and contemplative fashion to begin to justify the existence of that most fortunate among all professional classes—the salaried scholar of the State.

Endnotes

1   Charles Armitage Brown: *Shakespeare's Autobiographical Poems*, (1838), p. 100; Charles Knight (Ed.): *Pictorial Edition of the Works of Shakspere*, (1839), vol. 1, p. 433; Karl Elze: *Essays on Shakespeare* (1874), p. 315; A. H. Cooper-Pritchard: *The Shakespeare Pictorial*, (Feb. 1932), cited in C. Clark: *Shakespeare and National Character* (1932), p. 106; E. K. Chambers: *Shakespeare—A Study of Facts and Problems*, (1930), vol. 1, p. 61.

2   John Doherty, *The Ignorance of Shakespeare*, (2009), p. 198.

3   Richard Paul Roe, *The Shakespeare Guide to Italy*, (2011) pp. 28-33.

4   Benedikt Höttemann, *Shakespeare and Italy* (2011) p. 260.

5   Tubal is an Ashkenazi name; 16th century Ashkenazi are depicted in the "Jewish gabardine" (*Merchant of Venice* I, 3), and wore them long after other Jewish groups ceased to do so; the word *ashkenazi* was used in Hebrew to mean German, hence Roe's suggestion of the German synagogues, *Grande Tedescha* and *Scola Canton.* See Roe pp. 132-140.

6   Mario Praz: "Shakespeare's Italy" in *Shakespeare Survey 7* (1954), pp. 95-106; *Murray Levith: Shakespeare's Italian Settings and Plays* (1989). In "Ben Jonson's Italy" from *The Flaming Heart* (1958) pp. 168-185, Praz suggests that Shakespeare may have visited Italy with the Earl of Southampton in 1593, but appears to withdraw from this position in the reprint of "Shakespeare's Italy" for *A Shakespeare Encyclopaedia* (1966) *sub* Italy.

7   The phrase was used by Lee in his *Great Englishmen of the Sixteenth Century* (1904), p. 299, and repeated in his entry "Shakespeare" for the DNB (1917), Vol 17, p. 1294.

8   Chambers, vol 1, p. 330; Praz, p. 98; Levith, p. 89; Bate, p. 94, Schoenbaum p. 170, Höttemann, pp. 353 & 189; Doherty, p. 191, Foakes Introduction to *Comedy of Errors*, (1962) p. xxx; Matus: *Shakespeare in Fact* (2012), p. 249.

9   Edward Sullivan: "Shakespeare and the Waterways of North Italy" in *The Nineteenth Century*, (February 1908), pp.215-232.

10 *"De Lizafousina on peut aller si on veut par carrosse à Padoüe. Toutefois le cours de l'eau est plus*

plaisant à cause des beaux palais qui sont edifies à ses rives." Cited in Violet Jeffrey: "Shakespeare's Venice", *The Modern Language Review*, vol 27, No. 1 (Jan 1932), p. 32.

11 Scott McCrea: *The Case for Shakespeare—The End of the Authorship Question* (2005), p. 76.

12 See Oliver Kamm: "From Nonsense to Indecency" in *Jewish Chronicle Online* (4 Jan 2013); for Kamm's anxieties concerning anti-Semitic and anti-democratic conspiracies among non-Stratfordians see also his *Times* leader, 9 Feb. 2013.

13 Edward Sullivan: "Shakespeare and Italy" in *The Nineteenth Century*, (Jan 1918), pp. 138-153.

14 *The Taming of the Shrew* (I, i).

15 Vincentio: "O villain! He is a sailmaker in Bergamo" *The Taming of the Shrew* (V, i, 77).

16 Information gleaned from *Encyclopaedia Britannica* (9th Ed.), *sub* "Bergamo"; *OED*, *sub* "Bergamot"; *Edinburgh Gazetteer* (1822), *sub* "Bologna," "Retford," "Anhalt" and "Arzamas." See also Paolo Malanimi, *Pre-Modern European Economy: 10th – 19th Centuries*, p. 162.

17 *All's Well That Ends Well* (III.v.32-4).

18 Doherty, p. 199.

19 Roe (pp. 96-105), reproduces a 1718 map of Padua by Lorenzo Mazzi from the *Museo Civico di Padova* (F. 6330) that clearly identifies the port, nearby church of St. Luke's and the *Ostaria*. The University of Padua is situated a couple of blocks north.

20 Höttemann, pp. 211-2.

21 *Two Gentlemen of Verona* (IV, ii, 77).

22 Scott McCrea, p. 77.

23 For "St. Gregory's Well" see: Praz, 104; Höttemann, 187; Levith, 62; Davis and Frankforter *et al*. For a more considered account of what and where St. Gregory's Well was, see Roe, 72-77.

24 The word *tranect* appears only once and only in Shakespeare. It was once thought to apply to the Venetian *traghetto* that Shakespeare describes as the "common ferry," but is now known to refer to the dam at Liza Fusina which separates the fresh water of the river Brenta from the salt-water lagoon (possibly from "transect"), and/or the hoist, built in 1448, which pulled boats over this dam, known as the *transit* (possibly from an early spelling *trancet*). For further details of this and discussion of Shakespeare's "Sagittary" see Jeffery (1932).

25 *Two Gentlemen of Verona* (II, i, 24) and Praz, p. 99.

26 For ancient history and tradition of soul-cakes in Italy see *Venezia—Guide Rosse Italia*, p. 110.

27 See: *Le Pietre de Fuoco—Veronese Flintstones & the Flints of Europe* (1988) exhibition catalogue online.

28 John Gerard in his book *Herball* (1597) *sub*. "Fig Tree" (p. 1327) writes: *"Acer maior*—The great Maple, not rightly called the Sycamore tree… The great Maple is a stranger to England, only it groweth in the walkes and places of pleasure of noble men, where it especially is planted for the shadowe sake, and under the name of Sycomore tree."

29 Benvolio (*Romeo and Juliet*. I, i) says he had walked with troubled mind "underneath the grove of sycamore that westward rooteth from the city's side." In 2009 Roe found and photographed what he took to be remnants of that same grove. See Roe, pp. 8-10.

30 James Shapiro: *Contested Will* (2010), p. 311.

31 See Ernesto Grillo: *Shakespeare and Italy* (1949), p. 98. (This list unchecked by the present author); John Hamill identifies 10 further allusions to Mantua in "The Ten Restless Ghosts of Mantua" in *Shakespeare Oxford Newsletter*, Vol 39, Nos. 3 & 4 (Summer & Autumn 2003).

32 McCrea, 79.

33 Armin's naïve ballad, *The Italian Tailor and his Boy* (1609) was written in imitation of a fairy tale from *Nights of Straparola* (c. 1552) but Armin's version cannot, by any stretch, be considered a translation.

34 Frederick A. Keller: *Spearing the Wild Blue Boar* (2009), p. 76; variants of this claim may be found in Praz, 104; Schoenbaum, 169; McCrea 72; Höttemann, 167; and others.

35 G. S. Gargano: *Scapigliatura Italiana a Londra* (1923) p. 41: *"...a proposito del Vanni 'che va piu che mai al suo Piero del Giardino' aggiunge che 'se homo lo vol trovar bisogna che vadi là o in casa dell'Elefante.'"*

36 Many Stratfordian commentators further insist that the "Elephant Inn," mentioned as being in the "south suburbs" of some Illyrian city in *Twelfth Night,* is also a reference to the same Oliphant at Bankside. "The Elephant" was however a common name for an inn throughout Europe. There was an Elephant Inn on the via del Lupenare in ancient Pompeii; an Elephant Inn in the Piazza del Duomo at Catania; in 1516 a tavern in Rome was named *Hostaria del Leonfante* after the Pope's elephant, Hanno; Walsingham was asked to subscribe letters "at the sign of the Elephant, Rue St. Jacques, Paris" in June 1586. When in 1551 Emperor Maximilian II's elephant, Solomon, traveled through Genoa, Piacenza, Verona, Mantua, Venice, Bressanone and Trento several inns on the journey were renamed "at the sign of the Elephant." The "Elephant Inn" at Bressanone on the Adige was one of these. Mary Shelley stayed there in 1842 and it is still in business today.

37 Carol Chillington Rutter: "Shakespeare and School" in *Shakespeare Beyond Doubt* (ed. Edmondson and Wells, 2013), p. 143.

38 *Love's Labour's Lost* IV, ii, 97-8. Florio *First Fruites* (chapter 19) gives "Venetia, chi it vede, no ti pretia." Which he translates as "Venise, woo seeth thee not, praiseth thee not." See Catherine Alexander (ed.) *Cambridge Shakespeare Library*, vol 1, p. 67.

39 See Grillo, p. 32, for Shakespeare's use of *La Signora degli Stracci* in *Twelfth Night* and p. 126 for further examples of Shakespeare's Italian proverbs.

40 A.F. Falconer: *A Glossary of Shakespeare's Sea and Naval Terms* (1965); see introduction, p. vii.

41 Many published sources refute these statements: for Mantuan ships see Roe, 110; for Veronese ships see Magri: *Shakespeare and the Ships of the Venetian Republic*, DVSN (Mar 2011), p. 5; for the gate set in the north wall at Milan through which travelers passed to eastern destinations, see Roe 78; horse racing was banned in Venice in 1392 and Stratfordians report this as a permanent city-wide ban on all horses, but, for non-racing horses in 16th century Venice see David McPherson: *Shakespeare Jonson and the Myth of Venice* (1990), p. 123, Peter Ackroyd: *Venice—Pure City* (2010), p. 63, and Roe, 132; for the port at Florence see Roberto di Ferdinando: *I porti di Firenze*, http://curiositadifirenze. blogspot.co.uk/2011/01/i-porti-di-firenze.html; the Bentivoglii were banished from Bologna in 1506, but Stratfordians insist that Shakespeare's placing any of them outside Bologna is ignorant; Giulio Romano's tomb in Mantua praises him as a sculptor, but Stratfordians insist he wasn't one and that Shakespeare wrongly described him as such. For evidence supporting Shakespeare's view see Myron Laskin: "Guilio Romano and Baldassare Castiglione," *Burlington Magazine* Vol. 109, no 770, 1967, pp 300-303; *doge* means "duke" in Venetian dialect, for the Doge's influence over Venetian courts and Shakespeare's extraordinary precision in matters of Venetian law, see Magri: *Italian Legal System in Merchant of Venice,* DVSN (Feb 2009), p. 5.

Chapter 8:
Could Shakespeare Think Like a Lawyer?

By Thomas Regnier, J.D., LL.M.

In the late 18th century, Edmond Malone, an early editor of Shakespeare and a lawyer himself, may have been the first to comment on the frequent appearance of legal terms in Shakespeare's plays:

> [Shakespeare's] knowledge and application of legal terms, seems to me not merely such as might have been acquired by casual observation of his all-comprehending mind; it has the appearance of technical skill; and he is so fond of displaying it on all occasions, that there is, I think, some ground for supposing that he was early initiated in at least the forms of law. (Alexander 57–58)

The relevance of Shakespeare's legal knowledge to the authorship question is obvious. The more comprehensive and sophisticated Shakespeare's legal knowledge is shown to be, the more difficult it becomes to explain how William of Stratford could have acquired such knowledge. Some have theorized that he was a law clerk at one time, but no one has uncovered any external evidence that he served in such a capacity. If he had, it is odd that no document witnessed and signed by him as a law clerk has ever turned up, despite the ransacking of village archives by ardent Stratfordians in search of it (Greenwood 1908, 377–79). And although the Shakspere family was involved in many petty lawsuits in Stratford, this would not likely have taught young William about the law at a very sophisticated level (Greenwood 1908, 396–97). How, then, does one explain the apparent familiarity with the law that is evident in Shakespeare's plays?

Malone was not the last to be impressed by Shakespeare's legal acumen. In 1859, in *Shakespeare's Legal Acquirements Considered*, John Campbell, Lord Chief Justice of England, imparted his judgment on Shakespeare's legal terms:

> I am amazed, not only by their number, but by the accuracy and propriety with which they are uniformly introduced. There is nothing so dangerous as for one not of the craft to tamper with our free-masonry. . . . While Novelists and Dramatists are constantly making mistakes as to the law of marriage, of wills, and of inheritance,—to Shakespeare's law, lavishly as he propounds it, there can neither be [objection],[1] nor bill of exceptions, nor writ of error. (132-34)

Lord Penzance, another judge, noted in 1902 that, "[Shakespeare] seems almost to have thought in legal phrases—the commonest of legal expressions were ever at the end of his pen in description or illustration" (85-86).

In recent years, U.S. Supreme Court Justices John Paul Stevens, Sandra Day O'Connor, and Antonin Scalia have expressed doubt that the man from Stratford could have written the plays of Shakespeare (Bravin).

Great American writers Mark Twain and Walt Whitman also eloquently expressed skepticism about the disjunction between the Stratford man's lack of legal education and the depth of legal knowledge found in Shakespeare's plays. Twain said:

> Shakespeare couldn't have written Shakespeare's works, for the reason that the man who wrote them was limitlessly familiar with the laws, and the law-courts, and law-proceedings, and lawyer-talk, and lawyer-ways—and if Shakespeare was possessed of the infinitely-divided star-dust that constituted this vast wealth, *how* did he get it, and *where*, and *when*? (14)

Walt Whitman astutely recognized that Shakespeare's knowledge of law was on a grander scale than that of a mere practicing lawyer:

> Did you ever notice—how much the law is involved with the plays? . . . I had myself been conscious of the phrases, any characteristic turns, the sure touch, the invisible potent hand, of the lawyer—of a lawyer, yes: not a mere attorney-at-law but a mind capable of taking the law in its largest scope, penetrating even its origins: not a pettifogger, perhaps even technically in its detail defective—but a big intellect of great grasp. . . . I go with you fellows when you say no to Shaksper . . . . (52)

Malone, Campbell, Penzance, Twain, and Whitman did not go unchallenged, however, in their admiration for Shakespeare's knowledge of law. Over the last two centuries an intermittent, but sometimes fierce debate has gone on among those who found Shakespeare's legal knowledge impressive and those who tried to show it was run-of-the-mill.[2] The authorship controversy appears to have been an unmentioned subtext of the argument. Both sides were well aware that establishing that Shakespeare had a professional's knowledge of law, or something close to it, would cast doubt on the traditional theory that the Stratford man was the real author.

The key tactic of the detractors of Shakespeare's legal knowledge has been to play a numbers game in which they tally the number of legal references and allusions in Shakespeare's plays, then add up the number of legal references in the works of other playwrights of that era. They then report that other playwrights used legal terms at least as often as Shakespeare and conclude that the Elizabethan Age was obsessed with law, meaning that most playwrights knew enough law to be able to weave it into their plays.

But a serious and thoughtful study of Shakespeare's knowledge of law should concentrate on the quality, depth, accuracy, and technical expertise of his legal references and on the facility with which he could infuse an entire plot with legal resonance. After all, a playwright with a smattering of legal knowledge may take a few commonly known legal terms and pepper his dialogue with them, but that says nothing of the depth of his legal knowledge or his ability to reason with the law.

This is why, when examining Shakespeare's knowledge of the law, the real question is whether the works of Shakespeare show that the author could *think like a lawyer*. Whoever wrote the works thought like a person with sophisticated legal training because his use of legal allusions is frequent, accurate, and often highly technical. Entire plays, especially the English history plays, are often shaped by a legal inquiry. Shakespeare seems to have been so well-versed in the law that legal metaphors popped into his mind even when he wasn't writing about legal subjects. His legal acumen, as evidenced in his plays and poems, far surpasses that of other playwrights of his time.

Thomas Regnier, J.D., LL.M.

Scope of Shakespeare's Legal Usages

Shakespeare's understanding of law is not only highly accurate, but it is also broad in scope. This suggests someone who was trained to "think like a lawyer," as law professors say—someone who, as Lord Penzance said, had "legal expressions . . . ever at the end of his pen," and who could shape plots around legal questions. Legal references manifest themselves in Shakespeare's works in many ways. For example:

(1) *Law or justice as an overarching theme. Measure for Measure*, Shakespeare's most overtly legalistic play, best exemplifies this aspect of Shakespeare's law. Shakespeare uses the plot to illustrate the legal concepts of "law" and "equity." In England, the law courts would enforce the strict letter of the law, but equity courts could soften the harshness of the law in situations where strict adherence might have worked an injustice.

In *Measure for Measure*, Angelo, a new judge, begins to enforce laws against fornication that have lain dormant for years. Claudio, a young man who has impregnated his fiancée, is sentenced to death under the newly revived law. Claudio's sister Isabella, a novice nun, rushes to Lord Angelo to beg for her brother's life. A debate follows on justice, or law, versus equity, or mercy. Isabella admits her brother's fault but asks Angelo to be merciful. Angelo argues, among other things, that he is being merciful to a criminal's future victims when he prevents the criminal from committing more crimes. The play touches on the four classic theories of punishment—deterrence, incapacitation, rehabilitation, and retribution.[3]

(2) *Depictions of trial scenes, pleas, and other legal proceedings.* References to trials appear in 25 Shakespeare plays (Sokol 1). The trial scene in *The Merchant of Venice*, with its "pound of flesh" (a concept derived from ancient Roman law) (Keeton 110–11), is the most famous, and *Measure for Measure* includes depictions of legal proceedings, including the entire last act, in which Angelo, and later the Duke of Vienna, dispense justice. *King Lear* contains a mock trial scene in which Lear puts his two wicked daughters on trial, with a joint stool sitting in for the elder of the two absent daughters. *Henry VIII* depicts the trial of Catherine of Aragon. In *Romeo and Juliet*, the Prince of Verona metes out punishments in the public square after brawls between the feuding Montagues and Capulets end in death.

(3) *Extended metaphors using explicit legal terms.* Sonnet 46, for example, sets up a metaphor of a civil trial in which the heart sues the eye, the defendant, over who has the greater claim to the object of their affections. A jury (an inquest of thoughts) is empanelled to 'cide [decide] the verdict. It finds for the eye in terms of the loved one's outward form and for the heart in terms of the loved one's inner love. As Lord Campbell, the English Chief Justice said, "Surely [this] Sonnet . . . smells as potently of the attorney's office as any of the stanzas penned by Lord Kenyon while an attorney's clerk in Wales" (126–27). Examples of other sonnets steeped in legal metaphor include 87, 133, and 134.

(4) *Metaphors using implied legal concepts.* In *Merry Wives of Windsor*, Falstaff asks, "Of what quality was your love then?" Ford replies: "Like a fair house built on another man's ground, so that I have lost my edifice by mistaking the place where I erected it" (II.ii.214–17).[4] This is an illustration of the common law principle that *quicquid plantatur solo, solo cedit* (whatever is affixed to the soil belongs to the soil). The average person might think that if one inadvertently builds a house on another's land, mistakenly thinking the land is his own, he would be entitled to recover his building materials once he discovers the mistake. But, as Shakespeare apparently understood, once the building is attached to the soil, it becomes part of the land and belongs to whoever owns that land (Rushton 23–25).

This differs from an extended metaphor using *explicit* legal terms, as in the civil trial in Sonnet 46, in that no specifically legal terms or maxims are used in these lines. Nevertheless, the whole metaphor depends for its existence upon the understanding of a particular legal principle. As Mark Alexander says, "Shakespeare must have this kind of knowledge imprinted at the cellular level to access it so seemingly effortlessly in such a context. And how does one acquire such imprinting? Through training, through associations, through years of study" (105).

(5) *Gratuitous use of quasi-legal terms.* Often Shakespeare uses a term that has both a legal connotation and a non-legal meaning ("quasi-legal" terms), when he could have used a strictly non-legal term. For example, in Sonnet 30, he says, "When to the *sessions* of sweet silent thought/ I *summon* up remembrance of things past . . . ." The words "sessions" and "summon" do not necessarily strike one at first for their legal meanings, as they are often used in ordinary speech to refer to non-legal matters. Other quasi-legal terms in Sonnet 30 include waste, cancelled, expense, grievances, account, pay/paid. Indeed, the sonnet abounds with the language of accounting: "time's waste," "cancell'd woe," "th' expense of many a vanish'd sight," "sad account," "Which I new pay as if not paid before," "All losses are restored."

Additional examples of quasi-legal terms include "And summer's *lease* hath all too short a *date*," (Sonnet 18), "Her *pleading* hath deserved a greater *fee*," (*Venus and Adonis*), and "Hath served a dumb *arrest* upon his tongue" (*Rape of Lucrece*).

As Lord Penzance wrote of Shakespeare:

> At every turn and point at which the author required a metaphor, simile, or illustration, his mind ever turned to the law. He seems almost to have thought in legal phrases—the commonest of legal expressions were ever at the end of his pen in description or illustration. That he should have descanted in lawyer language when he had a forensic subject in hand, such as Shylock's bond, was to be expected. But the knowledge of law in "Shakespeare" was exhibited in a far different manner: it protruded itself on all occasions, appropriate or inappropriate, and mingled itself with strains of thought widely divergent from forensic subjects. (85–86)

(6) *Paraphrases of Latin legal maxims.* Anglo-American common law has a long tradition of legal maxims in Latin. In 1907, William Rushton, a lawyer, published a collection called *Shakespeare's Legal Maxims*. Rushton noted that while other Elizabethan writers quoted legal maxims *in Latin* in their plays, "Shakespeare never quotes legal maxims in Latin . . . he gives correct translations of them which are so embodied in his verse and prose that they have not the appearance of quotations" (9). For example:

"To offend and judge are distinct offices,/ And of opposed natures," in *Merchant of Venice* (II.ix.61–62) is based on the Latin maxim, "*Nemo debet esse judex in suâ propriâ causâ*" ("No one ought to be a judge in his own cause.") (Rushton 13–14).

"The law hath not been dead, though it hath slept," in *Measure for Measure* (II.ii.90) is based on the maxim, "*Dormiunt aliquando leges, moriuntur nunquam.*" ("The laws sometimes sleep, they never die.") (Rushton 25).

In 1929, Sir Dunbar Plunket Barton expressed a preference for the legal skill of those Elizabethan writers who actually quoted legal maxims in Latin, or at least in verbatim English translation. But why? Any layman could pull out a law book and copy from it, even in Latin. Lawyers must be able to summarize a case concisely *in their own words*. To do this, they must understand the case. And if they are arguing the law in front of a judge, the judge will not want to hear long quotations from a case, he will want to be able to discuss the case intelligently with the lawyer. Shakespeare's more subtle use of the principles enshrined in Latin legal maxims is an indication of a deeper understanding of law than is shown by playwrights who merely quoted from books.

In fact, Barton undercut his own argument when he said that Shakespeare's "legalisms were not more numerous and were less technical than those of the other poets and dramatists. Where he surpassed the others was in his *superior grace and ease in handling legal phrases*, which . . . flowed from his pen as part of his vocabulary, and as parcel of his thoughts" (141–42, emphasis added). When Barton spoke about the superior grace and ease with which Shakespeare handled legal phrases, he was speaking of exactly the kind of facility with legal terms that we expect of an experienced practitioner, not of an amateur. This ease and grace shows that Shakespeare had internalized the legal concepts, not just memorized the words.

(7) *Legal issues as a pervasive subtext.* A prime example of this is *Hamlet.* The play contains a subtle subplot concerning a struggle between Claudius and Hamlet over lands that Hamlet should have inherited from his father, as revealed in J. Anthony Burton's article on the subject, discussed later in this chapter. Additionally, R.S. Guernsey has analyzed how ecclesiastical law regarding suicide informs the writing of Ophelia's funeral. Thomas Glyn Watkin has demonstrated that the author of *Hamlet* must have been well aware of ongoing changes in the law of homicide that were occurring during the Elizabethan era. Law professor Carla Spivack has recently written on the relationship of the case of *Hales v. Petit* to Ophelia's death, in an article in the *Yale Journal of Law and the Humanities.*[5]

R.S. White, a professor of English and Cultural Studies, has shown that an understanding of the concept of natural law infuses such plays as *King Lear* and *Love's Labours Lost.*

Edna Zwick Boris, a professor of English, has argued that the English constitution, especially as articulated by Sir Thomas Smith, an outstanding Elizabethan legal scholar, is part of the subtext of Shakespeare's English history plays. Only those kings who guard their subjects' well-being and who respect important provisions established by legal tradition reign well in the plays. Kings who disregard these values soon face rebellion.

Jack Benoit Gohn, an attorney, wrote a 1982 article for *The Georgetown Law Journal* on *Richard II*, in which he compared the play to a legal brief. Gohn suggests that Shakespeare used the play as an example of how to resolve the problem of Queen Elizabeth's succession, by showing a nation in the midst of a constitutional crisis and the consequent breakdown of the legal order. Gohn concludes that "Shakespeare had both the legal and the historical sophistication to grapple with these problems" (955).

New York University law professor Theodor Meron uses medieval ordinances and Renaissance historical and legal sources to elucidate the historical context of *Henry V.* He shows that the play deals with war themes covered by such scholars of international law as Pisan and Gentili, who lived before or during Shakespeare's time.

Thus, Shakespeare's legal knowledge manifests itself in large ways and small, in both the grand theme and the tiny detail.

The Debate Over Shakespeare's Legal Knowledge

While a complete history of the debate on Shakespeare's legal knowledge is beyond the scope of this chapter, a brief summary will demonstrate the vacuity of the arguments proposed by detractors of Shakespeare's legal understanding. In 1899, for example, William Devecmon, a lawyer, wrote a slim volume called *In Re Shakespeare's "Legal Acquirements": Notes by an*

Unbeliever Therein, in which he criticized Lord Campbell, the Chief Justice, for his praise of Shakespeare's legal knowledge in *Shakespeare's Legal Acquirements Considered*.[6] Devecmon listed fourteen examples of what he considered "gross errors" in Shakespeare's use of the law. Devecmon, however, had no sense of metaphor or dramatic situation and often criticized legal usage in Shakespeare as if he were reading a legal memorandum, not a play. He did not understand that a dramatist would not want to have a character speaking with lawyerly precision when that character would not have been trained in the law.

For example, Devecmon criticized Shakespeare for having Dromio of Syracuse in *The Comedy of Errors* report that his master was arrested "on the case" (IV.ii.42), that is, for a "trespass on the case"—analogous to a charge of negligence in modern terms—when in fact he was arrested for a breach of contract for failing to pay money supposedly owed to a goldsmith (40). The literal-minded Devecmon didn't notice that Shakespeare's lower class characters, such as Dromio, often misstate the law. In fact, they usually get it exactly backwards, as Dromio does.

Likewise, Devecmon found fault with Shakespeare for having the Archbishop of Canterbury in *Henry V* say, "For all the temporal lands, which men devout/ By testament have given to the Church,/ Would they strip from us" (I.i.9–11). Devecmon complained that "testament" was used incorrectly since it refers to bequeathing personal property, whereas a "will" is used for devising real estate (41). First of all, Devecmon erred in expecting the Archbishop to speak like a lawyer instead of a religious man. "Testament," a word having stronger religious connotations than "will," may have come more readily to the Archbishop's lips. Secondly, while a myth persisted for some time in legal education that "testament" referred exclusively to personal property and "will" to real estate, modern scholars have dispelled that idea by showing that the terms were used interchangeably as far back as the records go (Dukeminier 37).

All of Devecmon's other examples of Shakespeare's "gross errors" have been fully addressed by such critics as Sir George Greenwood and Mark Alexander and thoroughly discredited (Alexander 69–76). In the early 20th century, Greenwood, a lawyer and a Member of Parliament, carried on a debate with J.M. Robertson, another M.P., about the quality of Shakespeare's legal knowledge. Greenwood found Shakespeare's legal knowledge profound and accurate, while Robertson disparaged it. Robertson, not being trained in law, was distinctly disadvantaged and often tripped himself up without realizing it (Alexander 82–92). For example, references to the legal concepts "fine" and "recovery" appear several times in Shakespeare's plays. The terms refer to special types of collusive lawsuits that underhandedly changed an *entailed* estate (one that was required to remain in the family bloodline) into a *fee simple* (an estate that could be freely sold by its owner). The word "fine" refers to the "final concord" in which the lawsuit results, a judgment that is binding even on third parties. A "recovery" is an even more complex type of collusive lawsuit, using legal tricks known as vouchers and double vouchers (Burton 104, Sokol 125–28, Bergin 31–32).

The allusions to "fine" and "recovery" in Shakespeare show that he understood this technical term. For example, in *The Merry Wives of Windsor*, Mistress Page speaks about the devil having Falstaff "in fee-simple, with fine and recovery" (IV.ii.209–12), as if to say that the devil will have outright ownership of Falstaff with all the legal tricks necessary to ensure a binding final judgment.[7]

Robertson set out to show that playwrights other than Shakespeare used "fine" and "recovery" and eagerly cited uses of those terms by other writers, but, alas, they were examples of "fine" used in the ordinary sense of money paid, or "recovery" referring to recovery of a debt (41, 46)—meanings that everyone understands regardless of legal training. Robertson's list thus gave no indication that the playwrights understood the technical meanings any more than Robertson apparently did. Greenwood had no trouble in demolishing Robertson's evidence (1916, 58–64). Yet, incredibly, some later commentators contended that Robertson won the debate![8]

In recent years, the book most often cited as authority for disparaging Shakespeare's legal knowledge[9] is Clarkson and Warren's *The Law of Property in Shakespeare and the Elizabethan Drama*, published in 1942. Clarkson and Warren set out to do a comprehensive study of references to the law of property, not only in Shakespeare's works, but also in the works of 17 other Elizabethan playwrights. Over an 11-year period, they studied all the known plays of the selected authors and catalogued every reference to property law on over 8,000 index cards (xxiii). In their 300-page book summarizing their study, the authors concluded that

> about half of Shakespeare's fellows employed on the average more legalisms than he did—some of them a great many more. For example, the sixteen plays of Ben Jonson (whose apprentice years were spent in laying bricks, and certainly not in copying deeds and drafting pleadings) have a total of over five hundred references from all fields of the law. This surpasses Shakespeare's total from more than twice as many plays. Not only do half of the playwrights employ legalisms more freely than Shakespeare, but most of them also exceed him in the detail and complexity of their legal problems and allusions, and with few exceptions display a degree of accuracy at least no lower than his. (285)

The difficulty with Clarkson and Warren's analysis, however, is that while it pretended to be as much about quality as quantity, it was really more about quantity. The flaws in their analysis of Ben Jonson's supposedly greater facility with the law can be seen in the way they assess the "skull of a lawyer" speech in *Hamlet* compared to Picklock's speech in Jonson's *Staple of News*. Picklock brags that he can "cant" in all the languages of the law courts and then reels off a string of legal terms:

> Fee-farm, fee-tail,
> Tenant in dower, at will, for term of life,
> By copy of court-roll, knights' service, homage,
> Fealty, escuage, soccage, or frank almoigne,
> Grand serjeantry, or burgage. (IV.iv)

Clarkson and Warren described Picklock's speech as a "*tour de force*" (174), but what does the speech really tell us about Ben Jonson's knowledge of the law? It tells us that Jonson was capable of compiling a list of legal terms, nothing more. It does not tell us that Jonson understood the terms, and even if he did, it doesn't tell us that he could relate one to another, or that he could intelligently use them in a legal argument. Much less does it tell us whether Jonson could critique the law or philosophize on its origins and goals. Anyone could easily make such a list by thumbing through a law book or jotting down random legal words one overhears in a discussion between lawyers.[10] Indeed, Jonson portrays Picklock as a show-off who merely spouts a torrent of legal terms to impress people.

Clarkson and Warren were much less impressed by Hamlet's use of legal terms in the "skull of a lawyer" speech. They believed that the legalisms in the speech, while no longer in common usage, were probably well known in Shakespeare's day (173–74). Another commentator, Arthur Underhill, thought some of the legal terms in the speech irrelevant to property law (I.406). What those critics missed is a subplot in *Hamlet* concerning property law that runs through the play and to which the "skull of a lawyer" speech is intimately connected. This subplot is revealed in J. Anthony Burton's "An Unrecognized Theme in *Hamlet*: Lost Inheritance and Claudius's Marriage to Gertrude," published in the *Shakespeare Newsletter* in 2000 and 2001. Burton discusses how, under the law, Hamlet would have expected to inherit some of his father's lands when his father died, even though Hamlet didn't get the kingship. But through some legal chicanery very similar to the "fine and recovery" that was used to cheat heirs of their estates, Claudius may have managed to stake a competing claim to Hamlet's lands through Claudius's marriage to Gertrude. After all, man and wife were, legally, one flesh.

Since Claudius happened to be king, his claim was superior to Hamlet's, as held in the 1562 case of *Hales v. Pettit*, which said that where a citizen and the monarch had competing claims on a piece of property, the crown's claim prevailed. A summary of *Hales v. Pettit* was available in Plowden's law reports, and there was also a manuscript report by Sir James Dyer. But neither was likely to be available to laymen, and both were written in Law French, the ancient language of the courts, a language not known to have been taught in the Stratford grammar school. The Gravedigger scene in *Hamlet* even parodies *Hales v. Pettit*. When one Gravedigger says that an act "hath three branches—it is to act, to do, to perform" (V.i.11–12), Shakespeare is spoofing the defense argument in *Hales v. Pettit* that an act has three parts— the imagination, the resolution, and the perfection, or execution. The relationship between the Gravedigger scene and *Hales v. Pettit* was first noticed in 1773 by Sir John Hawkins (Burton 71) and later noted by Lord Campbell (84–89). But Clarkson and Warren—inexplicably—did not cite the *Hales* case in their book (299), although their ostensible purpose in writing it was to analyze objectively the comparative mastery of the law among Elizabethan playwrights.

Burton argues that property is a constant theme of *Hamlet*, starting with the back story of Hamlet's father fighting and killing the King of Norway as part of a wager over land, to young Fortinbras's army's passage through Denmark to fight for a worthless piece of land in Poland. Claudius's legal maneuvers to usurp Hamlet's inheritance would leave Hamlet with very little income. This explains why Hamlet says, "Beggar that I am, I am even poor in thanks" (II.ii.272) and "I am most dreadfully attended" (i.e., he can't even get good servants) (II.ii.269). While looking at a skull in the graveyard, Hamlet speaks in the legal language of Elizabethan property law (legal terms italicized):

> Why may not that be the skull of a lawyer? Where be his *quiddities* now, his *quillities*, his cases, his *tenures*, and his tricks? . . . Hum! This fellow might be in 's time a great buyer of land, with his *statutes*, his *recognizances*, his *fines*, his *double vouchers*, his *recoveries*. Is this the *fine* of his *fines* and the *recovery* of his *recoveries*, to have his fine pate full of fine dirt? Will his *vouchers* vouch him no more of his *purchases*, and double ones too, than the length and breadth of a pair of *indentures*? The very *conveyances* of his lands will hardly lie in this box; and must th' inheritor himself have no more, ha? (V.i.98–112)

Burton's analysis gives thematic significance to the terms. Hamlet, who has been cheated out of his inheritance through Claudius's use of legal technicalities, is railing against such legal chicanery as the "fine" and "recovery" and the whole arsenal of lawyers' tricks—including vouchers and double vouchers, which were elements of "fine and recovery" cases—that could be used to deprive an heir of his inheritance (104).[11] Burton comments that the legal themes in *Hamlet* "run the gamut from points of common knowledge by landowners or litigants, to subtleties only lawyers would appreciate . . . . [T]he many legal allusions in the play suggest it was written with a legally sophisticated audience in mind. Who else, after all, but lawyers and law students would appreciate the Gravedigger's parody of legal reasoning in a forty-year old decision written in the corrupted version of Norman-English known as Law French?" (71)

Thus, the legal sophistication informing the "skull of a lawyer" far outweighs that of Picklock's speech in Ben Jonson's play. Clarkson and Warren, with their 8,000 index cards, entirely missed the boat in breathlessly favoring Picklock over "skull of a lawyer." Such a blunder casts withering doubt on their ultimate conclusion that Shakespeare was no more adept at the law than his fellow playwrights.

Not only did Clarkson and Warren fail to demonstrate greater mastery of the law by other playwrights, but in their entire 300-page book they listed only a tiny handful of alleged "errors" on Shakespeare's part, none of which survives scrutiny:

(1) The Host in *The Merry Wives of Windsor* (II.i.217–18) says *regress* where Clarkson and Warren thought *ingress* would be more appropriate (70). Here, they made the same mistake that Devecmon made with Dromio in *Comedy of Errors*: they expected a lower class, uneducated person to use legal terms precisely. This seldom happens in Shakespeare, as demonstrated by Dromio, Dogberry in *Much Ado About Nothing*, and the Gravediggers in *Hamlet*, who muddle their summary of the *Hales v. Pettit* case.

(2) In *Henry VI, Part 3*, King Henry says to York: "I here entail/ The crown to thee *and to thine heirs for ever,/* Conditionally that here thou take an oath/ To cease this civil war" (I.i.194–97). In response, Clarkson and Warren propounded an excruciatingly technical argument (58–60) based on the perceived error of King Henry's failing to use the magic words "and to the heirs *of thy body,*" which would have been necessary to create an entailed estate. The authors warned, "It must be borne in mind that the play purports to set out the actual conveyance, not an agreement to make a conveyance in which strict technical language would be unnecessary so long as the meaning of the parties was clear" (59). But Shakespeare was a dramatist first and a lawyer afterwards. Having Henry say that he entailed the crown to York, "and to thine heirs for ever," would certainly get the point across to his audience that Richard's bloodline would take over the crown after Henry's death, even if that precise language would not have stood up in a legal document. Here, Clarkson and Warren achieve a pedantry that rivals Devecmon's.

(3) Finally, Clarkson and Warren argued that in *Henry VI, Part 2*, Shakespeare erred by referring to Humphrey, Duke of Gloucester, as "heir-apparent" (I.i.147–52) to the English crown, when the correct term for Humphrey's status was "heir presumptive" (197–99). Clarkson and Warren were correct about the terminology, but again they made a foolish blunder in not looking up "heir presumptive" in the *Oxford English Dictionary*, as Alexander later pointed out (80–81). Had they consulted the *OED*, they would have learned that the term "heir presumptive" did not enter the language until decades after *Henry VI* was written. Shakespeare, brilliant as he was, cannot be faulted for failing to use a legal term that hadn't been invented yet.

Clarkson and Warren theorized that the reason that so many legal writers perceived Shakespeare as having been legally trained was that those writers wanted to see him as being one of their own. Samuel Schoenbaum, a Stratfordian scholar, would later quip about one of Sir George Greenwood's books that in it, "the talented attorney showed the plays to be the work of a talented attorney" (410). Clarkson and Warren suggested that this bias was not confined to lawyers and that a great many experts in other fields had looked into Shakespeare's works and seen themselves:

> Books by the score have been written to demonstrate the great poet's intimate and all pervading-knowledge of such diverse subjects as angling, hunting, falconry, and horsemanship; military life, tactics, and equipment; navigation, both of peace and of war; medicine and pharmacy; an almost philological erudition in classical mythology; folklore, and biblical lore; and a sweeping knowledge of natural history, flora as well as fauna . . . agriculture and gardening; music, heraldry, precious stones, and even typography. . . . jurisprudence—civil, ecclesiastical, common law, and equity. (xvi)

Clarkson and Warren cited at least one book, sometimes several, elucidating Shakespeare's knowledge of each of the subjects in their list, and they mentioned that they could have cited "numerous" books and articles for almost every subject (xvi–xvii, nn. 3–20).

Clarkson and Warren argued that the authors of these books and articles simply wanted so much to claim Shakespeare as their peer that they read into his works a knowledge and an expertise that the text didn't support. But did Clarkson and Warren draw the correct moral from their analysis? When a person becomes knowledgeable in a given field, isn't he more likely to notice other people's *mistakes* in that area? When people are trained in the law, they are much more likely to notice legal errors in novels, plays, films, and television shows.

As Mark Twain put it, in the context of Shakespeare's legal knowledge, "a man can't handle glibly and easily and comfortably and successfully the *argot* [jargon] of a trade at which he has not personally served. He will make mistakes; he will not, and cannot, get the trade-phrasings precisely and exactly right; and the moment he departs, by even a shade, from a common trade-form, the reader who has served that trade will know the writer *hasn't*" (15–16). The real lesson to be learned from all these books about Shakespeare's knowledge in a vast array of subjects is that the author had a thorough and broad-ranging education and experience, which he often called upon to advance his dramatic purposes.

Thus, Clarkson and Warren completely subvert their own argument in their attempt to establish that the plays could have been written by a person with minimal education. Professionals in law, medicine, mythology, or music will immediately spot small errors that give the writer away as an amateur. Yet no one has convincingly exposed a *bona fide* legal error in Shakespeare's works.

Far more thorough and persuasive than Clarkson and Warren's treatise is *Shakespeare's Legal Language: A Dictionary*, published in 2000 by B.J. Sokol, an Emeritus Professor of English at the University of London, and Mary Sokol, a lawyer. Sokol and Sokol, whose book is silent on the authorship question, show a far deeper appreciation than Clarkson and Warren for the way in which Shakespeare's legal knowledge could inform a complex metaphor, such as this passage from *The Rape of Lucrece*:

> My bloody judge forbade my tongue to speak,
> No rightful plea might plead for justice there.
> His scarlet lust came evidence to swear
> That my poor beauty had purloin'd his eyes,
> And when the judge is robb'd, the prisoner dies. (1648–52)

In elucidating this passage, Sokol and Sokol note that Lucrece herself was blamed for inspiring the lust of her rapist. They observe that judges, who wore scarlet, had summary jurisdiction over offenses committed in court; that robbery was a capital felony; and that defendants couldn't offer evidence, although the prosecutor could (2–3). Thus, Lucrece, whose beauty purloined (stole) the judge's eyes, must be sentenced to death by the judge, without a jury, and has no right to speak in her own defense. This passage can only have been written by someone whose legal knowledge was so thoroughly ingrained that it sprang to mind naturally in the service of his narrative. This is in sharp contrast to the shallowness of the legal knowledge informing Ben Jonson's Picklock speech.

Sokol and Sokol warn that because of the complexity of Shakespeare's legal usages, "sheer legal word-spotting" (Clarkson and Warren, take heed!) "is not a wholly reliable indication that Shakespeare took a precise or detailed account of substantive English law" (3). Sokol and Sokol conclude that Shakespeare's interest in law was both precise and serious:

> Yet, the overall impression given by this Dictionary may well contradict frequently reiterated claims that Shakespeare's interest in law was at best superficial, and that Shakespeare exploited legal ideas, circumstances, and language with no regard for any factor aside from 'poetic' effect. It is our view, derived from cumulative evidence, that on the contrary Shakespeare shows a quite precise and mainly serious interest in the capacity of legal language to convey matters of social, moral, and intellectual substance. (3)

Sokol and Sokol's book is an encyclopedic summary of legal concepts found in Shakespeare's works, with detailed explanations of how the concepts are used in the various plays and extensive references to legal sources. Compared to the Sokols, Clarkson and Warren barely scratched the surface of Shakespeare's legal expertise.

Conclusion

Dozens of books and many more articles have been written analyzing Shakespeare's use of legal terms, allusions, and themes—far more than have been written analyzing the legal expertise of Jonson, Marlowe, Webster, or any other Elizabethan playwright. This is because other writers have left us little to analyze in the way of legal understanding that compares with Shakespeare's all-encompassing view of the subject of law, from its mightiest themes, such as justice and mercy, to its most technical details, such as "fine" and "recovery."

Lord Campbell got it exactly right when he said, "to Shakespeare's law, lavishly as he propounds it, there can neither be [objection], nor bill of exceptions, nor writ of error."

Endnotes

[1] Campbell actually used the nearly archaic word "demurrer," which refers to an objection to the legal sufficiency of a pleading.

[2] For the best and most thorough analysis of the debate, see Mark Andre Alexander, "Shakespeare's Knowledge of Law: A Journey through the History of the Argument," *The Oxfordian*, 4 (2001): 51–119, *available at* http://www.shakespeare-oxford.com/?p=720.

[3] Deterrence: "Those many had not dar'd to do that evil/ If the first that did th' edict infringe/ Had answer'd for his deed" (II.ii.91–93). Incapacitation: "I show [pity] most of all when I show justice;/ For then I pity those I do not know,/ Which a dismissed offense would after gall" (II.ii.100–02). Rehabilitation: "Take him to prison, officer./ Correction and instruction must both work/ Ere this rude beast will profit" (III.ii.31–33). Retribution: "Like doth quit like, and *Measure* still *for Measure*" (V.i.411).

[4] References to Shakespeare's works are to the *Riverside Shakespeare*, 1974 edition.

[5] See also Regnier, 2003, 2011, for more on the law in *Hamlet*.

[6] To be sure, Lord Campbell's book had its flaws, as many critics have shown. But it was not intended to be a systematic analysis of Shakespeare's use of legal terms. The book was really a long letter in response to an inquiry about whether the knowledge of law in the plays indicated that Shakespeare might have been a law clerk. Lord Campbell's response amounted to a definite "maybe."

[7] The use of "fine" and "recovery" in *Hamlet* is discussed later in this chapter. See also the use of the terms in *The Comedy of Errors*, II.ii.72–76.

[8] D. Barton 10, Gibson 11–12, Keeton 20.

[9] Keeton 19–20, Phillips 191, Kornstein 237–38, Matus 272, Kathman 22.

[10] Shakespeare scholar Anne Barton notes that Jonson was a compulsive list-maker, but that his lists were "stifling and corrupt" compared to lists in Shakespeare, which evoke a world that is "fresh, creative, and young" (218–19).

[11] Other than Shakespeare, Clarkson and Warren cite only Thomas Middleton as having used "fine and recovery" in his plays (132–33), but Middleton studied law at Gray's Inn (Alexander 97).

WORKS CITED

Alexander, Mark Andre. "Shakespeare's Knowledge of Law: A Journey through the History of the Argument," *The Oxfordian*, 4 (2001): 51–119.

Barton, Anne. "A Midsummer Night's Dream," in *Riverside Shakespeare*, ed. G. Blakemore Evans (Boston: Houghton Mifflin Co., 1974) 217–21.

Barton, Dunbar Plunket. *Links Between the Law and Shakespeare*. Boston: Houghton Mifflin, 1929.

Bergin, Thomas F. & Paul G. Haskell, *Preface to Estates in Land and Future Interests,* 2nd ed. (Brooklyn: Foundation Press, 1984).

Boris, Edna Zwick. *Shakespeare's English Kings, the People and the Law: A Study in the Relationship Between the Tudor Constitution and the English History Plays*. Rutherford, NJ: Fairleigh Dickinson University Press, 1978.

Bravin, Jess. "Justice Stevens Renders an Opinion on Who Wrote Shakespeare's Plays," *Wall Street Journal*, Apr. 18, 2009.

Burton, J. Anthony. "An Unrecognized Theme in *Hamlet*: Lost Inheritance and Claudius' Marriage to Gertrude," *The Shakespeare Newsletter*, 50 (2000–2001): 71–106.

Campbell, Lord John. *Shakespeare's Legal Acquirements*. London: John Murray, 1859.

Clarkson, Paul S. & Clyde T. Warren. *The Law of Property in Shakespeare and the Elizabethan Drama*. Baltimore: Johns Hopkins, 1942.

Devecmon, William C. *IN RE Shakespeare's "Legal Acquirements": Notes by an Unbeliever Therein*. New York: Shakespeare Press, 1899.

Dukeminier, Jesse & Stanley M. Johanson. *Wills, Trusts, and Estates* (6th ed. Aspen 2000).

Gibson, H.N. *The Shakespeare Claimants*. New York: Barnes & Noble, 1962.

Gohn, Jack Benoit. "*Richard II*: Shakespeare's Legal Brief on the Royal Prerogative and the Succession to the Throne." *The Georgetown Law Journal* 70.3 (1982): 943–973.

Greenwood, George. *The Shakespeare Problem Restated*. London: John Lane, 1908.

_____. *Is There a Shakespeare Problem?* London: John Lane, 1916.

Guernsey, R.S. *Ecclesiastical Law in* Hamlet*: The Burial of Ophelia*. New York: Brentano Bros., 1885.

Hales v. Petit, 1 *Plowden* 253, 75 Eng. Rep. 387 (C.B. 1562).

Hales v. Petyt (1562), 1 *Reports from the Lost Notebooks of Sir James Dyer* 72, ed. J.H. Baker (London:

Selden Society, 1994).

Kathman, David. Letter, *The Elizabethan Review* 5.2 (1997): 21–23.

Keeton, George W. *Shakespeare's Legal and Political Background.* London: Pitman, 1967.

Kornstein, Daniel J. *Kill All the Lawyers? Shakespeare's Legal Appeal.* Princeton: PUP, 1994.

Matus, Irvin Leigh. *Shakespeare, IN FACT.* New York: Continuum, 1994.

Meron, Theodor. *Bloody Constraint: War and Chivalry in Shakespeare,* Oxford: OUP, 1998.

_____. *Henry's Wars and Shakespeare's Laws: Perspectives in the Law of War in the Later Middle Ages,* Oxford: Clarendon Press, 1993.

Oxford English Dictionary. CD-ROM. 2nd ed. 1995.

Penzance, Lord (Sir James Plaisted Wilde). *The Bacon-Shakespeare Controversy: A Judicial Summing Up.* London: Sampson Low, 1902.

Phillips, O. Hood. *Shakespeare and the Lawyers.* London: Methuen, 1972.

Regnier, Thomas. "Could Shakespeare Think Like a Lawyer? How Inheritance Law Issues in *Hamlet* May Shed Light on the Authorship Question," *University of Miami Law Review,* 57 (2003): 377–428.

_____. "The Law in *Hamlet*: Death, Property, and the Pursuit of Justice," *Brief Chronicles,* 3 (2011): 109–34.

Riverside Shakespeare, ed. G. Blakemore Evans (Boston: Houghton Mifflin Co., 1974).

Robertson, J.M. *The Baconian Heresy, a Confutation.* London: Herbert Jenkins Ltd., 1913.

Rushton, William Lowes: *Shakespeare's Legal Maxims* (Henry Young & Sons, 1907).

Schoenbaum, Samuel. *Shakespeare's Lives.* New edition. Oxford: Clarendon, 1991.

Sokol, B.J. & Mary Sokol, *Shakespeare's Legal Language: A Dictionary* (London: Athlone Press, 2000).

Spivack, Carla. "The Woman Will Be Out: A New Look at the Law In *Hamlet*," *Yale Journal of Law and the Humanities,* 20 (2008): 31–60.

Twain, Mark. *Is Shakespeare Dead?* New York: Harper & Brothers, 1909.

Underhill, Arthur. "Law," in *Shakespeare's England: An account of the Life & Manners of his Age.* Oxford: Clarendon, 1916.

Watkin, Thomas Glyn. "*Hamlet* and the Law of Homicide," *Law Quarterly Review,* 100 (1984): 282–310.

White, R.S. *Natural Law in English Renaissance Literature,* Cambridge: Cambridge University Press, 1996.

Whitman, Walt. *November Boughs,* London: Alexander Gardner, 1889.

Chapter 9:
How did Shakespeare Learn the Art of Medicine?

By Earl Showerman, M.D.

For 150 years physicians and Shakespeare scholars have written commendably about the comprehensive medical knowledge reflected in the Shakespeare canon. During this time, a remarkable number of rare medical texts have been identified as Shakespeare sources, including works on Hippocrates, anatomy, surgery, alchemy, infectious disease, and psychology. Further, the universal high regard for the playwright's medical acumen is mirrored in Shakespeare's high opinion of physicians, as reflected in a 1905 commentary in the *British Medical Journal*: "It is a curious fact that great writers, speaking generally, have been no lovers of the medical profession. Shakespeare, indeed, used them gently, as though he loved them … his large mind saw the nobility of (medicine's) aim."[1] Where did Shakespeare get his medical knowledge and empathy for physicians, and how did he access the rare medical literature confirmed by scholars as his likely sources? To date, no satisfactory answer has been provided. Traditional explanations strain credulity; nothing that is known about the Stratford man accounts for the author's vast medical knowledge.

New scholarship on Shakespeare's medical knowledge is still being reported, most recently in a 2011 BBC story headlined "Shakespeare could help doctors become better."[2] The article reported on Dr. Kenneth Heaton's research which demonstrated Shakespeare's unique and masterful representation of psycho-physiological phenomena such as fainting, vertigo, and hyperventilation. There is, in fact, a growing fascination with Shakespeare's clinical knowledge which has resulted in numerous publications over the past quarter century, and widely divergent theories put forward to explain Shakespeare's medical acumen.[3] Dr. John Brine's imaginative book-length homage, *His Medical Footprints* (2008) posits that medicine was not only integral to the playwright's way of thinking, but that he was himself a well-trained medical practitioner, while Dr. John Ross, in *Shakespeare's Tremor and Orwell's Cough* (2012), argues that the author's numerous allusions to sexual disease may be a key to explaining the scrawled penmanship of Shakspere's known signatures.

In "Shakespeare's Medical Knowledge: How Did He Acquire It?" Dr. Frank Davis summarizes how the author's impressive medical knowledge challenges the assumptions of the traditional attribution. Davis reviews three books by physicians who examined Shakespeare's medicine: J.C. Bucknill (1860), R.R. Simpson (1959), and Aubrey Kail (1986). Davis takes particular note of the fact that in the 16th century the "vast majority of medical works were published in Latin or Greek" (Davis 45), and he describes the primacy given to Galen's methods among English physicians, who generally lagged far behind the revolutionary medical discoveries being made in Italy, especially by the medical faculty at the University of Padua, whose famous English graduate, William Harvey, was the first to describe the circulation of blood.

In *Shakespeare and Medicine*, Dr. R.R. Simpson identified and dated 712 medical references in the plays. Davis cites Dr. Frank Miller's claim to have identified nearly twice that number. Shakespeare frequently refers to Galen's doctrine of the humors, but what is remarkable is the number of allusions to a wide array of clinical topics: anatomy, infectious disease, neurology, gerontology, psychology, toxicology, Paracelsian alchemy, and Hippocratic principles. In

Earl Showerman, M.D.

summarizing his own comparative survey of the canon, Davis agrees with Bucknill, Simpson and Kail that "medical imagery was an important component of the writing style of Shakespeare, and he used it more often than his contemporaries" (47).

The first scholar to examine this question systematically was Dr. John Charles Bucknill. In *Medical Knowledge of Shakespeare* (1860), Bucknill wrote "it would be difficult to point to any great author, not himself a physician, in whose works the healing art is referred to more frequently and more respectfully than in those of Shakespeare" (Bucknill 2). Dr. Bucknill was superintendent of a 600-bed psychiatric hospital in Devon, an outspoken advocate for the humane treatment of the insane, and a founding editor of the journal *Brain*. He dedicated his 300-page study on Shakespeare's medicine to Lord Campbell, the Lord Chancellor, who just a year earlier had written *Shakespeare's Legal Acquirements Considered*. Bucknill's volume includes detailed commentaries on the medical allusions in all the plays and poems, and represents the first attempt to identify the possible sources of Shakespeare's physic. Bucknill concludes that the poet-playwright must have been "a keen observer of men and an insatiable devourer of books" (8), and that he was clearly "influenced by medical trains of thought" (289). In the conclusion of his volume, Bucknill asserts:

> After a perusal of all the medical works of the period on which I have been able to lay hands, and the institution of a close comparison between them and the works of Shakespeare, I have arrived at the fullest conviction that the great dramatist had, at least, been a diligent student of all medical knowledge existing in his time. (290)

Almost exactly a century after Bucknill published his laudatory study, the Scottish physician R.R. Simpson published *Shakespeare and Medicine,* in which he also claims Shakespeare not only had "an astute knowledge of medical affairs but also a keen sense of the correct use of that knowledge" (Simpson 113). Like Bucknill, Simpson argued that the playwright was "not only well-acquainted with the medical knowledge of his day, but also with the literature" (113). With transparent admiration, Simpson concludes:

> No aspect of the study of Shakespeare shows more clearly his inspired poetic eye and mind . . . than the clinical descriptions to be found in his writings. The accuracy of his observation, his apt use of words, and the clinical picture he leaves in the mind of his audience, or his reader, are not only unsurpassed, they are not even approached in clinical value in any medical writings, however erudite. Here, indeed, is a large part of the Art of Medicine, written for us by a layman. (154)

Dr. Simpson asked the obvious question first raised by Bucknill: "Where did Shakespeare obtain all this medical knowledge?" By meticulously charting specific medical allusions in the plays against traditional dating, Simpson determined that at least two-thirds of these allusions were written prior to the marriage of Susanna Shakspere to Dr. John Hall in 1607. That date rules out Shakspere's relationship with his son-in-law, Dr. Hall, as the source of the medical content in most of the works. Ironically, Dr. Hall's copious Latin clinical notes, translated and published posthumously, never once referred to his famous father-in-law, whose medical knowledge was extraordinary (*if,* in fact, his relative was Shakespeare).

In *The Medical Mind of Shakespeare* (1986), Dr. Aubrey Kail expresses a similar opinion regarding Shakespeare's achievement, asserting that the plays display a profound knowledge of contemporary physiology and psychology and that Shakespeare "employed medical terms in a manner which would have been beyond the powers of any ordinary playwright or physician" (Kail 14):

> He exhibited the feelings associated with the tragedy of suffering and the influence of sympathy upon the patient, the relationship between hope and prognosis, the value of mirth, the evils of alcohol, the pangs of insomnia and the benefits of sleep, and, finally, the attributes of death. (14)

Neurology

Jean Marie Charcot, the 19th century French physician who founded modern neurology, urged his students, including authorship doubter Sigmund Freud, "to read Shakespeare for his insights into dementia, tremor, sleepwalking and hysterical symptoms" (Brine 16). Shakespeare's knowledge of neurological diseases was reviewed by Dr. Lance Fogan in his award-winning paper, "The Neurology in Shakespeare" (1988).[4] In a later iteration, "William Shakespeare: Renaissance Physician" (2009), Dr. Fogan illustrates the playwright's many clinically insightful descriptions of neuroanatomy, visual and auditory disturbances, tremors, paralysis, epilepsy, hysteria, malingering, and dementia. Fogan's review includes citations from the medical literature over the past century that addressed Shakespeare's knowledge of numerous other medical specialties including rheumatology, chest diseases, obstetrics, pediatrics, gerontology, dentistry, infectious disease, and psychiatry. Fogan concludes, "Shakespeare's apparent understanding of many signs and symptoms of neurological disease, will amaze the reader. His writing calls out the most clinical disease phenomena that couldn't be described any more accurately or succinctly, and for lovers of creative drama and literature, expressed more beautifully" (Fogan 119).

Dr. Davis is a retired neurosurgeon and has also noted Shakespeare's insight on neuroanatomy. Shakespeare refers to the *pia mater*, the ultrathin, innermost membrane surrounding the brain and spinal cord, in three different plays: *Twelfth Night* (I.v.123), *Troilus and Cressida* (II.i.77), and *Love's Labour's Lost* (IV.ii.70-1):

> Even more striking to me as a neurosurgeon is his acquaintance with the relationship of the third ventricle to memory. In *Loves Labour's Lost*, the pedant Holofernes states, 'these are begot in the ventricle of memory, nourished in the womb of *pia mater*.' A possible source might have been Vicary's *Anatomy of the Body of Man* (1548), which refers to the third ventricle as the 'ventricle of memory.' (Davis 51)

Davis also did comparative research, analyzing the medical content of fourteen plays by ten Renaissance playwrights, including Marlowe, Lyly, Jonson, Sidney, Sackville, Beaumont and Fletcher. Davis found, as did Dr. Heaton, that Shakespeare's medical references far outnumbered those of his contemporaries.

Physicians are not the only writers impressed by the author's medical intelligence. Carolyn Spurgeon recognized the unique sensitivity of Shakespeare's representation of sickness and the action of medicines on the body. In *Shakespeare's Imagery* (1952), Spurgeon notes that Shakespeare was ahead of his time regarding temperate living and avoiding overindulgence, but that his "understanding of the influence of mind on body is what, however, puts him nearest modern expert opinion…" (137).

Earl Showerman, M.D.

Recently published research in the *British Medical Journal* (2006) and *Medical Humanities* (2011) by Dr Kenneth Heaton extends Spurgeon's analysis of Shakespeare's grasp of the relationship between mind and body. Heaton's two reports describe the frequency with which Shakespeare depicts episodes of sudden death from high emotion (10), fainting (18), hyperventilation (11), vertigo, hyper- and hyposensitivity, temporary deafness, and physical collapse associated with grief. Heaton's survey of Shakespeare's contemporaries found no other playwright of the era who employed psycho-physiological phenomena with this frequency or variety. Dr. Heaton concluded that Shakespeare was exceptional in his use of sensory dysfunction to express emotional disturbances.

Davis is not alone in arguing that Shakespeare knew Thomas Vicary's *Anatomy*. Vicary, who was Sergeant Surgeon to Henry VIII, Edward VI, Mary and Elizabeth, compared the sealed womb to a purse in his book.[5] In *Shakespeare's Images of Pregnancy* (1980), author Elizabeth Sacks notes an important parallel to this purse metaphor in Iago's address to Cassio: "In my whole course of wooing, thou criedst, 'Indeed!'/And didst contract and purse thy brow together,/ As if thou then hadst shut up in thy brain/Some horrible conceit" (III.iii.112-15).

Psychiatry

In *The Mad Folk of Shakespeare: Psychological Essays* (1867), Dr. Bucknill took particular note of Shakespeare's unique representations of mental illness and compared his insights to the most advanced scientific principles of the 19th century psychiatry:

> That abnormal states of mind were a favorite study of Shakespeare would be evident from the mere number of characters to which he has attributed them, and to the extent alone to which he has written on the subject. On no other subject, except love and ambition, the blood and chyle of dramatic poetry, has he written so much. On no other has he written with such mighty power. (Bucknill xi)

Bucknill was a world-renowned psychiatrist and humanist. His observation that Shakespeare took a particular interest in mental illnesses is supported by the number of leading characters who commit suicide (Romeo, Juliet, Brutus, Mark Antony, Cleopatra, Othello, Timon), or suffer from alcoholism (Falstaff), melancholia (Hamlet, Jaques, Antonio) insanity (Lady Macbeth, Ophelia), visual and auditory hallucinations (Macbeth) and dementia (King Lear, King John).

In "Shakespeare's Shylock and the Strange Case of Gaspar Ribeiro" (2011), I presented evidence that Shakespeare's use of repetitive rhetoric in Shylock's speeches is unique and that this speech pattern is associated with senility. Professor Brian Pullen has presented compelling evidence that Shakespeare's Jew was actually based on Gaspar Ribeiro, a rich Marrano moneylender living in Venice, who was arguably demented according to recorded testimonies. Pullen recounts how many witnesses at Ribeiro's Inquisition trial commented on the decay in Gaspar's mental powers, and how he spoke with rudeness and rage and used "inconsequential and rambling speech."[6] In *Shylock Is Shakespeare* (2006), Professor Kenneth Gross specifically examined the psychological factors underlying Shylock's widely acknowledged rhetoric of repetition, which Gross argued is the key to appreciating Shylock's deep emotional disturbance: "The repetitions join revenge with mourning, aggressively embedding the lost object within a larger system of losses as if to outwit a loss he cannot control. There is a curious kind of dementia in his speech" (Gross 62).

Infectious Disease

Shakespeare alludes to any number of infectious diseases, including plague, malaria, smallpox, leprosy, measles, rabies and tuberculosis, but no infection captured the playwright's creative attention so vividly as syphilis, the *Morbus Gallicus*, commonly referred to as the "French pox" or the "Neopolitan disease." In *Shakespeare and the New Disease: The Dramatic Function of Syphilis in Troilus and Cressida, Measure for Measure and Timon of Athens* (1989), Greg Bentley demonstrates how Shakespeare repeatedly employed an "image cluster" around the manifestations of syphilis to define the major themes of these three plays: sexual commercialism, slander, and usury, respectively. In his 200-page study, Bentley argued that the image of syphilis served as a weapon of dramatic satire essential to the theme, unity, and design of these three plays. Syphilis provided what Bentley dubs an ultimate "word picture," one that satirizes "the physical, moral and spiritual degeneration of English society" (Bentley 4).

In *Troilus and Cressida*, Thersites' disease-inspired curses, start with the "rotten diseases of the South," and ends with the "incurable bone-ache, and the reviled fee-simple of the tetter," which are descriptions of secondary and tertiary syphilis. Timon of Athens' pox-inspired rant delivered to Timandra and Phrynia, Alcibiades' prostitutes, is especially rich in this imagery:

> Consumption sow
> In hollow bones of man, strike their sharp shins,
> And mar men's spurring. Crack the lawyers voice,
> That he may never false title plead,
> Nor sound his quillets shrilly. Hoar the flamen
> That scolds against the quality of flesh
> And not believes himself. Down with the nose,
> Down with it flat, take the bridge quite away
> Of him that, his particular to foresee,
> Smells from the general weal. Make curled-pate ruffians bald,
> And let the unscarred braggarts from the war
> Derive some pain from you.
>
> *Timon of Athens* (IV.iii.153-64)

In *Shakespeare's Physic* (1989), John Crawford Adams writes of this passage: "The destruction and deformity of bones…, the hoarse voice from laryngeal involvement, the destruction of the bridge of the nose, and the loss of hair—all classic features of syphilis—are so accurately described here that one feels that Shakespeare must have taken expert medical advice" (Adams 60).

Physiology and Forensics

As for Shakespeare's knowledge of Galen's classical doctrine of the four humors, Falstaff's inspired discourse of the effects of "sherris-sac" comprises, in Dr. Adam's opinion, "a veritable tutorial" (38) on Renaissance concepts of physiology:

> A good sherris sack hath a two-fold operation in it. It ascends me into the brain; dries me there all the foolish and dull and curdy vapours which environ it; makes it apprehensive, quick,

forgetive, full of nimble fiery and delectable shapes, which, delivered o'er to the voice, the tongue, which is the birth, becomes excellent wit. The second property of your excellent sherris is, the warming of the blood; which, before cold and settled, left the liver white and pale, which is the badge of pusillanimity and cowardice; but the sherris warms it and makes it course from the inwards to the parts extreme: it illumineth the face, which as a beacon gives warning to all the rest of this little kingdom, man, to arm; and then the vital commoners and inland petty spirits muster me all to their captain, the heart, who, great and puffed up with this retinue, doth any deed of courage; and this valour comes of sherris.

2 Henry IV (IV.iii.95-111)

Another Shakespearean medical monologue that reads like a script for a modern crime scene investigation is Warwick's description of the murdered Gloucester in *2 Henry VI*. Dr. Bucknill notes here that Shakespeare "describes the signs of a violent death, and especially of a death by strangulation, with a particularity which shows that the poet, whatever he might know of 'crowner's quest law,' was not ignorant of crowner's quest medicine" (Bucknill 174):

> But see, his face is black and full of blood,
> His eye-balls further out than when he lived,
> Staring full ghastly like a strangled man;
> His hair uprear'd, his nostrils stretched with struggling;
> His hands abroad display'd, as one that grasp'd
> And tugg'd for life and was by strength subdued:
> Look, on the sheets his hair you see, is sticking;
> His well-proportion'd beard made rough and rugged,
> Like to the summer's corn by tempest lodged.
> It cannot be but he was murder'd here,

2 Henry VI (III.ii.168-177)

Topical Toxicology

Several scholars have argued that Shakespeare's representation of the murder of King Hamlet may have been influenced by a passage from Pliny's *Natural History*, which describes the mental derangements caused by oil of henbane poured into a victim's ear. The "cursed hebonen" was a folk name for henbane, *Hyoscyamus niger*, a poisonous plant with anti-cholinergic effects known to cause hallucinations. Simpson considered henbane sufficiently toxic to cause clinical manifestations not unlike King Hamlet's grizzly description. Brine and Adams argue that the ear poisoning may also suggest that Shakespeare "had recently learned about Eustacchio's description of the auditory tube and wished to bring this anatomic novelty into the play" (Adams 33):

> Sleeping within my orchard,
> My custom always of the afternoon,
> Upon my secure hour thy uncle stole,
> With juice of cursed hebenon in a vial,
> And in the porches of my ears did pour
> The leperous distilment; whose effect

Holds such an enmity with blood of man
That swift as quicksilver it courses through
The natural gates and alleys of the body,
And with a sudden vigour doth posset
And curd, like eager droppings into milk,
The thin and wholesome blood: so did it mine;
And a most instant tetter bark'd about,
Most lazar-like, with vile and loathsome crust,
All my smooth body.

Hamlet (I.v.59-73)

What most physician writers have failed to note is the topical connection between King Hamlet's poisoning and an assassination by poison in 1538 of Francesco della Rovere, the Duke of Urbino, the patron of Castiglione and Giulio Romano. Urbino was reportedly killed by a poison rubbed in his ear by his barber as ordered of the Duke's nephew, Luigi Gonzaga. The assassination of Urbino is in all probability the source for Prince Hamlet's name for his "Mousetrap," the *Murder of Gonzago*.

The Greeks: Hippocrates, Hermes and Asclepius

Although Shakespeare only refers to Hippocrates but once, in *The Merry Wives of Windsor*, Bucknill and Simpson both proposed that Shakespeare was familiar with the Hippocratic *Aphorisms*. A passage from *Richard II* proclaims that spring was the best season for bleeding patients, reflecting the forty-seventh aphorism. Shakespeare scholar F. David Hoeniger, in *Medicine and Shakespeare in the English Renaissance* (1992), has noted allusions to Hippocrates' sixth aphorism: "For extreme diseases extreme strictness is most efficacious." Humphrey Llwyd's posthumously published work, *Treasury of Healthe* (1585), was the first English translation of the Hippocratic *Aphorisms* and was dedicated to William Cecil. Hoeniger also suggests that Shakespeare likely knew passages from Hippocrates' *Prognostic*, and speculates that Peter Lowe's *Whole Course of Chirurgerie* (1597), which included the first English translation of the *Presages of Hyppocrates*, was the author's likely source.

Although not reported in other physicians' studies, Shakespeare's medical representations should rightfully include the possibility of Hermetic influence, especially in the playwright's depictions of resuscitation and resurrection. In *Tragedy and After: Euripides, Shakespeare, Goethe*, Ekbert Faas recognizes that Hermione's miraculous emergence during the statue scene of *The Winter's Tale* is depicted in the style of Hermetic magic. Faas suggests that in this famous scene Shakespeare used imagery and dramaturgy of magic derived from the *Asclepius* dialogue of the Egyptian, Hermes Trismegistus, who was the reputed source of the *Corpus Hermeticum*, the text that proved to be the prime inspiration of the Florentine Neo-Platonists:

> This may or may not be a direct allusion "to the famous god-making passage in the *Asclepius*." But the notion, reported in the Hermetic text, of how the old Egyptian priests, frequently to the accompaniment of music, used to infuse their statues of the gods with life, was widely enough known to be recognized by at least some members of Shakespeare's audience. (Faas 144)

In *Majesty & Magic in Shakespeare's Last Plays*, Francis Yates argues that these Hermetic dialogues had a great influence in the Renaissance and were associated with the magical-religious teachings of Giordano Bruno. Suggesting that the "life-infusing" magic of the statue scene may be seen as a metaphor for the artistic process, Yates concludes that Shakespeare was not only familiar with the *Asclepius*, but also found it profoundly important, that "Paulina's daring magic, with its allusion to the magical statues of the *Asclepius*, may thus be a key to the meaning of the play as an expression of one of the deepest currents of Renaissance magical philosophy of nature" (Yates 91).

Similarly, when Lord Cerimon resuscitates Queen Thaisa in *Pericles*, his invocation begins, "Apollo, perfect me in the characters…" and the scene ends with the line, "Asclepius guide us," which mirrors the first line of the Hippocratic Oath: "I swear by Apollo, Asclepius, Hygeia and Panacea, and I take to witness all the gods…." Cerimon calls for fire to warm Thaisa and "the rough and woeful music that we have," and claims that "Death may usurp on nature many hours,/And yet, the fire of life kindle again,/The o'erpressed spirits. I heard of an Egyptian/That had nine hours lain dead, who was by good appliance recovered" (III.ii.83-7).

There can be little doubt that Cerimon's reference to the "Egyptian" points again to Hermes Trismegistus, the mysterious Alexandrian whose *Corpus Hermeticum* included the *Asclepius* along with a collection of other Greek texts written during the 2nd and 3rd centuries. *The Corpus Hermeticum* was translated into Latin by the Italian scholar Ficino in 1471, and during the Renaissance it was considered to reflect the apex of pagan philosophy. It included passages on Gnosticism, astrology, alchemy and magic, including the re-animation of sacred statues. Francis Yates concluded that there is a high probability that Shakespeare knew the god-making passage of the *Asclepius*.

Faas argued that Cerimon "has in Shakespeare been aggrandized to a semi-divine Renaissance Hermetic magus" (Faas 136), and Aubrey Kail wrote, "Shakespeare's greatest tribute to the medical profession is stated by Cerimon" (Kail 29). Many other writers have acknowledged the remarkable medical ethic of Cerimon's discourse:

> I hold it ever
> Virtue and cunning were endowments greater
> Than nobleness and riches. Careless heirs
> May the two latter darken and expend:
> But immortality attends the former,
> making the man a god. 'Tis known, I ever
> have studied physic, through which secret art,
> By turning o'er authorities, I have,
> Together with my practice, made familiar
> To me and to my aid the blessed infusions
> That dwell in vegetatives, in metals, stones;
> And can speak of the disturbances
> That nature works, and of her cures; which doth give me
> A more content in course of true delight
> Than to be thirsty after tottering honor,
> Or tie my pleasure up in silken bags,
> To please the fool and death.
>
> *Pericles* (III.ii.25-41)

Hoeniger observes, "There is no other speech like his devoted to medical art in the whole range of Elizabethan, Jacobean or Caroline drama…. Cerimon exemplifies the Hippocratic ideal in medicine" (Hoeniger 66). In *Shakespeare the Magus* (2001), Arthur Versluis similarly views Cerimon as a Hermetic master, leading initiates to rebirth, and concludes that "*Pericles* is finally a play of healing, not of loss; it is the play of Asclepius: it reveals the heart of medicine, of healing not just individual suffering, but our state in the cosmos" (Versluis 53).

Paracelsan Alchemy

Shakespeare specifically refers to the rival theories of Galen and Paracelsus in *All's Well* (II. iii.11). Paracelsan teachings challenged traditional Galenic medicine with an empirically based, homeopathic theory, associated with alchemy and the discovery of *arcana*, the healing virtues in nature. Paracelsans distilled herbs and employed minerals and metals, including antimony, arsenic, mercury, and vitriol, in their prescriptions.

Paracelsian alchemy in Shakespeare is discussed by David Hoeniger in *Medicine and Shakespeare in the English Renaissance*. Although he expresses doubts about Shakespeare's knowledge of Paracelsism, Hoeniger nonetheless cites a number of examples of alchemical imagery in the canon; *The Rape of Lucrece* passage, "The poisonous simple sometime is compacted/In a pure compound: being so applied, /His venom in effect is purified," has a marked "Paracelsian ring."

Hoeniger reviewed W.A. Murray's article, "Why Was Duncan's Blood Golden" (1966) on Shakespeare's use of Paracelsian images in Macbeth's description of the murdered Duncan, "His silver skin laced with his golden blood" (II.iii.108). Murray argued that this image is a specific reference to the *tincture* or *electrum*, representing the everlasting perfection of alchemical gold. Hoeniger further notes that in *Romeo and Juliet*, Friar Laurence refers to the "powerful graces that lie in herbs, plants, stones," and he grows a flower in which "Poison hath residence, and medicine power" (II.iii.20), both reflecting Paracelsian theory.

In his chapter, "The She-Doctor and the Miraculous Cure of the King's Fistula in *All's Well that Ends Well*," Hoeniger gives many details of the Paracelsian elements of Helena's approach to the French King's incurable fistula. Helena is described as an "empiric" practitioner who uses Paracelsian phrases such as "manifest experience," "general sovereignty" and "faculty inclusive." Bearing a "sanctified" remedy, and referring to herself as God's "minister," she accomplishes in a mere two days a cure that the King's physicians found hopeless. Helena claims her prescription is "fortified by divine grace."

> The attitude that medicine is a holy calling and the conviction that some virtuous practitioners were particularly favored by God in their skill, discoveries and cures were widespread among religious-minded physicians, surgeons, and women in Shakespeare's time. Their heaven-sent cures revealed God's love of humanity in new telling ways. When God created the earth, man, and woman, he hid in nature all sorts of herbal, animal and mineral remedies whose gradual discovery and application by virtuous doctors or more simple folk served to demonstrate anew the mystery and power of his grace. This conviction was asserted with vigor by Paracelsus and his followers, who claimed that their methods and remedies were Christian, not pagan or infidel like those of traditional Greek and Arabic medicine. (Hoeniger 300)

Hoeniger further notes that from 1570 to 1593, John Hester, "the man who would single-handedly bring Paracelsism across the English Channel,"[7] ran one of the largest apothecary shops in London as well as a distillery at St. Paul's Wharf. Under the influence of Continental practitioners, Hester published ten translations of Paracelsian tracts with long lists of new recipes. In 1596, Hester advertised in his book *The First Part of the Keye of Philosophie* two new secret medicines for the cure of fistulas: "...ye shall note it is good against all cankers, fistilowes, the wolfe, and such like; for it helpeth them al, though they were never so evil, as Paracelsus writes in his great Surgery..." (296).

Further discussion of Paracelsian influence on Shakespeare is found in Charles Nicholl's *The Chemical Theatre* (1980), in which over a hundred pages are devoted to an explication of alchemical imagery as the dominant motif in *King Lear*, as well as being found in *Cymbeline, The Tempest, Macbeth, The Merry Wives of Windsor* and *Romeo and Juliet*. Nicholl finds the most technical of Shakespeare's distillation metaphors to be in Lady Macbeth's assurance "That memory, the warder of the braine,/Shall be a fume, and receipt of reason/A lymbeck only" (I.iv.65-7). The romance of Imogen and Posthumous in *Cymbeline,* Nicholl concludes, is Shakespeare's most nuanced dramatization of the "*coniunctio* found in alchemical allegories..." (Nicholl 233).

Shakespeare's Medical Sources

In *Shakespeare and the Practice of Physic* (2007), Todd Pettigrew observes that some "Shakespeare plays draw considerable dramatic power from questioning and challenging the conservative narratives of the medical establishment" (Pettigrew 105), and that Shakespeare's medical practitioners often subvert the Galenist orthodox policies of the Royal College of Physicians. This should not be surprising given the number of medical sources used by Shakespeare that have been proposed by these physician writers and Shakespeare scholars.

The list could arguably include: *The Corpus Hippocraticum,* Thomas Elyot's *The Castel of Helth* (1539), Thomas Vicary's *Anatomy of the Body of Man* (1548, 1577), George Baker's *Newe Jewell of Health* (1576), Thomas Gale's *Galenic Treatises* (1567), William Clowes' *Morbus Gallicus* (1575), John Bannister's *Comendious Chyrugerie* (1585), Timothy Bright's *A Treatise of Melancholie* (1586), John Hester's *Keye of Philosophie* (1596), Peter Lowe's *Whole Course of Chirurgerie* [surgery](1597), Philemon Holland's translation of Pliny's *Natural History* (1601), Rabelais, and *The Asclepius* of *The Corpus Hermeticum*.

Aside from the medical faculties of Cambridge and Oxford universities, very few contemporaries of Shakespeare's acquired such a collection of medical texts. Among the aristocracy, however, there were a significant number of empiric medical practitioners, some with extensive libraries on medical topics. Sir Thomas Smith had over 1,000 books in his personal library, including many titles on diseases, alchemy, therapeutic botanicals, Galen, Paracelsus, veterinary medicine, and pharmacology. Dr. Davis noted that "It is evident that Smith was particularly interested in the theories attributed to Paracelsus regarding the use of distillates of herbal waters," and that he was also an "avid gardener who devoted much of his time to raising plants for the purpose of distilling into tonics and medicines" (Davis 53). William Cecil, Lord Burghley, also had a magnificent library with nearly 200 editions of books on alchemy and medical topics from all over Europe.

David Hoeniger provides a fascinating picture of the practice of medicine in Shakespeare's England, noting that only a small number of the sick were actually treated by physicians. "This was partly because trained physicians were scarce and partly because only the well-to-do could afford their usually high charges" (Hoeniger 17). Further, most Tudor noblemen were likely to own a few medical books, and several were noteworthy practitioners, including Edward Stanley, 3rd Earl of Derby (1508-72), who enjoyed unusual fame for "chirurgerie and bone-setting." Sir Thomas Elyot's *The Castel of Helth* (1539) was widely read for its medical information throughout the Elizabethan period.

Historical documents indicate that the women of the wealthier households also often knew about medicines and distillation. "In Shakespeare's time, the mother of Francis Bacon, daughter of Sir Anthony Coke; and also Lady Burleigh, wife of the great statesman, were among the women similarly knowledgeable in medicine. Queen Elizabeth often chose to prescribe for herself instead of depending on her personal physician" (26). Lady Margaret Hoby writes in her diary from 1599 to 1605 how she performed all sorts of medical activities, including surgery.

Speculations and Conclusion

Recently, physicians have published books with widely differing narratives on the significance of Shakespeare's medical content. In *Shakespeare's Tremor and Orwell's Cough: The Medical Lives of Famous Writers* (2012), John Ross argues that Shakspere's final signatures show a marked tremor. Ross speculates that the author's preoccupation with syphilis suggests he may himself have been infected and treated with mercury, which can cause neurologic symptoms including tremor. "Was there a connection between Shakespeare's syphilitic obsession, contemporary gossip about his sexual misadventures, and the only medical fact known about him with certainty – that his handwriting became tremulous in late middle age" (Ross x)? Dr. Ross's conclusion that the signatures show progressive deterioration is undermined by the fact that all six signatures date between 1612 and 1616, and all display similar poor penmanship. As for the frequency of allusions to syphilis, Dr. Ross fails to consider Greg Bentley's more scholarly explication that "the abundant and essential images of syphilis in these works[8] support the notion that they are primarily satires. Images of disease, especially venereal disease…are indeed important weapons of dramatic satire" (Bentley 3).

In *His Medical Footprints: Introducing Dr. William Arden Shakespeare* (2008), Dr. John Brine proposes that Mr. Shakspere had intensive medical training during the "lost years," possibly in Wales, and speculates that he travelled in Europe, possibly in the company of William Stanley, 6th Earl of Derby. Brine even claims grandiosely that the author likely "helped cement strong relationships between northern Italy and England" (Brine 128). What Dr. Brine promotes as "the imaginative and empathetic approach all Shakespeare scholars could follow" (112) is an unsupported attempt to reconcile the medical knowledge in the canon with the known life of Shakspere, which doesn't account for it.

That Shakspere did not gain his medical knowledge from his son-in-law, Dr. Hall, is clear from R.R. Simpson's dating of most of Shakespeare's medical allusions before Hall's arrival in Stratford. In chapter 4, "Shakespeare in Stratford and London: Ten Eyewitnesses Who Saw Nothing," Ramon Jiménez gives details of Dr. Hall's education and thirty-year medical career. Hall's patient records were written in Latin and posthumously translated and published. They include detailed commentaries on a number of his patients from as early as 1611, including the writers Michael Drayton and Thomas Holyoak and other regional notables. Nowhere, however, does he mention his famous father-in-law.

Thomas Lodge has also been suggested as a possible source of Shakespeare's medical knowledge. Lodge was an associate of writers John Lyly, Robert Greene and Thomas Nashe. He received medical training at the University of Avignon in the late 1590s and practiced in London from 1600 to 1604. Dr. Lodge is the author of *Rosalynde, Euphues Golden Legacie*

(1590), identified as the source for the plot of *As You Like It*. Although David Hoeniger admits, "no external evidence that Shakespeare and Lodge ever met has surfaced," he speculates that, "their acquaintance during the mid-1590s is highly probable in view of their shared interests" (Hoeniger 53). Lodge's practice in London, however, began after most of Shakespeare's medical references were written. Fifty years ago, Dr. Simpson could not offer a satisfactory explanation for Shakespeare's remarkable understanding of Renaissance medicine except to marvel at the playwright's natural intelligence.

> There is, indeed, no necessity to assume that Shakespeare's medical references, with all their strikingly apt and amazingly rich medical imagery, were any more influenced by a doctor than there is to make a comparable assumption about his references to naval and military matters, to music and law, and the many others. They were all the product of the mind of the genius Shakespeare. (Simpson 126)

The source of Shakespeare's medical knowledge remains a mystery. As we said earlier, nothing that is known about William of Stratford accounts for the author's vast medical knowledge. Traditional scholars have identified numerous medical texts that the author evidently read, and have noted his positive portrayal of physicians. Naturally we want to know how this happened; but speculation about "genius" and secret medical training, in the absence of supporting evidence, is unwarranted and unscholarly. Authorship studies offer explanations of Shakespeare's knowledge that hold up better under scrutiny and challenge the assumptions and imaginative digressions of tradition-bound scholarship.[9]

Works Cited

Adams, John Crawford: *Shakespeare's Physic* (London: Royal Society of Medicine: 1989, reprinted 2000).

Bentley, Greg: *Shakespeare and the New Disease: The Dramatic function of Syphilis in Troilus and Cressida, Measure for Measure and Timon of Athens* (New York, Peter Lang, 1989).

Brine, John: *His Medical Footprints: Introducing Dr William Arden Shakespeare – An Essay in Detection* (St. Thomas Place, Ely: Melrose Books, 2008).

Bucknill, John Charles: *Medical Knowledge of Shakespeare* (London, Longmans, 1860).

_____: *The Mad Folk of Shakespeare: Psychological Essays* (Cambridge: Macmillan and Co., 1867).

Davis, Frank: "Shakespeare's Medical Knowledge: How Did He Acquire It?" (*The Oxfordian* 3, 2000: 45-58).

Faas, Eckbert: *Tragedy and After: Euripides, Shakespeare, Goethe* (Montreal: McGill-Queen's University Press, 1984).

Fogan. Lance: "William Shakespeare: Renaissance Physician" (*Creativity and Madness: Psychological Studies of Art and Artists* 2, 2009, 118-46).

Gross, Kenneth: *Shakespeare Is Shylock* (Chicago: University of Chicago Press, 2006).

Heaton, Kenneth W.: "Faints, fits, and fatalities from emotion in Shakespeare's characters" (*British Medical Journal* 333, 2006, 1335-1338).

_____: "Body-consciousness Shakespeare: sensory disturbances in troubled characters" (*Medical Humanities* 37, 2011, 97-102).

Jiménez, Ramon: "Shakespeare in Stratford and London: Ten Eyewitnesses Who Saw Nothing" (*Shakespeare Oxford Society Fiftieth Anniversary Anthology 1957-2007*, 2007, 74-85).

Kail, Aubrey: *The Medical Mind of Shakespeare* (Balgowlah NSW: Williams & Wilkins, 1986).

Hoeniger, F.David: *Medicine and Shakespeare in the English Renaissance* (Newark: University of Delaware Press, 1992).

Hughes, Stephanie: "'Shakespeare's' Tutor: Sir Thomas Smith (1513-1577)" (*The Oxfordian* 3, 2000, 19-44).

Nicholl, Charles: *The Chemical Theatre* (London, Routledge & Kegan Paul, 1980).

Pettigrew, Todd: *Shakespeare and the Practice of Physic: Medical Narratives on the Early Modern English Stage (*Newark: University of Delaware Press, 2007).

Ross, John: *Shakespeare's Tremor and Orwell's Cough: The Medical Lives of Famous Writers* (New York: St. Martins Press, 2012).

Sacks, Elizabeth: *Shakespeare's Images of Pregnancy* (New York: St. Martin's Press, 1980).

Simpson, R.R.: *Shakespeare and Medicine* (Edinburgh: Livingston, 1959).

Stritmatter, Roger: "On the Chronology and Performance Venue of *A Midsummer Night's Dream*" (*The Oxfordian* 9, 2006, 81-90).

Showerman, Earl: "Shakespeare's Shylock and the Strange Case of Gaspar Ribeiro".
(*Shakespeare Matters* 10:3, 2011, 1-36).

_____: "Shakespeare's Medical Knowledge: Perspective from the E.R."(*Shakespeare Matters* 11:3, 2012, 1-26).

Spurgeon, Carolyn: *Shakespeare's Imagery* (Cambridge: Cambridge University Press, 1952).

Versluis, Arthur: *Shakespeare the Magus* (St. Paul: Grail, 2001).

Yates, Frances A.: *Majesty and Magic in Shakespeare's Last Plays* (Boulder: Shambala, 1978).

Endnotes

1 Reported in *British Medical Journal*, Vol 332, 25.2.2006, and included as a sidebar in *His Medical Footprints* (2008), p.9.

2 November 23, 2011, on-line BBC report.

3 Ross (2012), Showerman (2012), Heaton (2011), Fogan (2009), Brine (2008), Pettigrew (2007), Davis (2000), Hoeniger (1992), Bentley (1989), Adams (1989), and Kail (1986).

4 The paper appeared in *Archives of Neurology* 46: 922-924 (1989) and won the American Academy of Neurology History of Neurology Prize in 1988. Dr. Fogan is Clinical Professor of Neurology at the David Geffen School of Medicine at UCLA.

5 "The neck…in her concavitie hath many involutions and pleates, joined together in the maner of Rose leaves before they be fully spread or ripe, so they be shut together as a Purse mouth." From Sacks, p. 71.

6 Quote from Brian Pullen, *The Jews of Europe and the Inquisition of Venice, 1550-1670* (1983), p. 120. 'I'm not telling you anything. Do you want me to tell you things I don't know? I can't guess. I am not a wizard' and 'The attempt of witnesses to imitate Gaspar's eccentric mix of Portuguese and Italian duly found their way into print.' Pullen refers to Gaspar's advancing age and possible senile dementia on p.230.

7 Quote from Christopher Poltis, "John Hester: The First Paracelsan Translator in England" in *uScientia*: http://uscientia.ca/social-sciences/articles/john-hester-first-paracelsan-translator-england.

8 *Measure for Measure, Troilus and Cressida,* and *Timon of Athens.*

9 "See survey articles by Davis (2000), Fogan (2009) and Showerman (2012).

Part I, Section C
The First Folio and Stratford Monument

This section addresses the heart of the case for Mr. Shakspere as the author Shakespeare — the First Folio edition of the plays, and the Stratford monument, first alluded to in the First Folio in 1623. Without them, it seems very unlikely that anyone would ever have thought of him as the author in the first place. The two chapters on the First Folio both suggest that the so-called "testimony" in the front matter is deliberately deceptive. The chapter on the monument suggests that it was part of the initial deception and was modified later to make it even more deceptive.

The Declaration of Reasonable Doubt acknowledges the Folio and Stratford monument as key evidence, even admitting that they are part of a *"prima facie* case" for Shakspere. But it goes on to explain why both are problematic and shouldn't be taken at face value. These brief arguments have held up well; we quote them here almost in their entirety:

"The First Folio testimony does point to Shakspere as the author, but should this be taken at face value? . . . Neither Ben Jonson, nor Leonard Digges, ever wrote a personal reference to Mr. Shakspere while he lived. Not until the year Shakspere died did Jonson refer to "Shakespeare," and then only to list him as an actor. Other than their two brief allusions, neither Jonson nor Digges offered any further identifying information – not his dates of birth and death, or names of any family members, or any revealing episode from his life. Short on individualizing facts, they gave us generalized superlatives that describe the author, not the man.

"Perhaps the strongest link to Mr. Shakspere is the apparent testimony of actors Heminges and Condell. Neither of them was a writer, however, and several scholars doubt that they wrote the passages attributed to them. Some think their Folio testimony sounds like a sales pitch, urging readers to purchase. Most orthodox scholars are untroubled by the lack of corroboration, limited specifics, ambiguities, puffery and unclear role of Shakspere's fellow actors. Skeptics ask why the Folio is not more straightforward, and why such a great outpouring of eulogies occurred following seven years of silence after his death.

"Today's Stratford monument effigy depicts a writer; but it does not look the same as the one erected in the early 1600s. A sketch by a reputable antiquarian in 1634 shows a man with a drooping moustache holding a wool or grain sack, but no pen, no paper, no writing surface as in today's monument. Records show that the monument was "repaired." Apparently the effigy was also altered to depict a writer. The monument's strange inscription never states that Mr. Shakspere *was* the author William Shakespeare. For anybody living in Stratford, who may have known him, the epitaph could appear to say no such thing. It neither names, nor quotes from, any of the works; and it never mentions poetry, plays, acting or theater. Most orthodox biographers have little to say about the inscription, and some even describe it as enigmatic. Epitaphs of other writers of the time identify them clearly as writers, so why not Mr. Shakspere's epitaph?"

– Shakespeare Authorship Coalition, Declaration of Reasonable Doubt

Chapter 10:
Shakespeare's Impossible Doublet:
Droeshout's Engraving Anatomized*

By John M. Rollett, M.A., Ph.D.

Abstract

The engraving of Shakespeare by Martin Droeshout on the title page of the 1623 First Folio has often been criticized for various oddities. In 1911 a professional tailor asserted that the right-hand side of the poet's doublet was "obviously" the left-hand side of the back of the garment. In this paper I describe evidence which confirms this assessment, demonstrating that Shakespeare is pictured wearing an impossible garment. By printing a ridiculous caricature of the man from Stratford-upon-Avon, it would seem that the publishers were indicating that the implication that the Stratford man was the author of the works was a deliberate deception.

The Exhibition *Searching for Shakespeare,*[1] held at the National Portrait Gallery, London, in 2006, included several pictures supposed at one time or another to be portraits of our great poet and playwright. Only one may have any claim to authenticity – that engraved by Martin Droeshout for the title page of the First Folio (Figure 1), the collection of plays published in 1623. Because the dedication and the address "To the great Variety of Readers" are each signed by John Hemmings and Henry Condell, two of Shakespeare's theatrical colleagues, and because Ben Jonson's prefatory poem tells us "It was for gentle Shakespeare cut," the engraving appears to have the *imprimatur* of Shakespeare's friends and fellows. The picture is not very attractive, and various defects have been pointed out from time to time – the head is too large, the stiff white collar or wired band seems odd, left and right of the doublet don't quite match up. But nonetheless, the illustration is generally regarded as serving a valuable purpose in giving posterity some idea of what the playwright looked like.

The portrait's deficiencies are frequently ascribed to the incompetence of the engraver, usually assumed to be Martin Droeshout the younger, born in 1601, and aged twenty-one or twenty-two in 1623. It is unlikely that he would have seen Shakespeare (who died in 1616), and it is often supposed that the engraving of the face was based on a portrait from the life, now lost.

The doublet may have been copied from the same portrait, or may have been added by the engraver, perhaps working from a real garment. Although Mary Edmond proposed in 1991 that the engraver was probably the young man's uncle, of the same name

---

* First published under the same title in *Brief Chronicles*, Vol. II, 2010.

John M. Rollett, M.A., Ph.D.

Mr. WILLIAM
SHAKESPEARES
COMEDIES,
HISTORIES, &
TRAGEDIES.

Publiſhed according to the True Originall Copies.

Martin Droeſhout ſculpſit London.

LONDON
Printed by Iſaac Iaggard, and Ed. Blount. 1623.

**Fig. 1: Title page of the First Folio of
Shakespeare's plays, 1623.**

and aged around fifty-five,[2] this view is no longer tenable, following the publication by June Schlueter of fresh archival evidence which strongly supports the attribution to the younger Droeshout.[3] Notwithstanding the deficiencies of the engraving, it was evidently found acceptable by the publishers, since they approved it for the title-page of the First Folio.

Many commentators have drawn attention to the portrait's defects, most finding fault with the details of the face and hair, which will not concern us here. Several also point out errors in the costume, for example Sidney Lee refers to "patent defects of perspective"[4] in the dress, while M. H. Spielmann says that the shoulder-wings are "grotesquely large and vilely drawn."[5] The nature of the most elusive peculiarity was brought to light in 1911 by an anonymous tailor writing in *The Gentleman's Tailor*, under the title "A Problem for the Trade." After remarking that "it is passing strange that something like three centuries should have been allowed to pass before the tailor's handiwork should have been appealed to," he concludes that the doublet "is so strangely illustrated that the right-hand side of the forepart is *obviously* the left-hand side of the backpart; and so gives a harlequin appearance to the figure, which it is not unnatural to assume was intentional, and done with express object and purpose" (emphasis added).[6] Since what is obvious to a professional tailor may not be obvious to a layman, in the next section I shall analyze the doublet to see whether there is evidence to support this assessment.

Droeshout's Doublet

The doublet in the engraving displays a number of peculiarities. To begin with, the right shoulder-wing (onlooker's left, Figure 1) is smaller than the left shoulder-wing, when they should be (roughly) the same size, or at least balance pictorially. In addition, the right-hand front panel of the doublet is clearly smaller than the left-hand front panel, as is confirmed by the different lengths of the embroidery edges labeled "x" and "y" (Figure 2). To my knowledge, this is the first time this oddity has been pointed out.

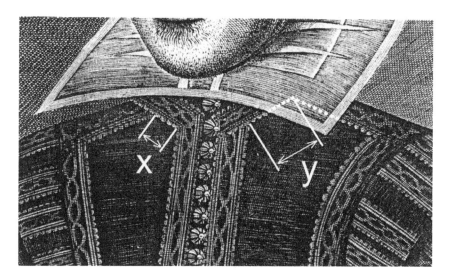

Fig. 2: The right-hand front panel is smaller than the left-hand front panel.

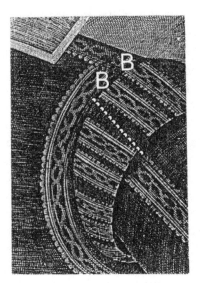 

Fig. 3: The embroidery on the right sleeve (right) is placed around twice as far down from the top of the shoulder-wing as that on the left sleeve (left).

More significantly, the embroidery on the right sleeve does not correspond to that on the left sleeve (Figure 3). On the left sleeve, the upper edge of the embroidery (when extended) meets the inside edge of the shoulder-wing (where it is joined to the doublet), a distance of just over two bands of embroidery (labeled "B") down from the top of the shoulder-wing. On the right sleeve, the upper edge of the embroidery meets the inside edge of the shoulder-wing a distance of rather over three bands, plus a wide gap (labeled "g," roughly the same width as a band),

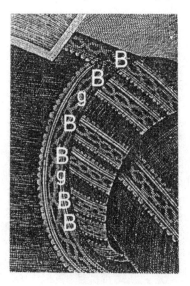 

Fig. 4: The embroidery on the right shoulder-wing does not match that on the left shoulder-wing.

down from the top of the wing. Instead of corresponding (at least approximately) with that on the left sleeve, the embroidery on the right sleeve is located around a distance of two bandwidths lower than that on the left sleeve, or nearly twice as far away from the top of the shoulder-wing. This too has not been noted before, as far as I know.

Most significantly, the embroidery on the right shoulder-wing *does not match* that on the left shoulder-wing. From the top of the left wing (Figure 4), moving down, there are two bands of embroidery close together, a wide gap, and then another pair of bands, and so on. On the right wing, starting at the corresponding place, there is only *one* band of embroidery, then a wide gap, then a pair of bands, and so on. Symbolically, the pattern of embroidery on the left wing, starting from the top, can be represented by "BBgBBgBB," etc., and that on the right wing by "BgBBgBBg," etc. These two patterns would match on a normal garment, but here they do not: clearly *this is not a normal garment*. This new piece of evidence, described here for the first time, is crucial to the analysis of the image.

These four points confirm the verdict of the tailor of 1911; the garment consists of the left front joined to the left back of a real doublet – a sartorial anomaly. The right-hand half of the front of the doublet (Figures 3 or 4) is clearly not the mirror image of the left-hand half (even after taking perspective into account), and the embroidery on the right sleeve indicates that this is in fact the *back* of the left sleeve, where it would be correctly placed. The smaller size of the front right-hand panel (shown by seam "x" being around half the length of seam "y", Figure 2) would be appropriate for the left-hand panel of the back of the doublet; the (non-matching) embroidery on the (smaller) right shoulder-wing would be what one would expect to see on the back of the left shoulder-wing, the "BBg" pattern being repeated regularly around it (Figure 5). It is now clear that no tailor-made doublet ever had such a counterchanged or "harlequin appearance." We are left wondering how this might have come about.

Fig. 5: A mock-up of the left shoulder-wing (left) from the front, (center) from the side and (right) from the back. Compare with Figure 3 or 4.

It has been frequently asserted that the engraver was incompetent and that the publishers, principally Isaac Jaggard and Edward Blount, were prepared to accept an imperfect image of the author and his doublet, despite the fact that such a costly undertaking (one of the most expensive to date by an English publisher) would surely demand a flawless frontispiece. Although incompetence in perspective drawing might possibly account for the first three points above, it cannot account for the last, the embroidery mismatch on the shoulder-wings. No tailor, dressmaker, painter or sculptor – or engraver – could ever commit such a gross error, unless it were expressly required by a patron or employer.

Thus, for whatever reason, the so-called "deficiencies" were apparently intentional, just as the tailor of 1911 supposed, and accepted as such by Jaggard and his colleagues (who would likely have approved initial sketches and might well have kept an eye on work in progress). If they didn't like what the engraver first produced, they had only to withhold payment until he produced something more acceptable. Moreover, a young man undertaking an important commission early in his career is going to make absolutely certain that the finished product is exactly what his patrons require. Anxious to gain a reputation and a living, he would strive to avoid errors at all costs, knowing that his work would be subject to severe scrutiny on account of his youth. That the engraver signed with his full name suggests he was fully satisfied with his achievement.

Nevertheless, the engraving was not found to be entirely satisfactory, since changes were made as printing proceeded. According to Peter Blayney, in the first stage (of which only a few examples survive), there was "so little shading on the ruff that Shakespeare's head appears to be floating in mid air." Shading was therefore added, and later small changes were made to the hair and eyes when the plate was modified a second time. Blayney adds, "It is unlikely that anyone but Droeshout would have considered those alterations necessary."[7] But despite such close attention to detail by the artist on going to press, none of the other peculiarities in the engraving were altered in any way. (Errors in draftsmanship could have been removed by use of the burnisher, at least in the early stages.)

The mismatch between the patterns of embroidery on the shoulder-wings can only have been achieved deliberately; to put it another way, even a child of ten would know that the bands of embroidery on the two shoulder-wings should be mirror images of each other. An artist or engraver, having completed one shoulder-wing, would *automatically* make sure the second wing matched the first, unless instructed otherwise. Together with the other peculiarities, this specific feature shows beyond doubt that the engraved doublet was carefully designed to consist of the left half of the front and the left half of the back of a real garment. It would appear that the artist had a real doublet in front of him; having depicted the front left half with the central fastenings and embroidery, he turned it round and drew the back left half. Why the engraver should have distorted reality in such a way as to produce a sartorial absurdity remains open to speculation, especially as other engravings signed with his name or monogram are executed with more than average competence.[8]

This departure from reality raises the question of whether anyone else has ever been portrayed in a similarly counterchanged or "harlequin" type of costume; and, if so, for what purpose? Alternatively, if there is no history of similar iconography, what would persons buying a copy of the First Folio in 1623 make of the engraving, assuming they spotted its peculiarities, which must have been far more readily apparent to them than to us? Leaving these questions aside, it comes as no surprise to find that the oddities of the portrait seem to have aroused a certain amount of skepticism when it was later used as the basis of another frontispiece. John Benson's 1640 edition of Shakespeare's *Poems* employs a reversed and simplified version of the engraving made by William Marshall (Figure 6).[10] The anomalous right-hand side of the doublet is covered by a cloak, and beneath the portrait are eight lines of verse, the first two of which read:

> This Shadowe is renowned Shakespear's? Soule of th'age
> The applause? delight? the wonder of the Stage.

The use of question marks rather than exclamation marks might appear to suggest that doubts about the engraving had already surfaced.

The learned will Confefs, his works are fuch,

Fig. 6: William Marshall's engraving of Shakespeare for the frontispiece of John Benson's edition of *Shakespeare's Poems*, 1640.

The Uncomely Frontispiece

To examine the strangeness of the doublet from a wider perspective, I shall quote from observations made by Leah S. Marcus in *Puzzling Shakespeare: Local Reading and Its Discontents*.[10] In the first chapter of her book, Marcus makes some trenchant remarks about the title page of the First Folio under the heading "The Art of the Uncomely Frontispiece." Compared with other folio volumes of the period she finds the Folio title page peculiar, to say the least. To begin with, she reports that the Droeshout portrait has been "the object of much vilification. It

has, we hear, a depressing 'pudding face' and a skull of 'horrible hydrocephalous development'"
(2). Readers, she says, "have delighted in pulling apart Droeshout's engraving. Shakespeare, it
is complained, has lopsided hair and a doublet with two left armholes, a displaced nose, eyes that
don't match, a head much too big for the body" (20). Compared with other portraits on title pages
of the period it is "extremely large." It is "stark and unadorned" – it has "no frame, no ornamental
borders" (even though such "embellishments" are found elsewhere inside the volume),

**Fig. 7: Frontispiece of Samuel Daniel's *Civil Wars*, engraved by Thomas
Cockson. London: Simon Waterson, 1609.**

and it is devoid of the allegorical figures and emblems which customarily surround such portraits
and are typical of the title pages of the age, including comparable volumes printed by William
and Isaac Jaggard (2).

Marcus compares the First Folio title page with those of Samuel Daniel's *Civil Wars* (1609), Samuel Purchas's *Pilgrims* (1625), John Taylor's *Works* (1630), Raleigh's *History of the World* (1614), and Jonson's *Works* (1616). In these books the author's engraving is surrounded by elaborate symbolical devices, designed to characterize the author and his book (3). As a representative example, consider the engraving of Samuel Daniel (Figure 7); note the modest costume appropriate to a middle class writer and poet, set off by complex ornamental designs. By contrast, the First Folio title page "appears stripped down to essentials," differing from all the others by offering "no particularizing details – only the raw directness of the image, as though to say that in this case, no artifice is necessary: this is the Man Himself" (18). Jonson's poem facing the portrait adds further to the puzzle. It begins:

> This Figure, that thou here seest put
> It was for gentle Shakespeare cut

and ends, "Reader looke / Not on his picture, but his Booke." Shakespeare, the verses tell us (according to Marcus), "is not to be found after all in the compelling image opposite" (8). It is a "Figure" cut "for" Shakespeare, and should be ignored (according to Jonson), in favor of the volume's contents.

Commentary

These findings reveal a puzzling discrepancy on the title page of the First Folio between what one should expect, and what one finds. In place of a lifelike or at least credible portrait of the "Soul of the Age," the "Star of Poets," dressed appropriately, we are offered a picture of a man wearing a nonsensical costume – a garment consisting of the left front and left back of a real doublet.[11] What can this mean?

If similar portraits or historical parallels exist which might supply an explanation, an exhaustive search has failed to produce a single example, and so we can only entertain a few conjectures. The idea that Martin Droeshout might have had a grudge against Shakespeare or the publishers of the First Folio, and set out to poke fun at him or them by producing an engraving full of faults (hoping no one would notice), can I think be discarded. Another possibility is that the two left sleeves symbolize the fact that Shakespeare was the servant of two masters, Queen Elizabeth and James I, badges of allegiance being worn on the left sleeve. But the man in the portrait, so far from wearing the clothing of a retainer or actor, is dressed in clothing appropriate to a landed gentleman such as Sir John Petre[12] (Figure 8). Shakespeare might have been given such clothing as a castoff to wear on the stage, but could hardly have worn it in ordinary life in view of the existing sumptuary laws. Another suggestion is that since left-handedness[13] is sometimes associated with covert dealings, the portrait may hint at some subterfuge connected with the publication, perhaps that his role was not what it appeared to be (that of author). A further possibility is that the depiction of the face was imaginary, and the anomalous doublet was thus intended to warn the onlooker that it was not to be regarded as a true portrait (that is, not to be taken at face value).[14]

John M. Rollett, M.A., Ph.D.

Fig. 8: Detail of the portrait of Sir John Petre (1603).

In the absence of a clear interpretation, perhaps something can be learned from other aspects of the engraving. Among the many peculiarities to which Marcus draws attention is that the portrait of Shakespeare is "extremely large" (2). In fact, it is around four times larger in area (six and a half inches by seven and a quarter) than the title page head-and-shoulders portrait of any other author of the period. Why is this? I would suggest that if the image had been of normal size (e.g. that of a playing card or postcard), the details, especially those of the embroidery, would have been so difficult to make out that the implication they were presumably designed to convey might never have been suspected. To ensure that the left-front left-back character would be noticed, the engraving had to be as large as possible; as a consequence no space was available for the conventional allegorical figures and emblems usually surrounding such an image.

Further evidence of the engraving's duplicity is provided by the starched white collar or wired band under the head (Figure 1). Its support, known as an "under-propper" or "supportasse" (made, e.g., from lightweight material covered in silk) shows clearly through the linen on the left side of the collar (onlooker's right), but is not visible on the right side; both Sandy Nairne[15] and Tarnya Cooper[16] draw attention to this curious omission in the National Portrait Gallery's publication *Searching for Shakespeare*. It is also worth noting that the collar conceals part of the embroidery edge labelled "y" (Figure 2), in such a way that the exposed part is the same length as the edge labeled "x". The left and right seams in the neck area therefore appear to match each other, creating a kind of *trompe l'oeil* effect which tends to obscure the

122

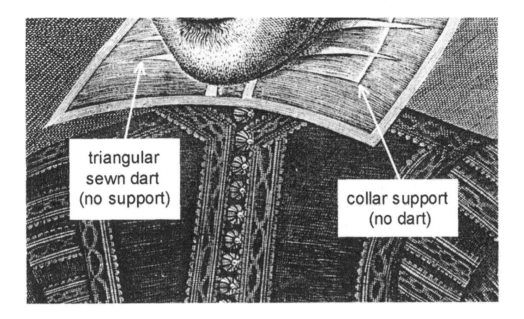

triangular
sewn dart
(no support)

collar support
(no dart)

Fig. 9: Showing the omission of the right-hand side of the collar support, and the lack of symmetry in the depiction of the triangular sewn darts in the wired band.

differing sizes of the front panels. In addition, the triangular sewn darts of the collar are almost comically unsymmetrical: left and right bear no kind of mirror relationship with each other, even allowing for perspective; Figure 9 draws attention to the chief mismatches.[17] It is no more a real collar than the doublet is a real doublet, and it is difficult to resist an impression that the person depicted is being gently and surreptitiously mocked. Although one or two peculiarities might be ascribed to carelessness, six or seven (some obvious at first glance) seem to point towards a deliberate agenda of some kind.

Conclusion

The engraving by Martin Droeshout on the title page of the First Folio shows a man, identified by Ben Jonson and Leonard Digges[18] as William Shakespeare of Stratford-upon-Avon, wearing an impossible garment which, it is reasonable to suppose, carries some symbolic implication. If no likeness of the poet had been available, the publishers could have commissioned an imaginary portrait properly costumed (as has sometimes been done, for example, with editions of Homer), or omitted one altogether; instead, they chose a course apparently intended to invite speculation.

If nothing else, this analysis of Shakespeare's doublet draws attention to an astonishing aberration at the heart of the First Folio. Whatever its interpretation, there can now be no doubt that the left-front/left-back anomaly is a fact. What is usually taken to be a poorly drawn portrait of the playwright turns out to be a skillfully executed depiction of a carefully designed enigma. Droeshout's engraving of Shakespeare has become, down the years, the most famous literary icon in the world, yet while ostensibly a portrait of our great poet, it hides beneath a more or less plausible surface a so far unresolved problem.

Perhaps light can be shed on this problem by examining other volumes of the period. Head-and-shoulder portraits of the following authors appear on title pages of their publications: John

John M. Rollett, M.A., Ph.D.

Florio, Walter Raleigh, Francis Bacon, Samuel Daniel, Michael Drayton, Ben Jonson, John Donne, John Weever, Samuel Purchas, John Taylor, John Milton; none show any peculiarities of costume and none are associated with questions of authorship. Only Shakespeare's dress is anomalous, and only Shakespeare's authorship is in doubt. Many people will be likely to conclude that by printing a ridiculous caricature of the man from Stratford-upon-Avon, the publishers were indicating that the implication that the Stratford man was the author was a deliberate deception.

Endnotes

[1] *Searching for Shakespeare*, Exhibition curated by Dr.Tarnya Cooper, National Portrait Gallery, London, March to May, 2006.

[2] Edmond, Mary. "It was for gentle Shakespeare cut." *Shakespeare Quarterly* 42 (1991): 339-344; "Martin Droeshout." *The Dictionary of Art*. Oxford: OUP, 1996; "Martin Droeshout." *Oxford Dictionary of National Biography*. Oxford: OUP, 2006.

[3] Schlueter, June. "Martin Droeshout Redivivus: Reassessing the Folio Engraving of Shakespeare." *Shakespeare Survey* 60 (2007): 237-251.

[4] Lee, Sidney. *A Life of William Shakespeare* (third edition of revised version). London: John Murray, 1922: 529.

[5] Spielmann, M.H. *The Title Page of the First Folio of Shakespeare's Plays: a comparative study of the Droeshout portrait and the Stratford bust*. London: H. Milford, 1924: 32.

[6] Anon. "A Problem for the Trade." *The Gentleman's Tailor* 46 (1911): 93.

[7] Blayney, Peter W.M. *The First Folio of Shakespeare*. Washington, D.C.: Folger Library Publications, 1991: 18.

[8] Martin Droeshout had a successful career as an engraver both in England and Spain, and engraved portraits of many well-known and distinguished people including John Donne, the Duke of Buckingham, the Bishop of Durham, the Marquis of Hamilton and Lord Coventry. In 1631 he was commissioned to illustrate the second edition of Crooke's *Mikrokosmographia* (over 1000 pages long), testifying to an excellent reputation. The title page of this work is given here: http://www.bpi1700.org.uk/jsp/zoomify.jsp?image=157307. Other examples of his work are included in June Schlueter's paper referenced above, and on the website of the National Portrait Gallery, http://www.npg.org.uk/collections/search/person.php?LinkID=mp06906&role=art.

[9] Shakespeare, William. *Poems: written by Wil. Shakespeare*, Gent. London: John Benson, 1640.

[10] Marcus, Leah S. *Puzzling Shakespeare: Local Reading and Its Discontents*. Berkeley: London: U. of California Press, 1988: 1-30.

[11] With plain material and bold colors, this is the style of dress of jesters.

[12] Detail from the painting of Sir John Petre, 1603. At the time he was Lord Lieutenant of Essex, and was later created Baron Petre.

[13] It may be relevant to note that the primary meaning of the word "ambodexter" or "ambidexter" (having two right hands) in the 16th-17th centuries was "double-dealer" (OED), in particular someone taking money from both sides in a dispute. The corresponding word, ambisinister, was very rarely used, though by inference it might convey the same meaning, especially as left-handedness is sometimes associated with underhand dealing. Characters named Ambodexter in dramas of the period were notably greedy for money.

[14] I am indebted to Phyllida McCormick for this suggestion.

[15] Nairne, Sandy. "Supportasse, 1600-1625." *Searching for Shakespeare*. London: National Portrait Gallery, 2006: 120.

[16] Cooper, Tarnya. "William Shakespeare, from the First Folio, c. 1623." *Searching for Shakespeare.* London: National Portrait Gallery, 2006: 48.

[17] In William Marshall's 1640 version of the engraving, Figure 5, the underpropper shows through on both sides of the collar, and the triangular darts on left and right are mirror images of each other. Through restoring symmetry, Marshall acknowledges – by correcting them – two of the more obvious peculiarities of the Droeshout original.

[18] In their poems prefaced to the first Folio, Ben Jonson addresses the poet as "Sweet Swan of Avon," and Leonard Digges refers to "Thy Stratford Monument."

Bibliography

Chambers, E.K. *William Shakespeare, a Study of Facts and Problems.* Oxford: Clarendon Press, 1930: i. 90; ii. 240.

Daniel, Samuel. *The Civil Wars between the Houses of Lancaster and York.* London: Simon Waterson, 1609.

Friswell, J. Hain. *Life Portraits of William Shakspeare: a history of the various representations of the poet, with an examination into their authenticity.* London: S. Low, son, & Marston, 1864: 36-45.

Greenwood, Sir George. *The Stratford Bust and the Droeshout Engraving.* London: Cecil Palmer, 1925.

Hind, Arthur M. *Engraving in England in the Sixteenth and Seventeenth Centuries.* Cambridge: at the University Press, 1952: Part II, 431-466.

Hinman, Charlton. *The Printing and Proof-reading of the First Folio of Shakespeare.* Oxford: at the Clarendon Press, 1963: vol. 1, 248-9.

Nevinson, J.L. "Shakespeare's Dress in his Portraits." *Shakespeare Quarterly* vol. 18 (1967): 101-106.

Schoenbaum, S. *Shakespeare's Lives.* Oxford: Clarendon Press, 1970.

_____. *William Shakespeare, a Documentary Life.* Oxford: Clarendon Press with The Scolar Press, 1975.

_____. *William Shakespeare, Records and Images.* Oxford, The Scolar Press, 1981.

Schuckmann, Christiaan. "The Engraver of the *First Folio* Portrait of William Shakespeare." *Print Quarterly* vol. VIII (1991): 40-43.

Chapter 11:
The Ambiguous Ben Jonson: Implications for Assessing the Validity of the First Folio Testimony

By Richard F. Whalen

Stratfordian academics generally claim, or simply assume, that the prefatory matter in the Shakespeare First Folio of 1623 provides conclusive evidence that William Shakspere of Stratford was the poet-dramatist. In particular, they cite allusions in Ben Jonson's eulogy to "Sweet swan of Avon" and in Leonard Digges' poem to "thy Stratford moniment," which, they believe, combine to prove the connection of Avon and Stratford to "Shakespeare."

They also point to the large, iconic portrait on the title page headed: *Mr. William Shakespeares Comedies, Histories & Tragedies* and on the facing page the ten-line poem by Jonson that says the portrait was "for gentle Shakespeare cut," as well as two letters over the names of John Heminge and Henry Condell, former actors mentioned in Shakspere's will, which state that they published the plays "onely to keepe the memory of so worthy a Friend & Fellow alive, as was our SHAKESPEARE."

Despite Jonson's reputation for deliberate ambiguity and his significant role in the publication of the First Folio, Stratfordian academics take this First Folio "testimony" at face value. For Jonathan Bate of Oxford University, author of *The Genius of Shakespeare*, Jonson's swan of Avon allusion "is the decisive link with Stratford-upon-Avon" (69-70). Stanley Wells of the University of Birmingham, and honorary president of the Shakespeare Birthplace Trust, points to it as "evidence that the author was the man of Stratford." His assertion appeared in his opinion article in the *Washington Post* in 2007. S. Schoenbaum of the University of Maryland called the dedication letter in the First Folio over the names of Heminge and Condell, which says they collected and published the plays, "the most crucial single document in the annals of authorship attribution" (*Internal*, 167).

Alan Nelson, Emeritus Professor of English at the University of California-Berkeley, said in *The Tennessee Law Review* that "the documentary evidence for [Shakspere], . . . in the First Folio of 1623 but also in standard historical sources . . . demonstrates the traditional claims [for him]" (149). He adds that doubters must believe that the First Folio "is not an honest tribute organized by Heminge and Condell, but a tissue of lies supervised by William and Philip Herbert [earls of Pembroke and Montgomery, to whom the First Folio was dedicated], with the voluntary or forced cooperation of Ben Jonson, who lied through his teeth both to his contemporaries and to posterity" (163).

More often, Stratfordian academics simply accept the prefatory matter in the First Folio as *prima facie* proof without further comment or analysis of the double meanings in it. For example, in *William Shakespeare, a Compact Documentary Life*, S. Schoenbaum devoted three pages to the prefatory matter without bothering to cite it as proof of the Stratford man's authorship (314-17). He took it as self-evident.

To accept unquestioningly the prefatory matter as proof of Shakspere's authorship is to ignore the fact that deliberate ambiguity was a common literary practice in the dangerous political climate of Jonson's day and that writers like Jonson resorted to it when expressing unwelcome truths that might offend and lead to reprisals or punishment. Stratfordian academics, however, choose to ignore Jonson's reputation for ambiguity and his role in preparing the First Folio for publication.

Master of ambiguity

Ambiguity is defined as "double-meaning, an expression that is equivocal" (OED 3.a. b., 4). It ranges from the simple pun that is relatively obvious and perhaps amusing to a misleading mistake in composition to artistic ambiguity for esthetic purposes to deliberate ambiguity meant to evoke alternative, multiple, even opposite reactions to the same piece of writing. In *Seven Types of Ambiguity*, William Empson says, "We call it ambiguous, I think, when we recognize that there could be a puzzle as to what the author meant, in that alternative views might be taken without sheer misreading" (x).

Quintilian, a first-century Roman rhetorician who had a major influence on Jonson, had this to say: "For it is time now to come to the very common device, which I am sure the reader is especially waiting for, in which we drop a hint to show that what we want to be understood is not what we are saying—not necessarily the opposite (as in irony) but something hidden and left to the hearer to discover. . . . You can speak as openly as you like against tyrants . . . as long as you can be understood differently, because you are not trying to avoid giving offense, only its dangerous repercussions. If danger can be avoided by some ambiguity of expression, everyone will admire its cunning" (*The Orator's Education 9.2*). Jonson was especially cunning in his use of deliberate ambiguity.

Such ambiguity by an orator or writer leaves the truth of a matter undetermined, providing immunity from blame, reprisals, prosecution or punishment. For discerning Elizabethan and Jacobean readers, as for Quintilian's Romans, deliberate ambiguity could also evoke an appreciation for the way in which the writer wittily avoids taking a dangerous public position while expressing something the reader knows or suspects to be true (see Empson, 1, 192).

Passages in Jonson's works can easily be identified as deliberately ambiguous—whether in the form of self-contradictions, rhetorically ambivalent language, equivocation, veiled meanings or sly falsehoods. Ambiguity was a significant feature of Elizabethan and Jacobean literature, especially to avoid censorship or offending authorities. It was used to blur dangerous or inconvenient truths, to give alternative or contradictory readings, and, according to one Jonson biographer, to create a "maze of seductive falsehoods," all while entertaining the reader or playgoer.

Ben Jonson was a master of ambiguity, but he was not alone. A survey of the use of ambiguity at the time is beyond the scope of this chapter but would include *Greene's Groatsworth of Wit*, Henry Chettle's *Kind Heart's Dream*, Philip Sidney's *Arcadia* and passages in Edmund Spenser and Thomas Nashe. The most creative use of ambiguity, both esthetically and to convey hidden meanings, is found in Shakespeare. Jonathan Bate notes, admiringly, that "Shakespeare gave Empson more examples of ambiguity than any other poet" (309).

In *Censorship and Interpretation: The Conditions of Writing and Reading in Early Modern England*, Annabel Patterson says that "I argue throughout this book that the unstable but unavoidable relationship between writers and holders of power was creative of a set of conventions that both sides partially understood and could partly articulate, conventions as to how far a writer could go in explicit address to the contentious issues of his day, and how, if he did not choose the confrontational approach, he could encode his opinions so that nobody would be required to make an example of him" (12). In other words, writers could express opinions in ambiguous language that could be understood by those in the know while preserving deniability.

Patterson describes what might be called the institutionalization of ambiguity: "What we can find everywhere apparent and widely understood, at least from the middle of the sixteenth century in England onward, is a system of communication ('literature') in which ambiguity becomes a creative and necessary instrument, while at the same time the art (and the theory) of interpretation was reinvented, expanded and honed." She calls it "functional ambiguity [that was] fully and knowingly exploited by authors and readers alike"—ambiguity with a political purpose (18).

Ben Jonson she describes as "this most complex of authors," adding that in his plays "there is evidence, if we look carefully, of a highly sophisticated system of oblique communication, of unwritten rules whereby writers could communicate with readers or audiences (among whom were the very same authorities who were responsible for state censorship) without producing a direct confrontation" (53, 62). Jonson learned his craft the hard way. He was imprisoned for his contributions to two plays, and five times he faced charges of libelous writings. The threat of prison and torture was a real incentive for Jonson to hone his skill for deliberate ambiguity that would permit deniability.

In a comment that could apply to the First Folio, Patterson notes the importance of prefatory matter that addresses the reader's expectations. "In general," she says, "late modern criticism has not paid enough attention to the interpretive status of introductory materials in early modern texts" (56).

In his biography of Ben Jonson, David Riggs of Stanford University describes many examples of ambiguity. He says the verse collection entitled "*The Forest* quietly but insistently addresses the tensions and ambiguities in Jonson's self-conception as a courtly amateur" (234). In "Inviting a Friend to Supper," the menu "is tantalizingly equivocal" (230). The poem "To Heaven" shows that "Jonson's [mental] state bristles with contradictions" (237). In *Catiline*, Jonson situates his own position on religion "beyond the reach of any recoverable meaning" (178). Jonson's poem "A Speech According to Horace," says Riggs, is a "mock encomium" full of irony and ambiguity (299). Jonsonian editor George Parfitt of Nottingham University wrote an article on the poem for *Studies in English Literature* (winter 1979). He titled it "History and Ambiguity: Jonson's 'A Speech According to Horace.'"

In a telling passage, Riggs writes: "Like *The Faerie Queene* and *Paradise Lost*, [Jonson's] *Volpone* forces its readers to work their way through a maze of seductive falsehoods; if they are any wiser at the end of the play, it is because they have withstood this assault on their moral bearings . . . Just as Volpone gulls his clients, Jonson gulls his audience; but Jonson's falsehood has the capacity to educate as well as delude" (136-7). Similarly, unwary readers of Jonson's prefatory poems in the First Folio risk being gulled by a maze of seductive falsehoods that make them lose their literary-historical bearings.

Ambiguity in the First Folio

Nothing in the First Folio provides straightforward biographical information that identifies the author unequivocally as Shakspere of Stratford. The Folio does not display the famous coat of arms that Shakspere and his father went to such trouble and expense to acquire. Nor does it include any tributes from fellow writers, still living, with whom he allegedly collaborated. Jonson and Shakespeare were rivals, and from later writings it is clear that Jonson was critical of Shakespeare's plays. It seems strange that Jonson should have been chosen to write the main eulogy to Shakespeare rather than one of his alleged collaborators such as Heywood, Dekker, Middleton or John Fletcher. Jonson had many more tributes from other writers in his own folio than did Shakespeare. In fact, Jonson is the *only* major writer to write a tribute—this for the man known as the "Soul of the age!"

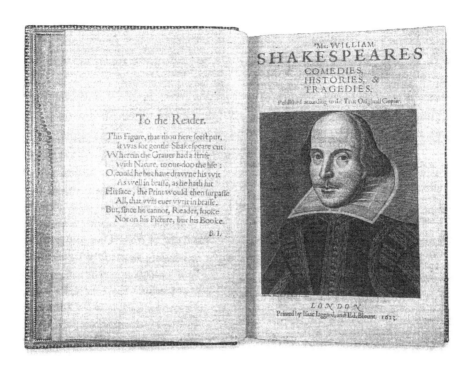

Fig. 1: title page with Droeshout engraving of Shakespeare, with Ben Jonson's poem "To the Reader" on facing page.

The most famous and significant First Folio passages, which have persuaded the unwary to accept the Stratfordian story line, are Jonson's allusion to "Sweet swan of Avon" and three pages later Digges' allusion to "thy Stratford moniment." Brought together they seem to point to Stratford-upon-Avon, but that is not necessarily the case. There were five rivers in England called Avon and at least ten towns or villages called Stratford. One of the Stratfords was a market town near London. Early readers of the First Folio would have thought first of the town on the outskirts of London, not the town three days away on one of the Avon rivers. To turn the allusions into Shakspere's hometown a reader had to take Digges' "Stratford" and put it in front of Jonson's "Avon" three pages earlier. It's unlikely that many readers would do that, and, if any did, Jonson could deny he meant for them to make the effort.

The oversize, iconic portrait on the First Folio title page and Jonson's accompanying poem "To the Reader" do not withstand scrutiny as valid evidence for Shakspere as the dramatist. The poem begins, "This Figure, that thou here seest put." "Figure," however, could have been read ambiguously either as a picture of someone or as "an imaginary form or phantom," a meaning now obsolete according to the OED (9 a. b.), which cites Chaucer's use of it in that sense.

Paradoxically, Jonson's poem rejects the portrait. It contradicts the title of the First Folio above the portrait and says that the portrait is not *of* the author but "for" him. A frontispiece

Richard F. Whalen

portrait in an author's collected works is *of* him, not *for* him. After several convoluted lines about the engraver's aborted effort "to out-doo the life," the ten-line poem closes by exhorting the reader to "looke / Not on his Picture, but his Booke." Here again, ambiguous language allows for two different meanings: either a poetic conceit suggesting that the true spirit of Shakespeare is in his plays and not to be found in his portrait, or an injunction to disregard the portrait as it is not a true representation of the dramatist.

In *Puzzling Shakespeare: Local Reading and Its Discontents*, Leah Marcus of Vanderbilt University devotes the first fifty pages to the portrait and Jonson's poem on the facing page. She reads them as contradicting each other, virtually abolishing Shakespeare as the man in the portrait.

She finds the portrait odd and unsettling. That's putting it mildly. It is strangely unbalanced. One eye is lower than the other. The hair is longer on one side than the other, and the tunic shoulders and sleeves are mismatched (see Chapter 10). It has dismayed almost all Shakespeare commentators. J. Dover Wilson called it a false image that the world turns from in disgust (6). Katherine Duncan-Jones referred to the "childish clumsiness" that produced "an inept and witless-looking image" (280). Schoenbaum said: "Droeshout's deficiencies are, alas, only too gross" (*Life*, 315).

Marcus begins by noting that "if the First Folio is considered in light of other English folios of the period . . . there is something quite odd about the way it starts out." She notes the "unsettling size and directness" of the portrait and its deficiencies. She suggests that it is saying "this is the Man Himself," but, she adds, "That, at least, is what the portrait seems to say; the verses on the facing page say otherwise . . . Shakespeare, the verses tell us, is not to be found in the image opposite" (18):

To the Reader.

> This Figure, that thou here seest put,
>   It was for gentle Shakespeare cut;
> Wherein the Graver had a strife
>   with Nature, to out-doo the life:
> O, could he have but drawn his wit
>   As well in brasse, as he hath hit
> His face, the Print would then surpasse
>   All, that was ever writ in brasse.
> But, since he cannot, Reader, looke
>   Not on his Picture, but his Booke.

B. I.

"The poem, Marcus continues, "undermines the visual power of the portrait by insisting on it as something constructed and "put" there. It is a "Figure" cut "for" Shakespeare (18).

She calls Jonson's poem "iconoclastic, shattering the power of the visual image in order to locate Shakespeare's identity elsewhere [namely] in 'wit.'" And therefore it "abolishes Shakespeare as an entity apart from his writings" (19). She concludes that "the First Folio opens with an implicit promise to communicate an authorial identity, which it instead repeatedly displaces: Shakespeare is somehow there, but nowhere definitively there" (20). If Shakespeare is not definitively there, it's not a portrait of the dramatist. Other Stratfordian academics rarely mention the portrait poem or print it. Schoenbaum merely said that "an

130

over-subtle reader will detect a latent irony in Jonson's conclusion [look at the book, not the picture] . . . but the advice is sound enough" (*Compact* 316-7). Ironically, Schoenbaum's "latent irony" and ambiguity are both forms of double-meaning.

Heminge, Condell and Jonson

Stratfordian academics also cite the two letters over the printed names of John Heminge and Henry Condell in the prefatory matter as evidence that Shakspere wrote the plays in the First Folio and that Heminge and Condell, two former actors and colleagues of Shakspere, edited and published the 900-page volume. For example, Michael Dobson and Stanley Wells in *The Oxford Companion to Shakespeare*, James Shapiro of Columbia University in *Contested Will: Who Wrote Shakespeare?* (29), and Jonathan Bate of Oxford in *The Genius of Shakespeare* (27), all assert that Heminge and Condell were the publishers. In the Norton edition of Shakespeare's works, the editors Stephen Greenblatt of Harvard and three other university professors say the First Folio was "edited by two of Shakespeare's old friends and fellow actors" (65). *The Reader's Encyclopedia of Shakespeare*, edited by Oscar J. Campbell of Columbia, calls them co-editors

The Heminge-Condell letters, however, were almost certainly ghostwritten by Ben Jonson, raising serious questions about the claims in them. The letters are sowed with so many deliberate ambiguities, contradictions and sly deceptions that they cannot be taken at face value as evidence for Shakspere. Heminge and Condell, moreover, were most unlikely editors and publishers of the First Folio. The Stratfordian academics do not explain how such a task, requiring literary skill, diligence and editorial experience, could have been accomplished by the two unlettered novices from the acting world.

Textual analysis by scholars reveals Jonson's hand in the letters. The parallels in them to his writings, first described in the eighteenth century, are striking. Sidney Lee recognized in his *Life of William Shakespeare* (1898 rev.1916) what he called a "theory" that Jonson may have written the Heminge-Condell letters and helped edit the First Folio (556). This idea was originally advanced by the distinguished eighteenth-century Shakespeare editor George Steevens. He produced twelve pages of examples comparing phrases in the Heminge-Condell letters to writings by Jonson. The parallels persuaded him that Jonson was the true author (In Malone-Boswell 2:663-75).

Lee was more cautious. He agreed that the letters appeared to use "phrases that crudely echo passages" in Jonson's writings but insisted that they do not reflect Jonson's "facility of style" and that Heminge and Condell, who had acted in Jonson's plays, got hints from his writings "for their unpracticed pens" (556-7). As for the First Folio, he suggested that they were only "nominally responsible for the design" and that they "made pretension to a larger responsibility for the enterprise than they probably incurred" (552, 556).

His conjectures against the theory, however, do not inspire confidence, for in addition to the parallels that Steevens found, the evidence for Jonson's hand is everywhere in the letters. They draw on Pliny and Horace, and Jonson was a classical scholar. The former actors were not. The letters are redolent of the kind of excessive rhetorical invention that is typical of Jonson's satirical writing. If they lack what Sidney Lee called Jonson's "facility of style," it is perhaps because Jonson was parodying what Heminge and Condell might have written with their "unpracticed pens," as Lee put it.

The first Heminge-Condell letter dedicates the First Folio to the earls of Pembroke and Montgomery, "the Most Noble and Incomparable Paire of Brethren," and does so with exaggerated servility and sanctimonious adulation, verging on open satire. Jonson has them saying that no one approaches the earls except "with a kind of religious address" like farmers offering milk, cream and fruits who "approach their Gods [with] the meanest of things made more precious, when they are dedicated to Temples." The discerning reader could have read this letter as an honest if somewhat bizarre dedication, or ambiguously as veiled satire of effusive dedicatory epistles to noble patrons by commoners.

The high-flown rhetoric in the dedication is not the sort of writing that would be expected from two former actors collaborating on a letter. In fact, neither Heminge nor Condell are known to have written anything or had any experience in publishing, much less a massive volume like the First Folio. What they thought of the letters with their names printed at the bottom can only be imagined.

The second Heminge-Condell letter is a bizarrely insistent sales pitch that has parallels to Jonson's writings. It is addressed "To the great Variety of Readers. / From the most able to him that can but spell, there you are numbered." Jonson would use similar language in the dedication of his comedy *The New Inn* (1631) "To the Reader. / If thou be such. . . . [meaning if you can read] if thou canst but spell and join my sense." Another example is in Jonson's *Discoveries* where he would write "how odde soever mens braines or wisdomes are." The Heminge-Condell letter to the reader has "how odde soever your braines be, or your wisdoms" (in Malone-Boswell 2:666).

The blatant and disingenuous sales pitch is addressed to the great variety of readers and "variety" in Jonson's day carried a connotation of fickleness (OED 1.b.) It acknowledges that the reader will claim the right to censure the plays and adds: "Do so, but buy it first. . . . Judge your six-pen'orth, your shillings worth, your five shillings worth at a time." Jonson's Induction to *Bartholomew Fair* has the phrase "to judge his six pen'orth, his twelve pen'orth, so to his eighteen pence, two shillings, half a crown, to the value of his place" (lines 75-80). This parallel to currency and other parallels found by Steevens seem persuasive for Jonson's authorship of the letter to the reader. Even Stratfordian Leah Marcus affirms that the language of the Heminge-Condell letter "so strongly echoes the Induction to Jonson's *Bartholomew Fair* that many are convinced Jonson wrote the preface himself" (22). She does not, however, examine the implications.

The letter even urges the reader a second time to buy: "But whatever you do, Buy. Censure will not drive a Trade." Even though insulted, the fickle reader is urged twice to buy the book, no matter what he thinks of it. This insistent commercialism contradicts the Heminge-Condell dedication letter on the previous page that insists that they are producing the folio "without ambition either of selfe profit or fame." Moreover, the insistence to buy the First Folio is genial hypocrisy, since a "great Variety of Readers" could hardly have afforded the expensive volume.

The Heminge-Condell letters also make obviously false statements that the discerning reader would be expected to catch. The letter to the reader makes a false claim about the condition of the plays collected for the First Folio. The letter says the plays were "maimed and deformed" but are now offered "cured and perfect" and "absolute in their numbers as he [the author] conceived them." This is not true. The plays in the First Folio are far from perfect; they are full of obvious errors and defects that an editor would have corrected. Jonson has Heminge and Condell uttering a falsehood as promotional puffery for their supposed editing and publishing skills, which the discerning reader would know is untrue. And so would the former actors.

In addition, "Maimed and deformed" contradicts the headline on the title page that says the plays were "Published according to the True Originall Copies." A meaning of "true" in the late 1500s was "exact, accurate, precise, correct" (OED 4.a.), the opposite of maimed and deformed. If Heminge and Condell were the editors and publisher, this contradiction could hardly have happened.

And as Marcus asks, "How can something be both an original and a copy?" (19). Jonson's deliberate ambiguity throughout alerts the perceptive reader to take nothing at face value.

Both letters claim that the dramatist did not have a chance to prepare the plays for publication before he died. The dedication letter tells the earls that the plays outlived the author who did not have the opportunity "to exequutor his own writings," that is, carry out or put into effect, "produce as an artist" (OED 5). The letter to the reader wishes "that the Author himself had liv'd to have set forth, and overseen his owne writings." But Shakspere died in the same year Jonson published his collected *Workes*, 1616, and according to tradition spent his last half-dozen years in comfortable retirement, plenty of time to prepare the plays for publication as his "collected works" if they were his. (See Appendix D for complete texts of the two letters.)

Ben Jonson not only had the reputation for deliberately ambiguous writing, he had the publishing experience, whereas Heminge and Condell had none. Seven years earlier he had published his *Workes of Benjamin Jonson*, the first English collection of plays (and some poems) in a folio volume. At the time, King James granted him an annual pension of sixty-six pounds for unspecified services. Jonson was involved in every aspect of his thousand-page folio, revising both its contents and presentation. "Jonson was tinkering with his folio text until the very last minute," says Riggs, his biographer (226). With this experience, Jonson was eminently qualified to shape the prefatory matter in the First Folio, and inject as much ambiguity, contradiction and subtle falsehood as he wanted.

His role in the publication of the First Folio gets indirect support from his close connections to the earls of Pembroke and Montgomery, brothers to whom it was dedicated. Pembroke was Jonson's patron, and Jonson dedicated his own *Workes* to him in 1616. As Lord Chamberlain, Pembroke oversaw the plays performed at court and in public theaters and the publication of plays. He supported Jonson's publication of his own "first folio," and he had the position and wealth to authorize and finance the Shakespeare First Folio and commission Jonson to work on it.

Finally, if ambiguous Ben wrote the Heminge-Condell letters, and the evidence seems very persuasive, he was setting up Heminge and Condell to convey indirectly the falsehood that Shakspere of Stratford, the sometime actor, was the author of the Shakespeare plays. He does this in the dedication letter to the earls, where he has Heminge and Condell claim that "we have collected them . . . onely to keepe the memory of so worthy a Friend & Fellow alive as was our SHAKESPEARE, by humble offer of his playes to your most noble patronage." This claim, however, cannot be taken as unequivocally true. There is no reason to accept it as valid testimony, given the deliberate ambiguities, equivocal rhetoric, contradictions and falsehoods that Jonson put into the two letters, beginning with the deception that John Heminge and Henry Condell wrote them. The Heminge-Condell letters are unreliable testimony and cannot be used as valid evidence for Shakspere of Stratford as the author of the thirty-six Shakespeare plays in the First Folio.

Summation

The Stratfordian reading of the First Folio prefatory matter as proof of Shakspere's authorship is literal and uncritical. It ignores abundant evidence of deliberate ambiguity that draws the reader into a maze of contradictions, equivocal language, veiled meanings and spurious falsehoods. Properly understood, the ambiguity and Jonson's role in the First Folio's publication render the prefatory matter invalid as evidence for the author's identity. Nothing in the First Folio provides straightforward biographical information that identifies the author unambiguously as Shakspere of Stratford, as Jonson surely intended. For example, it could have displayed the coat of arms that he and his father went to such trouble and expense to acquire and that would have identified him as the dramatist, but it does not, leaving the authorship of the Shakespeare plays open and undetermined.

The case for a more informed reading of the prefatory matter in the First Folio is made by anti-Stratfordian scholars and by Stratfordians Annabel Patterson (indirectly), Leah Marcus and Gary Taylor, who treat it more as a literary curiosity than evidence that would, if carefully considered, raise reasonable doubt about the identity of Shakespeare. The Folio prefatory matter should be interpreted in light of the prevalence of deliberately ambiguous writing during the Elizabethan and Jacobean periods, when readers were on the alert for ambiguous passages, especially in light of Jonson's reputation for ambiguity. He was not, "lying through his teeth." He was practicing the art of ambiguity in writing about a controversial matter—the identity behind the pseudonym William Shakespeare.

WORKS CITED

Bate, Jonathan. *The Genius of Shakespeare.* Oxford UP, 1998.

Campbell, Oscar James. *The Reader's Encyclopedia of Shakespeare.* New York: Crowell, 1966.

Chambers, E. K. *William Shakespeare: A Study of Facts and Problems.* 2 vols. Oxford UP, 1930.

Dobson, Michael and Stanley Wells. *The Oxford Companion to Shakespeare.* Oxford UP, 2001.

Duncan-Jones, Katherine. *Ungentle Shakespeare.* London, Thomson Learning, 2001.

Empson, William. *Seven Types of Ambiguity.* New York: New Directions, 1947.

Greenblatt, Stephen, et al., editors. *The Norton Shakespeare.* New York: Norton, 1997.

Jonson, Ben. *Bartholomew Fair* in *The Works of Ben Jonson*, vol. 4. 368. Chestnut Hill MA: Adamant, 2001.

___ .*The Workes of Benjamin Jonson.* London: Stansby, 1616.

Kay, Dennis. "Marlowe, *Edward II*, and the Cult of Elizabeth." *Early Modern Literary Studies 3.2* (September 1997).

Lee, Sidney. *A Life of William Shakespeare.* New edition, rewritten and enlarged, 1916. New York: Macmillan, 1924 reprint from the 1916 edition. First edition 1898.

Malone, the late Edmond. *Plays and Poems of William Shakspeare* (sic). Vol. 1. London: 1821. James Boswell the younger completed and edited the 21-volume work.

Marcus, Leah S. *Puzzling Shakespeare: Local Reading and Its Discontents.* University of California Press, 1988.

Nelson, Alan: "Stratford Si! Essex No! (An Open and Shut Case)." *The Tennessee Law Review*, vol. 72 No. 1 (fall 2004).

Oxford English Dictionary. 2nd ed. Oxford UP, 1989.

Parfitt, George. "History and Ambiguity: Jonson's 'A Speech According to Horace.'" *Studies in English Literature.* Vol. 19 No. 1 (winter 1979).

Patterson, Annabel. *Censorship and Interpretation: The Conditions of Writing and Reading in Early Modern England.* University of Wisconsin Press, 1984.

___ . "An Authorship Primer." *The Shakespeare Newsletter* (fall 2006).

Quintilian: *The Orator's Education*, 9-2. Ed. and trans. Donald A. Russell. Cambridge MA: Harvard UP, 2001).

Riggs, David: *Ben Jonson: a Life.* Harvard UP, 1989.

Schoenbaum, S.: *Internal Evidence and Elizabethan Dramatic Authorship*. Evanston IL: Northwestern UP, 1966.

___. *William Shakespeare, a Compact Documentary Life*. Revised edition. Oxford UP, 1987.

___. *Shakespeare's Lives*. New Edition. Oxford UP, 1991.

Shakespeare, William: *Mr. William Shakespeares Comedies, Histoires & Tragedies*. London: Jaggard and Blount, 1623. The Riverside edition supplies a facsimile of the prefatory matter pages that are almost as large as in the folio itself.

Shapiro, James. *Contested Will: Who Wrote Shakespeare?* New York: Simon & Schuster, 2010.

Weis, Rene. *Shakespeare Unbound*. New York: Holt, 2007.

Wells, Stanley, and Gary Taylor: *William Shakespeare, a Textual Companion*. New York: Norton, 1997.

Wells, Stanley: "There's No Doubt It's Will." *Washington Post* March 18, 2007.

Wilson, J. Dover: *The Essential Shakespeare*. London: Cambridge University Press, 1932.

Author's note: For this chapter I drew on two earlier works: my article "Look Not on this Picture': Ambiguity in the Shakespeare First Folio Preface" in *Shakespeare Matters* (summer 2011), and chapter 5 "The Ambiguous Testimony of the First Folio" in my book, *Shakespeare: Who Was He?* (1994). It also includes new material, thanks primarily to Alexander Waugh. The significance of Ben Jonson's ambiguity in the First Folio has been discussed and analyzed in books and articles for two centuries. For more recent treatments, see especially the chapters in *The Man Who Was Never Shakespeare* (2011) by A.J. Pointon, and *Shakespeare's Unorthodox Biography* (2001) by Diana Price.

Chapter 12:
The Stratford Bust: A Monumental Fraud

By Richard F. Whalen

Today's monument to a writer in the Stratford church is one of two defining images of William Shakspere of Stratford-upon-Avon for those who believe he was the author of the Shakespeare plays and poems (the other being the engraved image in the First Folio). The monument is in Holy Trinity Church in the town of his birth and death, and it shows a writer with pen, paper, and, as a writing surface, a cushion of all things. The plaque on it says it's for "Shakspeare." According to the Stratfordian story line, this effigy of a writer is the same effigy in the monument that was erected four centuries ago.

Fig. 1: Today's Stratford monument effigy.

It is not. An analysis of the historical evidence demonstrates that it is not the original, nor does it resemble the original, which depicted a man holding a sack—likely meant to depict a bag of wool or grain, suggesting an agricultural commodity trader—without pen, paper or writing surface. The effigy in today's monument is primarily the result of work by two nineteenth-century Shakespeare Bardolators with civic leaders of Stratford. Their work of repair and alteration provided ample opportunity to change the original man holding a sack into today's writer.

The principal witnesses against the authenticity of today's effigy are a respected antiquarian who made an eyewitness sketch of the man holding a sack in the original monument, the curate of the Stratford church who protested too much that he did not change the effigy when he "refurbished" the monument to "old Billy our Bard," and the two enthusiasts who cited decay of the effigy that they refurbished. Although various records over the centuries mention decay and damage to the effigy requiring repairs and "beautification," today's effigy is alleged to be the original, surviving for four centuries untouched by time or beautification. The historical record does not support that view.

There are two fundamental issues: First, whether the antiquarian, Sir William Dugdale, was accurate when, in 1634, he sketched the effigy in the monument as a dour man with a down-turned moustache clutching a large sack—not a writer with pen and paper as in today's monument; and second, if Dugdale was accurate, how and when the man holding a sack was transformed into a writer. Stratfordian academics either avoid the whole issue or say Dugdale must have been mistaken.

The Dugdale and Hollar images

Fig. 2 (left): Dugdale's sketch of the Stratford monument made in 1634 during his visit to Stratford. Courtesy of Sir William Dugdale, a descendant. Photo courtesy of Gerald Downs. Fig. 3 (right): Hollar's engraving of the monument in Dugdale, published in 1656, 1730 and 1765 editions.

Richard F. Whalen

The earliest and most important witness in the case against the authenticity of today's effigy of a writer is Sir William Dugdale of Warwickshire, author of the mammoth *Antiquities of Warwickshire* (1656). The prolific antiquarian sketched the monument when he visited Stratford on July 4, 1634, within two decades of the death of the Stratford man (Lee 484, 522). His sketch, found in his papers, shows a man with a dour visage holding a large sack of wool or grain. His arms are akimbo, nowhere near a writing position. There is no pen, paper or writing surface. The effigy of the man holding a sack, with a narrow face and down-drooping mustachio, is entirely different from today's monument to a writer with an upturned moustache and goatee. Dugdale's sketch is the first eyewitness description of the original monument, and it shows that he was not looking at the effigy of a writer. Confirmation of Dugdale's accuracy is the engraving based on it that Wenceslaus Hollar made for Dugdale's *Antiquities*. Hollar's engraving of the Stratford monument shows the same image of a man holding a sack (Dugdale 523). The monument to "Shakspeare" in the early 1600s did not depict a writer.

Although Stratfordians insist that Dugdale and Hollar were mistaken, scholars of the two men all agree that both were very experienced and successful and that their work is reliable. Writing about Dugdale's *Antiquities of Warwickshire*, his biographer was "filled with admiration at the general correctness of its details" (Hamper 483). Theodore D. Whitaker, a nineteenth-century antiquarian, referred to Dugdale's "scrupulous accuracy, united with stubborn integrity" (Greenwood's *Problem Restated* 247-8 fn 1). The original *Dictionary of National Biography* (ODNB) called Dugdale "remarkable for general accuracy." An illustrated history of Dugdale and Hollar by Marion Roberts in 2002 refers to Dugdale's "careful observation of details of costume or armor" in his *Antiquities* (15).

Hollar also has a reputation for accuracy. Roberts says that "Hollar's disciplined observation, his willingness to copy and his considerable skill at rendering detail to obtain accurately informative illustrations suited Dugdale's quest" (24). Hollar was "a master of precise and detailed renderings," according to a book published by the Folger Shakespeare Library with an exhibition of his works (Doggett, 9). For another exhibition of his works, the Smithsonian Institution described him as a "dispassionate reporter" with an "exacting eye and skillful hand" and a "prodigious talent for copy work, topography and mapmaking" (January 1995).

Supporting Hollar's reputation is his engraving of Dugdale himself. It shows Dugdale the writer at a desk with notebooks, books, paper, pens and ink. Commenting on this etching, Vladimir Denkstein notes in *Hollar's Works* that "for all the care he took over the scholar's features, Hollar seems to have been even more fascinated by the objects around him" (67). The only object that Hollar depicted along with the effigy in his engraving of the Stratford monument is a sack, nothing that would signify a writer.

The objection might be raised that Dugdale made his sketch in the Stratford church when the light was bad or he was somehow distracted. Dugdale, however, was close enough and the light was good enough that he could transcribe the words of the epitaph under the effigy. That there are mistakes in Dugdale's voluminous work is not in question, but they turn out to be few and not material, or they are mistranscriptions of town records by assistants. Dugdale's sketch stands as primary source evidence.

Confirming the Dugdale-Hollar image of the man holding a sack as the authentic image of the effigy in the original monument is its appearance unchanged a century later in the 1730 edition of Dugdale's *Antiquities*. This second edition was "from a copy corrected by the Author himself," according to the editor, William Thomas. Thomas, also a Warwickshire man, added that he himself had "visited all the churches" (Title page, ix). If during his visit to the Stratford church Thomas had seen the effigy of a writer, it is inconceivable that he would have left the effigy unchanged in his edition of Dugdale.

In his book, Dugdale is suspiciously reticent about the Stratford man. He wrote more than three thousand words on the town of Stratford, but he refers to the monument only very briefly as an afterthought in the last sentence: "One thing more in reference to this ancient town is observable, that it gave birth and sepulture to our late famous poet Will. Shakespere, whose monument I have inserted in my discourse of the church" (523). A half-hearted, belated mention of the Stratford man as the great poet-dramatist, tacked on to the end of a long article. Another sign of Dugdale's peculiar reticence is the title he gave to Hollar's engraving in his book. It does not identify the monument as Shakespeare's. It says simply: "In the North wall of the Chancell is this Monument fixt." The name "Shakspeare" appears only in Dugdale's transcript of the verse epitaph.

The abstruse epitaph

The abstruse eight-line epitaph on the Stratford monument also argues against its having been erected to a writer. The epitaph never mentions poems, plays or the theater. It opens with two lines in Latin referring to Nestor, Socrates, Virgil and Olympus. But Nestor and Socrates were not writers. Virgil was much less important than Ovid for Shakespeare, and Mount Olympus should have been Mount Parnassus, home of the Muses and literature, since the lines are supposed to be for a writer. Olympus was the home of the gods. Only for those not in the know, but expecting to find a monument to Shakespeare in Stratford, would this Latin inscription seem to suggest that this is it.

JVDICIO PYLIVM. GENIO SOCRATEM, ARTE MARONEM,
TERRA TEGIT, POPVLVS MÆRET, OLYMPVS HABET.

STAY PASSENGER, WHY GOEST THOV BY SO FAST,
READ IF THOV CANST, WHOM ENVIOVS DEATH HATH PLAST
WITH IN THIS MONVEMENT SHAKESPEARE: WITH WHOME,
QVICK NATVRE DIDE WHOSE NAME DOTH DECK y^s [THIS] TOMBE,
FAR MORE, THEN COST: SIEH ALL, y^s [THAT] HE HATH WRITT,
LEAVES LIVING ART, BVT PAGE, TO SERVE HIS WITT.

OBIT ANO DO^I 1616
ÆTATIS 53 DIE 23 AP^R

Fig. 4: Inscription on Stratford monument.

The six-line verse tells the viewer to "stay, passenger" and "read if thou canst," a peculiar thing to say—why question the reader's ability to read, or is it questioning the reader's ability to understand what is being read? Given its nature, the latter seems more likely. The last two lines with the words "sieh all [that] he hath writt" have defied explication:

FAR MORE, THEN COST: SIEH ALL Ys [THAT] HE HATH WRITT,
LEAVES LIVING ART, BVT PAGE, TO SERVE HIS WITT.

It seems to suggest a writer, for anyone expecting to find a monument to Shakespeare, but without actually saying that he was, or naming or quoting from anything he wrote. Seemingly baffled by it, Stratfordian commentators usually omit mention of the epitaph or decline to explain it. Rarely, they try to imagine what it must mean. E. K. Chambers offers no explanation in his two-volume *William Shakespeare: a Study of Facts and Problems* (2:182). Nor does S. Schoenbaum in his *Documentary Life* (254). In his chapter on "Shakespeare's Epitaphs" in *Shakespeare's Lives*, Schoenbaum does not mention the epitaph in the Stratford church even though it should be primary source evidence for what contemporaries thought about the man for whom it was written and engraved.

A possible explanation for the monument's cryptic inscription is that it's another example of Ben Jonson's work. There is no record of anyone in Stratford having erected it. We saw in the last chapter that Jonson was a "master of ambiguity," and both the two lines in Latin and the six lines in English beneath them are worthy of his talents. Many phrases and usages in Jonson's poem in the First Folio and in other epitaphs are similar to the monument's inscription (Green, 2001). The First Folio contains the first reference to the monument. Just as Jonson's claims in the First Folio are not to be believed, neither is the cryptic inscription on the monument credible evidence for Shakspere as the author.

Hammond, Langbaine and Rowe

Another visitor to the Stratford church in 1634 also assumed that the monument had been erected to the poet-dramatist. He was a Lieutenant Hammond. In a travel diary, he wrote that in August or September he saw "a neat Monument of the famous English poet, Mr. William Shakespeere; who was born heere" (Chambers 2:242-3). By that time, a decade after publication of the Shakespeare First Folio, people were starting to believe that Shakspere was the poet-dramatist Shakespeare, despite the sack-holder effigy.

Toward the end of the 1600s, the historian and biographer Gerard Langbaine was the first to describe the sack of wool or grain as a cushion: "In the north wall of the chancel is a monument fixed which represents his true effigies, leaning upon a cushion" (Ingleby 2:356). He does not mention pen, paper or writing surface, and his mention of "leaning upon a cushion" suggests that he could not accept that his beloved "Shakespeare" would be shown simply holding a sack. Since his wording is almost identical to Dugdale's title over Hollar's engraving in *Antiquities*, Langbaine's description is no doubt based on the engraving in *Antiquities*.

The validity of the Dugdale-Hollar image drew significant support in Nicholas Rowe's edition of the Shakespeare plays in 1709. For his edition, he wrote the first attempt at a biography of the Stratford man as the poet-dramatist, and he included with it a close copy of the Dugdale-Hollar image. He had sent Thomas Betterton, the leading actor of the day, to Stratford "to gather up what remains he could of a name for which he had so great a veneration" (Rowe in Pope xvi). Betterton looked into the records of the Stratford church and could not have failed to look at the monument. If the effigy had been a writer as in today's monument, not a man holding a sack as by Dugdale-Hollar, Betterton would have alerted Rowe to the discrepancy. He was known for his "integrity, respectability and prudence" (ODNB). Rowe, however, ordered a copy of the Hollar image for his 1709 edition and used it again in his 1714 edition.

First depiction of a writer

The first depiction of a writer in the Stratford monument is George Vertue's engraving in Alexander Pope's 1723-5 edition of the Shakespeare plays. In Vertue's engraving, the effigy, dressed as a commoner, holds pen and paper and is preparing to write on a thin, tasseled cushion, just as in today's monument. He wears an earring, and the face resembles that of the man with an earring in the so-called Chandos portrait. Vertue could have replaced the dour visage of Dugdale-Hollar with a face like that in the First Folio, but he chose to copy the Chandos portrait, probably because he had heard a report that it was painted by "a player who acted for Shakespear" (Schoenbaum *Lives*, 204). At the time, the Chandos was thought by many to be an authentic portrait of the poet-dramatist. Although scholars today question its pedigree and authenticity, it is still one of the most popular of the many different "Shakespeare" portraits.

**Fig. 5: George Vertue's engraving in Alexander Pope's
1725 edition of Shakespeare's works.**

For Pope's edition, Vertue could have used a copy of the engraving in Dugdale's *Antiquities*, or Nicholas Rowe's close copy in his second edition of Shakespeare's works a decade earlier. Pope must have seen it; he used most of Rowe's short biography of the Stratford man as "Shakespeare." Vertue, however, created for Pope the first image of a writer in the Stratford monument. This image of a writer fits with Pope's idolization of Shakespeare. As the decades passed, Vertue's imaginary writer in Pope's edition would become the prototype for illustrations of the effigy in the Stratford monument. A writer should have pen, paper and something to write upon, and so Dugdale's man holding a sack became a writer and his lumpy sack became a thin cushion with decorative tassels. The image could only have been the product of Vertue's imagination. He would not visit Stratford for the first time until fourteen years later.

Pope's edition included another portrait by Vertue, and it is the first image of "Shakespeare" that the reader would see. The frontispiece of the book, it is a large portrait of a man under a banner proclaiming that he is "William Shakespeare." He has a moustache, a short, pointed beard, and the Chandos earring. He wears a large, stiff, elegant, white ruff typical of aristocratic garb. A century later a dismayed James Boaden, who wrote on the merits of the many Shakespeare portraits, would note in passing "Mr. Pope publishing to the world a head of King James, and calling it Shakespeare" (131). Schoenbaum would call it a "monumental lapse" in his *Shakespeare's Lives* (212).

Greene's "repairs" of the monument

Fourteen years after Pope's edition appeared, a new curate was installed in Stratford's Holy Trinity Church. He was Joseph Greene (1712-90), and he would play a major role in the first refurbishing of the Stratford monument in his church. Greene was not a shy and retiring parson. Besides being curate, he was the schoolmaster, a civic booster, a theater buff, a versifier, an antiquarian, "a great scribbler in books," librarian for a wealthy neighbor and an outspoken writer of letters (Fox in Greene, 3-21). He was also partial to "a bottle of old Stingo." Shortly after his arrival in 1737, he created a great stir in town. He eloped with the daughter of Stratford's druggist and former mayor. He would also find Shakspere's will, which he described as "dull and irregular" (59).

When an acting company performed *Othello* in Stratford as a benefit for the "repairing of the Original Monument of the Poet" (57), Greene wrote a 45-line prologue for the performance, which included these lines:

> Hail, happy Stratford! Envied be thy name!
> What City boasts, than thee, a greater fame?
> Here, his first infant-lays great Shakespeare sung
> Here, his last accents faultered on his tongue!
> His Honours yet with future times shall grow,
> Like Avon's streams, enlarging as they flow!
> Be these thy trophies, Bard, these might alone
> Demand thy features on the Mimick* Stone,

His asterisk refers to a note that he is "alluding to the Design in hand" (Greene, 59). He does not explain what design he had in hand or whether it had anything to do with the "features on the Mimick Stone." To mimic is to imitate, including, for example, "expressions of countenance" (OED 1.b. and A.2), as a mime does in performance. But mimic carries connotations of "ridiculous imitation" and contempt (OED v. 2.a.), including ridicule of "inanimate things personified" (OED v.2.c.). It would seem the man holding a sack did not please Greene. Later on, he would refer to "repairing and beautifying the monument" (168).

Greene also wrote the playbill for the performance, and his language is telling. The benefit, he wrote, was for "the curious original monument and bust (that)...is through length of years and other accidents become much impaired and decayed" (Greene 57, 164). He finds the original monument "curious," and this is the first time anyone says on the record that the monument was decayed. It would not be the last.

Fundraising began, but apparently a dispute about the extent of the work to be done delayed the project. Months passed and two years later Greene wrote of "repairing and re-beautifying" the monument. He proposed that the painter John Hall do the work provided "that the monument shall become as like as possible to what it was when first erected" (168-9). This is the first of four times that Greene says that the monument either would not be, or was not, changed. It seems he was worried about being challenged.

Greene had the monument repaired and beautified early in 1749, and within months he was protesting again that he did not change it. A fellow alumnus of Oxford had questioned him about the stone used in the original. Greene replied: "I can assure you that the bust and cushion before it (on which as on a desk this our poet seems preparing to write) is one entire limestone...." He then took care to add that "as nearly as could be, not to add to or diminish what the work consisted of, and appeared to have been when first erected. And really except changing the substance of the architraves from alabaster to marble, nothing has been changed, *nothing* [his emphasis] altered, except the supplying with the original material (saved for that purpose) whatsoever was by accident broken off, reviving the old coloring and renewing the gilding that was lost" (171). The sack, however, has become a cushion to serve as a writing surface.

A decade later, antiquarian James West asked him about an irregularity of features, an "unnatural distance in the face," in the mask (or mold) that Greene had had made. Greene answered that he had made the mask with "Heath the carver" when they took the bust down and laid it on the floor. Greene says the mask "answers exactly to our original bust" and is a "thorough resemblance" to the Droeshout engraving in the First Folio (77).

It might be argued that in this letter of 16 January 1758 (and elsewhere in his correspondence) Greene testifies to the authenticity of the cast that he and Heath made. His testimony, however, is suspect. Dugdale's gloomy man holding a sack in no way resembles the face in the Droeshout portrait in the First Folio. If the mask resembled the Droeshout, it can only be because Greene made it so. Moreover, Greene's recollections decades later of when he had the cast made are inconsistent, and his repeated protests over the years that he changed nothing ring hollow.

The following year, Greene placed a short article in *The Gentleman's Magazine* (June 1759), a very popular periodical. Greene begins: "A Doubt, perhaps not unworthy of notice, has arisen among some whether the old monument Bust of Shakespeare in the Collegiate Church of Stratford upon Avon Warwickshire, had any resemblance of the Bard" (Greene 172-3). He notes that such doubts did not arise until installation of the life-size statue in Westminster, which Pope had helped to commission in 1741. The statue in Westminster is so idealized it's difficult to see why Greene felt impelled to answer doubts about the authenticity of his Stratford monument when compared to it. In his opinion, the face of the statue in Westminster is "venerable and majestic" expressing an intensity of serious thought that the Bard "undoubtedly *sometimes* had" (Greene's emphasis).

He then draws an odd contrast with the Stratford bust. Its thoughtfulness, he says, "seems to arise from a *chearfulness* of thought." The Bard retired "and liv'd chearfully amongst his friends" (172). His disposition was *"chearful"* (Greene's emphases). At another point, he refers to him fondly, even possessively as "old Billy our Bard" (115). His cheerful Shakespeare can only have been the result of his repair and beautification in 1749 of the gloomy effigy that Dugdale saw and sketched for Hollar to engrave.

The cheerfulness of the new effigy did not go unremarked. The eminent painter Thomas Gainsborough called it "a silly, smiling thing" and refused to make a painting of it for David Garrick's Jubilee in Stratford in 1769 (Deelman 68-9). Stratford's town historian, R. B. Wheler, in 1806 said the effigy was indeed somewhat thoughtful "but then it seems to arise from a *cheerfulness of thought*" (his emphasis), and since the Bard's disposition was cheerful the effigy properly depicts him (72-3). His book's engraving from his own drawing shows an effigy that is neither gloomy like Dugdale's nor vacant as today, but with a somewhat wan smile (70, 73).

James Boaden, a London theater buff, said the effigy showed the Bard "in his gayest mood," an expression of "facetiousness... decidedly intended by the sculptor of the bust" (30-1, 34).

"The face indicates cheerfulness, good humor, suavity, benignity, and intelligence," wrote John Britton just two years after 1814, when his agent took the effigy down for four or five days so that a cast could be made (14). Britton, a prominent London antiquarian, had instigated the work. Two pages later, he quotes Washington Irving, who said of the effigy, "I thought I could read in it a clear indication of that cheerful social disposition" (16). In 1825, Abraham Wivell, a London portrait painter, quoted the aforementioned Wheler and Boaden on the effigy's cheerfulness, apparently approvingly (10, 18). And later in the century, Matthew Arnold (1822-88) would begin his 14-line poem, "Shakespeare:"

> Others abide our question. Thou art free.
> We ask and ask: Thou *smilest* and art still,
> Out-topping knowledge. (Emphasis added)

The Dugdale-Hollar effigy was decidedly gloomy, and today's effigy has never been called cheerful or smiling. Mouth agape, expressionless eyes staring into the middle distance, today's effigy has drawn harsh words even from Stratfordian scholars: "A clumsy piece of work. . . . [with] a mechanical and unintellectual expression," said Sidney Lee (522). "Curious and at first sight stupid," said M. H. Spielmann even as he tried valiantly to defend it as authentic (9). Having "a general air of stupid and self-complacent prosperity," said J. Dover Wilson, who concluded that the task was "quite beyond the workman's scope" (5, 6). It's difficult to escape the conclusion that Joseph Greene had his workman create a smiling Bard and that it was changed at least once again to give the world the "stupid" effigy seen in the Stratford monument today.

Twenty-eight years after he published his article, Greene again expressed some concern about representations of the effigy. In a letter to his brother, he said he would send him a small, slightly damaged painting on pasteboard that Hall made of the monument. But first he noted at some length that it was "exceedingly difficult" to make an accurate painting of a carved bust, which "may perhaps in some measure account for the dissimilitude of a painted head as opposed to a carved bust of the same person" (145). It's not clear why Greene would ruminate about the accuracy of the painting, but he seemed quite concerned. All in all, Greene protests too much. A review of his letters gives the distinct impression that he was dissembling about his work on the monument.

A painting resembling today's monument to a writer, with a note on its back that said it was painted by John Hall before he worked on the bust in 1749, came to the attention of Spielmann in 1910 (24). He argued that it proved the original monument held the effigy of a writer. George G. Greenwood, however, noted several discrepancies that cast doubt on the authenticity of the painting and the note on the back. In his book, *The Stratford Bust and the Droeshout Engraving* (1925), he concluded that, "It seems much more probable that Hall should have painted it—if, indeed, he did paint it—*after* rather than *before* he had helped to 'repair and beautify' it" (33, his emphases).

The question arises as to who did the sculpture work for Greene to refurbish the "much impaired and decayed" monument. Hall was a painter. No record says the town hired a sculptor. Not generally recognized is that letter of 1758 to his patron, wherein Greene mentions "Heath the carver." Greene says Heath was with him and Hall when they took the effigy down from the wall. That's all that is known about him. The Shakespeare Centre Library in Stratford has no information on Heath the carver (Bearman email 24 May 2004).

The evidence strongly supports the view that in 1749 Greene engineered changing the effigy from a gloomy man holding a sack to a cheerful writer. Greene the antiquarian and civic booster, Heath the carver and Hall the painter had as models Vertue's engraving of a writer in Pope's edition and, as Greene implicitly acknowledges, the Droeshout engraving in the First Folio. Greene also had two other precedents: Thomas Hanmer's recent edition of Shakespeare (1744) with Gravelot's engraving of a writer in the monument modeled on Vertue's engraving in Pope's edition, and the very popular editions of Shakespeare (1733 and 1740) by Lewis Theobald, which Greene twice expressed interest in buying (56). Theobald described the effigy as having "a cushion spread before him, with a pen in his right hand, and his left resting on a scroll of paper" (13). No evidence puts Theobald or Hanmer in Stratford. Theobald certainly saw Vertue's engraving in Pope, for he was an outspoken critic of Pope's editing of Shakespeare.

Joseph Greene had the motive, the opportunity and the means to create a fraudulent bust of "Shakespeare" in the Stratford monument, although he probably felt he was doing it for the best of reasons—to show his hometown hero as the famous writer and a cheerful one at that. But Greene's cheerful effigy would not survive for posterity. Another refurbisher arrived in the early nineteenth century.

More "repairs" of the monument

In 1814, two men from London must have replaced the cheerful, smiling face with the more serious, stolid visage in today's effigy, along with any other changes they might have made. The evidence is persuasive. They were George Bullock, who "began his career as a sculptor" and later went into business making furniture (Thornton, 6), and John Britton, a prolific London antiquarian and writer who admitted that he idolized the Bard. Britton commissioned Bullock to go to Stratford and take a mold of the effigy so plaster casts could be made (5-6). One of the plaster casts is in Sir John Soane's Museum in London. On the back is inscribed, "Moulded by Geo: Bullock from the original in the church at Stratford, Decr. 1814" (Thornton, 96). Britton was an old friend of Sir John Soane (ix).

The bust at the Soane Museum looks very much like today's effigy of a writer with a cushion. It is not cheerful or smiling, which raises questions about what happened to Joseph Greene's cheerful, smiling effigy that was so widely noticed and how Bullock was able to make a mold from a decayed effigy for a plaster cast that appears to be in such good shape.

The answers to those questions may be found in Britton's account of what happened when Bullock took a mold of the Stratford bust. Although the evidence is indirect, it seems quite likely that Bullock and civic leaders in Stratford created the effigy seen in the church today. Britton supplies the evidence in his 1849 book (6-7, 12).

In his account, Britton describes how the Stratford civic leaders were involved and how long it took Bullock supposedly just to take a mold of the bust:

Mr. Bullock's visit to Stratford [in December 1814] was made under the most favourable auspices. Through the influence of my old friend, Mr. Robt. Bell Wheeler, the historian of Stratford, (a most devoted Shaksperian,) Mr. Bullock readily obtained permission from the Vicar, (the Rev. Dr. Davenport,) and the parochial authorities, to take a mould of the Bust; and many and interesting were the comments of the Artist on that precious memento of the Immortal Bard. He was much alarmed on taking down the "Effigy" to find it to be in a decayed and dangerous state, and declared that it would be risking its destruction to remove it again. (6)

Richard F. Whalen

He then quotes from Bullock's December 1814 letter wherein Bullock indicates that he may have done more than just make a mold of the effigy. It reads in part:

> I had every preparation made, and assisted in erecting a sort of scaffolding, before I was aware of the difficult task I was going to perform. In short, instead of one day's work, I have found four or five; as I mean to mould the whole figure.

Four or five days seem excessive just to take a mold of the bust, and it is hardly credible that Bullock would take a mold of a decayed and crumbling bust and not repair it. He was a sculptor. More likely, he and his associates made some repairs and improved the face, although they would not say so, and then took the mold of their finished product. The plaster cast of it in the Soane Museum shows no sign of decay. Although the reports by Britton and Bullock cannot be taken to prove that Bullock and the Stratford civic leaders changed Gainsborough's "silly smiling thing" to today's stolid, staring figure before making a mold of it, the evidence for such a change fits the historical records of the fate of the Stratford bust over the centuries. This is especially true since Britton two decades later would say nothing about what was done to the bust, if anything, in his long description of renovations to the chancel that he directed in 1836-7.

Over the years, Britton vigorously defended the authenticity of the 1814 bust. Two years after Bullock made casts for him, Britton dismissed various paintings of "Shakespeare" and defended the bust as having "all the force of truth...a family record...raised by the affection and esteem of his relatives...consecrated by time" (12). Thirty-three years later, he would repeat his "firm conviction that the Stratford Effigy was the most authentic and genuine Portrait of the Bard" (6).

Britton the proactive Bardolator, Bullock the sculptor and agent, Wheler the town historian, the Vicar of Holy Trinity Church and the other "parochial authorities" of Stratford had the obvious motivation to make sure the effigy looked like a writer, namely, Shakespeare's importance to England as a national hero and the understandable civic pride and commercial ambitions of the Stratford businessmen. The stakes were high, and the renovation could be rationalized as a well-intentioned desire to ensure that the effigy properly depicted their "Immortal Bard."

Bullock's mold spawned several different casts. Abraham Wivell said that one entrepreneur made three new molds from one of Bullock's casts, a cast of the entire effigy, one "without the hands" and one of the head only. He said that Wheler of Stratford had one of the head and shoulders and that Britton had a sculptor make a half-size head and shoulders bust and had a mold made of that. Bullock's mold, he said, "was afterwards destroyed, and the casts soon became scarce" (17-18 fn), and not incidentally more valuable.

Two decades later, the Shakespearean Club of Stratford wanted to renovate and restore the monument and the chancel. According to Charlotte Carmichael Stopes, a Stratfordian, who examined records in Stratford, the club noted that it had "long beheld with regret, the disfigurement of the Bust and Monument of Shakespeare, and the neglected condition of the interior of the Chancel which contains that monument and his grave" (121). The club resolved to raise funds "for the Renovation and Restoration of Shakespeare's Monument and Bust, and of the chancel." The king and the town each contributed fifty pounds. Britton, who led the fundraising in London, was determined to renovate the whole chancel, especially the roof, and he hired an architect to make drawings. It's possible that work was also done, as the club intended, to renovate and restore the reportedly disfigured bust that Bullock had worked on. Britton, however, makes no mention of it in his long description of the 1836-7 work on the entire chancel (28-32). Stopes refers to seemingly extensive records in Stratford (118, 120, 122).

Further research may clarify how much work, if any, was done on the monument following the initiative of the Shakespearean Club of Stratford.

In 1973, thieves reportedly looking for manuscripts in the monument removed and damaged the three-hundred-pound bust. Levi Fox, director of the Shakespeare Birthplace Trust, is quoted as referring to a "restoration," but records, if any, about how much restoration and repair work was done have not been made public. Shortly afterward, Schoenbaum examined the effigy and said only that it had been slightly damaged (*Documentary* 256 fn 2). And John Michell wrote in his 1996 book on the authorship question that "modern experts have closely examined the bust which is made of one block of stone, and find no evidence that it has ever been substantially repaired" (97). That report would seem to preclude any repairs to the effigy in 1973.

Today, the effigy appears to be in good shape. No one has noted any signs of decay, damage, or disfigurement. It's very unlikely that today's unblemished effigy is the one erected almost four centuries ago that suffered periodic decay, according to sculptors and others who took it down for repairs. It must date to more recent times, probably to Bullock's work in 1814, and perhaps again in 1836-7, when more modern materials would have been used, although there is no record of repairs to the effigy when work was done on the chancel.

Stratfordians reject Dugdale-Hollar effigy

The few Stratfordian academics who have recognized the problem conclude that Dugdale was mistaken and dismiss his sketch as inaccurate. The first was probably the antiquarian John Britton. In 1816, he summarily dismissed Hollar's engraving in Dugdale's book as "tasteless and inaccurate" (13). In 1853, J. O. Halliwell-Phillipps called it "evidently too inaccurate to be of any authority" (in Greenwood's *Problem Restated* 247 fn 1).

Charlotte Stopes was the first to analyze the evidence in detail. A dogged researcher, she published dozens of articles and several books on Stratford and its famous son. In an article in 1904, she argued that Hollar's engraving was an accurate depiction of the dramatist but when he was old and near death, "a tired creator of poems, exhausted from lack of sleep... weary of the bustling London life" (114). The effigy, she said, was later fundamentally changed to depict a writer in his prime, "necessarily something very different from the original" (113, 120). To her dismay, she found herself caught between the Baconians, who had seized upon the Hollar effigy as evidence against the Stratford man, and her Stratfordian colleagues, who said she failed to understand that Dugdale and Hollar were mistaken and that the original monument depicted a writer (115). Ten years later, she would also be the first scholar to see the Dugdale sketch among his notes at the Dugdale ancestral home, where the sketch remains. In her 1914 book, she reprinted her 1904 article, reported on additional research in Stratford and said Dugdale's sketch and others in his diary show that "he was very careful as to significant details" (123).

The Stratfordian biographer Sidney Lee rejected Dugdale as inaccurate and Stopes as ineffectual. He saw Dugdale's drawing for Hollar among Dugdale's papers and wrote that "it differs in many details, owing to inaccurate draughtsman-ship, from the present condition of the monument" (496-7). Like others who call Dugdale inaccurate, he does not explain how today's monument could possibly be the standard of accuracy for the original monument that Dugdale saw and sketched in 1634. And he summarily dismisses Stopes: "There is very little force in her argument to the effect that Dugdale's sketch faithfully represents the original form of the monument, which was subsequently refashioned out of all knowledge" (522-3).

M. H. Spielmann, who wrote widely on art, was the only Stratfordian to address the authenticity problem head-on. In a slim, vitriolic volume published in 1924, he argued at length and with examples that both Dugdale and Hollar were unreliable and mistaken. He maintained that both made errors in other works and that Dugdale was "victimized both by his helpers and his artists" (16). He claims that Hollar's workshop, not Hollar himself, may have produced the engraving of the Stratford monument, and he notes errors in three other Hollar engravings (18-9). The engraving of an equestrian statue shows the horse with the wrong forefoot raised. In Dugdale's *Antiquities,* the Clopton monument in the Stratford church has several details reversed or omitted and the Carew monument engraving reverses the positions of the husband and wife. Stopes and Lee, however, had noted that the Carew sketch was not among Dugdale's papers, indicating that someone else drew it. None of the errors, however, changed what the subject looked like—a horse and the prone figures of wife and husband. Dugdale's sketch of a man holding a sack and Hollar's engraving from the sketch, stands as primary source evidence of what the effigy looked like in 1634.

Spielmann found a determined critic in George Greenwood, barrister, member of Parliament and an anti-Stratfordian. In his 1908 book, he had agreed with Stopes that Dugdale-Hollar represented the original effigy, but not that it represented "Shakespeare" as weary, old and near death. He commended her attempt to explain the discrepancy, but concluded, "It seems absolutely certain that this Stratford bust...is in reality not the original bust at all," adding that "the whole thing is changed" (*Problem Restated* 245-6).

Returning to the issue in 1925 with *The Stratford Bust and the Droeshout Engraving*, Greenwood noted the "vast amount of discussion and disputation" about the bust. He argued again that Dugdale's drawing, which he had now seen, "is absolutely unlike the effigy as it exists today" (10). He critiqued Spielmann at length. For example, he corrects Spielmann's claim that the 12 pounds 10 shillings paid to a local painter, John Hall, was too little for a major renovation of the effigy, and he suggests that the moustache on today's bust did not come into fashion until decades after Shakspere died (15-17, 21-2). Point by point, he rebuts Spielmann, who remained silent.

In 1930, E. K. Chambers alleged in an uncharacteristic overstatement that other illustrations in Dugdale's book also "completely misrepresent the originals," probably based on his reading of Spielmann. Citing Stopes and Greenwood, he concludes, "But the whole theory seems to me a mare's nest....It seems to me incredible that the monument should ever have resembled Dugdale's engraving" (2:185).

The Reader's Encyclopedia of Shakespeare (1966), edited by Oscar J. Campbell of Columbia University, recognizes the problem but sidesteps it. Its short entry "monument" includes illustrations of the Hollar engraving of the effigy of the man holding a sack in Dugdale's book and next to it today's effigy in the Stratford church. The Dugdale-Hollar effigy, the entry says, "differs radically from the monument as we know it. Either Dugdale's illustration is inaccurate or the monument has been overhauled since the seventeenth-century. There was a certain amount of alteration and repair which took place in 1748 [*sic*], but the extent and nature of these alterations have never been determined."

One of the very few Stratfordian scholars to publish the Hollar engraving was Schoenbaum. He allowed in 1975 that the engraving of the man holding a sack is "perplexing rather than helpful" and hard to reconcile with today's monument. But he concluded rather lamely that it is "authentic enough" *(Documentary Life,* 255). In his compact 1987 edition, he added a provocative, parenthetical possibility to his text: "(A comparison of the engraving [by Hollar] with the drawing [by Dugdale]–perhaps still extant–on which it is based might be revealing)" (313). The drawing, of course, was extant. Schoenbaum had overlooked the fact that Stopes, Greenwood and Lee had seen it and reported on it, although it had not yet been published. Chambers also mentioned its survival (2:184). More recently, independent scholar Gerald Downs took the first photograph of it. If Schoenbaum had seen Dugdale's drawing or Downs' photograph of it, perhaps he might have changed his opinion from "authentic enough" to "not authentic enough" as a representation of Shakespeare the poet-dramatist.

Most Stratfordian academics simply ignore the problem. They include the editors of the various collected works of Shakespeare and biographers such as Stephen Greenblatt (2004), Michael Wood (2003), Park Honan (1998) and Stanley Wells (1995). *The Oxford Companion to Shakespeare* (2001), edited by Michael Dobson and Stanley Wells, has entries for "Dugdale" and "monument," but does not even mention Dugdale's sketch or Hollar's engraving of the man holding a sack.

A notable exception to the position of Stratfordian academics is Brian Vickers, research fellow at the Institute of English Studies, University of London, and the author or editor of a dozen books on Shakespeare's works. A Stratfordian himself, he wrote in *The Times Literary Supplement* (18-25 August 2006) that the "well-documented records of recurrent decay and the need for extensive repair work to the monument in 1749, 1814, 1835 and 1861 make it impossible that the present bust is the same one that was in place in the 1620s." He and Peter Beal, a colleague at the institute, are the first Stratfordians to acknowledge that the effigy of a writer in today's monument is not the original, although without acknowledging the implications.

Vickers also expressed support for Richard Kennedy's theory (2005) that the original monument in the Dugdale sketch was to William's father, John Shakspere. Vickers writes as follows:

> The subject looks elderly with a gaunt face and a drooping moustache; the columns enclosing the monument are crowned with leopards' heads; and he is shown arms akimbo, resting his hands on a woolsack. As Richard Kennedy has argued, the woolsack suggests the original monument was erected to John Shakespeare (sic) (1530-1601), father of the poet who had been 'a considerable dealer in wool.' Shakespeare senior had also held various civic offices between 1557 and 1571 . . . before falling on hard times. Following his son's acquisition of a coat of arms in 1596, he regained his place on the borough council. Kennedy also showed that the leopards' heads were far from 'irrelevant', as E.K. Chambers judged, since they are found in Stratford's coat of arms, another detail making this monument more suitable for the father than for the son. (TLS, 2006)

Finally, despite the inscription's claim that "Shakspeare" is buried in the monument, he is not. It is too small for anyone to be buried in it. Tradition has it that he is buried beneath a slab in front of the monument that does not bear his name, but, rather, the following four lines of doggerel verse:

GOOD FREND FOR JESUS SAKE FORBEARE,
TO DIGG THE DUST ENCLOSED HERE
BLESTE BE THE MAN WHO SPARES THESE STONES
AND CURST BE HE THAT MOVES MY BONES.

Stratfordian academics would have us think that Shakespeare himself wrote these lines. In fact, we do not know for sure to this day whether Mr. Shakspere was buried beneath this slab or elsewhere on the church grounds, but it seems certain that if he had been the poet-playwright he would not have been buried in a grave that didn't even bear his name.

Summation

The cumulative power of the evidence is persuasive. Dugdale's eyewitness sketch of the man holding a sack in the original monument for "Shakspeare," Hollar's engraving of it through two editions of Dugdale's book, Rowe's copy of it almost a century later for his Shakespeare edition, Vertue's "Shakespeare" as both a nobleman in a ruff and an imaginary writer in the monument for Pope's edition, Greene's suspect refurbishing that resulted in a cheerful, smiling effigy, reports over the centuries of the monument's decay in contrast to the good condition of the effigy today, Bullock's work on the effigy for four or five days ostensibly just to make a mold of it, and the failure of Stratfordians to mount a credible defense of today's monument as the original—all lead to the conclusion that today's Stratford monument is not the original and that William Shakspere of Stratford was not a writer, much less the great poet-dramatist William Shakespeare.

WORKS CITED

Boaden, James. *An Inquiry into the Authenticity...Portraits of Shakspere.* London: Triphook, 1824.

Britton, John. *Essays on the Merits...Shakspere...his Monument.* London: 1849. Includes his 1816 "Remarks on the Monumental Bust of Shakspere."

Chambers, E. K. *William Shakespeare: A Study of Facts and Problems.* 2 vols. Oxford: Clarendon, 1930.

Craig, Harden. Ed. *The Complete Works of Shakespeare.* Chicago: Scott, Foresman, 1951.

Dobson, Michael. *The Making of the National Poet.* Oxford: Clarendon Press, 1992.

Doggett, Rachel, Julie L. Biggs and Carol Brobeck. *Impressions of Wenceslaus Hollar.* Washington DC: Folger, 1966.

Denkstein, Vladimir. *Hollar Drawings.* New York, Abaris, 1977.

Dugdale, William. *The Antiquities of Warwickshire, Illustrated.* London: Thomas Warren, 1656. Second edition "printed from a copy corrected by the author himself and with the original copper plates." Ed. William Thomas. London: Osborn and Longman, 1730.

Greene, the Rev. Joseph. *Correspondence.* Ed. Levi Fox. London: Her Majesty's Stationery Office, 1965.

Green, Nina. *Edward de Vere Newsletter,* No. 9, February 2001

Greenwood, Sir George G. *The Shakespeare Problem Restated.* London: John Lane/the Bodley Head, 1908.

___. *Is There a Shakespeare Problem?* London: Lane, 1916.

___. *The Stratford Bust and the Droeshout Engraving.* London: Cecil Palmer, 1925.

Hamper, William. Ed. *The Life, Diary and Correspondence of Sir William Dugdale.* London: Harding, Lepard, 1827.

Hanmer, Thomas. *The Works of Shakespear.* Oxford: At the Theater, 1744.

Honan, Park. *Shakespeare: A Life.* Oxford: OUP, 1998.

Ingleby, C. M. et al. *The Shakspere Allusion Book.* 2 vols, London: Chatto & Windus, 1909.

Kennedy, Richard. *The Woolpack Man:* (http://webpages.charter.net/stairway/woolpackman.htm, 2005).

Langbaine, Gerard. In *The Shakspere Allusion Book*. Eds. C. M. Ingleby and John Munro, 2 vols 1909.

Lee, Sidney. *A Life of William Shakespeare*. New York: Macmillan, 1898. New edition 1924.

Michell, John. *Who Wrote Shakespeare?* London: Thames and Hudson, 1996.

National Portrait Gallery, London. See Piper.

Piper, David. Ed. *O Sweet Mr. Shakespeare I'll Have His Picture: The Changing Image of Shakespeare's Person 1600-1800*. [London]: National Portrait Gallery, 1964. Introduction [and commentary] by Piper, an art historian who became the gallery's director in 1964.

Pope, Alexander. *The Works of Shakespear*. London: Tonson, 1723-5.

Roberts, Marion. *Dugdale and Hollar: History Illustrated*. Newark NJ: University of Delaware Press, 2002.

Schoenbaum, S. *William Shakespeare: A Documentary Life*. New York: Oxford UP, 1975.

___ *William Shakespeare: A Compact Documentary Life*. New York: Oxford UP, 1977.

___ *Shakespeare's Lives*. New edition. Oxford: Clarendon, 1991.

Spielmann, M. H. *The Title Page of the First Folio of Shakespeare's Plays: A Comparative Study of the Droeshout Portrait and the Stratford Monument*. London: Oxford UP, 1924.

Stopes, Charlotte Carmichael. "The True Story of the Stratford Bust" in *Murray's Monthly Review* (April 1904), reprinted in her *Shakespeare's Environment* with a "P.S." adding much new information. London: Bell, 1914.

Theobald, Lewis. *The Works of Shakespeare*. London: Bettesworth and Hitch, 1733.

Thornton, Peter, and Helen Dorey. *A Miscellany of Objects from Sir John Soane's Museum*. [London]: Laurence King Publishing, 1992.

Vertue, George. *Note Books*. Oxford: Walpole Society, 1930. Vols 18, 20, 22, 24, 26 and 30 are the *Vertue Note Books*, vols 1-6. In an undated note ca. 1737, Vertue said he got a cast of the face, but this was a decade after his engraving of the writer with the Chandos face for Pope (1:73). Vickers, Brian. "The Face of the Bard?" *The Times Literary Supplement*. London: 18-25 August 2006.

Walpole, Horace. *Anecdotes of Painting in England*. Strawberry Hill: Farmer, 1762-3. New edition by Ralph N. Wornum. London: Chatto and Windus, 1876.

Wheler, Robert Bell. *History and Antiquities of Stratford-Upon-Avon*. Stratford-Upon-Avon, J. Ward, [1806].

Wilson, J. Dover. *The Essential Shakespeare*. Cambridge UP, 1935.

Wivell, Abraham. *An Historical Account of the Monumental Bust of William Shakspeare*. London: By the author, 1827. Includes much from Wheler [1806] unattributed.

Wood, Michael. *Shakespeare*. New York: Basic, 2003.

(This article updates and revises an article first published in *The Oxfordian 8* (2005), which expanded on the author's paper "The Stratford Bust, a Monumental Fraud," delivered at the eighth annual Edward de Vere Studies Conference, April 2004, at Concordia University, Portland, Oregon.)

Part II:

Exposing an Industry in Denial: The Coalition responds

to

The Shakespeare Birthplace Trust's "60 Minutes with Shakespeare"

Exposing an Industry in Denial: The Coalition responds to the Shakespeare Birthplace Trust's *'60 Minutes with Shakespeare'*

Organized and Edited by John M. Shahan, Chairman
The Shakespeare Authorship Coalition
Claremont, California, U.S.A.

Date of first publication (pdf download at the Coalition website): November 21, 2011

Organizations endorsing the rebuttals

Organizations neutral about the identity of the author:

Shakespeare Authorship Coalition (doubtaboutwill.org)

Shakespeare Authorship Research Center (www.authorshipstudies.org)

Shakespeare Authorship Roundtable (www.shakespeareauthorship.org/)

Shakespearean Authorship Trust

(www.shakespeareanauthorshiptrust.org.uk/)

Organizations favoring specific candidates:

Francis Bacon Research Trust (http://www.fbrt.org.uk/)

De Vere Society of Great Britain (http://www.deveresociety.co.uk/)

International Marlowe-Shakespeare Society

(http://www.marloweshakespeare.org/)

Mary Sidney Society (www.MarySidneySociety.org)

Neue Shake-speare Gesellschaft (Germany) (http://shake-speare-today.de/)

Shakespeare Fellowship (U.S.) (http://www.shakespearefellowship.org/)

Shakespeare Oxford Society (U.S.) (http://www.shakespeare-oxford.com/)

Websites favoring other prominent candidates:

Sir Henry Neville as Shakespeare (http://www.henryneville.com/)

William Stanley, 6th Earl of Derby (http://www.rahul.net/raithel/Derby/)

CONTENTS

List of "60 Minute" questions, and SBT and Doubter responders   **155**

I. Introduction and challenge to the Shakespeare Birthplace Trust   **157**

II. Rebuttals to Birthplace Trust's "60 Minutes with Shakespeare"   **158**

Five key questions the SBT did not ask and cannot answer   **218**

    1. What is the basis of claims that there is "no room for doubt" about who wrote the works?

    2. What do the six signatures often attributed to the Stratford man tell us about his writing?

    3. What do scientific studies of genius say about the sort of person who wrote the works?

    4. What about the many people who knew the Stratford man, and knew about the author Shakespeare, but never connected the two?

    5. Why did the author say he didn't expect, and didn't want, his name to be remembered?

Six common myths about the works and authorship doubters   **222**

    1. As long as we have the plays and poems, the identity of the author does not matter.

    2. Doubters argue that a man from humble origins could not become a great writer.

    3. Doubters who support aristocratic candidates are motivated by snobbery.

    4. The phenomenon of doubt about Shakespeare's identity is a psychological aberration.

    5. The authorship controversy is just another conspiracy theory, no different from others.

    6. Doubters don't use the same methods as other scholars in attributing authorship.

Letter from SAC Chairman to SBT Chairman Stanley Wells   **223**

List of "60 Minute" Questions (abbreviated), and SBT and Doubter Responders

"60 Minute" Question – SBT Responder	Doubter Responder
Q1: Books in Stratford? – Sylvia Morris	Virginia Renner
Q2: Attend grammar school? – Lois Potter	Robin Fox
Q3: Reflect university education? – Carol Rutter	Robin Fox
Q4: Reflect Strat grammar school? – Perry Mills	Robin Fox
Q5: Family's illiteracy relevant? – Elizabeth Woledge	John Shahan
Q6: Richard Field connection? – Nick Walton	William Rubinstein
Q7: Links to Stratford in plays? – David Kathman	Michael Egan
Q8: Works reflect life in Stratford? – Michael Wood	Ramon Jiménez
Q9: When first appear on the scene? – Andrew Dickson	Frank Davis
Q10: Seen as author of specific works? – Charles Whitworth	Pat Buckridge
Q11: Other writers dispraise his work? – Emma Smith	Pat Buckridge
Q12: Plays in own name in his lifetime? – Laurie Maguire	Felicia Londré
Q13: Name used to sell plays he wrote? – Andrew Murphy	John Hamill
Q14: If fraud, what about the evidence? – AJ Leon	Richard Joyrich, John Shahan
Q15: Shakespeare famous in life-time? – Tiffany Stern	John Hamill
Q16: Concerned about gaps in record? – Andrew Hadfield	Mike Rubbo
Q17: Where did he get his money? – Boika Sokolova	William Rubinstein
Q18: What was his social status? – René Weis	Richard Joyrich
Q19: Author never left England? – Margaret Drabble	Mark Anderson
Q20: Actor names in printed texts? – Harriet Walter	Peter Dawkins
Q21: Know theatrical practice? – Tina Packer	Bonner Cutting
Q22: Shakespeare's personality? – Simon Callow	John Plummer
Q23: Conspiracy theory reaction? – Janet Suzman	Kristin Linklater
Q24: Extent of collaboration? – Gary Taylor	Ramon Jiménez, Robin Williams
Q25: Collaboration in minor ways? – Eric Rasmussen	Ramon Jiménez, Robin Williams
Q26: Collaboration common? – Peter Kirwan	Ramon Jiménez, Robin Williams
Q27: Multiple author methods? – MacDonald Jackson	Ramon Jiménez, Robin Williams
Q28: His verse vs. Marlowe's? – Antony Sher	Ros Barber, Ph.D.
Q29: Any aristocratic patron? – Michael Holroyd	Tony Pointon
Q30: Aristocracy and theatre? – Farah Karim-Cooper	Michael Cecil

Exposing an Industry in Denial

"60 Minute" Question – SBT Responder	Doubter Responder
Q31: How presented in fiction? – Paul Franssen	John Shahan, Kurt Kreiler
Q32: Other writers in question? – Martin Wiggins	Robert Detobel
Q33: Authority of First Folio? – David Bevington	Richard Whalen
Q34: Prefatory poems in Folio? – Ewan Fernie	Richard Whalen
Q35: Does his will shed light? – Mairi Macdonald	Bonner Cutting
Q36: Absence of books in will? – Diana Owen	Bonner Cutting
Q37: Commemorated at death? – Peter Kyle	Richard Whalen
Q38: Does bust tell profession? – Paul Edmondson	Peter Dawkins
Q39: What learn from Jonson? – Greg Doran	Peter Dawkins
Q40: When questions started? – Lena Cowen Orlin	Frank Davis, Peter Dawkins
Q41: Reasons for questioning? – Stuart Hampton-Reeves	Robin Williams
Q42: Psychological impulse? – Anouchka Grose	The Magnificent Seven
Q43: James Wilmot's role? – Stanley Wells	Daniel L Wright
Q44: Delia Bacon's role? – Graham Holderness	Carole Sue Lipman
Q45: Francis Bacon plausible? – Alan Stewart	Peter Dawkins
Q46: Agree with Mark Twain? – Jay Halio	Keir Cutler
Q47: Why did Freud doubt? – Paul Prescott	Jan Scheffer, Richard Waugaman
Q48: Why did Henry James doubt? – Adrian Poole	Ren Draya
Q49: Oxford's theatre connection? – Michael Dobson	Earl Showerman
Q50: Factual objections to Oxford? – Alan Nelson	Oxfordian societies: DVS, NSG, SF, SOS
Q51: Factual objections to Marlowe? -- Charles Nicholl	Peter Farey
Q52: Who else suggested as author? – Matt Kubus	Robin Williams
Q53: Brunel, Concordia programs? – Victoria Buckley	Daniel L. Wright
Q54: Mainstream scholar attitude? – Peter Holland	Tony Pointon
Q55: Typical conspiracy theory? – Kate McLuskie	John Shahan, James Broderick
Q56: Why Conspiracy Theories? – Simon Palfrey	The Editor
Q57: What Stephen Fry thinks? – Stephen Fry	A few disappointed admirers
Q58: The Indian perspective? – K.S. Vijay Elanqova	James W. Brooks
Q59: Why Emmerich doubts? – Roland Emmerich	Roland Emmerich
Q60: Reputation being stolen? – Dan Snow	Alex McNeil, Tom Regnier
Q61: Links to royalty of his day? – HRH Prince Charles	Shakespeare Authorship Doubters

I. Introduction

On September 1, 2011, the Shakespeare Birthplace Trust (SBT) in Stratford-upon-Avon announced "a campaign to debunk the 'conspiracy theories' surrounding the authorship of Shakespeare's works" prior to the release of Roland Emmerich's film, *Anonymous*, scheduled for October 28. The campaign featured an audio website, "60 Minutes with Shakespeare," with 60 actors, writers and scholars, each addressing one of 60 questions in 60 seconds each.

The purpose of the site was not to inform but, rather, to create the illusion that there is a consensus about the identity of the author William Shakespeare and dupe the public into ignoring the issue. If the SBT had genuinely wanted to inform people, they would have posted the full text. Instead, most people will likely read it for the first time in this book, along with our rebuttals.

The SBT people are very homogeneous. Twenty-five (42%) hold academic positions in English literature or Shakespeare studies. Twenty (33%) are board members or employees of the SBT or the Shakespeare Institute. At least four SBT trustees are not listed as such in their 60 Minutes profiles—Margaret Drabble, Life Trustee; Carol Rutter, University of Warwick Trustee to the SBT; René Weis, University of London Trustee to the SBT; and Michael Wood, Life Trustee.

Another ten are actors and/or theater professionals. There is no historian except SBT Life Trustee Michael Wood; no social or behavioral scientist; no expert in creativity or genius. Oh yes, and there is film director Roland Emmerich, who made the feature film *Anonymous* about the issue. Despite this exception, it is the response of a single industry.

The Shakespeare Authorship Coalition (SAC) quickly began a collaborative effort to write rebuttals to all of the "60 Minutes." This report, "Exposing an Industry in Denial" ("Exposing") presents the rebuttals that resulted from this effort. The full version of *Exposing* is available at the SAC website at DoubtAboutWill.org/exposing. The version shown here omits doubter rebuttals to the answers given by SBT people to questions 28, 45, 49, 50, 51 and 57 because they deal with specific alternative candidates. Supporters of those candidates were given an opportunity to respond in *Exposing*, but we want to keep the focus of this book entirely on the evidence relating to Mr. Shakspere.

In the following pages we give our rebuttals to the remaining 55 questions asked and answered by the SBT responders. Given the diversity of our coalition, with a dozen major authorship organizations and thirty-seven rebutters, we had a remarkable degree of unity. Not everyone agrees with each rebuttal, but that is to be expected. Orthodox scholars, all of whom agree that the Stratford man was the author, differ greatly on specific details.

Birthplace Trust questions and replies

We are not impressed with the SBT replies to its questions. If the purpose was to present incontrovertible evidence that Shakspere was the author, they failed. For anyone familiar with the evidence, their replies reveal ignorance of important facts—perhaps a result of having suppressed dissenting views, isolating themselves. We can only speculate, but the problem of Stratfordian ignorance is real, and should be clear from many of our rebuttals.

Ignorance of relevant historical facts is not the only problem. There are examples of generalizing from single observations. How many people today would take seriously a survey based on a sample of one? The SBT generalizes from individuals selected to be mouthpieces. They point out isolated examples, suggesting that they are representative. For people who claim to be scholars, while doubters are not, they don't act like scholars.

The SBT makes extensive use of *ad hominem* attacks. If the evidence were as strong as they say, there would be no need for this. There is an old adage among lawyers that says: "If the facts are on your side, you argue the facts; if the law is on your side, you argue the law; and if neither is on your side, attack your opponent." Judging from how much the SBT attacks doubters they must not have much else going for them.

In addition to our rebuttals, we ask and answer "Five key questions that the SBT did not ask and cannot answer," and we address "Eight myths about the Works, doubters and Will Shakspere." It is only fair that we should get to ask and answer a few questions, too.

Challenge to the Shakespeare Birthplace Trust

We have written a definitive statement of our position—the *Declaration of Reasonable Doubt About the Identity of William Shakespeare*, issued in 2007, and now (April 2013) signed by over 2,600 people—more than 400 with doctoral degrees, and 444 current or former college/ university faculty members. If we did it, English professors should be able to write a statement of their position and have people sign it. We challenge them to do so.

We hereby request that the Shakespeare Birthplace Trust write a definitive statement of the reasons why it claims there is no doubt about the identity of the author of the plays and poems of Shakespeare and post it along with the names of those who have signed it. With all of the questions that have been raised, the issue calls for a definitive treatment.

Shakespeare vs. Shakspere

There is a consistent difference between the spelling of the name "Shakspere," or close variants, on all eight church records relating to the Stratford man, from baptism to death, and the spelling of the name "Shakespeare" (or "Shake-speare"), with minor exceptions, on the works. So it appears these are two different names, implying two different persons.

Note that SBT people always use "Shakespeare" for both the author (whoever he was) and the Stratford man. They pretend there is no difference between the name of the author and of Shakspere. Until early last century it was common for orthodox scholars to spell the name as it appears on his baptismal record, on his monument, and in his will. But then they abandoned the original spelling, because it suggests there were two different men.

Regardless of whether the names are the same, some convention is required to distinguish them. The convention we use is that "Shakespeare" always refers to the author and "Shakspere" always refers to the Stratford man. Whether the two are one and the same is what the debate is about.

Most authorship doubters think the name "Shakespeare" was a pseudonym that the real author used to conceal his identity. Some also believe that Mr. Shakspere, evidently an actor and theater entrepreneur in London, was a front for the real author, making it easy later to perpetuate the myth that he had been the author all along. Be aware of these differences when reading the answers of the SBT responders, who make no distinctions.

II. Rebuttals to "60 Minutes with Shakespeare"
(http://60-minutes.bloggingshakespeare.com/conference/)

Question 1: How would Shakespeare have had access to books growing up in Stratford-upon-Avon?

Well, religious books like the prayer book and Bible would have been kept at the church he attended every week, and at Stratford's grammar school he would have been taught from books including William Lilly's *Latin Grammar* and Ovid's *Metamorphoses.*

Some people owned their own books. The vicar who baptised Shakespeare left a Latin-English dictionary specially for the use of the school children. The curate in a neighbouring village left one hundred and sixty-eight books on subjects including stories and hobbies as well as religion, and a man from Anne Hathaway's village, Shottery, owned law books.

Even in the unlikely setting of the isolated Cumbrian village of Troutbeck is a yeoman's farmhouse still containing books dating from Shakespeare's lifetime. Nobody knows how they got there, but it's thought they came from local markets, so books were probably also bought and sold at Stratford's fairs and markets.

Books were a source of entertainment and instruction not just for the rich.

—Sylvia Morris, independent Shakespeare researcher, formerly Head of Shakespeare Centre Library and Archive.

Doubter Response

The issue is not what books might have been in Stratford-upon-Avon, but whether contemporaneous evidence documents Shakspere's aptitude for reading and writing in English and foreign languages, and the wide-ranging knowledge found in the author's works. After forty years as a librarian, I am acquainted with many of the sources used in this author's published works and have helped researchers to use rare and modern editions of them, or even to expand that list. It is a phenomenally long bibliography.

The author must have spent significant time reading and learning in his early life to have written with the profound understanding demonstrated in these works. Scholars have searched in vain for documents, not only from those first 28 "lost years," but also through 1616, for traces of Mr. Shakspere's writing and reading. There are no letters by him; documents concerning him are about taxes, business transactions and his will. Yet his works employ sources written in Latin, Greek, French, Spanish, and Italian not yet translated into English at the time. This man evidently relished words. He must have had access to books at some university, or at private libraries, to have gained knowledge of classical literature, history, philosophy, law, astronomy, mathematics, court protocol in France and Italy, as well as in England, and his familiarity with aristocratic pastimes.

From the years he traveled between London and Stratford, presumably writing poetry and plays, there should be definitive evidence. Other English authors of the period have left paper trails. Neither the idea of "genius," nor speculation about talk in some tavern, dispels my reasonable doubts about the orthodox biography of this man from Stratford.

—Virginia J. Renner, retired head of the Reader Services Department, Huntington Library; signer of the Declaration of Reasonable Doubt with ten former colleagues.

Question 2: Did Shakespeare attend the King Edward VI Grammar School in Stratford-upon-Avon?

The school's records for that period haven't survived, but he must have been there. His father was an alderman and he could have had a free education and the plays show that he knew the basic text books. For instance, in *Much Ado About Nothing*, Benedick has the rather odd line—"What, interjections? Well, then, some be of laughing, as Ha ha he he". That comes from the section on interjections in William Lily's grammar book, which every teacher in the country was supposed to use. Students also had to memorise a lot of proverbs and short sayings. So Leontes in *The Winter's Tale* tells his son, "We must be neat." His son is seven, and he would have just begun learning very short Latin phrases like "Mundus esto", which means "Be neat". In *The Merry Wives of Windsor* a schoolboy named William is asked Questions about grammar. He doesn't do very well, but his mother is pleased anyway.

—Lois Potter, former Ned B. Allen Professor of English at the University of Delaware.

Doubter Response

It's impossible to know now whether he attended the "King's New School" in Stratford, or how long he was actually there if he did. All of the records are lost. He probably did attend for a time—at least long enough to learn to read; but judging from his six extant signatures (if they are all his), he didn't stay long enough to develop good writing skills. At the end of his life, his detailed will, drawn up by law clerks, gives no hint of a writer. This is consistent with the strange absence of manuscripts, or even a letter, in his hand.

As for references to William Lily's *Latin Grammar* in the works, that hardly narrows down the field of possible authors. The law required that this work be used by beginners, and every child who got an education studied the same grammar school curriculum, including members of the upper nobility, and even the royal family of whose education we have detailed records. The main difference is that aristocrats had the best tutors, and lots of special attention. Such advantages were unavailable to others, although they could get a good education. Marlowe did well enough in grammar school that he won a scholarship to Cambridge. Why did Shakspere not win a scholarship? Why was his alleged talent not recognized?

As an example of an alternative explanation of the references to Lily's *A Short Introduction of Grammar*: William Lily (or Lyly) was the grandfather of the novelist and playwright John Lyly who was the 17th Earl of Oxford's secretary, collaborator and steward. John Lyly, Anthony Munday and others in Oxford's retinue, were all grammar-school boys. Oxford himself was the patron of a grammar school in Earls Colne, which he oversaw. The Lyly references hardly point only to Shakspere and the Stratford Grammar School. (See *The Oxfordian* 11: 113-136.)

—Robin Fox, Ph.D., D.Sc., University Professor of Social Theory, and Research Professor of Anthropology (founder of the Department of Anthropology in 1967), Rutgers University; Former Director of Research, H. F. Guggenheim Foundation; Former Senior Overseas Scholar, St. John's College, Cambridge; Member of the National Academy of Sciences.

Question 3: Is there anything in the *Works* which require their author to have been educated at a university?

Certainly not. In the early 1590s there was a clutch of university-educated playwrights who were hopping mad that a new generation of writers, equipped with only their grammar school training, reading Ovid, Virgil and Cicero, were supplying the players with brilliant scripts for the stage. Shakespeare was one of these smart grammar-school lads. Ben Jonson was another.

And Dekker, Heywood, Webster. None of the big books that informed Shakespeare's mind and writing was even on the university syllabus: Holinshed's *Chronicles*, Plutarch's *Lives*, Montaigne's *Essays*, Ovid's *Metamorphoses*.

What students on the university arts course studied was Latin, Greek, rhetoric, and overwhelmingly logic, for careers in the church, civil service, Inns of Court. You can see in Shakespeare what kind of men the university fashioned: tedious logic-choppers like Polonius, dubious schoolmasters like Lucentio in the *Shrew*, and caviar-to-the-general playwrights like Hamlet in "The Mousetrap". If you want to know what kind of playwright Shakespeare was, have a look at Peter Quince in *A Midsummer Night's Dream*.

—Carol Rutter, Birthplace Trust Representative Trustee from the University of Warwick, Professor of Shakespeare and Performance Studies at the University of Warwick and a National Teaching Fellow.

Doubter Response

The works may not "require" that the author received a university education, but they clearly suggest that he spent some time at Cambridge or at least had connections there. Yes, he mocked pedants, but clearly respected university men like Hamlet and Horatio. *Titus Andronicus*, *2 Henry IV* and *Timon of Athens* all contain specific, identifiable college jargon—clearly the strange idiomatic language unique to Cambridge University. Frederick Boas, remarking on *Timon of Athens* in his *Shakespeare and the Universities*, wrote that "The misanthropist talks as if he had graduated on the banks of the Cam."

Love's Labor's Lost features an extended reference to a real debate that was conducted by university dons mostly at St. John's College, Cambridge. Holofernes rebukes Don Armado for his pronunciation of English in some detail. His argument accurately reflects the terms of the erudite "pronunciation debate" among Sir Thomas Smith, Sir John Speke, William Cecil (Lord Burghley), Arthur Golding and others. (*The Oxfordian* 12: 56:64.) It's difficult to imagine how the Stratford man could have learned of this debate without any connection to Cambridge.

Also suggesting a Cambridge connection, a book published by Cambridge University authorities in 1595, entitled *Polimanteia*, and written by William Clerke, a reputable Cambridge scholar, specifically lists "Shakespeare" as an alumnus of the University.

—Robin Fox, Ph.D., D.Sc.

Question 4: Do the plays reflect the education the boys in the Stratford grammar school received?

Of course! Lessons at the "Kynges New Scole" provided all the Latin (and "less Greek") he needed to know. He was not just taught to read Latin but to write and speak it. A popular exercise was *ethopoeia*, or Impersonation—where the student was expected to express himself in the style and voice of someone else, often a woman such as Ariadne or Hecuba; a useful skill for the trainee playwright, no doubt.

And Shakespeare's men habitually remember Ovid's *Metamorphoses* and *Heroides*, two central texts on the Elizabethan set-book list, along with the standard textbook Lyly's Latin Grammar.

Perhaps the pupils did not always show the "consistent application" demanded by us teachers. Witness the scene in *Merry Wives* when young Will (*nota bene!*) is instructed in basic vocabulary by the Welsh pedagogue and windbag Sir Hugh Evans—or should that be Thomas Jenkins, Master from 1575–1579?

—Perry Mills, Assistant Headmaster and Director of Specialism at King Edward VI Grammar School, Stratford-upon-Avon

Doubter Response

As we've already pointed out, there was nothing unique about "the education the boys in the Stratford grammar school received," such that the works point only to that school. In fact, we don't know for sure what was taught there, and just assume the curriculum was the same as at other grammar schools. If Mills' examples come from other schools, why assume that the author Shakespeare, whoever he was, must have attended the Stratford grammar school, and not some other grammar school, such as the one where Mills found his examples? It could have been any grammar school, or anyone tutored in the grammar school curriculum.

The scene in *Merry Wives* where Hugh Evans instructs young Will in basic vocabulary could easily have been written by someone tutored in the lesson, and who was familiar with grammar school boys and teachers. The humor of the scene comes as much from Evans' Welsh accent as from the Latin. Stratford schoolmaster Thomas Jenkins was an Oxford-educated born Londoner, and could not have been a model for Evans. There is, however, another likely model for Hugh Evans: The theater troupe known as Oxford's Men included a well-known Welshman named Henry Evans, who trained boy players.

And since the boy is called "Will," and was not good in basic Latin, he could be seen as a reference to a certain newcomer from Stratford, trying to make it big in the London theater world. The scene is included for laughs, and has nothing to do with the plot. Was "Will" the author's depiction of his own front man, and his academic prowess?

—Robin Fox, Ph.D., D.Sc.

Question 5: Are charges of illiteracy against members of Shakespeare's family relevant to his own identification as a writer?

Literacy—the ability to read and write—is nothing more than a function of education; it tells us nothing about the person's intelligence, imagination or creativity. [Being illiterate] tells us only that no one taught that person to make or recognize a symbolic mark to represent a word. Shakespeare's father and mother may not have been able to sign their names, but they were perfectly intelligent individuals, John handling local affairs and Mary being the executor of her father's will. It is probable that both parents could read, although they were not skilled in pen craft. Reading and writing were taught as separate skills in Renaissance England, not linked as they are for us today.

But literate or not, Shakespeare's parents were perfectly capable of producing and raising a son who became one of the most gifted writers ever—writing is far more than pen craft alone, and literacy is no determinant of intelligence or creativity. Many of us can write, though few of us have yet written anything approaching Shakespeare's brilliance. Incidentally, there are surviving signatures of Shakespeare's daughter and granddaughter; by that time pen craft was a far more universally taught skill.

—Elizabeth Woledge, Outreach and Informal Learning Development Manager at The Shakespeare Birthplace Trust.

Doubter Response

We agree with Elizabeth Woledge that being illiterate tells us nothing about a person's "intelligence," but that's not the question. The question is not about "intelligence," but rather about whether growing up in an illiterate family is relevant to identification as a "writer." The answer is yes, of course it is relevant. Is it more likely that a great writer will come from an illiterate family, or from a highly literate one? As we mention under Key Question 3 in Appendix A, one of the characteristics that typifies literary geniuses is having "enriched home environments during childhood." This is an established fact.

Doubters make no claim that a man from humble origins cannot become a great writer. As stated in our Declaration, "Scholars know nothing about how [the author] acquired the breadth and depth of knowledge found in the works. This is not to say that a commoner, even in the rigid, hierarchical social structure of Elizabethan England, could not have managed to do it somehow; but how could it have happened without leaving a single trace?" That is the issue: it would have been a remarkable achievement, and it should have been much commented upon at the time, leaving a trail of evidence. It is one thing to claim it "could have happened," but quite another to find evidence of it, and still another to assert that there is no room to doubt that it did happen.

There is also the matter of particularity. Samuel Clemens (Mark Twain) rose from humble origins to become a great writer, but he wouldn't have written the works of Shakespeare. That's how the controversy began: with a perceived disconnect between "the sublimity of the subject and the mundane inconsequence of the documentary record" for the supposed author, as Sam Schoenbaum put it. Or, as Ralph Waldo Emerson said, "Other admirable men had led lives in some sort of keeping with their thought, but this man in wide contrast."

We agree that there's no reason to think Mr. Shakspere's genetic inheritance from his parents would have precluded him from become an outstanding writer, given the right circumstances. Certainly his parents' lack of writing ability doesn't mean this. Where we disagree is in the critical importance of environment to the development of creative genius—especially artistic-literary-poetic genius (see Appendix A, Question 3). There is no evidence that Shakspere grew up in an environment conducive to literary genius.

—John M. Shahan, Chairman and CEO, Shakespeare Authorship Coalition

Question 6: Did any of Shakespeare's boyhood contemporaries achieve intellectual and professional distinction?

One of Shakespeare's boyhood contemporaries, called Richard Field, who grew up on Bridge Street just a stone's throw away from Henley Street, achieved intellectual and professional distinction as a prominent London publisher. Richard oversaw the printing of the first full edition of Edmund Spencer's *The Faerie Queene*, and in 1598 he published an edition of Sir Philip

Sidney's *Arcadia*. He also published works such as *Orlando Furioso* and *Pandosto*, which served as primary sources for Shakespeare's *Much Ado About Nothing* and *The Winter's Tale*, respectively.

Shakespeare himself chose Richard's shop in Blackfriars as the printing house for his first two printed works, *Venus and Adonis* and *The Rape of Lucrece*. By the early 1590s, Richard was beginning to make a name for himself in London. Having served an apprenticeship to the esteemed French printer Thomas Vautrollier, Richard acquired a reputation for printing sophisticated books, including language instruction manuals for English speakers trying to learn French.

—Nick Walton, Executive Secretary to The International Shakespeare Association, and Shakespeare Courses Development Manager at The Shakespeare Birthplace Trust.

Doubter Response

Whether the Stratford man's boyhood contemporaries achieved intellectual or professional distinction has no bearing on whether he wrote the works of Shakespeare. This depends entirely on independent evidence. Adolf Hitler and philosopher Ludwig Wittgenstein were in the same elementary school class in Linz, Austria; this does not mean that Wittgenstein (who was Jewish, and taught at Cambridge) is likely to have been a Nazi, or that Hitler is likely to have been a philosopher. It is difficult to see the point of this question, except to show that Stratford residents weren't all semi-literate yokels, and it was not anomalous for the author Shakespeare to have been born there.

Richard Field was indeed a prominent publisher in London, but his prominence today consists in having published Shakespeare's first two poems. It is not hard to place this fact in the context of someone else having written Shakespeare's works—if Shakspere was "fronting" for the real author, he may have suggested using Field as his publisher. Or, if the real author had already settled on Field, but needed a front man, Field may have suggested his fellow townsman, the actor.

There is no documentary evidence for Walton's claim that "Shakespeare himself chose [Field's print shop]." Field published none of Shakespeare's quartos, had no role in the First Folio, and wasn't mentioned in Shakspere's will. Isn't it strange that Shakspere didn't remember the man, right in his own town, who published the poems that first made him famous, launching his career?

Claims that Shakespeare used the books in Field's office as the basis for his plays are sheer supposition, and highly implausible. Field was running a business, not a library.

—William D. Rubinstein, Professor of History, University of Wales, Aberystwyth

Question 7: Are there any clear links to be made between Shakespeare's plays and the area around Stratford-upon-Avon?

Shakespeare wrote his plays primarily for a London audience, but they still contain plenty of signs that the author came from the area around Stratford-upon-Avon. For one thing, they're peppered with dialect words from Warwickshire and the West Midlands, such as "wappered", meaning tired, and "geck", meaning fool. But there are also many specific references to people and places from the area around Stratford, as in *Henry the Fourth Part Two*, where Silence calls Falstaff "Goodman Puff of Barson", referring to a Warwickshire village. The induction to *The Taming of the Shrew* is full of such allusions, including Barton-on-the-Heath, where Shakespeare's aunt and uncle lived, and "Marian Hacket, the fat alewife of Wincot", referring to a village four miles from Stratford where a real Hacket family lived in the 1590s. These references are consistent with the frequent rural imagery in the plays, reflecting Shakespeare's lifelong fondness for the area where he grew up.

—David Kathman, independent scholar and co-founder of the Shakespeare Authorship web page.

Doubter Response

David Kathman is wrong: the plays are not "peppered" with Warwickshire dialect words. In point of fact, Warwickshire and West Midlands references and dialect words form a distinct minority among the places and people Shakespeare refers to and in the speech forms he uses. The overwhelming majority of settings are royal courts, castles, noble houses and associated forests and parkland, primarily in England, France and Italy. There are more references to St. Albans in Hertfordshire than to the Stratford area. The same could be said of many parts of England. Stratford is way down on the list.

Despite the fact that in 1900 Appleton Morgan was surprised to find not a single Warwickshire word in *Venus and Adonis*, the view that Shakspere was Shakespeare continues to be reinforced by false claims of dialect words typical of Warwickshire. This apparently goes back to C.T. Onions, who in 1911 mistakenly claimed to have identified 24 Warwickshire words in the plays.

"Mobled," for example (referring to Priam's distraught queen in *Hamlet*), which Onions said was a Warwickshire word meaning "muffed," is actually a Herefordshire term for "disarrayed." "Ballow" and "batler" were misreadings, while other instances he cited turned out not to be specific to Warwickshire at all. The archaic "tarre," found in *King John*, meaning "to urge on," was used in both London and Warwickshire. Tellingly, Onions' list was not included in the 1986 revised edition of his book.

In 1938, Fripp argued that the First Folio's "kisse" and "sonne" were unique Warwickshire spellings; in fact, these forms were found throughout Elizabethan England. Similarly "Cotsall," incorrectly identified as a local version of "Cotswold," was in fact a Staffordshire word, "Codsall," still locally pronounced "Cotsall."

Kokeritz acknowledged in 1953 that the accent implicit in Shakespeare's works is inconsistent with Warwickshire. Brook confirmed this when he observed that the playwright's colloquialisms mainly reflected usages in the southwest and London.

Yorkshire, East Anglia, Scotland and Ireland also contributed substantially to Shakespeare's vocabulary. The modern linguist David Crystal notes that "original pronunciation" performances of *Romeo and Juliet* and *Troilus and Cressida* at The Globe bear no traces of the Warwickshire accent. As A.J. Pointon remarks, "Of all the regions of Britain, Warwickshire…had the least influence on Shakespeare's language."

Despite this evidence, the error persists. *The Oxford Companion to Shakespeare* notes:

> It is somewhat strange that Shakespeare did not…exploit his Warwickshire accent, since he was happy enough to represent, in phonetic spelling, the non-standard English of French and Welsh speakers, and the national dialects of Scotland and Ireland.

Kathman is also wrong about "Wincot," a farm near Stratford, not a village. It had no "alehouse"—no place for "Marian Hacket, the fat alewife of Wincot" to live. Sly likely refers to the village of Wilnecote, still pronounced "Wincot," 30 miles from Stratford. It had five ale-houses and more Hacketts than anywhere else in the region.

Furthermore, what about the main character in that scene, Christopher Sly? He says that he is "by education a Cardmaker, by transmutation a Beare-heard, and now by present profession a Tinker." Cards were used for combing wool; bear-herds looked after the bears used for public displays; and tinkers included itinerant performers. What an unlikely series of occupations! Yet we know of someone whose father (John), dealt in wool, and who apparently later worked for a man who ran a bear-baiting arena (Philip Henslowe), and who became an actor—one William Shakspere. Could it be that Christopher Sly represents the Stratford man? Why would Shakspere portray himself as a drunken tinker who woke up one day to find himself treated as someone he wasn't?

References

G.L. Brook, *The Language of Shakespeare* (Andre Deutsch 1976)

David Crystal, *Pronouncing Shakespeare* (CUP 2005)

Dobson, Michael and Stanley Wells, *Oxford Companion to Shakespeare* (OUP 2000)

E.I. Fripp, *Shakespeare Man and Artist* (OUP 1938)

H. Kokeritz, *Shakespeare's Pronunciation* (Yale UP 1953)

J. Appleton Morgan, *A Study of the Warwickshire Dialect* (Shakespeare Press 1900)

C.T. Onions, *A Shakespeare Glossary* (OUP1911 rev. ed. Eagleson 1986)

A.J. Pointon, *The Man Who Was Never Shakespeare* (Parapress 2011)

Induction to *Taming of the Shrew*

—Michael Egan, Ph.D., Editor, *The Oxfordian* and *The Shakespeare-Oxford Newsletter*; author, *The Tragedy of Richard II, Part One: A Newly Authenticated Play by William Shakespeare with an Introduction and Variorum Notes*, Winner, 2006 Adele Mellen Award for Distinguished Contribution to Scholarship.

Question 8: Do Shakespeare's *Works* reflect aspects of life in Stratford-upon-Avon during his time?

In the end the Shakespeare Authorship Question all boils down to a simple matter of judging historical sources. To deny Shakespeare's authorship is to deny the primary sources, above all his will.

But the plays themselves also tell us about their author. They show that he was a grammar-school boy from the Stratford area. They have local dialect words, and spellings; they show specialist knowledge of wool dealing and gloving, the two trades his father did in Stratford. (Think of Feste's joke in *Twelfth Night* about chevril, the soft kidskin used in glove making). The plays show an intimate knowledge of people and places around Stratford, like the Hackets of Wilmcote (his mother's village) in *Taming of the Shrew*, or real life Cotswold wool-men like George Vizer and Clement Perkes in *Henry IV*.

So you can see from the plays themselves that the author came from the Stratford region, as all Shakespeare's contemporaries of course knew. And they knew it because it was true.

—Michael Wood, Birthplace Trust Life Trustee, broadcaster, writer and historian, and author of *In Search of Shakespeare*.

Doubter Response

As "primary sources" go, the Stratford man's will is actually the one document that's most damaging to claims that he was the author of the Shakespeare canon. It contains no reference to any Shakespeare play or poem, nor to writing, nor writers, of any kind. Nor does it contain any reference to books or bookshelves, papers, manuscripts, letters, or any intellectual property—things any professional writer would mention in his will.

The plays do not reveal "a grammar-school boy from the Stratford area." They show us that he was a highly educated, well-read, well-travelled intellectual, familiar with the latest thinking in the fields of astronomy, philosophy and medicine, and with the political issues of the time. He was also competent in Greek and Latin, and fluent in French and Italian. In other words, a Renaissance man, not a "grammar-school boy."

The most striking "specialist knowledge" in the plays is not of wool dealing and gloving, but of the sea and seamanship, ancient and modern warfare, and the law. Nothing shows that Shakspere had any knowledge of these subjects, nor any opportunity to acquire it. As for "intimate knowledge of people and places," the town of Windsor is mentioned two dozen times in four different plays. Maybe "Shakespeare" was a Berkshire boy. And let's not forget that the town of Stratford-upon-Avon itself is never mentioned.

There is not the slightest bit of evidence that Shakespeare's contemporaries "knew he came from Stratford." They did not know it, of course, because it wasn't true. No one, during his lifetime, connected Mr. Shakspere of Stratford with the Shakespeare canon.

—Ramon Jiménez, author of two books about the Roman Republic, plus numerous authorship-related articles in *The Oxfordian* and the *Shakespeare-Oxford Newsletter*.

Question 9: When did Shakespeare first appear on the literary scene?

The earliest surviving reference to Shakespeare as a writer comes from one of his rivals, playwright Robert Greene. In a pamphlet from 1592, called Greene's *Groatsworth of Wit*, Greene sneers at a rival author who is "in his own conceit the only Shakes-scene in a country". Although Greene doesn't deign to name Shakespeare directly, "Shake-scene" is quite obviously a pun on his name.

The interesting thing, I think, is that Greene's *Groatsworth of Wit* appears to be the remnant of some long-lost literary feud—Greene goes on, without, it has to be said, much evidence, to accuse Shakespeare of plagiarism.

Did Shakespeare borrow from Greene's work? Well, perhaps—but, more likely, Greene was simply annoyed that a young "upstart" from the sticks was writing plays every bit as good as his.

In any case, it's because of Greene that we can be confident that Shakespeare was on the scene from the early 1590s, and he was doing well enough to have acquired some bitter literary enemies.

—Andrew Dickson, Guardian theatre editor, author of *The Rough Guide to Shakespeare*, and contributor to *The New Cambridge Companion to Shakespeare.*.

Doubter Response

Although orthodox Shakespeare scholars now generally accept the identification of the "upstart crow" in *Groatsworth* with Shakespeare of Stratford, both orthodox and non-orthodox scholars have questioned this identification. Among the alternatives proposed are actors Edward Alleyn, Will Kemp and Ben Jonson. Also, there has been much discussion of whether *Groatsworth* was, in fact, a forgery by Henry Chettle, the publisher who claimed that he found *Groatsworth* with Greene's papers after he died.

Seldom mentioned is that the source of the identification of the "upstart crow" with William Shakespeare in *Groatsworth* is in the second of three parts of the pamphlet. But if we accept the identification of the crow with Stratford's Mr. Shakspere in the second part of *Groatsworth*, what do the first and third parts tell us? In Part One we find a "gentleman" whose character must also be a representative of the "upstart crow;" and in Part Three an "Aesope ant" also representing the "crow." This gives us a clearer picture of the "upstart crow." The portrait is one of a miserly, plagiarizing pretender—hardly a flattering picture of the person thought to have been the young Shakespeare.

Another piece of the puzzle is Henry Chettle's response published in a work called *Kind-Heart's Dream*, responding to "one or two" writers "offensively taken" by *Groatsworth*. These are presumed to be Christopher Marlowe, accused of atheism, and Thomas Nashe. The latter, upset that he was accused of writing *Groatsworth*, wrote a scathing complaint in an epistle attached to his *Pierce Pennilesse* with charges of forgery. Chettle apologized to one writer (Nashe) but not the other (Marlowe), saying he did not know either. Modern Shakespeare biographers, in a transparent effort to enhance Shakespeare's standing, continue to claim that the apology was to Shakespeare when the text clearly does not have that implication. Noted Shakespeare scholar Prof. Lukas Erne correctly points that out:

"The cumulative effect of the evidence against Shakespeare [as recipient of the Chettle apology] is such that it partakes of mythology, rather than biography, to keep drawing inferences about Shakespeare's early years in London from Chettle's apology."

References

Erne, Lukas. "Biography and Mythology: Rereading Chettle's Alleged Apology to Shakespeare." *English Studies*, No. 5, pp. 430-440 (1998)

—Frank Davis, M.D., Past President, Shakespeare Oxford Society.

Question 10: Do writers of Shakespeare's time identify him as an author of specific works?

There are many references to Shakespeare as the author of specific works. For example, in 1598 Francis Meres lists a dozen plays by name, attributing them to Shakespeare, and praising the "mellifluous and honey-tongued" poet for his *Venus and Adonis, Lucrece*, and sonnets. In the same year the poet Richard Barnfield praises Shakespeare for those same narrative poems. At around the same time, John Weever, in a sonnet addressed to Shakespeare, mentions the poems and both "Romeo" and "Richard"; and the scholar Gabriel Harvey cites "Shakespeare's *Venus and Adonis...Lucrece*, and his tragedy of *Hamlet, Prince of Denmark*". But the earliest specific allusion occurs in a 1592 pamphlet by the writer Robert Greene, who warns fellow dramatists about the "upstart crow" who "with his tiger's heart wrapped in a player's hide" imagines himself "the only Shake-scene in a country". The parody of a line from Act I of *Henry VI, Part 3*, and the pun on Shakespeare's name, linking him to the theatre, make the attribution unmistakable.

—Charles Whitworth, Professor of English at the University of Montpellier, founding director of the IRCL (a CNRS-affiliated centre for Early Modern research).

Doubter Response

No one disputes that there are contemporary references to a writer named "Shakespeare." Not one of them, however, establishes his real identity, just as a reference to "Mark Twain" does not prove the existence of a real person by that name, and a reference to the Oscar-winning writer "Robert Rich" (one of the blacklisted screenwriter Dalton Trumbo's fronts in the 1950s) does not prove that "Rich" was the true writer.

It is not at all surprising that Meres, Barnfield and Harvey refer to "Shakespeare" as the author of the two long narrative poems, *Venus and Adonis* and *The Rape of Lucrece* (1593, 1594), the first works to appear with the name "William Shakespeare" on them. It proves nothing, except that they accepted the two printed attributions at face value. Interestingly, however, the name was under the dedications, and not on the title pages.

Six of the plays were then published anonymously, until Meres, in 1598, said that this "Shakespeare" was also a great playwright, naming twelve of his plays. Nobody up to then had associated the name Shakespeare with anything but the two narrative poems. The poems were very popular; why publish six of his plays without his name on them? The way these events unfolded is strange, and suggests people did not know the author.

So while some contemporary writers name "Shakespeare," whoever he was, as the author of specific works they do not specifically identify him as the Stratford man. Orthodox scholars simply assume that every reference to "Shakespeare" is a reference to Mr. Shakspere, but not a single reference during his lifetime specifically identifies him as such. The name could just as easily have been a pseudonym, and/or the name of a front man. Not until the *First Folio* was published in 1623, seven years after he died, did anyone claim that the Stratford man had been the author, and even then by no means unambiguously.

Charles Whitworth claims that Robert Greene's parody of a line from Act I of *Henry VI, Part 3*, plus the "Shake-scene" pun on the actor's name "make the attribution unmistakable." It may well be a reference to Shakspere, but this doesn't necessarily mean he wrote the play. To the contrary, Greene suggests the actor wasn't an author, but was pretending to be.

—Patrick Buckridge, Ph.D., Professor of English, Griffith University, Australia.

Question 11: Do Writers of Shakespeare's time dispraise his work?

Do contemporary writers dispraise Shakespeare? Not much. There's that early reference, perhaps by Robert Greene, describing Shakespeare as "an upstart Crow beautified with our feathers," but by quoting Shakespeare this becomes an anxious compliment to the newcomer's ability.

From some writers he gets faint praise: fellow playwright John Webster, writing in 1612, admires "the right happy and copious industry of Master Shakespeare, Master Dekker, and Master Heywood".

The most explicit criticism of Shakespeare comes from his rival Ben Jonson. Jonson is scornful of Shakespeare's error in giving Bohemia a seacoast in *The Winter's Tale*, and laughs at a line from *Julius Caesar*—that remark seems to have stung, since the text of the play doesn't include the offending line. He wishes, in contrast to the claim that Shakespeare never blotted a line, that he "had blotted a thousand". But in the end, Jonson notes that there "was ever more in him to be praised than to be pardoned".

—Emma Smith, Fellow and Tutor in English at Hertford College, Oxford.

Doubter Response

We agree that writers of Shakespeare's time rarely "dispraise" his work, but so what? The truth is that most of his fellow writers seldom said anything at all about his works. He appears to have been a relatively shadowy figure throughout his career as a writer. He wrote no commendatory verse to anyone, and nobody wrote any to him, until 1623. In an age known for its lavish dedications, nobody dedicated anything to Shakespeare.

There's little doubt that "Shake-scene" and the "upstart Crow" refer to Mr. Shakspere. Stratfordians usually assume Greene was attacking him for plagiarizing his own works and works of other "University Wits." But as Andrew Dickson mentions in his reply to Question 9, there is little evidence for this. Further, in this context "beautified with our feathers" (in the absence of any evidence of plagiarism) is more likely to mean that he was profiting from their plays, which he bought and brokered to the acting companies, probably taking a commission for himself that writers and actors considered excessive.

Emma Smith mentions Ben Jonson's criticisms, but omits that they are all posthumous and impersonal, as though Jonson never actually knew this writer named Shakespeare. Jonson first mentions Shakespeare in his own collected works in 1616, the same year Shakspere died. Jonson lists him as an actor in two of his own plays, from years earlier. That's all; nothing on the passing of his friend and fellow writer, William Shakespeare. It's not as if Jonson didn't have time to reflect on the matter; Shakspere died in April, and Jonson's works were published over six months later.

Jonson was a great master of ambiguity, as several of his biographers have pointed out. Some say his praise of Shakespeare in the First Folio subtly suggests two different men. Then there's Jonson's epigram entitled "On Poet-Ape," often thought to be Shakspere, also from 1616:

> He takes up all, makes each man's wit his own.
> And told of this, he slights it. Tut, such crimes
> The sluggish, gaping auditor devours;
> He marks not whose 'twas first, and after-times
> May judge it to be his as well as ours.

As indeed they have! Jonson was right.

—Patrick Buckridge, Ph.D.

Question 12: Were Shakespeare's plays published under his own name in his lifetime?

There's nothing unusual about an Elizabethan play reaching print without its author's name. The important name on the title page was the theatre company's, so Shakespeare's plays were first published in editions that identified the playing company but did not name the author. *Titus Andronicus* in 1594, *Richard II*, *Richard III*, and *Romeo and Juliet* in 1597—none of them said they were written by Shakespeare. But then a change crept in. When *Richard II* and *Richard III* were reprinted in 1598, their title pages advertised Shakespeare as the author. This change was not consistent. In Shakespeare's lifetime there were 39 editions of 16 of his plays: only 66 per cent of these editions say "Written by William Shakespeare," or "Newly corrected," or "Newly augmented by William Shakespeare".

—Laurie Maguire, Professor of English at Oxford University, and a Tutorial fellow of Magdalen College.

Doubter Response

Plays were published under the name "Shakespeare" while Mr. Shakspere was alive, but none under "Shakspere," the family name of the Stratford man. In any other field that would be taken as evidence that Shakspere did not write the plays, not that he did. Nor was the name on the works ever "William Shakespeare of Stratford-upon-Avon."

Anonymous publication was the norm for authors of plays throughout the entire period. Roughly 80% of plays were published anonymously; it could be risky to publish things. There were no freedoms of speech, assembly, religion, or of the press, as we know them. Writers and theater companies could, and occasionally did, run afoul of the authorities. It should not be surprising that some writers might have published under pseudonyms.

What's odd about Shakespeare is the on-off pattern of publication of works over time: first the two narrative poems, *Venus and Adonis* and *The Rape of Lucrece* (1593, 1594), both very popular; then nothing in this popular poet's name until 1598, when twelve of his plays are named at once, and he is thus identified as a playwright for the first time; then a flood of quartos with his name on them over a span of six years; then just a few new quartos until 1609; then none until *Othello* in 1622, and eighteen plays for the first time in 1623 in the First Folio!

Why were Shakespeare's first six plays published anonymously if he was a popular poet? Maguire claims that "the important name on the title page was the theater company's," but *Venus and Adonis* and *The Rape of Lucrece* did well under the name "Shakespeare," and not that of a theater company. Why didn't the author, the printers, and the theatre company seek to exploit his name? Why the sudden change in 1598, which amounts to a sort of "coming out" for Shakespeare? Why the drop-off in new quartos after six years? And why hold back many valuable plays until 1623, seven years after Shakspere died? Doubters find these questions difficult to answer if the Stratford man was the author.

—Felicia Hardison Londré, Curators' Professor of Theatre, University of Missouri-Kansas City.

Question 13: Was Shakespeare's name used as a selling point on works we now don't believe he wrote?

Yes, it was. When plays first began to be published, writers were rarely credited on the title pages. For example, the first play of Shakespeare's that survives—the 1594 edition of *Titus Andronicus*—makes no mention of him as author.

However, his name did very quickly become a selling point, so the title page of the 1608 edition of *King Lear*, for instance, features Shakespeare's name at the very top of the page, in large, bold letters.

Some publishers do seem to have tried to cash in on Shakespeare's growing popularity by issuing texts under his name that he hadn't actually written. In 1599, a collection of poems titled *The Passionate Pilgrime* was identified as being by Shakespeare when, in fact, only a small number of the poems were his.

Likewise, various plays, such as *The London Prodigal* (in 1605) and *A Yorkshire Tragedy* (in 1608), appeared with Shakespeare's name on the title pages, though evidence suggests that he hadn't actually written them.

—Andrew Murphy, Professor of English, University of St Andrews, and author of *Shakespeare in Print: A History and Chronology of Shakespeare Publishing.*

Doubter Response

We welcome Professor Murphy's admission that a name on a play didn't necessarily mean that a person with that name wrote the play. We suspect that Shakspere wrote none of the plays with the name "Shakespeare" on them—a name similar to, but not necessarily the same as his own. If Shakspere did write and publish plays with his name on them, why did this otherwise litigious man never sue over a fraudulent publication? The fact that it never happened suggests a hidden author who could not come forward.

As for Murphy's statement that "the name did very quickly become a selling point," it depends on what "quickly" means. We cannot agree that the name on the 1608 quarto of *King Lear*, eighteen years into, and near the end of his alleged career, was "quickly." But more to the point, perhaps Murphy can address the questions we've raised in our response to Question 12, and especially why the name wasn't a selling point until 1598.

—John Hamill, Independent Scholar, Past President, Shakespeare Oxford Society; author of numerous authorship related articles in *The Oxfordian*, and *The Shakespeare Oxford Newsletter.*

Question 14: If Shakespeare is a fraud, what about the historical evidence?

What I cannot understand is the way people who say he didn't write the *Works* have to ignore all the evidence that shows he did. Let's get this story straight. We aren't talking about a belief that can be interpreted differently depending on our point of view. The evidence for William Shakespeare of Stratford-upon-Avon is not circumstantial. It is factual and multifaceted. Sure, we don't have personal letters or diary entries, but that's not all that unusual for people of that period. At least fourteen other writers mentioned him by name as a playwright and poet and discussed his work. Printers and publishers worked with him. Seven of his plays were co-authored, for God's sake. Readers, actors, and theatre audiences were part of the living and breathing testimony of thousands of people. On his death he was memorialized as a writer, and his reputation grew. To claim that Shakespeare of Stratford didn't write the plays is no less than to deny history and slap the greatest writer the world has ever known in the face.

—A. J. Leon, Senior Digital Advisor to The Shakespeare Birthplace Trust.

Doubter Response

First, yes, many people do say that "he did not write the works," but what we all agree on is that there's "reasonable doubt," so it is a legitimate question for people to pursue. The Birthplace Trust should stop trying to stigmatize and suppress a legitimate historical question.

Second, we do not "ignore" evidence that suggests he did. For example, the Declaration of Reasonable Doubt outlines "four main reasons to identify Mr. Shakspere…with the author William Shakespeare." It says they seem to amount to a *prima facie* case for him. But it explains why each of the four is problematic, and then outlines some reasons why "We Say the Evidence Does Not Fit." What we can't understand is why Leon ignores it.

Third, it is extremely unusual that we have not a single letter in Mr. Shakspere's hand. If A. J. Leon thinks otherwise, he is the one who is ignoring the evidence. He should read *Shakespeare's Unorthodox Biography*, by Diana Price (esp. "Literary Paper Trails").

Fourth, the fourteen other writers who, "mentioned him by name as a playwright and poet and discussed his work," never associate him with Stratford, and never indicate that they knew or met him personally.

Fifth, no document shows that the author worked directly with printers and publishers. He may have, but this says nothing about who he was. If such people keep the identities of pseudonymous authors and ghostwriters secret today, why wouldn't they have then?

Sixth, it is not certain that any of the plays was co-authored; but even if some were, it's not certain that the collaborators knew the author personally, or knew his true identity. Plays can be started and completed by different authors working independently. They can be written by one and revised by another, or completed, but revised posthumously. Any of these could easily account for several jarring inconsistencies in certain plays. It's also hard to distinguish collaboration from an author revising his own early works. The more scholars claim collaboration, the harder it is to explain the absence of letters, or other documentation of the alleged collaboration, especially with a man in Stratford.

Seventh, there's no "living and breathing testimony of thousands of people." Nonsense!

Eighth, on his death the Stratford man was not "memorialized as a writer," although many poets and playwrights of the time were, sometimes within days of their deaths. Francis Beaumont, for example, who died the month before Shakspere, received many tributes and was interred in Westminster Abbey. No tributes exist for Shakespeare.

Ninth, we have as much respect for the author Shakespeare, whoever he was, as anyone. It is disgraceful that A.J. Leon uses, and the Birthplace Trust condones, such inflammatory language.

Tenth, Leon has misrepresented the issue, the evidence, our positions and our motives—all too typical of Stratfordians; if the evidence is so clear, why the need for such tactics?

—Richard Joyrich, M.D., President, Shakespeare Oxford Society; John M. Shahan

Question 15: Did Shakespeare become famous in his lifetime?

Shakespeare was first known as an erotic poet because of *Venus and Adonis*, *Rape of Lucrece* and his "sugred sonnets": in 1595 he's heralded as "sweet Shakespeare" and "Honie-tong'd Shakespeare".[*]

But from 1598 onwards, Shakespeare's name is found on playbooks. Known as an actor-writer, "Mr... Shakespeare" was lauded for having "plaide... Kingly parts in sport", while being "our English Terence" (Terence was a famous classical playwright).[**]

He was seen, however, as not highly educated. Fellow playwright, Beaumont, "would... from all Learninge keepe these lines as [cl]eere as Shakespeares'; more positively, *Returne from Pernassus* maintains "Few of the university pen plaies well" and concludes "Shakespeare puts them all downe".[***]

Though thought less brilliant than Ben Jonson, Shakespeare had a solid reputation. By 1630, a jest book calls "Stratford upon Avon...remarkable for the birth of famous William Shakespeare".[****]

Notes
[*]Frances Meres, *Palladis Tamia* (1598), 281; William Covell, *Polimanteia* (1595), R2r. John Weever, "Ad Gulielmum Shakespeare", Epigrammes (1595), E6r.
[**]John Davies, "To our English Terence, Mr. Will: Shake-speare", *The Scourge of Folly* (1611), 76.
[***]Francis Beaumont, "To Mr B: J:" (c. 1615), Holgate MS, Pierpont Morgan Library, f. 110, quoted in E.K. Chambers, *William Shakespeare*, 2 vols (Oxford: Clarendon Press, 1930), 2: 222-5; *The Returne from Pernassus* (1606), G2v.
[****]*A Banquet of Jeasts* (1630), 157.

—Tiffany Stern, Professor of Early Modern Drama at Oxford University, and author of several books on Shakespeare performance.

Doubter Response

The name "Shakespeare" was famous during the lifetime of William of Stratford, but there's no evidence that anyone indentified him with Shakespeare until seven years after he died. Apart from the assumption that he was the author, nothing shows that he was famous. (See Ramon Jiménez' answer to Key Question 4 below.) As stated in the Declaration, "Contrary to the traditional view that the author became a prominent public figure, there is no record that he ever addressed the public directly, either in person or in writing...and nothing shows that either Elizabeth I, or James I, ever met Shakespeare, or spoke or wrote his name. Almost uniquely among Elizabethan poets, Shakespeare remained silent following the death of Elizabeth. Early in the reign of James I, records place Shakspere in Stratford while plays were staged in London for the court. Why was the popular playwright and leading actor of the King's Men not part of such events?"

Further, "Nobody, including literary contemporaries, ever recognized Shakspere as a writer during his lifetime; and when he died in 1616, no one seemed to notice. Not so much as a letter refers to the author's passing. If Shakspere was Shakespeare, surely something dating from 1616 should mention the author's death. Even Heminges, Condell and Richard Burbage, whom he mentioned in his will, had no recorded reaction. Nor did those who held rights to previously published editions of plays or poems rush new ones into print." It is difficult to argue that this man was famous.

Finally, it is ironic that Tiffany Stern quotes Davies about Shakespeare being "our English Terence," since the Roman writer Terence was credited with other writers' works! Terence himself said that some thought that he was taking the credit for plays written by two noble Romans. Davies may well have had this in mind when he wrote the poem.

—John Hamill

Question 16: Should we be concerned that there are gaps in the historical record?

It always astonishes me that people are so surprised at gaps in the records of the lives of early modern people and that they demand, often stridently, that these be explained, or else they will assume there has been some sort of cover up. But we know so little about most people outside the very upper echelons of society. And what biographies were written were designed to tell exemplary stories, so hardly any survive of writers until things changed in the later seventeenth century. Hardly any personal letters survive, paper being scarce and invariably reused, so we should not read anything into the lack of a cache of Shakespeare letters. Nor should we be surprised that Shakespeare's will does not include some objects, such as books, as wills tended to mention only important and valuable items, everything else going to the next of kin. My favorite non-fact is that, although Thomas Nashe is, I think, the only English writer ever to have forced the authorities to close down the theatres and printing presses, making him something of a celebrity, we do not know when or how he died. Traces of Shakespeare, though scanty, do not require special explanation. Or, alternatively, we could imagine that a whole host of writers who emerged in the late sixteenth century, were imposters.

—Andrew Hadfield, Professor of English at the University of Sussex, and author of *Shakespeare and Republicanism*, and *Edmund Spenser: A Life*.

Doubter Response

It's true that we should expect gaps in the records for Elizabethan and Jacobean times. But gaps are different from total silence, especially when records for others do survive. Occupations leave traces; though some will disappear over 400 years, some should not.

In *Shakespeare's Unorthodox Biography* (2001), Diana Price studied the literary paper trails of twenty-five writers of the period, using all of the extant published biographies. She organized the various kinds of evidence used to document their writing careers into ten general categories—evidence of education, books owned or borrowed, letters about literary matters, etc. Only for Ben Jonson could she find evidence in all ten categories.

As expected, for some writers there are major gaps. For ten of the twenty-five, we have no record of correspondence; for fifteen no extant original manuscript or evidence of books owned, borrowed, given or written in. Price's data show that for Thomas Nashe there is indeed no "notice at death as a writer." But Nashe still left the most substantial literary paper trail after Jonson's, with evidence in all of the remaining nine categories.

Edmund Spenser left seven out of ten; and even Marlowe, who officially died at age 29, hit four of the ten categories (with Francis Beaumont, John Fletcher and Thomas Kyd). John

Webster would be last on the list, with evidence in only three categories, except for one extreme outlier, with nothing at all in any of the ten categories: William Shakspere. In other words, no unambiguous evidence from his lifetime proves that he was a writer. Given the amount of time and effort devoted to searching for evidence relating to him, the lack of a substantial literary paper trail cannot be dismissed as some sort of fluke.

He did leave a substantial paper trail—just not a literary one. Some seventy documents show he bought and sold land, properties, grain and tithes, lent money, recouped debts. Any objective observer might conclude that he was a successful businessman, an actor, a theater shareholder, perhaps some sort of theatrical wheeler-dealer, but not a writer. How could so many and varied documents survive, and yet none for his writing career?

A Stratfordian commonplace says that "absence of evidence is not evidence of absence." Absence of expected evidence is indeed evidence of absence. Not only can Stratfordians not explain this remarkable lack of expected evidence for their man's supposed career (based on what we find for other writers), they remain in denial about the entire issue.

References

Shakespeare's Unorthodox Biography: New Evidence of an Authorship Problem, by Diana Price (Greenwood Press, 2001).

—Michael D. Rubbo, M.A., Stanford University; Director, *Much Ado About Something*, the award-winning documentary on the case for Christopher Marlowe as Shakespeare.

Question 17: Where did Shakespeare get his money?

Shakespeare was an actor, playwright and poet with lots of opportunities to earn an income in the new theatre business. As a young actor, he would have been paid a weekly wage. As a playwright he could sell his plays to a company at £6-£8 apiece. (For comparison, the annual income of a goldsmith was about £8.) As a resident playwright for about twenty years, he would have had a salary, plus a benefit for each performed new play.

Unlike other playwrights, he was also a shareholder in a most successful London theatre company, which ended up owning two theatres, the Globe and Blackfriars. This is likely to have brought him around £150 a year. Performances at Court were another good source of money, as was patronage. Among his patrons were Lord Strange, the Earl of Southampton (to whom he dedicated *Venus and Adonis*), and King James. In addition, Shakespeare prudently invested in land and other business ventures.

—Boika Sokolova, who teaches Shakespeare and the drama of his contemporaries at the University of Notre Dame in London

Doubter Response

Boika Sokolova does not answer the question. Rather than tell us where Mr. Shakspere "did" get his money, she says he had "lots of opportunities" to earn an income; that he "would have been" paid a weekly wage; he "could" sell his plays to a theater company; that as a resident playwright for about twenty years, he "would have had" a salary...; and being a shareholder in two theater companies, "is likely" to have brought him..." The reason why she resorts to hypotheticals when it comes to his theatrical and alleged literary career is that, in fact, no record shows he ever received a payment for writing.

This is very strange. Philip Henslowe, in his records of payments to writers and actors, or "Henslowe's diaries" (his account books), never mentions Shakespeare, even though Henslowe staged some of his plays. There are records for other writers and actors, and there's lots of evidence for Shakspere's business transactions; but not for literary work. There are approximately 70 documents relating to Shakspere, but all are non-literary. They reveal a businessman in Stratford, and a theater entrepreneur/actor in London.

Sokolova makes one unequivocal statement—that "among [Shakspere's] patrons were Lord Strange, the Earl of Southampton...and King James;" and that statement is false. No document shows that any of these supposed "patrons" ever paid William Shakspere for writing. The closest one comes is a grant of "red cloth" by King James to the actors to participate in his coronation procession through the city of London. The King's Men received payment for plays put on at court, but nothing shows any patronage payments. Southampton's biographers have searched in vain for evidence he bankrolled the Bard, assuming that he must have, since Shakespeare dedicated two narrative poems to him. Not only did they find no evidence of patronage, they found no evidence they ever met.

—William D. Rubinstein, Ph.D.

Question 18: What was Shakespeare's social status?

William Shakespeare was the son of a successful yeoman glover who had served a term as mayor of Stratford-upon-Avon. Through his mother Mary Arden, Shakespeare may have been related to the ancient Arden family of Park Hall. In 1596 the Shakespeares successfully applied for a coat of arms, which formally gentrified the family. From now on William Shakespeare, player and London playwright, was Master Shakespeare. He was mocked for his apparent pretentiousness by his friend Ben Jonson.

Shakespeare was socially ambitious, hence his purchase, a year after the coat of arms, of New Place, a large mansion house in Stratford. It seems that he, who was only ever a lodger in London, was keen to be lord of the manor in his home town. Throughout his life he astutely invested in land, tithes, and property; and he did not remit debts. Shakespeare's evident concern with money and status may have its roots in his father's long struggle with debt which confined John Shakespeare to his family home at a time when his teenage son was living there.

—René Weis, Birthplace Trust Representative Trustee from the University of London, teacher of Shakespeare at UCL, Editor of *Romeo and Juliet* for Arden.

Doubter Response

René Weis's assessment of "Shakespeare's" social status (meaning the Stratford man's) is mostly correct, except in saying he was a "London playwright." It's not clear he was. The problem is that the author's social status appears very different from Shakspere's. All but one of the plays (*Merry Wives of Windsor*) is set among the uppermost nobility. It's hard to imagine how Shakspere could have understood the upper classes so well.

Weis speculates about Shakspere's father's "long struggle with debt which confined John Shakespeare to his family home at a time when his teenage son was living there." In fact, we do not know for sure that Shakspere and his father lived together when the former was a teen. All we have for the first 28 years of his life are a few church records. Shakspere may have been motivated by his father's situation, but nothing supports this.

If Shakspere was "socially ambitious," and succeeded in his ambitions in London, why did he retire to Stratford at the end of his career, rather than remain in London in the company of some former social superiors who now welcomed him as their social equal? Surely that was a big comedown in status for the lead dramatist of the "King's Men." Why did he never own a home in London, or settle into retirement among the many high-status people who would have found it fascinating to have him as their friend?

Further, why did he evidently not keep in touch with any of them, so when it came time to make out his will he remembered none of his fellow writers, or any prominent person other than his three fellow actors, not even his alleged patron the Earl of Southampton?

—Richard Joyrich, M.D.

Question 19: Could the plays have been written by someone who never left England?

Shakespeare's geography was patchy. He gave Bohemia a seacoast and a desert, which many, including Ben Jonson, have delighted to ridicule; but *A Winter's Tale* is a romance, and accuracy was not his aim. Illyria in *Twelfth Night* is also a mythical place of dreams, a version of Elysium. His Italian cities, particularly Verona and Venice, glitter with Renaissance glamour, and one would like to think he might have been there; but equally he could and would have talked to travelers, seen paintings, read accounts, and constructed from them the lively cities we see on stage. It was not necessary for him to go to Rome to write his Roman tragedies: he found the Forum and the Capitol in Plutarch. He travelled in books and in his imagination, as writers do; and as the greatest writer of them all, he did it supremely well. His Egypt, with its flies and gnats of Nile, is as real as the Forest of Arden.

—Margaret Drabble, Birthplace Trust Life Trustee, educated at Cambridge and briefly an RSC actress, before authoring seventeen novels and various works of non-fiction.

Doubter Response

Shakespeare's knowledge of geography was not "patchy." Rudolf II, King of Bohemia, did in fact reign over territory that included some Adriatic seacoast from 1575 to 1611. A new book virtually proves that Shakespeare did leave England. The book is *The Shakespeare Guide to Italy: Retracing the Bard's Unknown Travels*, by Richard Paul Roe (HarperCollins, 2012). Roe found

> ...a secret Italy hidden in the plays of Shakespeare. It is an ingeniously-described Italy that has neither been recognized, nor even suspected—not in four hundred years, except by a curious few. It is exact; it is detailed; and it is brilliant.

Shakespeare studies will never be the same.

Roe isn't the first to conclude that Shakespeare must have traveled extensively in Italy. The orthodox Italian scholar Ernesto Grillo wrote that

> When we consider that in the north of Italy he reveals a profound knowledge of Milan, Bergamo, Verona, Mantua, Padua and Venice, the very limitation of the poet's notion of geography proves that he derived his information from an actual journey through Italy and not from books.

Independent scholar Noemi Magri wrote many articles on the Italian plays, showing that they held detailed knowledge that could only have been acquired by being there. British scholar Kevin Gilvary made the same point. Roe's landmark book all but seals the case.

That said, we agree that nothing about the Egyptian settings in *Antony and Cleopatra*, or Viennese settings in *Measure for Measure* or Cyprian settings in *Othello*, suggests that the author must have been to Egypt, Vienna or Cyprus. Not every locale depicted in the plays argues that the author surely witnessed it first hand. Some are, to trained eyes knowledgeable in a particular local geography, more vividly depicted than others.

—Mark Anderson, author, *"Shakespeare" By Another Name* (Gotham Books, 2005; 2011, 2nd Ed.)

Question 20: Why is it important that actors' names appear in some of the early printed texts of Shakespeare's plays?

Shakespeare knew many of the actors he wrote for throughout his career. The names of the principal actors are printed at the front of the 1623 First Folio, and Shakespeare's own name is first among them.

He knew how his fellow actors worked. He wrote some of the greatest of all theatrical parts for his friend Richard Burbage: *Hamlet*, *Othello*, and *King Lear*.

Some of the early play texts are revealing about Shakespeare's thought-processes. Exits are often missed out. He knew the actors would know when to leave. Occasionally characters are named who don't speak: Violenta in *All's Well That Ends Well*. There were probably second thoughts in rehearsal.

In the first edition of *Much Ado About Nothing* the names of the much-loved comic actors Will Kemp and Richard Cowley appear as speech prefixes instead of their characters' names: Dogberry and Verges. He was writing with the actors themselves in mind. These are texts written by a poet and actor, and have the DNA of the playhouse running through them.

—Harriet Walter, actor in all media, author of 3 books, performer in 17 Shakespearean roles.

Doubter Response

It was routine to rewrite scripts in various forms after they were delivered. That an actor's name might appear in some version says nothing about the author's original. But there is no reason to think that only an actor in the company could have written these plays. A genius playwright who attended and observed plays could have done it. There is also no reason to assume a different author wouldn't have known the players. He may even have been an actor himself during his career, working closely with them.

Harriet Walter claims that the plays have "the DNA of the playhouse running through them." It is a specious analogy, invoking the idea of DNA evidence, as if it couldn't be wrong. Public playhouses were hardly the only places where plays were written and performed. A large majority of all documented performances of Shakespeare plays were not in the public playhouses at all, but elsewhere, such as at court, the great houses of the nobility, Oxford and Cambridge universities, the London law schools known as "The Inns of Court," and the private Blackfriars theater.

The Inns of Court, especially Gray's Inn, were renowned for writing and producing their own plays, with their own acting companies. Many playwrights of the time had attended the Inns of Court, which required students to participate in entertainments. Several Shakespeare plays were written specifically for Inns of Court entertainments, such as *The Comedy of Errors*, first staged during the 1594 Gray's Inn Christmas revels. Shakspere's company, The Lord Chamberlain's Men, were performing a different play before the Queen at Greenwich at that time. Nothing about the plays requires that they could only have been written by Shakspere, or by another actor in some public theater.

—Peter Dawkins, M.A., Principal of the Francis Bacon Research Trust; and Trustee, Shakespearean Authorship Trust; Author, *The Shakespeare Enigma* (Polair Publishing).

Question 21: In what ways are the plays revealing about Shakespeare's knowledge of theatrical practice?

As a theatrical poet, Shakespeare knew all about stagecraft. There are implied stage-directions within the speeches which help the actor to move. Volumnia speaks to her companions about her son, Coriolanus, "He turns away. / Down ladies. Let us shame him with our knees."

Music cues are integrated into the main action; music and its effects become part of Shakespeare's stories.

Nearly all of the plays can be performed with a company of around 14 people, and were adaptable for touring.

Plays allow for meaningful doubling of roles: the two brothers in *Hamlet*—Claudius and the Ghost of the brother he has murdered.

There is time for stage descents and for costume changes from the upper playing space.

And in the later plays, his writing draws on the resources of the new, smaller, indoor theatres like the one at Blackfriars which opened in 1608.

Shakespeare knew what it is to direct and to act, as well as to write.

—Tina Packer, founder of Shakespeare & Company (1978), whose work crosses the States, and focuses equally on performance, education and training.

Doubter Response

Nobody disputes the consummate stagecraft in the plays, but this is hardly an argument for the Stratford man. Do only professional actors understand practicalities of theater? Every successful dramatist is familiar with theatrical practice, and most are not actors. All we can infer from the stageworthiness of the plays is that whoever wrote them had firsthand knowledge of the theater, and that he may well have known the main actors.

Tina Packer's statement that "music and its effects become part of Shakespeare's stories" suggests an author with musical training, as scholars have noted. It is even harder to explain how Shakspere could have gotten musical training in Stratford than how he could have gotten training in foreign languages like French, Italian and Greek; and of course both foreign languages and facility with music are most easily acquired while young, not later in adulthood. Shakspere's will mentions no musical instruments, nor any other intellectual property.

—Bonner Miller Cutting, M.M., Independent Scholar; Board Member, Shakespeare Fellowship, and Shakespeare Authorship Coalition.

Question 22: As an actor, what is your sense of Shakespeare's personality?

I think that as an actor you get a very clear sense of an author's personality and that of Shakespeare is above all open—open and receiving rather than judging or controlling. He allows his characters to have their own life, and he observes human life with absolute clarity, and some compassion.

It's exactly the opposite sensation that you get from, for example, acting in the plays of Ben Jonson, in which you have a strong sense of him controlling everything, judging everything, condemning everything, a hard, intemperate personality. Shakespeare is all yielding, all experiencing, and nothing human is alien to him, and that's an extraordinarily warm and generous feeling.

—Simon Callow, actor and writer, and performer in the one-man play, *Being Shakespeare*.

Doubter Response

The Birthplace Trust often criticizes doubters for looking to the works for evidence of the author's identity, so it's odd that here they ask for an actor's "sense" of the author's personality. How is he to respond, except in terms of how he sees the author reflected in the works? Of course it's appropriate to look to the works, or they would not ask such a question.

Simon Callow's subjective response is fine, as far as it goes; but his is hardly the only possible answer, nor necessarily the most authoritative and insightful. Actors more experienced at playing Shakespeare, like Derek Jacobi or Mark Rylance, might see him differently. To get a scholarly, methodologically sound answer, one would have to do a legitimate study, with carefully selected actors and scholars, and a well designed set of questions. Unfortunately, the Birthplace Trust does not appear at all interested. They already know what sort of answer they want, so one suitable response is all they need for their present purpose.

While it would, in fact, be interesting to do such a study to see what light it might shed on the sort of person who wrote all the works, it couldn't possibly provide any support for the Stratford man, because we know almost nothing about his personality anyway.

—John Christian Plummer, Artistic Director, World's End Theatre, director of the version of *Twelfth Night* featured in the PBS documentary *Shakespeare on the Hudson*.

Question 23: How do you respond as an actor and director to the Shakespeare authorship conspiracy theory?

I wonder why people think one must experience something to write about it. That's not what authors do. You don't have to be a king in order to play one. If we don't expect it of actors to have been something that they play, then why of the poet himself? It doesn't make any sense. And then, you know, he's a surrealist, or a super-realist, his figures, his thoughts, his apperceptions about humanity are much larger than life. They may be true, but they're not exactly documentary realism. And documentary realism has nothing to do with this poet. He's out of that sphere. He writes so much about appearance and reality—it's perhaps something that we should take on board, when you think of somebody who can't do that. And then I don't understand why those people in that period might have stopped gossiping, human nature gossips all the time.

—Janet Suzman, adequately trained in the classics, and who sees Shakespeare as a modern playwright (ref. production of *Othello* in apartheid South Africa).

Doubter Response

Authors write from their imaginations, but their imaginations are commonly based on their experiences. Eugene O'Neill, Tennessee Williams, Ibsen, Strindberg, Aphra Behn, Ben Jonson and Geoffrey Chaucer (to offer a few examples) drew on their life experiences. Shakespeare's plays reveal firsthand knowledge of the court, politics, military tactics, seamanship and foreign travels, suggesting an author very unlike the Stratford man.

A playwright need not have been a king, queen, courtier, soldier or sailor to write about them, but the most successful characterizations are those rooted in detailed observation. Actors need not know anything about the playwright; but when they do, the characters and other complex aspects are more easily fleshed out from the playwright's biography. Knowing that the author may have been close to kings and queens, and may have been to Italy and lived in Venice, grounds the actor's imagination in a more lifelike reality.

Shakespeare's "super-realism" is powerful because the poet is not cut off from reality. His eloquent characterizations derive from a deep experience of life, which then soars. One gossips with one's peers. The young Shakspere, newly arrived from Warwickshire, must have been a very upwardly mobile gossip to obtain the inside information found in certain relatively early plays, like *Love's Labor's Lost*, or *A Midsummer Night's Dream*. Only one steeped in courtly ways—no mere gossip—might seem to be the true author of plays such as these, fanciful as they may be.

—Kristin Linklater, Professor of Theatre Arts, Columbia University School of the Arts.

Question 24: To what extent can collaboration be identified in the Shakespeare canon?

Shakespeare was a star, but he was also a team player. He formed temporary partnerships with other professional playwrights to work on specific projects. Elizabethan professions were normally based on an apprenticeship system, so at the beginning of his career Shakespeare worked with older, more experienced, better educated authors. For instance he teamed up with George Peele to write *Titus Andronicus*. Peele got the ball rolling; Shakespeare ran with it. At least three different writers got together to produce *Henry VI Part I*: Thomas Nashe, Christopher

Marlowe and Shakespeare. When he got older, Shakespeare himself became the veteran, teaching his trade to promising younger men. He paired with Thomas Middleton on *Timon of Athens*, with George Wilkins on *Pericles*, with John Fletcher on *Cardenio, All is True* and *The Two Noble Kinsmen*. After his death, Shakespeare's company commissioned Thomas Middleton to update two of Shakespeare's plays: *Macbeth* and *Measure for Measure*. None of Shakespeare's plays is the product of an isolated genius.

—Gary Taylor, editor of the works of Shakespeare, and of Thomas Middleton, for Oxford University Press.

Doubter Response

Except for the 1634 edition of *The Two Noble Kinsmen*, published 18 years after William Shakspere's death, there is no documentary or bibliographic evidence that Shakespeare ever collaborated with anyone.

The alleged evidence for collaboration is based on a wide variety of stylistic analyses, but the results routinely contradict each other. Over the past 100 years, as just one example, authorship attribution studies have "proven" that *Edward III* was written by George Peele alone; by Christopher Marlowe with George Peele, Robert Greene, and Thomas Kyd; by Thomas Kyd alone; by Michael Drayton; by Robert Wilson; by William Shakespeare alone; by William Shakespeare and one unknown other; by William Shakespeare and Christopher Marlowe; by William Shakespeare and several others, excluding Marlowe; and most recently and very specifically by Thomas Kyd (60 percent) and William Shakespeare (40 percent).

There is no reliable evidence that Shakespeare "teamed up with George Peele" or with anyone else. Gary Taylor's statements are opinions, not facts.

—Ramon Jiménez
—Robin Williams, President, Mary Sidney Society; doctoral candidate in English, Brunel University, London

Question 25: Is it possible that Shakespeare collaborated in minor ways with other authors?

We know from a wide body of evidence, related both to Shakespeare and to other theatre workers (notably the stable of playwrights that worked for Phillip Henslowe at the Rose Theatre), that drama was, as it remains, an essentially collaborative art form. Shakespeare was a frequent collaborator in the writing of scripts, especially at the beginning and the end of his career. Recent attribution studies have provided compelling evidence that Shakespeare got a toehold in the profession by contributing a few scenes to plays such as *Edward III* and *Arden of Faversham* in the early 1590s. Shakespeare then collaborated with George Peele on *Titus Andronicus*, with either Thomas Nashe or Thomas Kyd on *1 Henry VI*, with Thomas Middleton on *Timon of Athens*, and with George Wilkins on *Pericles*. He later passed the baton of principal dramatist for the King's Men to John Fletcher by collaborating with the younger playwright on *Henry VIII*, *The Two Noble Kinsmen*, and the lost *Cardenio*.

—Eric Rasmussen, Chair of English at the University of Nevada, and co-editor with Jonathan Bate of the *RSC Complete Works of Shakespeare*.

Doubter Response

Henslowe's Diary (mentioned obliquely above) is a 17-year record of plays performed and payments made, in which 28 playwrights are mentioned by name. Although the titles of several Shakespearean plays are included in the Diary, Shakespeare's own name does not appear in any of the collaborations by two or more playwrights. In fact, Shakespeare's name is never mentioned in Henslowe's Diary, nor in any other document related to playwriting. This suggests he worked alone, outside the well-known fraternity of Elizabethan playwrights.

The term "collaboration" implies, as Rasmussen wishes it to imply, that Shakespeare actively worked with other writers. Rasmussen neglects to mention that attribution studies provide theories based on stylistic interpretations, not facts—not one scrap of documentary evidence that Shakespeare actively worked with a writing partner has ever been found. Although there are clear signs of interpolations in several plays, it was an easy task in the theater for someone to add text to any play at a later date. The version of Christopher Marlowe's *Doctor Faustus* printed in 1616 is almost a third longer than the version printed in 1604. If Marlowe had been alive at the time, it would now be called a collaboration—but the records tell us that Marlowe had been dead 23 years when the 1616 version appeared. This is but one example to illustrate that what is assertively called "collaboration" does not prove that every collaboration is a result of writers sitting in a room together writing a play.

—Ramon Jiménez
—Robin Williams

Question 26: Was collaboration common in Shakespeare's time?

Collaboration was arguably the default form of writing in the early theatre. Our best source, Philip Henslowe's diary, gives us a snapshot of several decades in which nearly two thirds of plays had multiple authors. Shakespeare's contemporary, Thomas Heywood, claimed to have a finger in over 200 plays; and all of the major writers—including Jonson and Marlowe—worked with others.

It's not just about words, though. Anthony Munday was known as "the best plotter" of the day. Some writers specialized in stories, others patched up dialogue or worked out backstage practicalities. The manuscript of *Thomas More*, with some seven different hands, shows us the range of collaborations.

We know that the plays of Shakespeare were performed, and we also know that the sheer number of collaborators involved in creating plays meant that they were inherently social productions.

The idea of a single artistic mind presiding over a whole body of work is at odds with the very nature of professional theatre.

—Peter Kirwan, tutor, blogger and researcher, and who has undertaken doctoral work at the University of Warwick on plays of disputed authorship.

Doubter Response

Collaboration may have been common with some playwrights, but this in itself does not prove that any other writer collaborated with—or even met—the man William Shakespeare.

Peter Kirwan (above) mentions that almost two-thirds of the payments recorded in Henslowe's Diary are for collaborations. The Diary records 282 plays; almost two-thirds is about 180. But Henslowe's Diary is a record of only one of at least seven playhouses active during the time—we know the names of more than 1500 plays (there is evidence of more than 3000 plays produced on stage during Shakespeare's life); of these 1500, only about one-eighth are known collaborations. This does not prove anything one way or another except that the emphasis on collaboration is perhaps misplaced, or has another agenda.

How odd that we acknowledge Shakespeare's genius as towering high above every other author; that his works are different from all others, such that we can pick out scenes, even individual lines, that he did not write because they do not have that Golden Touch; that he alone is master of this medium, to the extent that we don't even hold him to the same standards of other authors as far as documentary evidence. Yet suddenly, in this area of collaboration, Shakespeare is as common as every hack writer of the Elizabethan age. What is really going on here?

—Ramon Jiménez
—Robin Williams

Question 27: What methods are used to find evidence of multiple authorship in Shakespeare's plays?

Shakespeare and his fellow playwrights all had different styles. Their verse, vocabulary, grammar, sentence structure, imagery, phrasing and ideas can be analyzed, and specific features counted in order to identify their contributions to a play. In *The Two Noble Kinsmen*, published as by Shakespeare and Fletcher, even trivial details help distinguish the two men's shares. Unlike Shakespeare, Fletcher prefers "ye" to "you" and avoids old fashioned "hath" and "doth". Fletcher adds an extra unstressed syllable to the end of a verse line far more often than Shakespeare. From numerous such preferences, evident in plays written alone, we build up distinct authorial profiles.

—MacDonald Jackson, Professor Emeritus of English at the University of Auckland, and a Fellow of the Royal Society of New Zealand.

Doubter Response

As Jiménez points out (Question 24), we have documentary evidence in the 1634 publication of *The Two Noble Kinsmen* that it is co-authored by John Fletcher and William Shakespeare (albeit 18 years after Mr. Shakspere's death). Even on that score, one should keep in mind that several plays were issued with title pages erroneously identifying the author as Shakespeare. The attribution to "Fletcher and Shakespeare" is not necessarily accurate. There is no other evidence that the two authors collaborated. Whether they ever met and actively collaborated, we cannot know.

There is no such documentation for any of the other alleged Shakespeare collaborations. Attribution studies are notoriously unreliable and consistently contradict each other. In the absence of documentary evidence, the validity of attribution studies is uncertain.

Although the studies can help to pinpoint differences in styles, and it is easily acknowledged that there are clear interpolations in several plays, it is not at all certain that a collaborator/

interpolator/editor knew the original author personally. Plays may be started and completed by different authors working independently; they can be written by one and revised by another; they can be completed and revised posthumously; what appears to be collaboration can be an author revising his own early works.

The more that scholars claim collaboration, the harder it is to explain the absence of documentary evidence such as letters, especially at times when Mr. Shakspere was in Stratford—collaboration requires correspondence. We have letters and documents for other writers—why not for the greatest of them all?

—Robin Williams

Question 28: Does Shakespeare's dramatic verse seem to be different from Marlowe's?

[See DoubtAboutWill.org/exposing.]

Question 29: did Shakespeare have an aristocratic patron?

Shakespeare had a romantic view of the aristocracy. They seemed to inhabit an altogether different world from his own. The obsequious dedications he wrote to his patron, the Earl of Southampton, for his narrative poems have disturbed some of his admirers (especially when compared with Webster's dedication of *The Duchess of Malfi* to Baron Berkeley—"I do not altogether look up to your title"). But there was calculation as well as deference in Shakespeare's "well-sugared" words. It was rumored he had been given money by Southampton to join the Chamberlain's Men, and he received 44 shillings in gold for designing the impresa which the Earl of Rutland wore in the annual Accession Tilt at Whitehall. Though he appears to have regretted crooking "the pregnant hinges of the knee" for aristocratic patronage, his posthumous First Folio was dedicated to the Earls of Pembroke and Montgomery.

—Michael Holroyd, biographer and former President of The Royal Society of Literature.

Doubter Response

There's no evidence that Shakespeare had a patron, or that Shakspere had one either. Notice that Michael Holroyd never gives a direct answer. If he had to prove Shakespeare had a patron, he couldn't; so he talks about the aristocracy and Shakespeare's dedications to Southampton instead, plus a mere "rumor" that Southampton once gave him money to join the Chamberlain's Men. He simply assumes that Southampton was Shakespeare's patron, even though there's no document that proves he was. Southampton biographer Charlotte Stopes spent years trying to find evidence of a relationship in Southampton's voluminous personal papers, and failed. Subsequent biographers have fared no better.

The only "evidence" for the supposed relationship is the two dedications; but they are not evidence so much as the basis for an inference based in turn on an assumption that the author of the dedications, "William Shakespeare," was, indeed, the Stratford Man, not the pen name of someone else to whom Southampton was not a patron but a friend.

It's unclear what point Holroyd is trying to make in his last sentence. Is he suggesting that Shakspere had something to do with dedicating the First Folio to Pembroke and Montgomery? Seven years after he died is a bit late to be flattering potential patrons. More likely the First Folio dedication was due to political considerations at that time.

—A. J. (Tony) Pointon, Emeritus Professor, former Director of Research, University of Portsmouth; Author, *The Man who was Never Shakespeare* (Parapress, 2011).

Question 30: What Was the relationship between the aristocracy and the theatre in Shakespeare's time?

The aristocracy was very important to Elizabethan theatre, not least because the theatre companies needed influential members of the court and government to advocate for them against the city authorities, who were opposed to the commercial repertory companies. For example, the Shakespeare company patron, Henry Carey, wrote to the Lord Mayor of London in October 1594 to ask if the theatre company could perform within the city walls (which was prohibited at the time).

Acting was not a highly respected trade when the theatres first opened in the 1570s, so the patronage system was crucial for the theatrical profession as a whole. To have the financial and ideological support of influential members of the Elizabethan aristocracy would ensure that the profession of theatre would thrive. Many playwrights and poets would formally recognize their patrons in print through dedications.

Shakespeare was supported not only by the Lord Chamberlain, patron of his theatre company, and later in 1603 King James I, but his gifts as a poet were recognized early in his career by the Earl of Southampton, whose name as dedicatee is on Shakespeare's first publications, *Venus and Adonis* (1593) and *The Rape of Lucrece* (1594).

—Farah Karim-Cooper, Head of Research & Courses, Globe Education.

Doubter Response

Yes, the aristocracy was very important to Elizabethan theater. What does this have to do with the question of authorship? Henry Carey, Lord Hunsdon—a close associate of my famous ancestor, William Cecil, the first Lord Burghley—was indeed the patron of the Lord Chamberlain's Men, renamed the "King's Men" early in the reign of James I. There was nothing unusual in this. Each theater company needed a sponsor to function. But sponsorship did not necessarily entail "patronage" in the sense of financial support.

Similarly, the fact that a poet or playwright dedicated a work to a prominent nobleman did not necessarily mean that the nobleman was the writer's patron, or even necessarily that the writer was seeking patronage. Thus, the fact that "Shakespeare" dedicated both *Venus & Adonis* and *Lucrece* to the Earl of Southampton proves nothing, in and of itself. If, in fact, Southampton was Shakespeare's patron, there should be clear evidence for it. There is none— no documentary evidence that Shakespeare ever met Southampton, or that he ever received any payment or patronage from the Earl, and certainly none that, as Karim-Cooper claims, Southampton recognized his gifts as a poet early in his career.

Farah Karin-Cooper is correct in claiming that "Many playwrights and poets would formally recognize their patrons in print through dedications." But does it not strike her and her Birthplace Trust colleagues as odd that Shakespeare never dedicated a play to anyone, and that the only epistle to one of his plays (*Troilus and Cressida*) was written by some other person? Why would a poet-playwright motivated by profit, as they say Shakespeare was, never seek patronage again after dedicating the two early narrative poems to Southampton? One could hypothesize that he needed no other patron, but there's no evidence of this. Orthodox Shakespeare scholars should acknowledge what they do not know for sure.

—Michael Cecil, Baron Burghley, Marquess of Exeter.

Question 31: How has the Shakespeare authorship discussion been presented in fiction?

Apart from scholarship, anti-Stratfordians have also produced fiction about the authorship question. Some of these works focus on the preferred candidate—Bacon or Oxford—and suggest that the name "Shakespeare" was just his pseudonym. But sometimes Shakespeare does exist, as the real author's front man. Then he is usually portrayed as a country bumpkin, without any talent or manners, and Stratford as the back of beyond. That Shakespeare's father was a respectable tradesman, and Stratford's former mayor; that the town boasted a good grammar school; those inconvenient facts are ignored. The reason is obvious: the entire anti-Stratfordian case rests on the assumption that the Man from Stratford could not possibly have had the knowledge needed to write his plays, that only an aristocrat could have done so. To make this scenario look more likely, Shakespeare is ridiculed as an ignoramus, and facts that suggest otherwise are swept underneath the carpet.

—Paul Franssen, lecturer in English Literature at Utrecht University, the Netherlands.

Doubter Response

Paul Franssen says that "the entire anti-Stratfordian case rests on the assumption that "the Man from Stratford could not possibly have had the knowledge needed to write his plays." No, this is not our position. As stated in our response to Question 5, the issue is "not" that a commoner, "even in the rigid, hierarchical social structure of Elizabethan England, could not have managed to do it some-how; but how could it have happened without leaving a single trace?" Also, "it would have been a remarkable achievement, and should have been much commented upon at the time...That is not what one finds."

Franssen only addresses fictional works by authorship doubters, not by Stratfordians. He does not mention, for example, the fictional so-called biography, *Will in the World*, by Harvard English Professor Stephen Greenblatt. The book begins, "Let us imagine," and Greenblatt admits that it is not a work of biography, but of his personal fantasies. He was criticized for this by his colleague, James Shapiro, in his book, *Contested Will*, and ridiculed by perhaps our best living English Renaissance scholar, Alastair Fowler.

Greenblatt slipped up in 2004, committing an uncharacteristic act of candor, reported in an article in *Harvard Alumni Magazine* (Sept-Oct, 2004). Referring to the authorship controversy, Professor Greenblatt said:

the process of writing the book…has made me respect that preposterous fantasy, if I may say so, rather more than when I began…because I have now taken several years of hard work and 40 years of serious academic training to grapple with the difficulty of making the connections meaningful and compelling between the life of this writer and the works that he produced.

Greenblatt found it "difficult" to make meaningful connections between the writer and the works! This is our point, and the reason why so many people have expressed doubt. Yet despite this insight, a year later Greenblatt wrote as follows in a letter to the editor of the *New York Times*:

> The idea that William Shakespeare's authorship…is a matter of conjecture, and the idea that the "authorship controversy" should be taught in the classroom are the exact equivalent of current arguments that 'intelligent design' be taught alongside evolution. In both cases an overwhelming…consensus, based on a serious assessment of hard evidence, is challenged by passionately held fantasies whose adherents demand equal time. The demand seems harmless enough until one reflects on its implications. Should claims that the Holocaust did not occur also be made part of the standard curriculum?

Now that is fiction! An "overwhelming consensus"? Two years later, on April 22, 2007, the *New York Times* reported the results of a survey it conducted among Shakespeare professors in the U.S. Eighty-two percent said that there is "no good reason" to question whether William Shakespeare of Stratford-on-Avon was the principal author of the poems and plays attributed to him; but 6% said that there is "good reason," and an additional 11% said there is "possibly good reason." One would not find that 17% of biology professors harbor doubts about evolution, or that 17% of history professors doubt the Holocaust. But one does find that 17% of U.S. Shakespeare professors have doubts about the Bard. Doubters are in the minority, but not such a small minority that they should be ignored, or prohibited from teaching their students about the issue, as Prof. Greenblatt suggests.

In fact, nearly every biography of Shakespeare should be considered a work of fiction. Orthodox Shakespeare scholars have the wrong man, as seen in the seemingly endless stream of fanciful so-called biographies, trying to put flesh on the bones of what Mark Twain termed "a brontosaur—nine bones and six hundred barrels of plaster of Paris."

—John M. Shahan
—Dr. Kurt Kreiler, author of *Anonymous SHAKE-SPEARE: The Man Behind.*

Question 32: Are there any other writers whose authorship is questioned?

In 1647, The King's Men—the acting company which owned and performed the plays of Shakespeare—published a collection of plays by their other great authorial brand, Francis Beaumont and John Fletcher. The book contained plays by Beaumont and Fletcher, plays by Beaumont writing on his own, and Fletcher on his own, and it contained plays written by neither. Many plays of this period were published with no author's name on the title pages, but Shakespeare's plays were probably not among them.

In 1599, or thereabouts, there appeared *The Passionate Pilgrim*, a collection of poems with Shakespeare's name on the title page. But according to the playwright Thomas Heywood, Shakespeare was "much offended" with the publisher "that altogether unknown to him presumed to make so bold with his name." The King's Men may not have cared very much about dramatic authorship later in the seventeenth century, but Shakespeare cared, and Shakespeare was really careful.

—Martin Wiggins, Senior Lecturer and Fellow at The Shakespeare Institute, University of Birmingham.

Doubter Response

Martin Wiggins ignores the question, to which the answer is "many." But it is not very relevant to the question of authorship. Wiggins' point that "The King's Men may not have cared much about dramatic authorship...in the seventeenth century, but Shakespeare cared" is interesting because, contrary to what he says, the opposite is true, as he should know. Frank Arthur Mumby, a leading expert on publishing history, wrote

> it is a remarkable fact that not only were all his plays published without the slightest sign of interest on his part, but his Sonnets as well...

Mr. Shakspere is regarded by historians as having been litigious in his business dealings, but strangely not when it came to his poems and plays. E.K. Chambers observed, not without astonishment, that other writers "were far from adopting Shakespeare's attitude of detachment from the literary fate of his works."

—Robert Detobel, co-editor of the German *Neues Shakespeare Journal.*

Question 33: What kind of authority is the 1623 folio collection of Shakespeare's plays?

The 1623 Folio edition of Shakespeare's plays, published seven years after he died, is an extraordinarily important authority in establishing what he wrote. Approximately half of the plays it contains, including *Macbeth*, *Antony and Cleopatra* and *The Tempest*, had not been published prior to 1623 and might otherwise be lost to us. The lists of plays corresponds to many other pieces of evidence as to what plays were his. The editors, John Heminges and Henry Condell, Shakespeare's long time colleagues in the King's acting company, had access to drafts and scripts of the plays that had been used in production. They prefaced it with tributes from prominent intellectuals and writers, notably Ben Jonson, who publicly proclaimed in the Folio volume that he regarded Shakespeare as a genius of tragedy equal to Sophocles, Euripides and Aeschylus, and the greatest writer of comedy the world had ever seen. This is stirring praise indeed, coming from a man of such fierce intellectual integrity. That Ben Jonson, and so many others, could have been bamboozled into praising Shakespeare if the plays were not his, or would have consented to a widespread conspiracy to perpetuate a lie about the authorship, is simply inconceivable.

—David Bevington, Phyllis Fay Horton Distinguished Service Professor Emeritus in the Humanities at the University of Chicago.

Doubter Response

We agree with the first 80 per cent of what David Bevington says about the significance of the First Folio. Ben Jonson, however, was not "bamboozled." He praised Shakespeare and rightly so. The plays were his, appearing as by William Shakespeare, just as the works of Mark Twain were his and appeared under his pen name. The authorship question is whether "William Shakespeare" was a pen name. Note that nothing in the First Folio clearly and unambiguously attributes the plays to Shakspere of Stratford-upon-Avon.

There is no evidence of a "widespread conspiracy to perpetuate a lie." Doubters make no such claim, and no "widespread" conspiracy would have been required. This is an assumption that Stratfordians impose on doubters for the sake of argument. If a writer uses a pseudonym, does this mean that he, his family, friends and publisher are part of a "widespread conspiracy" to conceal his identity? What is "widespread"? There is little evidence that people knew who the author Shakespeare was in the first place.

However the claim that actors Heminges and Condell wrote the introductory material in the First Folio, or edited the plays, was shown to be false by George Steevens in 1770. His conclusion has been accepted by most Shakespeare scholars ever since. Would they and Ben Jonson have helped to perpetuate a myth for some good reason? Probably yes. We know that this claim by the two actors is false. Why assume everything else is true?

—Richard F. Whalen, Past President, Shakespeare Oxford Society; author of numerous research articles and book reviews in Oxfordian publications over nearly two decades.

Question 34: The 1623 Folio includes poems in praise of Shakespeare by other writers. Do these support Shakespeare's authorship of the *Works*?

The poems in praise of Shakespeare from the 1623 Folio couldn't do more to point at the man behind, and, indeed, in the work. Ben Jonson first meditates on the engraving of Shakespeare on the facing page, insisting a better likeness—the lively figure of his wit—is revealed not in "his picture, but his book". In their "Epistle to the Great Variety of Readers", Shakespeare's fellow actors, Heminge and Condell, speak of the care and pain they have taken to present Shakespeare's writings to the world "as he conceived them". And they, too, imagine Shakespeare's works as a triumph over death. The consolation and joy in Jonson's chattier [!] poem to the memory of his "beloved, the Author" also derives from the continued life his friend enjoys in print, shaking a lance "as brandish't at the eyes of ignorance".

"Shake a lance" is a pun on Shakespeare of course. The "eyes of ignorance," unsuspected by Jonson, are those who dare to doubt he wrote the plays.

—Ewan Fernie, Professor of Shakespeare Studies at The Shakespeare Institute, University of Birmingham, Stratford-upon-Avon.

Doubter Response

The poems in the First Folio praising Shakespeare do *not* point unambiguously to the man Fernie accepts as the dramatist. As was often the case in Elizabethan-Jacobean times, the poems about the author are ambiguous, and cannot be taken at face value. Ben Jonson was a "master" of ambiguity, as noted by Annabel Patterson of Yale and Leah Marcus of Vanderbilt—both well-respected English Renaissance scholars—and by Jonson's biographer, David Riggs of Stanford.

Even the references to "Stratford" and "Avon" are found on two different pages. Other than these two brief allusions, neither Ben Jonson nor Leonard Digges provides any identifying information—not his dates of birth and death, or names of any family members, nor any revealing episode from his life. Short on individualizing facts, they gave us generalized superlatives that describe the author, but nowhere is the man. If the Folio "couldn't do more," where is the coat of arms that Shakspere was so proud of?

Ewan Fernie's claim that the Folio "couldn't do more" is belied by the fact that Shakspere's home town is identified only via widely separated allusions that one must combine by putting "Sweet swan of Avon" together with "time dissolves thy Stratford moniment." To get the town, the words get reversed, hyphens get added, and also the word "upon." "Stratford-upon-Avon" does not appear. If he was from Stratford, why not just say so?

—Richard F. Whalen

Question 35: Does Shakespeare's will shed any light on his professional practice?

Shakespeare's will contains virtually no references to his theatrical life in London. He describes himself as "William Shackspeare of Stratford-upon-Avon...gent", and the only direct reference to the capital is to the Blackfriars property, part of the extensive real estate left to Susanna. With hindsight, we know that "my ffellowes John Hemynges, Rychard Burbage & Henry Cundell," to whom he left 26s 8d each for a mourning ring, were professional colleagues; but intriguingly their legacies are a belated insertion in the middle of purely local remembrances. More relevant to an idea of his theatrical life would have been mention of his theatre shareholding, but shares and leases were regarded as personal estate and would have been recorded in the inventory of Shakespeare's moveable property taken after his death. This, sadly, does not survive; and we are left, in his will, with virtually no evidence of his professional life or practice.

—Mairi Macdonald, former Head of Local Collections at the Shakespeare Birthplace Trust, and contributor to *The New Dictionary of National Biography* and *The Oxford Companion to Shakespeare*.

Doubter Response

Mairi Macdonald is correct in saying that Shakspere's will "contains virtually no reference to his theatrical life in London." She might have thought from that alone that there is reason to doubt he was the author. Actually it contains no references whatsoever to theatrical life: no costumes, no theatrical memorabilia, no bequests to apprentices. Only the monetary gift to fellow actors Heminges, Burbage and Condell "to buy them rings," and she acknowledges that this was an interlineation. It's odd that Shakspere the actor only remembered his fellow actors as an afterthought, and then with nothing special.

But since he was an actor, how does Shakspere's will compare to those of other actors? *Playhouse Wills*, edited by E.A.J. Honigmann and Susan Brock, sheds light on that question. Thomas Pope, Augustine Phillips, John Underwood, John Shank, Henry Condell and John Heminges all bequeathed shares in the premises of the theaters and/or shares in the theatrical proceeds in the main bodies of their wills—where such valuable assets belong. If Shakspere owned theater shares, they should have been in the body of his will, too.

The assertion that "shares and leases were regarded as personal estate and would have been recorded in the inventory of Shakespeare's moveable property...after his death" is wrong. Personal property appears in the main body of wills of testators of all occupations. Only appraised values of items are usually listed in inventories. The missing inventory is a handy device for explaining away missing property one would expect in the will of a literary man, and Stratfordians resort to it often; but it doesn't explain as much as they would like to think.

—Bonner Miller Cutting

Question 36: Is it suspicious that no books are mentioned in Shakespeare's Will?

Books were not often mentioned in wills; they might have been listed in inventories. Sadly, the inventory of Shakespeare's possessions doesn't survive. Those of his possessions that are not named as bequests were inherited by his daughter and son-in-law, Susannah and John Hall; and in John Hall's 1635 will, he bequeathed what he called a "study of books" to his son-in-law, Thomas Nashe, "to dispose of them as you see good."

In 1637 the study of New Place (Shakespeare's home) was broken into as part of a legal dispute, and "divers books" and "other goods of great value" were taken away.

In the collections of The Shakespeare Birthplace Trust are two books which might have belonged to Shakespeare. One is Plutarch's *Lives of the Noble Grecians and Romans* of 1579. Our copy belonged to Lord Strange, 5th Earl of Derby, whose company of actors performed some of Shakespeare's early works. Perhaps this is the very copy that Shakespeare used to write his Roman plays. In 1643, Queen Henrietta Maria (whose husband Charles I loved Shakespeare) visited Stratford and was given the life of Katherine de Medici [*sic*] by Susannah Hall, possibly from her late father's own library.

—Diana Owen, Director of The Shakespeare Birthplace Trust.

Doubter Response

All the conjectures ("might have," "perhaps," "possibly") do not mitigate the fact that no books are mentioned in the will. Then as now, testators made specific bequests of their most precious possessions; thus the absence of books, at the very least, is an indication that books were not important to this person.

There is also no mention of any bookshelves, cabinets or cases that could contain books, tables or desks on which to write or study from books, manuscripts, papers, correspondence, maps, musical instruments—nothing suggesting in any way that this was a writer. This is surprising, and contrary to our expectation of a profoundly learned individual associated with the creation of the Shakespeare canon.

It is indeed surprising that no books appear in this will in light of the sheer number, and also the rarity of many of the books used as sources in the plays. Many were expensive, leather-bound books. It is highly unlikely that such prized items would have been relegated to an inventory, something usually prepared by neighbors. If so, they would have been listed with livestock, crops, and mundane household items.

Moreover, there is no bequest for the education of anyone! He left bequests for five minor children, but never suggested that the money be used for their education, even though it was common to do so. He had a sizable estate, but left no money to educate anyone in Stratford. He made no bequests to the town grammar school, allegedly the source of the education that enabled him to write the Shakespeare canon; this at a time when ordinary people left bequests to educate others in their community. In fact, the early 17th century reached a high point in philanthropic giving in England. (*When Death Do Us Part*, Arkell, ed). Yet Shakespeare, of all people, was an exception? The Birthplace Trust should stop pretending that the only problem with the will is the absence of books.

—Bonner Miller Cutting

Question 37: How was Shakespeare commemorated on his death?

Shakespeare was commemorated on his death in 1616 by a fine monument which was erected in Holy Trinity Church. It carries inscriptions praising him as a writer comparable to great figures of antiquity. The Dutch-born sculptor, Gerard Janssen, had a workshop in Southwark, near The Globe Theatre, and produced the stone effigy for Shakespeare's Stratford friend, John Coombe, for Holy Trinity Church in 1614.

The First Folio of 1623 is itself a great memorial to Shakespeare made possible by his friends and fellow actors John Heminges and Henry Condell. Shakespeare had left money to both of them to buy mourning rings.

At the front of the First Folio Heminges and Condell write a touching letter to Shakespeare's "Great Variety of Readers". There are commendatory poems from the writers Ben Jonson, Hugh Holland, Leonard Digges, and James Mabbe. In an edition of Shakespeare's poems in 1640, there is an elegy by William Basse of which there are also many early manuscript versions, one of them headed "On William Shakespeare, buried at Stratford-upon-Avon, his town of nativity.'"

—Peter Kyle, Chairman of the Shakespeare Birthplace Trust, Director General of the English-Speaking Union, and former Chief Executive of Shakespeare's Globe.

Doubter Response

"Shakespeare," the author, was *not* commemorated on the death of Mr. Shakspere in 1616. Contrary to what Peter Kyle says, the death of the Stratford man went unnoticed until 1623. The plain slab under which he is said to have been buried does not even carry his name. If he was the author, he should have been eulogized and buried in Westminster Abbey. That would have been a suitable commemoration, but nothing like it happened. The earliest reference to Shakspere's monument is in 1623, not in 1616 as Kyle implies. There is no evidence at all that it was built in 1616, or that anyone saw it prior to 1623.

According to antiquarian William Dugdale, the original effigy at Holy Trinity Church depicted a man with a drooping moustache clutching a sack of wool or grain to his belly, likely a businessman, with no pen, no paper, no writing surface as in today's monument. This is what Dugdale drew during his 1634 visit to Stratford, and what Hollar engraved for Dugdale's Antiquities of Warwickshire (1656). Records show that the monument was repaired and "beautified" several times in the 1700s. So yes, today's effigy clearly does depict a writer—with pen, and paper, and a pillow (of all things!) as a writing surface.

The inscription never specifically says that it is a monument to the writer Shakespeare. To anyone living in Stratford who may have known the man, the epitaph could appear to say no such thing. It neither names, nor quotes from, any of the works, and it never mentions poetry, plays, acting or theater. Shakespeare's biographers often ignore the epitaph. Epitaphs of other writers of the time identify them clearly as writers; why not Shakespeare's epitaph?

No document says that actors Heminges and Condell "made possible" the First Folio. They were not men of letters, or editors capable of undertaking a publishing project. Ben Jonson was qualified, having published his own folio in 1616. Most scholars have long thought that Jonson probably wrote the epistles signed by Heminges and Condell.

The elegy that Peter Kyle says was by William Basse was not by him. It first appeared in 1633 in a posthumous volume of poems by John Donne, where it is attributed to him. It was entitled "An Epitaph upon Shakespeare," and said nothing about Basse or birth and death in Stratford. Basse didn't include the poem in either of two anthologies of his own poems, probably because it wasn't his. Three dozen manuscript copies of the poem have turned up, but only eight have titles mentioning Stratford, or death in 1616. None indicates who added these references to Stratford, or to his burial in Stratford in 1616. They were likely added to the eight copies after 1633, almost two decades after he died.

—Richard F. Whalen

Question 38: Does the memorial bust of Shakespeare tell us anything about his profession?

A memorial bust for Shakespeare was erected in Holy Trinity Church, Stratford-upon-Avon, between his death in 1616, and 1623, when Leonard Digges refers to it as Shakespeare's 'Stratford monument' in a poem at the front of the First Folio. The bust was installed during the lifetime of his widow, two daughters, and his son-in-law. Anne Shakespeare died in 1623. Its inscription starts with two lines in Latin, comparing Shakespeare with famous classical writers: calling him "a Socrates" in mind (after the Greek philosopher) and "a Virgil in art" (after the Roman poet). In English we go on to read that "all that he hath writ, leaves living art but page to serve his wit." Shakespeare is here honored as a great writer. "Living art" refers to his work as a dramatist, and the image of a page serving him is also a pun on the page of a book. The monument and its inscription were presumably approved by the vicar, the surviving members of Shakespeare's family, and many townspeople who had known Shakespeare.

—Paul Edmondson, Head of Research and Knowledge for The Shakespeare Birthplace Trust, co-author (with Stanley Wells) of *Shakespeare's Sonnets*, and a priest in the Church of England.

Doubter Response

At least Paul Edmondson doesn't say that "Shakespeare was commemorated on his death in 1616 by a fine monument…," as Peter Kyle does. Rather, he says that it was "erected…between his death in 1616, and 1623," when it's referred to in the First Folio. Okay so far. But then he claims that the "bust" was installed "during the lifetime of his widow…Anne Shakespeare died in 1623." This is sheer speculation. We do not know exactly when the monument was built, or precisely when Anne Shakspere died, either. The First Folio was published in December, 1623, although its printing began a year earlier.

195

Nor does anything show that the vicar, surviving family members, or any townspeople approved the monument, as Edmondson asserts we may presume. It is all supposition. There is no record of anyone in Stratford saying they thought Shakspere was a writer, and no record of his family, the vicar or townspeople objecting to the sack-holder bust.

The monument's inscription is rarely quoted, probably because it seems too weak and laconic for the greatest poet-playwright of the time (or its implications too dangerous!). The lines in Latin liken the author to Nestor, Socrates and Virgil in terms of judgment, genius and art, respectively. Nestor was a counselor in the Trojan War; Socrates was a philosopher in Plato; but neither was a writer. Virgil was a poet (and he may even have used a pseudonym for some of his poetry), but he was not Shakespeare's favorite poet. It should have been Ovid, who had by far the most influence of anyone on Shakespeare. The inscription does not even give Mr. Shakspere's full name, referring to him only as "Shakspeare." And again, there is no name at all on his gravestone nearby on the floor. Why would the greatest writer of the time have been buried in a grave without a name?

—Peter Dawkins, M.A.

Question 39: What do we learn about Shakespeare from Ben Jonson?

Ben Jonson loved Shakespeare this side idolatry, calling him "Thou star of poets," and of course: that he was "Not for an age but for all time". But he was also critical of his friend: he insisted that Shakespeare lacked art, citing how he had described a sea-shore in landlocked Bohemia. The players say he never blotted a line, "would he had blotted a thousand," he writes. And he even gets in a dig at his fellow grammar school boy's poor grasp of the Classics: "And though thou hadst small Latin and less Greek".

Jonson was not a man to keep a secret. William Drummond recorded his friend's drunken conversation, late at night before he sank into a stupor, imagining Tartars fighting Turks around his great toe; and he could be pretty indiscreet. But in all his writing, Jonson never reveals even the slightest hint that the man he refers to fondly as "My gentle Shakespeare" is anything other than the "Sweet Swan of Avon".

—Gregory (Greg) Doran, Chief Associate Director of The Royal Shakespeare Company, and director of many plays by Shakespeare and his contemporaries.

Doubter Response

Again, Jonson was a master of ambiguity and put this to use in the Shakespeare Folio. In his tribute to the author, he famously said, "And though thou hadst small Latin and less Greek," which is often thought to mean Shakespeare knew little Latin and Greek. But then Jonson immediately compares him to Aeschylus, Euripides, and Sophocles. If he did not know much Greek, why compare him to these famous Greek playwrights? In this context a truer meaning of Jonson's grammatical construction is "And *even if* thou hadst small Latin and less Greek." Shakespeare sometimes used "though" in the same way, as for example: "I'll follow thee, though Hell itself should gape" *Hamlet* 1.ii.247. So Jonson also suggests that Shakespeare knew Latin and Greek, which he clearly did. As seen in the works, he knew Latin and Greek well (also French, Italian and Spanish). Throughout the prefatory matter, Jonson practices his skill at deliberate ambiguity, even at times speaking of the author, and the actor Shakspere, as different persons.

Here is another instance of Jonson speaking of author and actor as different persons: In his tribute to "The author, Mr. William Shakespeare," in the First Folio, Jonson is full of praise, likening the author to Apollo, god of light, renowned for his inspiration and illumination, and to Mercury, messenger of the gods, renowned for his eloquence. But in the only contemporary reference to the actor that could be called biographical (*Timber: or Discoveries; Made upon Men and Matter*, in *Jonson's Workes*, 1641, 97-8), Jonson likens him to the Roman orator Haterius, a highly ineloquent, unenlightened man with a reputation for getting so carried away with words that he muddled them, speaking so much that he had to be stopped. This is not the man praised in the Folio. About Bohemia, Jonson was wrong and Shakespeare was right. It did have a coastline on the Adriatic at one time. Robert Greene also gave Bohemia a coastline in *Pandosto*.

—Peter Dawkins, M.A.

Question 40: When did people start to question Shakespeare's authorship of the *Works*?

In 1623, Leonard Digges predicted that Shakespeare's plays would outlive his "Stratford monument." Eleven years later, a traveler to Stratford wrote that he'd seen the funeral monument of that "famous" poet. Further on in the century, there was a rumor that the writer William Davenant was Shakespeare's illegitimate son. What made the story credible was that Davenant was born in Oxford, and Oxford was a stopover point for Shakespeare's frequent trips between Stratford and London. Stratford vicar John Ward, who ministered to Shakespeare's descendants, was told that when Shakespeare came home to Stratford for good, he still sent new plays back to London twice a year. For the first biography of Shakespeare in 1708, Nicholas Rowe dispatched a man to Stratford to research the playwright's life in town and parish records. In other words, everyone connected the author Shakespeare with the town of Stratford. All the facts were there. It wasn't until 250 years later that anyone questioned the facts.

—Lena Cowen Orlin, Professor of English at Georgetown University.

Doubter Response

First, let's get a few facts straight:
\

1. Stratford "monument" is incorrect. The word used in the First Folio is "moniment." It may have been intended as monument, based on 17th century phonetic spellings, but "moniment" could carry a different meaning—it could mean a collection of documents.

2. The Davenant "rumor" is just that: a rumor. No document shows that Shakspere ever stayed over at Oxford during his frequent trips between Stratford and London.

3. Vicar John Ward said,

> Mr. Shakespeare was a natural wit, without any art at all; hee frequented the plays all his younger time, but in his elder days lived at Stratford, and supplied the stage with two plays every year, and for itt had an allowance so large, that hee spent at the rate of 1,000 £ a-year, as I have heard.

So he said the man had "no art;" and also implied that he did much of his writing after retiring to Stratford. This counts as evidence for Mr. Shakspere? It was hearsay, as Ward himself admits.

4. Yes, Rowe wrote his biography (in 1709 actually) using information from Stratford obtained by his actor friend, Thomas Betterton. Is it not important that he wrote that Shakspere did not even complete grammar school, and gained no proficiency in Latin? If so, how could he have been the author, given the many Latin, Greek, French and Italian source works reflected in the plays—works not yet translated into English?

Lena Cowen Orlin says "everyone connected the author Shakespeare with the town of Stratford," but all of her examples postdate the First Folio in 1623 when that story was put out. There is no evidence that anyone thought the author was from Stratford before then.

Orlin is wrong; questioning of the authorship began in Shakespeare's own time, and in several cases by other writers who were likely in a position to know the truth. The first questioning of authorship was by Robert Greene in Greene's *Groatsworth of Wit* (1592) (see our response to Question 9), even before the name first appeared in print. Then it continued almost immediately after the name appeared on his earliest published poems. In his *Scourge of Villainie*, first printed anonymously in 1598, poet John Marston wrote as follows:

> Far fly thy fame,
> Most, most of me beloved, whose silent name
> One letter bounds. Thy true judicial style
> I ever honour, and if my love beguile
> Not much my hopes, then thy unvalu'd worth
> Shall mount fair place when Apes are turned forth.

It sounds as if Marston knew of some great, concealed author who had a "silent name." The unknown author of the last of three satirical plays entitled *Return from Parnassus*, acted by the students of St. John's College, Cambridge, during the Christmas revels of 1601-2, seems to refer to Shakspere, as indicated by the title "esquire" he had recently acquired, and calling him a "mimick ape" who mouths words better wits have framed.

Poet John Davies of Hereford, in his book of epigrams, *The Scourge of Folly* (1610), includes an epigram addressed to "Mr. Will Shakespeare," referring to Shakespeare as "our English Terence." Terence was a Roman slave who allegedly acted as a mask for the writings of great men who wished to keep their authorship of works concealed.

In 1624 (post-Folio) the second edition of Thomas Vicars' manual of rhetoric gave a list of outstanding English poets, including Geoffrey Chaucer, Edmund Spenser, Michael Drayton, and George Wither, but omitting Shakespeare! Surely he must have known about Shakespeare in 1624. In the third edition (1628), Vicars corrected the omission with a peculiar new sentence inserted after the list:

> To these I believe should be added that famous poet who takes his name from 'Shaking' and 'Spear.' (Schurink, Fred, "An unnoticed early reference to Shakespeare," *Notes and Queries*, March 2006, 72-74).

Here is a reference to Shakespeare implying that the name is a made-up or pen name. The logical explanation is that Vicars knew the First Folio's attribution was incorrect, and didn't want to acquiesce in the misattribution of the plays to the Stratford man in 1623; so he made no mention of Shakespeare in his 1624 publication the following year. By the time of the 1628 edition, he had figured out a way to include Shakespeare while revealing that it was a pen name, but without assuming the risk of openly saying so.*

The Glasgow University copy of the First Folio shows annotations next to the names of several of the "Principal Actors in all these plays." Next to Shakespeare's name is what appears to be a contemporary annotation, reading "leass for making." After consulting the Oxford English Dictionary, the author of the article reporting the discovery wrote:

> Although there is no specific entry for *leass* there are multiple meanings for "lease" spelled various ways. As a noun or adjective, the word may be spelled *leas, laes, lese, les, lees, lesse, less, leace, leis(s)*, leas(s)e, *leys*, and *lase*.*

Note particularly the spelling "leas(s)e." What is important, of course, is the meaning. As an adjective, it means: **"untrue, false, lying,"** as a noun, **"untruth, falsehood, lying"** (3). It was also not uncommon to drop the terminal "e" from words during this period. The article concluded (based on more than what is shown here) that

> in this original Shakespeare *First Folio* [we have] contemporary documentary evidence of someone who knew certain actors and knew of actors of the…period, [and who] stated his opinion that the actor, William Shakespeare, was "untruthful or lying for making" [plays)!" **

George Wither, a poet who would have known Shakespeare, in a poem of his titled, *The Great Assizes holden in Parnassus by Apollo and his Assessours* (1645), declared that the actor Shakspere was a mimic who pretended to be the author Shakespeare.

So there are seven examples showing that even during the period there were doubters. And finally, we have the author's own words, in which he himself says that he did not want, and did not expect, his name to be remembered (Sonnets 72 and 81, respectively). As we point out in Key Question 5, "None of this makes sense, unless his name was not associated with his works at the time." So here we have a contemporary statement in the author's own words that calls the identity of the author into question.

*Donald Frederick Nelson, "Schurink's Discovery of a Century," *Shakespeare Oxford Newsletter*, Vol. 44, No. 1, Spring 2008, 10-11.
**Frank Davis, M.D. "'Leass for Making': Shakespeare Outed as a Liar?" *Shakespeare Oxford Newsletter*, Vol. 43, No. 2, Spring 2007, 3-5.

——Frank Davis, M.D.
——Peter Dawkins, M.A.

Question 41: What reasons do people give for questioning Shakespeare's authorship of the plays?

Of course there are as many reasons for doubting Shakespeare's authorship as there are people who doubt them. And I think some people just love a good story and like to challenge accepted conventions. And I think those people who feel particularly strongly about this often start with a genuine passion for Shakespeare. It's more like a love affair. But when they turn to the archives, and look at the records that have survived about the man, they find very little in there to fall in love with. They don't find the voice of Romeo, or the voice of Hamlet, or the tragic absurdity of Lear. What they find instead is a story about what seems to be a fairly ordinary man, living an ordinary life. And since Shakespeare cannot live up to the author that they've fallen in love with, they turn to the archives to look for other, more colorful characters. I think this is a function of the way that Shakespeare writes. He was able to speak with many different voices, and the only conspiracy of silence is the conspiracy to silence his own voice in his works.

—Stuart Hampton-Reeves, Professor of Research-informed Teaching at the University of Central Lancashire, Chair of the British Shakespeare Association, and author of several books on Shakespeare in performance.

Doubter Response

To say that "there are as many reasons for doubting…as…people who doubt" is false. There is a great deal of agreement about the main reasons to doubt Shakespeare's authorship. These reasons are outlined in the Declaration of Reasonable Doubt, first issued in 2007, and now signed by more than 2,600 people.

There is no mystery about why many people question Shakespeare's authorship, except among those who are in denial, refusing to read the Declaration, or even acknowledge its existence. One reason that is not in the Declaration is that people find "very little to fall in love with" in the records relating to the Stratford man, as Hampton-Reeves says. No matter how much the Birthplace Trust tries to pretend that doubt about the authorship is due to the psychology of doubters, it is, always has been, and always will be, about the evidence.

Originally the issue was based on a lack of connection between the man and the work. Since then, extensive research has found (1) no documentary evidence that Shakspere was a writer, (2) no record that he was ever paid as a writer (although he was an actor), (3) no letter in which he is recognized as a writer, (4) no record of anyone referring to him personally as a writer, (5) no one in his family who acknowledged him as a writer, and (6) he himself left no record that he was a writer. In fact, all we have in his hand are six signatures on legal documents, but otherwise no manuscript, letter, or even a poem. As a doubter once said, Shakespeare was "a singularly taciturn fountain of eloquence."

We have twenty-one references to works attributed to "Shakespeare," but no personal reference to Shakspere as the author of any of them, or as the author of anything else. References to the Stratford man as an actor do not prove, or even suggest, that he was also a writer. In fact, no other professional playwright of that period is known to have been a professional actor. A few, Ben Jonson included, acted in plays at the beginnings of their careers, but as soon as they were established as writers, they abandoned acting. Thus, the main reason for doubt is not some romantic search for "the voice of Hamlet," but, rather, the fact that "the greatest battery of organized research that has ever been directed upon a single person," as one Oxford history professor put it, came up empty.

—Robin Williams

Question 42: What psychological impulse might lie behind the questioning of Shakespeare's authorship?

Doubting Shakespeare's authorship might be a way of dealing with envy and competition. So if great people aren't actually that great, then you don't have to feel quite so measly in relation to them. Then there's also the fact that conspiracy theories often try to give rational explanations for things that are just too sublime or irrational. So the famous figure who dies in a stupid accident must have been killed by the CIA, or whatever. So the idea that Shakespeare was able to do so many things—to know so much about the world, and about the interior lives of human beings, and then to be able to articulate all of that, using strict rhyme and meter, across such a huge body of work—makes him a kind of uncanny figure. And it might be more comforting to think that his works were written by a group of writers (maybe including men and women), or that he actually only wrote a couple of the plays himself.

—Anouchka Grose, writer and psychoanalyst, practising in London.

Doubter Response

The correct answer is that the underlying "psychological impulse" is a search for truth. Is this not the same "impulse" that underlies many of humanity's intellectual pursuits? Anouchka Grose gives no hint in her comments that she considered this rather obvious possibility. The impulse of the Birthplace Trust would appear to be to try to suppress this truth-seeking, using Anouchka Grose to assist in its efforts to stigmatize the issue as a "conspiracy theory." It is outrageous, considering who has signed the Declaration of Reasonable Doubt, that doubters still get labeled as "conspiracy theorists." A quick glance at the signatory list negates this negative stereotype— U.S. Supreme Court Justices; Shakespearean actors; more than 900 advanced degrees; 444 current or former college faculty members; 375 English literature graduates. Does it make sense to think that all of these people are deranged conspiracy theorists? No, it makes no sense at all. So what is going on here? For years, up until last April, the Birthplace Trust had a page on its website that said the following:

> The phenomenon of disbelief in Shakespeare's authorship is a psychological aberration of considerable interest. Endorsement of it in favor of aristocratic candidates may be ascribed to snobbery—reluctance to believe…works of genius could emanate from a man of relatively humble origin—an attitude that would not permit Marlowe to have written his own works, let alone Shakespeare's. Other causes include ignorance; poor sense of logic; refusal, willful or otherwise, to accept evidence; folly; the desire for publicity; and even certifiable madness (as in the sad case of Delia Bacon, who hoped to open Shakespeare's grave in 1856).

Outraged that the Birthplace Trust would define all doubters, without any valid scientific evidence, as psychologically aberrant—implying that doubters are all mentally defective one way or another, on April 5, 2010, the Shakespeare Authorship Coalition sent a letter to then SBT Chairman Stanley Wells, calling attention to the above paragraph and saying that

> If these allegations are true, it should be possible for qualified experts in the disciplines of psychiatry, psychology and sociology to validate your claims with empirical evidence. I hereby challenge you to either obtain such expert validation, or stop making the claims. Specifically, I challenge you to either back up your claims on the SBT website with data worthy of the high scholarly standards you claim to represent, or remove them forthwith.

The complete text of the letter appears at the end of this document. The SAC has received no reply, but the Birthplace Trust did take the authorship page down last spring. It has been replaced, however, by an even more aggressive campaign against doubters. Their label of "psychologically aberrant" has been replaced with "conspiracy theorist," and all doubters, even our best Shakespearean actors, are now "anti-Shakespeareans."

The inclusion of Anouchka Grose, a lone psychoanalyst among an otherwise strikingly homogeneous group of English professors and theater professionals, suggests that they wanted to support their claims with someone who would be perceived as an authority. But looking at Grose's testimony (if she can be thought of as a sort of "expert witness"), how credible is she? "A writer and psychoanalyst, practicing in London" the Birthplace Trust says. There is no mention of any particular expertise in the diagnosis of mental disorders, using psychological testing or any other objective methods. There is no mention of any academic position. Not even any mention of knowledge in the subject she's addressing. Her website and books say nothing about conspiracy theories/theorists that we can see. Nor is there any indication that she has any knowledge about the authorship question.

Having a lone psychoanalyst offer a subjective opinion on the "psychological impulse" that "might" lie behind questioning authorship and expecting this to be taken seriously strikes us as bizarre—like asking any single actor to sum up Shakespeare's personality, or allowing a single Indian journalist to speak for everyone on the Indian subcontinent. And we are supposed to take these methodologically-challenged people seriously when they say that there is "no room for doubt" about the identity of William Shakespeare? This is not only an issue of competence, important as that is; there is a moral dimension. The letter to SBT Chairman Stanley Wells of April 5, 2010 also points out the following:

> You appear to label as "psychologically aberrant" anyone who disagrees with your view. You appear to be exploiting prejudices against the mentally ill to discredit your opponents. The use of such tactics is morally reprehensible, and those who would resort to them are unworthy of being regarded as legitimate stewards of the legacy of William Shakespeare.

Finally, let us not forget that Shakespeare, more than other writers, created characters who struggled with madness, portraying them so realistically and sympathetically as to suggest that he understood their maladies from firsthand experience. The list includes Hamlet, Ophelia, Titus, Timon, King Lear, and Edgar/ Tom O'Bedlam. Yet people who present themselves as the guardians of the legacy of Shakespeare have no qualms about exploiting the stigma against the mentally ill as a weapon to use against their opponents.

To those at the Birthplace Trust responsible for claims that doubt about Shakespeare's authorship is a "psychological aberration," and that doubters are ignorant snobs, and/or publicity hounds with poor senses of logic, who refuse to accept evidence and may be certifiably mad, that we are "anti-Shakespeareans," "intellectual thieves," "conspiracy theorists," "pursuing a poisonous, insidious agenda," there is a question we would like to ask you: Why, in the face of so much evidence for reasonable doubt, and so many well-regarded people who see it as such, do Birthplace Trust people refuse to consider any alternatives, and reply with worn-out clichés, cheap insults, pop psychoanalysis and *ad hominem* arguments?

The answer is that they are defending both a quasi-religious orthodoxy and a fat living. If they allowed themselves to doubt at all, regardless of the evidence, it would threaten both their flush incomes and the beliefs in which they have invested their identities. If they can so glibly accuse doubters of snobbery and parricidal tendencies, we can accuse them of being authoritarian personalities and/or hypocrites. The truth is that they are afraid of the scholarship of doubters, rarely read it, and continue to think that poking fun at Delia Bacon's infirmity and J. Thomas Looney's name is a substitute for honesty and scholarly integrity. Asking the Birthplace Trust to honestly research the Authorship Question is like asking a religion's high priests to honestly research their basic beliefs. The issue for them is long-settled, and like all good authoritarians they prefer to keep it that way. If English professors can diagnose mental disorders, then that is our diagnosis of the Birthplace Trust.

—John M. Shahan
—Frank Davis, M.D.
—Robin Fox, Ph.D., D.Sc.
—Richard Joyrich, M.D.
—Jan Scheffer, M.D., Psychiatrist and Psychoanalyst, Utrecht, The Netherlands
—Earl Showerman, M.D., President, Shakespeare Fellowship
—Richard Waugaman, M.D., Clinical Professor of Psychiatry, Georgetown University.

Question 43: What part does James Wilmot play in the authorship story?

James Wilmot was a Warwickshire clergyman who lived from 1726 to 1807. There's a manuscript in the Senate House Library of the University of London which seems to represent two lectures given to the Ipswich Philosophical Society in 1805 by a man called James Corton Cowell. According to this, Wilmot had started trying to write a biography of Shakespeare, but, finding little evidence, decided that the works must have been written by Francis Bacon, which would make Wilmot the first anti-Stratfordian. But people now have questioned the authenticity of this manuscript. There's no evidence that either Cowell or the Ipswich Philosophical Society ever existed. And in 2010 James Shapiro, in his book *Contested Will*, showed conclusively that the manuscript is a forgery, done probably in the early twentieth century. And that means that the beginnings of the authorship debate can now be said to date not from the late eighteenth century, as had been supposed, but with Delia Bacon, some fifty years later.

—Stanley Wells, Honorary President of The Shakespeare Birthplace Trust, Professor Emeritus at the University of Birmingham, author of many books about Shakespeare, and general editor of the Oxford and Penguin Shakespeares.

Doubter Response

The answer is that the James Wilmot episode sheds no light on the origins of the authorship question. The first person to investigate the manuscript in the Senate House Library of the University of London was not Professor James Shapiro, or any orthodox Shakespeare scholar, but, rather, Dr. John Rollett, a prominent authorship doubter and researcher, himself living in Ipswich. It was Rollett, in 2002, who noticed the absence of any record of either the Ipswich Philosophic [*recte*] Society or the said James Corton Cowell. Educated middle-class men— such as Cowell was supposed to be—left numerous records among those that survive: births and deaths, marriages, voting lists, property transactions, legal cases, newspaper reports, wills. After many hours of research in the Suffolk Record Office, Dr. Rollett drew a complete blank. He then asked an eminent local historian (and past President of the Society of Antiquaries) to investigate; he too could find no trace of the man.

Rollett followed this up, involving Dr. Dan Wright, Director of the Shakespeare Authorship Research Centre at Concordia University in Portland, Oregon, Dr. Daniel Mackay, and Dr. Alan Nelson, a noted documents and handwriting expert in the English department at U.C. Berkeley. Professor Nelson, an orthodox scholar, also involved two additional document experts in assessing the Wilmot address. The consensus was that the document was either a later copy of a genuine manuscript, or a later forgery. But since no trace of James Corton Cowell could be found in the local records, the evidence strongly favored forgery.

Professor Wright gave an account of these findings at a conference in April 2003, concluding that the manuscript was a Baconian forgery. His presentation was written up and published in *Shakespeare Matters* (Vol. 2, no. 4; Summer 2003). Professor Shapiro refers to this account on page 284 of his book *Contested Will* (2010), but his announcement on page 12 of his "discovery" that the manuscript was a forgery makes no mention of the fact that this conclusion had been documented in print seven years earlier. It would be appropriate for Professor Shapiro to give full credit to Dr. Rollett for being the first to question the manuscript's authenticity, and to acknowledge Rollett and Wright's determination to initiate a formal scientific investigation into the authenticity and provenance of the manuscript prior to any orthodox scholar.

In any case, Shakespeare's authorship was first questioned in his own time (See Question 40).

—Daniel L. Wright, Ph.D., Professor of English; Director, Shakespeare Authorship Research Centre, Concordia University, Portland, Oregon.

Question 44: What part did Delia Bacon play in the Shakespeare authorship discussion?

The Shakespeare Authorship controversy really begins with a remarkable New England scholar, Delia Bacon, who in the middle of the 19th century concluded that there was an inexplicable gap between the Shakespeare biography and the philosophical understanding to be found in the works. The plays must therefore have been written by a group of educated and worldly courtiers, including Francis Bacon and Walter Raleigh, who hoped to replace monarchical tyranny with republican liberty, but in defeat turned to literature, writing under cover of the Shakespeare disguise. Bacon used remarkably modern methods of literary analysis, argued that the plays were written collaboratively, and that they contained a radical political agenda, all many years before these ideas became current. But her intellectual isolation forced her into the pursuit of a "monomania", and her unfortunate collapse into mental illness enabled her opponents cruelly to label her as a madwoman. In every respect her career shaped the future of the Shakespeare Authorship Question.

—Graham Holderness, writer, Professor of English at the University of Hertfordshire, and author of *Nine Lives of William Shakespeare* (Continuum, 2011).

Doubter Response

Graham Holderness has written a nice summary, and we thank him for it. Delia Bacon was a most remarkable woman. She burst onto the scene by winning first prize ($100) in a *Philadelphia Saturday Courier* writing contest, besting the young Edgar Allan Poe. She was widely recognized as a brilliant historian on the New England lecture circuit. Friends and patrons included Ralph Waldo Emerson, Thomas Carlyle and Nathaniel Hawthorne, all of whom supported her work. Their prolific correspondence is extant.

Her first article about Shakespeare appeared in *Putnam's Magazine* in 1856. Its success encouraged her to publish *The Philosophy of the Plays of Shakespeare Unfolded* in 1857. Some blame her, while others credit her, for being first to devote a book to the subject. It includes a brilliant analysis of three plays: *King Lear*, *Julius Caesar*, and *Coriolanus*. Bacon was no madwoman—not when she worked out her theories and wrote her book. But she became physically ill from stress and malnutrition, traveling alone in England—uncommon for a woman at the time—pursuing her search for Shakespeare's identity. She suffered what we would today call a nervous breakdown, and died at the age of 48.

Bacon was challenging a quasi-religious myth—an enterprise for which there were few precedents or sources of intellectual and moral support. She paid a terrible price for it. Defenders of orthodoxy, including the Birthplace Trust, have used Bacon's tragic end to stereotype doubters and suppress most dissent, imposing a strict conformity on much of academia. A side effect is that non-academics and scholars from other disciplines now fill the void.

In 2000, Elliott Baker edited an abridged edition of *Shakespeare's Philosophy Unfolded*, making the thoughts of this remarkable woman, Delia Bacon, easily accessible to us all.

—Carole Sue Lipman, President, Shakespeare Authorship Roundtable of Los Angeles.

Question 45: Is it plausible that Sir Francis Bacon wrote the plays attributed to Shakespeare?

[See DoubtAboutWill.org/exposing.]

Question 46: Do you agree with Mark Twain that you have to experience something in order to write about it?

Twain may be right, but only up to a point. Surprisingly, he obviously fails to account for the autonomy of the imagination. How did Swift experience Gulliver's travels to Lilliput, for example, or the voyage to the Hounyhms [*sic*], but through the imagination, the most powerful attribute of the human intellect? Consider also Shakespeare's contemporaries: Edmund Spenser and

The Faerie Queen, Marlowe's *Faustus* and *Tamburlaine*. How else could they have been experienced but through the imagination? Shakespeare's imagination carried him everywhere, through time as well as place, and has never been surpassed.

—Jay Halio, Professor Emeritus at the University of Delaware, and who has published widely on Shakespeare.

Doubter Response

What Twain really said was that you have to know something about a subject in order to write about it, and that most people write about what they know.

Professor Halio speaks of "the autonomy of the imagination," and says "Shakespeare's imagination carried him everywhere…" Everywhere? So knowledge does not have to be learned, it can be imagined? Twain focuses on the Bard being "limitlessly familiar with the laws, and law-courts, and law-proceedings, and lawyer-talk, and lawyer-ways…" He claims that the legal expertise in the plays reflects practical experience that cannot be connected with the presumed writer. How can a writer "imagine" legal knowledge?

Furthermore, the depth and breadth of many disciplines of knowledge found in the works is staggering. Lengthy lists can be found in various places, such as in the Declaration of Reasonable Doubt, and in other rebuttals in this document. Is it credible to think that all of that knowledge could have been acquired via imagination?

"Imagination" and "genius" are mystifications used to shore up a house of cards based on the assumption that Shakespeare's works could have been written by someone who left no trace of evidence that he had done so. There are no plays, no poems, no letters, or diaries in the supposed author's own hand. Twain said that the Stratford myth is based on "guesses, inferences, theories, conjectures—an Eiffel Tower of artificialities rising sky-high from a very flat and very thin foundation of inconsequential facts."

—Keir Cutler, Ph.D. (doctorate in theatre), Actor, Playwright; adapter of Twain's book, *Is Shakespeare Dead?*

Question 47: Why did Sigmund Freud doubt Shakespeare's authorship?

It's fun to psychoanalyze the founder of psychoanalysis. Why was Freud a doubter? Was it a professional sense that the truth is always obscure and never self-evident? Was it because the facts of Shakespeare's life were irreconcilable with Freud's crassly biographical reading of *Hamlet*? Or was it a form of revenge on the only writer with a greater understanding of psychology than his own?

Why do we relate to Richard III? Because, Freud wrote, he magnifies something in all of us: "We all reproach Nature for congenital disadvantages...Why did She not give us the lofty brow of genius or the noble profile of aristocracy? Why were we born in a middle class home instead of in a royal palace?", Freud asked.

There's a submerged anti-Stratfordian logic here: To come from a middle-class home is not something to be envied. But we envy Shakespeare. Ergo Shakespeare cannot have come from a middle-class home.

Whatever lay behind Freud's doubts, it's an attempted patricide—an unconscious retaliation against an overwhelming father figure. Perhaps, after all, Freud was right about Oedipus, if very wrong about William Shakespeare.

—Paul Prescott, Associate Professor of English at the University of Warwick, and Associate Academic in the RSC-Warwick Centre for Teaching Shakespeare.

Doubter Response

How ironic that an English professor in that fraternity of Shakespeare scholars which is so territorial about its supposed area of expertise would frivolously encroach on ours. Paul Prescott is wrong about Freud. He offers nothing credible to back up his subjective opinion. Here again it's unclear what qualifications he has to render such an opinion, or what his methodology may be, other than to continue the pattern of *ad hominem* attacks against anyone who dares question Shakespeare's authorship, no matter how respected.

Prescott may find it "fun" to psychoanalyze Freud, but he should still get his facts right. There is no mystery about it. Freud was curious, as many other skeptics were, about the Stratford man's background. What impressed Freud was the methodology presented in J. Thomas Looney's book, not some distortion of psychology. Freud recognized that the psychology of Shakespeare, as found in his works, is not the psychology apparent in the detailed but mundane record of William of Stratford, and that should surprise no one. It is the same reason that orthodox scholars keep denying: Mr. Shakspere does not fit.

Freud's reputation is based on his willingness to ignore conventional wisdom in pursuit of truth. Consequently he has always been controversial. But he did much to synthesize our knowledge of the unconscious mind, and to expand it by practicing psychoanalysis. One core finding of psychoanalysis is that people defend themselves against disturbing realizations through the ego's defense mechanisms. One of the most unhealthy of these defense mechanisms is denial. In our opinion much of the Shakespeare industry is just what the title of this document says it is: "An Industry in Denial"—about the fact that there are good reasons to doubt the identity of the author of the works of Shakespeare.

—Jan Scheffer, M.D., Psychiatrist and Psychoanalyst; Board Member, Society for Psychoanalysis and Culture, Utrecht, Netherlands
—Richard Waugaman, M.D., Clinical Professor of Psychiatry, Georgetown University; Training and Supervising Analyst, Emeritus, Washington Psychoanalytic Institute.

Question 48: Why did Henry James doubt Shakespeare's authorship?

Henry James told a friend he thought it "almost as impossible to conceive that Bacon wrote the plays as to conceive that the man from Stratford, as we know the man from Stratford, did." Almost, but not quite. By the early 1900s, a great deal was known about the man from Stratford. The Romantic idea of Shakespeare's transcendent genius had collided with the distinctly Victorian image of a hard-headed businessman. How could the man who wrote *Hamlet* go on to sue a Stratford neighbor for an unpaid debt? Henry James pretended to be shocked, but he was also fascinated. Did Shakespeare harbor some general truth about artists, even the greatest?—that they are always divided, their creativity always a mystery? This is why late in his own career James described the author of *The Tempest*, unforgettably, as "the monster and magician of a thousand masks".

—Adrian Poole, Professor of English Literature at the University of Cambridge.

Doubter Response

Why did James doubt? For the same reason Freud doubted, and thousands of others. He does not fit! Mr. Poole's transparent effort to minimize the views of Henry James omits the famous statement:

> I am a sort of haunted by the conviction that the divine William is the biggest and most successful fraud ever practiced on a patient world. The more I turn him around and round the more he so affects me.

James cut to the chase. Poole, on the other hand, barely begins to engage the question. Rather, he obfuscates. According to Leon Edel, James believed that Shakespeare's power and contributions had "withstood the siege of the years; he had survived as invulnerable granite. James had always mocked the legends of Stratford-on-Avon. He argued that the facts of Stratford "spoke for a common-place man; the plays for the greatest genius the world had ever known," calling the question of authorship "the most attaching of literary mysteries." (See his story "The Birthplace," cited in our response to Question 55.)

—Ren Draya, Ph.D., Professor of British and American Literature; Chair of the Department of English and Communications, Blackburn College, Carlinville, Illinois.

Question 49: Does the Earl of Oxford have any connection with the theatre?

[See DoubtAboutWill.org/exposing.]

Question 50: Are there any factual objections to the belief that the Earl of Oxford wrote the work attributed to Shakespeare?

[See DoubtAboutWill.org/exposing.]

Question 51: Are there any factual objections to the belief that Christopher Marlowe wrote the work attributed to Shakespeare?

[See DoubtAboutWill.org/exposing.]

Question 52: Who else has been suggested as the possible author of the works attributed to Shakespeare?

Woody Allen comically warned us in an essay some years ago that when you ask the average man or woman who wrote the plays of William Shakespeare you should not be surprised "if you get answers like Sir Francis Bacon, Ben Jonson, Queen Elizabeth and possibly even the Homestead

Act." You may laugh at Mr. Allen's hyperbole, but is it any less improbable than some of the other candidates put forth? The case has been made for no fewer than 77 persons or groups of people to be the true dramatist or dramatists of those plays attributed to William Shakespeare. A list of those unusual suspects—those lesser-known individuals—would read as such: William Alexander, Lancelot Andrews, Richard Burbage, Edmund Campion (who died in 1581), Miguel de Cervantes, The Jesuit priests, Thomas Kyd (who died in 1594), Sir Thomas More (who was beheaded in 1535), Cardinal Wolsey, and even King James I himself.

The list goes on, and suddenly the Homestead Act looks more plausible than ever.

—Matt Kubus, doctoral researcher at The Shakespeare Institute, and a regular contributor to Blogging Shakespeare.

Doubter Response

Matt Kubus uses ridicule to make a spurious argument that does not address the issue. The number of candidates proposed is irrelevant to whether the question itself is valid. The number of candidates shows that the doubts are widespread. Kubus omits some major candidates, but lists obscure ones who have no support at all. There are really just a few leading candidates who have gained any significant support.

—Robin Williams

Question 53: Degrees are awarded to those doubting Shakespeare's authorship at Brunel and Concordia, OR, universities. What is the intellectual justification for this?

(a) Concordia University's Shakespeare Authorship Research Centre regards traditional Shakespeare scholarship as "an industry in denial" and invites enthusiastic amateurs to, Horatio-like, assist in the process of "reporting the cause aright". For $125 a year anyone with an undergraduate degree can become an associate research scholar. $10,000 buys the title of Life Scholar.

—Victoria Buckley, whose work includes doctoral research on Shakespeare and the Gunpowder Plot at the University of Sussex

Doubter Response

Victoria Buckley evidently wants people to think something is misguided at Concordia University. Not so. We merely act in the interest of, and on requests from, our alumnae and others who wish to prolong their Shakespeare studies after attaining their degrees. We provide access to our databases so they can study and do research on a fascinating topic they otherwise could not easily pursue in many of their post-collegiate vocations and locales.

Associate research scholars, for a small annual fee that helps defray the university's costs, gain 24/7 access to journals and other publications that otherwise often aren't easily accessible in print or readily available online. Our Life Scholar program provides support to the university, enabling us to expand our resources and extend them to others who may have limited or no access to them. Does the University of Sussex not do this?

The Birthplace Trust and its academic allies may not like that their exclusive control of access to published, juried scholarship may be coming to an end, but they have no cause to chide us for meeting former students' needs rather than restricting their access to published knowledge. Why are the Birthplace Trust and its allies so worried? Of what are they so afraid?

—Daniel L. Wright, Ph.D.

(b) Brunel's Master's program in Shakespeare Authorship Studies propounds the view that it was the desire for a national and global icon which produced the Shakespeare industry, and argues Shakespeare was not one, but many authors. While there is certainly intellectual justification for serious enquiry into the early modern collaborative writing process, both institutions seek to disprove the research of generations of scholars, and are in danger of obfuscating long-established critical approaches to the history and literary production of the period.

—Victoria Buckley

Doubter Response

Heaven forbid that any college or university should ever disprove "the research of generations of scholars," or challenge "long-established critical approaches." Don't people sometimes win Nobel Prizes for exactly that?

If, as the Birthplace Trust says, their evidence is so clear and strong that there can be "no room for doubt," then they have nothing to fear. The Stratfordian theory could not possibly be displaced. All they have to do is make it clear, by writing it up and presenting it for all of us to see. The problem, of course, is that they cannot, because their assertions are not anything as clear as they say.

What is at stake here is whether a highly defensive, self-interested industry, based on Stratford tourism, can defend itself from a small minority of truth-seekers by imposing strict demands for conformity, with biases favoring their tradition and legends, on academia. Whatever else one may think of our two universities, we have no such conflicts of interest in protecting vested interests or tenured traditions. Our universities exist to serve the needs of our students, not an industry—or a tradition uncritically examined. Our position:

> Berowne: What is the end of study? let me know.
> King: Why, that to know which else we should not know.
> Berowne: Things hid and barr'd, you mean, from common sense?
> King: Aye, that is study's godlike recompense.
> Berowne: Come on then; I will swear to study so,
> To know the thing I am forbid to know.
> —*Love's Labor's Lost*, I.i.55-60.

—Daniel L. Wright, Ph.D.

(c) Schoenbaum's assertion that the Looney Oxfordian theory derives in part from a medium, channelling the disembodied voice of Shakespeare in 1942, neatly demonstrates why it deserves no place in academic Shakespearean curricula.

—Victoria Buckley

Doubter Response

Schoenbaum's assertion is wrong. The Oxfordian theory is based on factual evidence and logical inference. The use of mediums by Percy Allen in the 1940s has nothing to do with it. This is yet another example of the Birthplace Trust using highly unrepresentative narratives and anecdotes to mischaracterize, discredit and smear the entire authorship movement. Just because one may find a few such examples of unscientific eccentricity amongst a handful of enthusiasts, that does not mean they are representative of the larger community. Certainly J.T. Looney was never influenced by such nonsense. He published his book, *Shakespeare Identified* in 1920; how could it have been influenced by some other person using a medium in 1942?

A theory should be evaluated based on the best arguments of its strongest proponents. The strongest arguments of the proponents of doubt about Shakespeare's authorship are very compelling indeed. They should be read.

—Daniel L. Wright, Ph.D.

Question 54: What is the attitude of mainstream Shakespeare scholars towards the authorship discussion?

For a long time, Shakespeare scholars ignored the authorship controversy, treating it as a bizarre, marginal phenomenon. After all, the proponents of other candidates don't develop their arguments according to the standards of scholarship developed in so many fields of academic study (history, biography, textual analysis and so on). Discussing the details of their case with anti-Stratfordians was and continues to be frustrating, because the kinds of evidence they adduce—hypothesis piled on speculation, built on conspiracy theories and secret codes—can't be met with logical argument. But those of us intrigued by the ways in which popular beliefs develop (Elvis lives, Barack Obama wasn't born in the USA, and so on) are fascinated by why it should be that some people might think that Shakespeare couldn't have written Shakespeare. The strange passion that drives these theories is a powerful fact about our society's need to believe.

—Peter Holland, McMeel Family Professor in Shakespeare Studies in the Department of Film, Television and Theatre, and Associate Dean for the Arts at the University of Notre Dame.

Doubter Response

Asking a Stratfordian about the attitude of mainstream Shakespeare scholars to the authorship issue is like asking a priest about the attitude of the Pope toward atheists. Peter Holland is wrong in claiming that authorship doubters do not develop their arguments "according to the standards of scholarship developed in many fields of academic study." Indeed, a substantial proportion of doubters come from those fields of study, including English departments. This is easily verified by visiting the website of the Shakespeare Authorship Coalition and checking the backgrounds of Declaration signatories there. Declaration signatories are as impressive as any of the 60 Birthplace Trust responders.

—A. J. (Tony) Pointon

Question 55: What other theories might be compared to the Shakespeare authorship conspiracy theory and why? [Referred to only as the "authorship issue" in the transcript].

Shakespeare knew: telling and believing stories is the best, and the worst, way to get at the truth: his plays are full of figures telling stories, and lies; and the most unlikely truth of all—that Banquo's ghost could come to the banquet—is dismissed as a woman's story by a winter's fire.

Small wonder, then, that the tale of a Stratford glover's son who became the greatest poet-playwright in England, might be misbelieved. The stories that are believed always involve dark and sinister forces, hidden truths, stolen documents.

From the death of Diana to the president's complicity in 9/11, the stories of conspiracy always seem more satisfying than the messy complexity of truth. They certainly make for better movies. If we prefer to believe that fair is foul, and foul is fair, the case for Shakespeare's authorship of his plays will remain a mystery. Alternatively, you can engage with the more removed mysteries of the plays themselves.

—Kate McLuskie, Director of The Shakespeare Institute, University of Birmingham, from 2005 to 2011, and author of *Writers and their Work: Macbeth*.

Doubter Response

Calling it the "Shakespeare Authorship Conspiracy Theory" is a PR ploy by the Birthplace Trust. Interestingly, they refer to it as the "authorship issue" in the transcript, showing how unnatural it is even for them to call it a "conspiracy theory." We must be very special. Indeed, they don't even bother to define the term, so they can use it just as they please. The examples they offer seem intended to suggest that all conspiracy theories are false, but of course this is not so. Why does the word exist in our language if there are none?

The historical record is clear: actual conspiracies are often uncovered by people willing to tolerate derision, even threats, for calling attention to something that doesn't add up. Woodward and Bernstein were pilloried for saying Nixon was engaged in a conspiracy. Those who tried to expose the "Iran Contra scandal" were mocked and ridiculed for it. Investigators who exposed a long-term study of poor black men in Tuskegee, Alabama, infected with syphilis were called "kooks," "anti-American."

Conspiracies are common. Fortunately most are also relatively benign. As George Bernard Shaw said, for example, "all professions are conspiracies against the laity." Is the Birthplace Trust a conspiracy? Henry James certainly seems to have thought so, based on his story, "The Birthplace" in his book, *The Better Sort* (Charles Scribner's Sons, 1903). This seems worth considering.

Those replying to all of the questions the Birthplace Trust has asked on this subject (why so many?) do not appear to have any particular expertise. One of us spent years researching and writing a book on popular conspiracy theories:

> What I discovered is that most do not hold up under scrutiny. The more one digs, the shakier and less credible they become. The Authorship Question was different. The more I dug, the more credible it seemed, until I became fully convinced of its validity.

What I had set out expecting to debunk turned out to be the most compelling, fact-based "conspiracy" I had ever researched.

—John M. Shahan
—James Broderick, Ph.D., Associate Professor of English and Journalism, New Jersey City University; author with Darren Miller of *Web of Conspiracy: A Guide to Conspiracy Theory Sites on the Internet*.

Question 56: Why conspiracy theories?

Conspiracy theories began once the Bard had been sainted. We like our saints to have a touch of the impossible about them. They are not merely human. Conspiracy is another word, then, for God, delivering something astonishing and then kicking over the traces.

In this way of thinking, our fancies about authorship express our deep-rooted need for magic. There may only be a few conspiracy theorists, but how many of us long for just one of their conspiracies to be true?

But we don't want the wrong kind of magic. Just as the princess is in truth a shepherdess, we don't want our lowborn heroes to be inveterately plebeian. We might think we do, but we don't.

Or maybe Coleridge had it right: Shakespeare must have remained a child, some sort of changeling. Had he been a real flesh and blood man, he would have been a monster. Or maybe our blank-faced nobody was in on it from the start: stealing into unknown spaces; seeing everything and everyone before a soul has even noticed him; and then disappearing. He was his own conspirator.

—Simon Palfrey, Professor of English Literature and Fellow of Brasenose College, Oxford.

Doubter Response

Having tried, and failed, to find anything about this worthy of a response, we pass on it. Anyone interested in our response to charges that the Shakespeare authorship issue is a "conspiracy theory" (whatever that means) should see our replies to Questions 42 and 55. We find it odd that the Birthplace Trust could claim doubters are unscholarly and then publish this.

—The Editor.

Question 57: What does Stephen Fry think about the Shakespeare authorship issue?

[See DoubtAboutWill.org/exposing.]

Question 58: What about the Indian perspective of the Shakespeare Authorship conspiracy theory?

I come from a remote part of India, and the first book I ever read (at the age of 13) was Shakespeare in old spelling. I have loved Shakespeare all my life, and I remember always wanting to visit his birthplace. Therefore, I do not understand where this conspiracy theory comes from. Genius can come from humble origins. Ben Jonson's father was a bricklayer. Many of our Indian writers came from poor backgrounds—perhaps with a humble heart their inspiration was greater. Subramania Bharethi was from a poor family, but was able to impress the king with his poetry. He knew fourteen languages, including French and English. He was inspired by Shakespeare, Shelley, Byron, and Keats. In India we are aware of all these conspiracy theories, but we do not support them ever. We have a high respect for our two-thousand year old written history. Shakespeare's contemporaries did not doubt his authorship or the great minds for 300 years. I am concerned that today's younger generation should not be misled by this insubstantial, inconsequential and ridiculous theory. We all love Shakespeare from Stratford.

—K.S. Vijay Elanqova, journalist for *The Hindu*, writer and a poet.

Doubter Response

We find Mr. Elanqova's statement sincere, and can easily identify with his sentiments. We, too, love Shakespeare. The great majority of us learned to love the author and his works long before hearing that there was any question about who actually wrote them. The idea is counter-intuitive and disturbing; few people come to doubt quickly or easily, and fewer still doubt because they do not want to believe the myth of the Stratford man. It's a very appealing story, especially for people steeped in liberal democratic traditions. But historical truth is about evidence, and too much of the evidence just doesn't add up.

Elanqova says that he does "not understand where this conspiracy theory comes from." He should look into it. It's not as if it's a new theory and little has been written about it. There are literally hundreds of books in print, and thousands of pages available online. A good place to start is the Declaration of Reasonable Doubt, followed by Diana Price's book, *Shakespeare's Unorthodox Biography: New Evidence of an Authorship Problem* (Greenwood-Praeger, 2001). Both are neutral about the true identity of the author. As for it being a "conspiracy theory," please see our replies to Questions 33, 42, 55 and 56.

We would like to correct two common misconceptions in what Mr. Elanqova has said. As we say elsewhere in this document, we do not argue that great writers cannot come from humble beginnings. This is a mischaracterization promulgated by our opponents. The issue is not that it could not have happened, but that there is so little contemporary evidence that it did happen in the case of Shakspere. It would have been a remarkable achievement, and should have left a convincing paper trail for how it happened; but there is no such paper trail. Second, he says that "Shakespeare's contemporaries did not doubt his authorship...for 300 years." In fact, doubts about his identity began during his lifetime. See Question 40.

Finally, we find it strange that the Birthplace Trust would ask a single Indian journalist to give "the Indian perspective," as if any one person could speak for the entire Indian subcontinent. How can he represent something like a billion people based on his subjective viewpoint? A number of Indian nationals have signed our Declaration. What about their opinions?

—James W. Brooks, Jr., Ph.D. (Physics).

Question 59: Why don't you believe that Shakespeare wrote Shakespeare?

SAC Note: Roland Emmerich, director of films including *Anonymous*, outnumbered 59 to 1, with no script to read from like the rest, and whose first language is not English, gave the following answer during a debate at the English Speaking Union in London, where this answer was recorded:

I don't think that William Shakespeare of Stratford, you know, like, wrote these plays because in his will he left not one book. Lots of works of Shakespeare's are, like, kind of, based on other material. Secondly, you know, his father was illiterate, his two daughters were too—very unlikely for a big author of this magnitude, you know, to not, like, teach his children how to write and read.

There's also this fact, you know, in a way, you know, he retired early and became a grain merchant. And there's one thing which always got me because I'm a very visual person. When you look at his eight [sic] signatures, they look not [like] the signature of a learned man or writer, when you, like, compare them with all the other signatures.

SAC Note: Here is Roland Emmerich when given the same opportunity to prepare as others:

For me there are many reasons to doubt the traditional attribution of the works of William Shakespeare to the man from Stratford. The points that strike me most are his signatures—all poorly executed, and hardly a sign for true penmanship; his detailed will, that famously mentioned his "second best bed," but fails to include anything that gives the slightest hint that the man from Stratford had a literary career; and the fact that his two daughters were functionally illiterate. And why did nobody seem to notice the great poet's death in 1616, which was followed by complete silence? The Declaration of Reasonable Doubt, which contains more arguments on this debate, is what everybody should read to learn more about this subject.

Question 60: What do you think about Shakespeare's reputation being stolen and passed off as someone else's?

I was amazed to discover the other day that a distant ancestor of mine was the Earl of Southampton, who was Shakespeare's literary patron.

And one of the points that's not often made is that the Shakespeare Authorship Conspiracy Theory is actually a shameless act of intellectual theft. The whole thing is motivated, I think, by an insidious jealousy, by people who, unfortunately, can't accept and rejoice in another man's talent.

All of the alternative nominees—77 different people the last time I looked (including, one person thinks, my ancestor)—are actually imposters. They themselves can't help being nominated; I'm sure they'd actually be appalled at the thought of having the finger pointed at them.

And of course none of it began until the nineteenth century, and I think perhaps the theory can be understood as part of the Victorian quest for points of origin—as unsettling as Darwin's theory of evolution was for scripture. But it's moved on, and it's turned nasty.

I think intellectual fraud is a very serious offence, and I'm naming it when I see it.

The fact is that all the historical evidence does point to William Shakespeare of Stratford-upon-Avon—a market-town lad, developed by Elizabethan schooling and the culture at the time—who had enormous talent, and who has enjoyed more success than any other writer who has ever lived.

—Dan Snow, television presenter and writer.

Doubter Response

First we want to correct two factual errors. It is not true that "none of it began until the nineteenth century." Doubts about the author's identity started during his own lifetime. See our response to Question 40. It is not true that "all the historical evidence does point to William Shakespeare of Stratford-upon-Avon." See our responses to Questions 1-59, and then the Declaration of Reasonable Doubt About the Identity of William Shakespeare.

The Birthplace Trust has chosen to end its "60 Minutes" with a biased, loaded question that assumes the truth of their indefensible position, and launches a slanderous attack on those with whom it disagrees. This hardly represents the spirit of a collegial inquiry into the truth, but then that's obviously not what they are after if they regard us as intellectual thieves.

Let's get this straight: First the Birthplace Trust and its allies charge repeatedly throughout their "60 Minutes" that authorship doubters are poor, deluded and deranged conspiracy theorists, but then at the last minute they change their tune and say we are all common criminals. If one outrageous false allegation will not stick, then maybe another false allegation will! Which is it? Hasn't it occurred to them that these two scenarios are mutually exclusive? And don't tell us Snow speaks for himself. The Birthplace Trust chose what to include and what not.

This is what the Authorship Question is all about. The Birthplace Trust and its allies promote a man as the author Shakespeare who palpably does not fit; then they attack anyone who tries to find the person who does fit. And they harm their allies by exposing them to ridicule. The fact that they would resort to such an accusation suggests they will deny to the end. Calling us criminals relieves them of any obligation to engage with us in mutual inquiry. That appears to be the point of their entire "60 Minutes" campaign—demonize then shun.

Snow says doubt is motivated "by an insidious jealousy, by people who, unfortunately, can't accept and rejoice in another man's talent." He provides nothing to back this up. What evidence does he offer? None. Is he an expert psychologist or psychoanalyst? No. Is he a neutral, unbiased, disinterested observer with no personal stake in this? Hardly. We therefore feel justified in concluding that his charge is a desperate attempt to divert attention from the weakness of the case for Shakspere by hurling mud at his opponents. At the very least the Birthplace Trust should have considered his qualifications to be psychologizing.

We doubters are truth seekers; we believe in robust, unbridled questioning of authority. Can't rejoice in another man's talent? We revel in the greatness of his plays and poems! Loving them as we do, we feel obligated to pursue, discover and tell the truth about him. Knowing his identity will enlighten us about literary creativity and the nature of genius. It is entirely fitting and proper that we should put forth alternative theories to be tested. Some will be right, some not; this is in the spirit of inquiry—how we expand knowledge.

The question of Shakespeare's authorship should be open to all—to debate the evidence openly and amicably, without fear of being labeled "conspiracy theorists," or "thieves." The notion that anyone would "steal" credit for writing Shakespeare's works is absurd. Only one with a proprietary interest in controlling or capitalizing on him would say so. The Birthplace Trust seems to think they "own" Shakespeare, but Shakespeare belongs to all of us.

—Thomas Regnier, J.D., LL.M., author, "Could Shakespeare Think Like a Lawyer?", University of Miami Law Review (2003)
—Alex McNeil, J.D., Past President, Shakespeare Fellowship; Former Administrator (retired), Massachusetts Appeals Court; author, *Total Television*.

3. What do scientific studies of genius say about the sort of person who wrote the *Works*?

Orthodox scholars often reduce the Question of whether Shakspere had the background to become a genius to whether he attended the Stratford grammar school. They say that as the son of a former town official he could have attended for free. They assume he did, and so case closed, as if this were enough to account for the great genius of Shakespeare. Academic research on genius says otherwise. There should be more, and it is not there.

Dean Keith Simonton, Ph.D., Distinguished Professor of Psychology at the University of California at Davis, and a leading expert on creativity and genius, describes the characteristics one would expect to find in *Origins of Genius, Darwinian Perspectives on Creativity* (1999). The research he summarizes is based on the biographies of other well-known geniuses (not including Shakespeare because too little is known about him—especially his youth). Typical characteristics are (1) enriched home environments during childhood, (2) living in diverse locales during childhood, (3) family reversal of fortune—especially loss of one or both parents early in life, (4) self-educated, with unusually broad interests, (5) a tendency to be independent, autonomous, unconventional, rebellious, iconoclastic, (6) later-born children, not first-borns or "functional" first-borns, (7) emotionally and psychologically unstable, (8) multicultural and bilingual (*Origins*, Chapters 3 and 4).

Looking over these characteristics, it is difficult to make a case that Shakspere fits. He was a functional firstborn (two older siblings died before he was born). Nothing points to an enriched home environment. Both of his parents signed with a mark, and chances are that they had no books. He seems to have spent his entire youth living in Stratford. His father fell on hard times, but there was no great reversal of family fortune during his childhood. Both parents lived until he reached adulthood. He was not multicultural, and nothing suggests he ever left England. Nor does anything suggest he was bilingual. Some assume he was self-educated, without documentary evidence. Nothing shows that he was particularly unconventional or rebellious, or mentally or emotionally unstable.

The idea that Shakspere was our greatest literary genius seems to contradict much of what we thought we knew about the developmental and personality characteristics of literary geniuses. How could all of the scientific evidence be so wrong in this one case? The fact that Mr. Shakspere does not seem to fit is one of the most important reasons for pursuing the authorship question—to resolve the nature of literary creative genius.

4. What about the many people who knew the Stratford man, and knew about the author Shakespeare, but never connected the two?

The failure of anyone in Stratford-upon-Avon to connect their neighbor William Shakspere to the well-known and admired Shakespeare canon is a key question that has never been answered, or even addressed, by orthodox scholars. Sir Fulke Greville, a poet and dramatist himself, was born and raised in the area and was related to the Ardens, the family of Shakespeare's mother. He was an important man in Stratford-on-Avon, and on the death of his father in 1606 was appointed to the office his father had held—Recorder of Warwick and Stratford-upon-Avon. His closest friends were the poets Edward Dyer and Philip Sidney, and he was a patron of Samuel Daniel. Yet nowhere in any of Fulke Greville's reminiscences, or in the letters he wrote or received, is there any mention of the well-known poet and playwright, William Shakespeare, who supposedly was living right under his nose.

The poet and dramatist Michael Drayton was born and raised in Warwickshire, only about twenty-five miles from Stratford-upon-Avon. He wrote plays that appeared on the London stage in the late 1590s, about the same time as those of Shakespeare. In 1612 Drayton published his poem *Poly-Olbion*, a county-by-county history that included well-known men of every kind. In it he referred often to Chaucer, to Spenser, and to other English poets. But in his section on Warwickshire, he never mentioned Stratford-upon-Avon or Shakespeare, even though by 1612 Shakespeare was a well-known playwright. During the last 30 years of his life he spent many summers visiting a household in Clifford Chambers, a village about two miles from Stratford-upon-Avon. He was also an occasional patient of Dr. John Hall, William Shakspere's son-in-law. Yet nowhere in his substantial correspondence did Michael Drayton ever refer to William Shakespeare until more than ten years after Mr. Shakspere's death. When he finally did, he wrote four lines about what a good comedian he was. It is unclear whether he was referring to him as a playwright, an actor, or in some other capacity.

Mr. Shakspere's own son-in-law, Dr. John Hall, kept hundreds of anecdotal records about his patients and their ailments. He frequently noted their characteristics and achievements, remarking, for instance, that Michael Drayton was an "excellent poet." Dr. Hall surely treated his wife's father during the ten years they lived within minutes of each other. But nowhere in his notebook is there any mention of William Shakspere, not even at his death in 1616. It is indeed strange that in the early 1630s, as he was collecting the cases he wished to publish, he should neglect to include any record of his treating his supposedly famous father-in-law whose collected works had been published only a few years earlier.

The eminent historian and antiquary William Camden was deeply involved in the literary and intellectual world of his time. He knew Philip Sidney, was a valued friend of Michael Drayton, and is said to have been a teacher of Ben Jonson. In 1597, in his position of Clarenceaux King of Arms, he was one of the two officials in the College of Arms who approved the application of John Shakspere, William's father, to have his existing coat of arms impaled with the arms of his wife's family, the Ardens of Wilmcote. Thus, William Camden was acquainted with the Stratford Shakspertes, father and son.

In 1607 Camden published the sixth edition of *Britannia*, his county-by-county history of England. In the section on Stratford-upon-Avon, he described this "small market-town" as owing "all its consequence" to two natives—John de Stratford, later Archbishop of Canterbury, who built the church, and Hugh Clopton, later mayor of London, who built the Clopton bridge across the Avon. He failed to mention the well-known playwright William Shakespeare, who supposedly lived in the same town.

The theater-owner Philip Henslowe and the noted actor Edward Alleyn were leading members of the Elizabethan stage community for several decades. In their surviving diaries, letters and other papers, they mention dozens of actors, playwrights, plays, and playing companies. Yet in none of these documents does the name "William Shakespeare" appear. If Shakespeare really were the busy actor and playwright we are told he was, then Henslowe and Alleyn would surely have known him, and mentioned him in their diaries and letters. This body of evidence, none of which has ever been refuted, suggests that there is at least a reasonable doubt that the Stratford businessman was England's greatest dramatist.

—Ramon Jiménez

5. Why did the author say that he did not expect, and did not want, his name to be remembered?

Orthodox scholars say no one questioned the author's identity until long after he died. But they fail to note that the author himself said that he neither wanted, nor expected his name to be remembered; and his works could immortalize others, but not himself. None of this makes sense, unless his name wasn't associated with his works at the time. He says repeatedly that he is in disgrace, beyond recovery (Sonnets 29, 37, 112, 121, 72, 81). Is it hard to imagine that such a man would want his name kept separate from his works?

Sonnet 72

O! lest the world should task you to recite
What merit lived in me, that you should love
After my death,--dear love, forget me quite,
For you in me can nothing worthy prove.
Unless you would devise some virtuous lie,
To do more for me than mine own desert,
And hang more praise upon deceased I
Than niggard truth would willingly impart:
O! lest your true love may seem false in this
That you for love speak well of me untrue,
My name be buried where my body is,
And live no more to shame nor me nor you.
   For I am shamed by that which I bring forth,
   And so should you, to love things nothing worth.

Sonnet 81

Or I shall live your epitaph to make,
Or you survive when I in earth am rotten,
From hence your memory death cannot take,
Although in me each part will be forgotten.
Your name from hence immortal life shall have,
Though I, once gone, to all the world must die:
The earth can yield me but a common grave,
When you entombed in men's eyes shall lie.
Your monument shall be my gentle verse,
Which eyes not yet created shall o'er-read;
And tongues to be your being shall rehearse,
When all the breathers of this world are dead;
   You still shall live, such virtue hath my pen,
   Where breath most breathes, even in the mouths of men.

Six myths about the *Works*, doubters and the Stratford man

1. As long as we have the plays and poems, the identity of the author doesn't matter.

If the identity of Shakespeare does not matter, whose identity does matter? Of course his identity matters. As long as these works are important, so is the author. They can't be fully understood and appreciated without understanding his viewpoint. So it is a critical question for anyone seeking to understand the works, the formative literary culture in which they were produced, or the nature of literary creativity and genius. Even orthodox scholars no longer say, as they once did, that it doesn't matter.

2. Doubters argue that a man from humble origins could not become a great writer.

This is a false stereotype promulgated by defenders of orthodoxy to discredit doubters. They never quote any doubters who hold this view; they should be asked for a citation. An accurate statement is the one that is found in the Declaration of Reasonable Doubt: "Scholars know nothing about how [Mr. Shakspere] acquired the breadth and depth of knowledge displayed in the works. This is not to say that a commoner, even in the rigid, hierarchical social structure of Elizabethan England, could not have managed to do it somehow; but how could it have happened without leaving a single trace?" That is the issue: It would have been a remarkable achievement; it should have been noted and left evidence for how it happened. That is not what one finds in the case of Mr. Shakspere.

3. Doubters who support aristocratic candidates are motivated by snobbery.

It is absurd to think that all of the many outstanding authorship doubters are motivated by snobbery. Was Walt Whitman, the poet of democracy and the common man, a snob? This *ad hominem* argument is a red herring invented by defenders of orthodoxy. Those who resort to it should be asked to provide evidence to back up the claims. They cannot. It is a means for them to avoid having to deal with evidence that does not support them. As U.S. Supreme Court Justice Antonin Scalia has pointed out "It is … more likely that [Stratfordians] are affected by a democratic bias than [supporters of given aristocrat] are affected by an aristocratic bias." (*The Wall Street Journal*, April 19, 2009.)

4. The phenomenon of doubt about Shakespeare is a psychological aberration.

This claim, which appeared on the website of the Shakespeare Birthplace Trust, is false. The Birthplace Trust, when challenged, has failed to back up its claim. See the letter to then-SBT Chairman Stanley Wells below.

5. The authorship debate is just another conspiracy theory, no different from others.

It is absurd to think that all of the many outstanding doubters are conspiracy theorists. Too many very credible people have expressed doubts, focusing just on this one author. This *ad hominem* argument is a red herring used by Stratfordians to change the subject. Those who resort to it should be asked for the names of independent experts who agree. It is a means for them to avoid having to deal with evidence that does not support them.

6. Doubters do not use the same methods as other scholars in attributing authorship.

There may be some authorship doubters who use methods that are not acceptable to mainstream scholars, but they are exceptions, not the rule. It is absurd to think this of all of the many outstanding doubters, many of whom are mainstream scholars themselves. More than 800 signers of the Declaration of Reasonable Doubt have advanced degrees. Where is the evidence that all of these people use methods unacceptable to…whom?

Letter from Shakespeare Authorship Coalition (SAC) Chairman John Shahan to Shakespeare Birthplace Trust (SBT) Chairman Stanley Wells

April 5, 2010

Dear Professor Wells,

I am writing on behalf of the Shakespeare Authorship Coalition to challenge your claim on the SBT website (see "Shakespeare's Authorship" page, bottom) that the phenomenon of widespread doubt about William Shakespeare's identity is "a psychological aberration of considerable interest," attributable to a variety of causes, including "snobbery" based on class prejudice, or "even certifiable madness (as in the sad case of Delia Bacon…)."

If these allegations are true, it should be possible for qualified experts in the disciplines of psychiatry, psychology and sociology to validate your claims with empirical evidence. I hereby challenge you to either obtain such expert validation, or stop making the claims. Specifically, I challenge you to either back up your claims on the SBT website with data worthy of the high scholarly standards you claim to represent, or remove them forthwith.

Any theory should be evaluated based on the best arguments of its strongest proponents. There will, of course, be some level of aberrant thinking and behavior in any population; but to prove your claims, not only must you show that the prevalence of these conditions and behaviors is much greater among authorship doubters than in the general population, or in a control group, such as orthodox Shakespeare scholars, but that they are pervasive.

The enclosed "Declaration of Reasonable Doubt" names twenty prominent past doubters, including Mark Twain, William and Henry James, Tyrone Guthrie and Sir John Gielgud. On what basis do you claim that their doubts were due entirely to the defects you allege? Over 1,700 people have signed the Declaration. Of these, over 300 are current or former college/ university faculty members. Some of them are much better qualified to diagnose psychological disorders than you are. On what basis do you claim that they are aberrant?

You appear to label as "psychologically aberrant" anyone who disagrees with your view. You appear to be exploiting prejudices against the mentally ill to discredit your opponents. The use of such tactics is morally reprehensible, and those who would resort to them are unworthy of being regarded as legitimate stewards of the legacy of William Shakespeare. If you continue to make such allegations, on your website or elsewhere, with no credible evidence to back them up, you should assume that the SAC will pursue this issue further.

Sincerely,

John M. Shahan

Conclusion and request to read and sign the
Declaration of Reasonable Doubt
About the Identity of William Shakespeare

This book is in response to the Stratfordian book *Shakespeare Beyond Doubt*, in which the Shakespeare Birthplace Trust argues that not only is there "no room for doubt" about the identity of the author William Shakespeare, but that the evidence for their home-town favorite, William Shakspere of Stratford, is so clear and incontrovertible that anyone who disagrees, no matter how well-educated, reputable and upstanding they otherwise might be, should be vilified as a "conspiracy theorist," as "insane," and as "anti-Shakespeare." Their aim is to delegitimize the issue, making it a taboo subject so that even Shakespeare students will fear to raise it. They have set a high bar for themselves, and we believe the evidence and arguments presented in this book show there is clearly room for doubt and that the Declaration is now vindicated. Doubters are the rational ones. It is Stratfordians who are in denial—out of touch with reality.

It is not often that a book on such a controversial issue provides an easy way for those who feel strongly about it to take a stand in a way that could make a difference. Quotes from the Declaration are sprinkled through this book as epigraphs to chapters that back up most points. We think the Declaration has held up extremely well, and we now invite you to go online and read it in its entirety for the first time, and, if you agree, to sign it. Here are the closing lines that the Birthplace Trust finds so threatening:

> We make no claim in signing this declaration to know exactly what happened, who wrote the works, nor even that Mr. Shakspere definitely did not. Individuals have their own views about the author, but all we claim here is that there is room for doubt and other reasonable scenarios are possible. If writers and thinkers of the stature of Henry James, Ralph Waldo Emerson, Walt Whitman, Mark Twain and all the rest of the outstanding people named above have expressed doubt that William Shakspere of Stratford wrote the works attributed to him, why is it even necessary to *say* that there is room for doubt? There clearly *is* doubt, as a matter of empirical fact—*reasonable* doubt, expressed by very credible people. Reasonable people may differ about whether a preponderance of the evidence supports Mr. Shakspere, but **it is simply not credible for anyone to claim, in 2007, that there is no room for doubt** about the author.

> Therefore, in adding our names to those of the distinguished individuals named above, we hereby declare that the identity of William Shakespeare should, henceforth, be regarded in academia as a legitimate issue for research and publication and an appropriate topic for instruction and discussion in classrooms.

The Declaration can be read and signed online at our website at DoubtAboutWill.org. Thanks for reading this book.

Appendix A:
William Shakspere's Last Will and Testament

The will is shown line by line, displaying interlineations between the lines. Cancelled passages are in italics and have been crossed out. No punctuation is added. Spelling is modernized for easier reading. Proper names and places, plus capitalizations, are as they appear in the original document.

Martii
Vicesimo Quinto die ~~Januerii~~ /\ Anno Regni Domini nostri Jacobi nunc Regis Anglie
&c decimo quarto & Scotie xlix° Annoque domini 1616

In the name of god amen I William Shackspeare of Stratford upon Avon in the county
of Warr gent in perfect health & memory god be praised do make & Ordain this
my last will & testament in manner & form following That is to say first I Commend
my Soul into the hands of god my Creator hoping & assuredly believing through
the only merits of Jesus Christ my Savior to be made partaker of life everlasting
And my body to the Earth whereof it is made   Item I Give & bequeath
unto my ~~son in L~~ daughter Judith One Hundred & fifty pounds of lawful
English money to be paid unto her in manner & form following that is to
in discharge of her marriage portion
say One Hundred Pounds /\ within one year after my decease with consideration
after the Rate of two shillings in the pound for so long time as the same
shall be unpaid unto her after my decease & the fifty pounds Residue thereof
of
 upon her Surrendering /\ or giving of such sufficient security as the overseers of
this my will shall like of to Surrender or grant All her estate & Right that
that she
shall descend or come unto her after my decease or /\ now hath of in or to one
Copyhold tenement with the appurtenances lying & being in Stratford upon Avon
aforesaid in the said county of Warr being parcel or holden of the manor of
Rowington unto my daughter Susanna Hall & her heirs for ever
Item I Give & bequeath unto my said daughter Judith One
Hundred & fifty Pounds more if she or Any issue of her body be
Living at the end of three Years next ensuing the day of the date
of this my will during which time my executors to pay her consideration from
my decease according to the Rate aforesaid And if she die within the said
term without issue of her body then my will is & I do give & bequeath
One Hundred Pounds thereof to my Niece Elizabeth Hall & the fifty
Pounds to be set forth by my executors during the life of my Sister
Johane Harte & the use & profit thereof Coming shall be paid to my said
Sister Jone & after her decease the said l^li shall Remain Amongst the
children of my said Sister Equally to be divided Amongst them But
if my said daughter Judith be Living at the end of the said three Years or
any issue of her body then my will is & so I devise & bequeath the
by my executors & overseers
said Hundred and fifty pounds to be set out /\ for the best benefit of her & her

the stock   to be
issue & /\ not /\ paid unto her so long as she shall be married & covert Baron
~~by my executors & overseers~~ but my will is that she shall have the consideration
yearly paid unto her during her life & after her decease the said stock and
consideration to be paid to her children if she have Any & if not to her
executors or assigns she living the said term after my decease provided that if
such husband as she shall at the end of the said three Years be married unto or attaine
after do sufficiently Assure unto her & the issue of her body lands Answerable to
the portion by this my will given unto her & to be adjudged so by my executors
& overseers then my will is that the said cl^{li} shall be paid to such husband as
shall make such assurance to his own use Item I give and bequeath unto my said
sister Jone xx^{li} and all my wearing Apparel to be paid & delivered within one year
the house
after my decease And I do will & devise unto her /\ with the appurtenances in Stratford wherein
she dwelleth for her natural life under the yearly Rent of xij^d Item I give and bequeath
unto her three sons William Harte   Hart & Michaell Harte
five pounds A piece to be paid within one Year after my decease
~~to be set out for her within one Year after my decease by my executors~~
~~with the advice and directions of my overseers for her best profit until her~~
~~Marriage and then the same with the increase thereof to be paid unto~~
the said Elizabeth Hall   except my broad silver & gilt bowl
~~her~~ Item I give & bequeath unto /\ ~~her~~ All my Plate /\ that I now
have at the date of this my will   Item I give & bequeath unto
the Poor of Stratford aforesaid ten pounds to mr Thomas
Combe my Sword to Thomas Russell esquire five pounds &
to ffrauncis Collins of the Borough of Warr in the county of Warr
gent thirteen pounds Six shillings & eight pence to be paid within
Hamlett Sadler
one Year after my decease Item I give & bequeath to ~~mr Richard~~ /\
to Wiliam Raynoldes gent xxvj^s viij^d to buy him A Ring
~~Tyler the elder~~ xxvj^s viij^d to buy him A Ring /\ to my godson William
Walker xx^s in gold to Anthonye Nashe gent xxvj^s viij^d & to Mr
& to my fellows John Hemynge Richard Burbage & Henry Cundell xxvj^s viij^d
viij^d A piece to buy them Rings
John Nashe xxvj^s /\ ~~in gold~~ Item I Give Will bequeath & Devise unto
for better enabling of her to perform this my will & towards the performance thereof
my daughter Susanna Hall /\ All that Capital Messuage or tenement
in Stratford aforesaid
with the appurtenances /\ Called the new place wherein I now dwell
& two messuages or tenements with appurtenances scituat lying and being
in Henley street within the borough of Stratford aforesaid And all
my barns stables Orchards gardens lands tenements & hereditaments whatsoever
scituat lying & being or to be had Received perceived or taken
within the towns Hamlets villages fields & grounds of Stratford
upon Avon Oldstratford Bushopton & Welcombe or in any of them

in the said county of Warr And also All that Messuage or
tenement with the appurtenances wherein John Robinson dwelleth scituat
lying & being in the blackfriers in London near the Wardrobe & all
other my lands tenements & hereditaments whatsoever To Have & to hold All &
singular the said premises with their Appurtenances unto the said Susanna
Hall for & during the term of her natural life & after her
Decease to the first son of her body lawfully issuing & to the
heirs Males of the body of the said first Son lawfully
issuing & for default of such issue to the second Son of her
body lawfully issuing & to the heirs Males of the body of the
said Second Son lawfully issuing & for default of such
heirs to the third Son of the body of the said Susanna
Lawfully issuing & of the heirs Males of the body of the said third
son lawfully issuing And for default of such issue the same so
to be & Remain to the fourth ~~son~~ fifth sixth & seventh
sons of her body lawfully issuing one after Another & to the heirs
Males of the bodies of the said fourth fifth Sixth & Seventh sons
lawfully issuing in such manner as it is before Limited to be & Remain
to the first second & third Sons of her body & to their heirs Males
And for default of such issue the said premises to be & Remain to my
said Niece Hall & the heirs males of her body Lawfully
issuing & for default of such issue to my daughter Judith
& the heirs Males of her body lawfully issuing And for
default of such issue to the Right heirs of me the said William
Item I give unto my wife my second best bed with the furniture
Shackspere for ever /\ Item I give & bequeath to my said daughter
Judith my broad silver gilt bowl All the Rest of my goods Chattels
Leases plate Jewels & household stuff whatsoever after my debts and
legacies paid & my funeral expenses discharged I give devise
& bequeath to my Son in Law John Hall gent & my daughter
Susanna his wife whom I ordain & make executors of this my
the said
Last will & testament And I do entreat & Appoint /\ Thomas
Russell Esquire& ffrauncis Collins gent to be overseers hereof And
do Revoke All former wills & publish this to be my last
will & testament In witness whereof I have hereunto put my
hand
~~Seal~~ the day & Year first above Written

By me William Shakspeare

Witness to the publishing
Hereof   Fra: collyns
Julyus Shawe   Hamnet Sadler
John Robinson   Robert Whattcott

227

Appendix B:
Stylometrics: How Reliable is it Really?

A book review by Ramon Jiménez

Shakespeare, Computers, and the Mystery of Authorship
Hugh Craig and Arthur F. Kinney
Cambridge University Press 2009

Arthur F. Kinney, the venerable editor of *English Literary Renaissance*, and Hugh Craig, an English professor at the University of Newcastle in Australia, have teamed up with two of their graduate students to produce a group of essays that focus on the authorship questions surrounding more than a dozen plays and parts of plays both in and out of the Shakespeare canon. More than half of the play-texts examined appeared in Shakespeare's First Folio; two others—*The Two Noble Kinsmen* and *Edward III*—were added to the canon in the last thirty years. Four other anonymous plays and fragments make up the balance.

Citing Georges Braque's remark that "One's style is one's inability to do otherwise," (10) the authors claim that " . . . writers leave subtle and persistent traces of a distinctive style through all levels of their syntax and lexis," (xvi) the former being the writer's arrangement of words, and the latter his vocabulary or word stock. Their objective is to " . . . resolve a number of questions in the Shakespeare canon, so that the business of interpretation, which is so often stymied by uncertainty of authorship, can proceed." Their studies supply considerable additional evidence of Shakespeare's participation or lack of it in the selected texts, but in most cases that evidence falls short of resolving the question.

They lay out the case, with considerable biological detail, for the absolute individuality of verbal expression. This leads them to conclude that "a scene or an act will become uniquely identifiable" (4). To accomplish such identification, Craig and Kinney use "computational stylistics" to calculate the probability that a particular author wrote or did not write a particular body of text. Roughly speaking, their method is to compare an author's use of two types of common words in his known works—function words and lexical words—with the use of the same words in an anonymous work or disputed section of text. It may be summarized in this series of steps:

- Select an appropriate "control group" of an author's acknowledged plays and divide it into 2000-word segments, regardless of speech, act or scene divisions.

- For each segment, obtain a numerical score for the author's use and non-use of a group of the 200 most common *functional* words occurring in Early Modern English drama, words such as *and, you* and *through*, etc. that have syntactical rather than semantic uses.

- For each segment, obtain a numerical score for the author's use and non-use of a group of 500 selected *lexical* words. These are the words in a writer's vocabulary that have semantic meaning.

- On two scatter plots, graphically display the individual scores for each test for each segment of 2000 words.

- The result is two scatter plots, on one of which a cluster of points indicates the author's typical use and non-use of the 200 functional words. On the other scatter plot, the cluster indicates the author's typical use and non-use of the 500 selected lexical words. The statistical center of each cluster is the *centroid*.

- Conduct the same two tests for similar 2000-word blocks from an anonymous play or questionable fragment, and superimpose the scores on the scatter plots for the proposed author of the text.

- The physical distance of the scores for the subject segment of text from the *centroid* of the selected author's cluster, and the size of the sample, indicate the degree of probability that he wrote it.

The result is a mixed bag of conclusions, many of which confirm today's scholarly consensus about what Shakespeare wrote and what he didn't, but many others that conflict with recent studies by other scholars who also use methods of stylometric analysis, such as Sir Brian Vickers, Thomas Merriam, Eric Sams, and Ward Elliott and Robert Valenza. In spite of their use of an array of statistical tools, such as Principal Component Analysis, the *t* test, the "Zeta" test, and discriminant analysis, Craig and Kinney's conclusions raise the same doubts and questions as other methods of determining authorship that rely on detailed textual analysis.

One problem is the selection of the "control group" from a dramatist's accepted work to develop the criteria to apply to questionable texts. In the case of Shakespeare, the authors chose 27 "core" plays— excluding in their entirety the three *Henry VI* plays, the Folio *King Lear, Macbeth, Measure for Measure, The Taming of the Shrew, Henry VIII, The Two Noble Kinsmen, Timon of Athens, Titus Andronicus*, and *Pericles*. Also excluded are *Edward III, Edmond Ironside*, and *Thomas of Woodstock* (*1 Richard II*), each of which has been attributed to Shakespeare in a full-length study by a reputable modern scholar. Admittedly, many of these plays, or parts of them, remain disputed, and are the actual subjects of Craig and Kinney's analyses. But to exclude the entirety of half-a-dozen of Shakespeare's earliest plays when attempting to establish his linguistic peculiarities is to limit and distort the definition of his style. This is particularly important in the case of Shakespeare because much of the apocrypha, the disputed texts, are obviously his earliest work.

Shakespeare and Marlowe

The authors applied their function word and lexical word tests to each of the three *Henry VI* plays, using as their baseline the results from a control group of six undisputed Shakespeare plays, three histories and three comedies, that "he wrote about the same time" (47). Test results for Part 3 were sufficiently vague to cause them to discontinue any further analysis, but the results for Parts 1 and 2 suggested that portions of each play were not by Shakespeare. In the case of Part 1, their tests confirmed the opinions of numerous commentators, including Malone, Wilson, Cairncross and Taylor, that the Temple Garden scene and the scenes involving John Talbot and his son were Shakespeare's work. But Acts I, III and V, and three scenes in Acts II and IV were the work of another writer or writers.

Although they acknowledge that a third dramatist was probably involved, most likely Thomas Nashe, the authors assert that Marlowe was Shakespeare's earliest collaborator, and that he and Shakespeare worked together on *Parts 1* and *2* of *Henry VI*. Marlowe was responsible for, at least, "the middle part" of *Part 1*, involving Joan of Arc, as well as the Cade rebellion scenes in *Part 2* (77).

This analysis of *1 Henry VI* conflicts with the recent conclusion of Sir Brian Vickers that Thomas Kyd was the author of the play ("Kyd" 13). In light of Vickers' attribution, Craig and Kinney compared *1 Henry VI* to a Kyd corpus of *The Spanish Tragedy* and *Cornelia*, and found "no affinities between Kyd and *1 Henry VI*." (See Figure 3.8.) After expanding the Kyd corpus to include *Soliman and Perseda*, they found that "the *1 Henry VI* segments remained firmly in the non-Kyd cluster" (58).

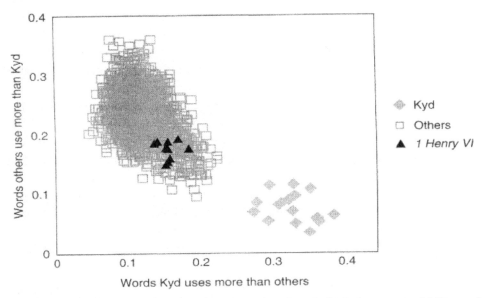

Figure 3.8 Lexical-words test: 2000-word segments from 2 Kyd plays versus 2000-word segments from 134 plays by others, with 2000-word segments from *1 Henry VI*.

Three Anonymous Plays

The anonymous *Arden of Faversham*, published in 1592, is the play in the Shakespearean Apocrypha that has most often been ascribed to him, although it has been assigned to at least six other authors. The most recent attribution was by Sir Brian Vickers, who agreed with T. S. Eliot that the author was Thomas Kyd. *Arden* was extravagantly praised and ascribed to Shakespeare by A. C. Swinburne, and more recently MacDonald P. Jackson has published several papers suggesting that Shakespeare had a major hand in it, most assuredly in scene vi and scene viii, the admirable "quarrel scene." Craig and Kinney tested the author's use of lexical words against the Shakespeare pattern obtained from the 27-play control group. The results suggest that Shakespeare was responsible for scenes iv, v, vi, vii and xvi, but the scores for the two longest scenes (i and xv), and most of the rest of them, fall clearly out of the Shakespeare cluster (94). Further tests "gave no support for the idea that Marlowe or Kyd were collaborators in writing *Arden of Faversham*" (97). Craig and Kinney's scores for scene viii place it in the "non-Shakespearean" category, in direct disagreement with Jackson.

The chapter on the anonymous *Edmond Ironside* reviews all the literature on the play, focusing especially on that since 1986, when Eric Sams published his extensive study claiming that it was Shakespeare's apprentice work, and his alone, in about 1588. Most other critics have derided Sams' attribution and instead asserted that the author was heavily indebted to Shakespeare. The function word and lexical word tests that Craig and Kinney applied to *Edmond Ironside* suggest that none of it was by Shakespeare. Furthermore, the application of similar tests comparing the *Ironside* sections against plays by Lyly, Peele, Greene, Marlowe and seven other playwrights produced no positive results. Thus, the authorship of *Ironside*, dated by most scholars in the 1590s, remains a mystery to everyone except those who agree with Sams' convincing attribution to Shakespeare.

The authors subjected the two major episodes of *Edward III*—the so-called Countess scenes (I.ii through II.ii) and the French campaign scenes (III.i through IV.iii)—to the same function word and lexical word tests. Each segment makes up a third of the play. The results indicated that Shakespeare wrote the Countess segment, echoing a conclusion arrived at by most critics. But the authors' results for the French campaign segment fail to support Shakespeare's authorship. Further tests of word usage in both segments against that in undisputed plays by Marlowe, Peele and Kyd did not "support the idea" that any of them wrote either segment. Craig and Kinney thus consign two-thirds of *Edward III* to an unknown collaborator with Shakespeare. They describe as "flawed" the studies of Wentersdorf (1960), Lapides (1980), Slater (1988) and Sams (1996), all of whom concluded that Shakespeare wrote the entire play.

Further complicating the issue are the findings of Sir Brian Vickers, who in late 2008 asserted that his analysis of three-word collocations in the "non-Shakespearean" portions of *Edward III* (I.i, III, and V) revealed that they were by Thomas Kyd. A few months later, Thomas Merriam, another advocate of Shakespearean co-authorship, published the results of his "multi-dimensional analysis of relative frequencies of function words" in the same "non-Shakespearean" passages of *Edward III*. He found that Shakespeare's collaborator was none other than Christopher Marlowe. But all these theories of co-authorship contradict the findings of Jonathan Hope, who had in 1994, using "socio-historical linguistic evidence," found little or no evidence of divided authorship in the play. He considered it likely that Shakespeare wrote all of *Edward III* (137, 154).

King Lear and *The Spanish Tragedy*

Various critics have speculated about the passages that were added to the first quartos of these two plays, *Lear* being firmly in the Shakespeare canon, and *The Spanish Tragedy* attached by a tenuous thread to Thomas Kyd.

The authors found "a consistency in the distribution of some common function words" in both the Quarto *Lear* (1608) and the Folio *Lear* (1623), indicating that a single person (or persons) was responsible for the entirety of each text (194). When they then examined the approximately 900 words in F that did not appear in Q, they found that both function word and lexical word tests indicated that these passages were by Shakespeare. This is the view of most editors and critics.

The analysis of *The Spanish Tragedy* (Q1 1592) consisted of tests of the five passages of the Additions, comprising less than 500 lines, that appeared in the edition of 1602. These have been attributed to Dekker, Webster, Shakespeare and, most often, to Ben Jonson. Craig and Kinney found sufficient similarities in the frequency of common function words and of simple lexical words between the Additions to *The Spanish Tragedy* and the Shakespeare canon to come to the carefully-stated conclusion that the "readiest explanation" was that Shakespeare was the author of the Additions (180). But in his recent book on Kyd, Lucas Erne calls the attribution of the Additions to Shakespeare "groundless" (172). What a shame that Craig and Kinney didn't test the rest of the play! There are plenty of questions about its author, and the attribution to Kyd rests on shaky grounds. Several scholars, especially C. V. Berney, have adduced substantial evidence that it is a Shakespeare play.

Sir Thomas More

Craig and Kinney tested the approximately 1200 words in Additions II (Hand D) and III (Hand C) in the manuscript of *Sir Thomas More* against texts from the Shakespeare canon, as well as those by other dramatists, such as Dekker, Jonson and Webster. The results were clearly consistent with Shakespeare's authorship of these additions, and no one else's. This led the authors to conclude that "the threshold from conjecture to genuine probability has been crossed" (161). They assert that this "creates a presumption in favour" of the proposition that the handwriting of Hands C and D is the same as that in the six extant signatures of Shakspere of Stratford, and that this is now "among the surest facts of his biography." Considering the astonishment that many experts have expressed that the six extant signatures of Shakespeare of Stratford represent the efforts of a fluent, or even literate, writer, it is hard to believe that anyone could assert such a thing with a straight face. Although Craig and Kinney's conclusions are not unusual, they contradict those of Elliott and Valenza, who applied their "new optics methodology" to the Hand D portion of *Sir Thomas More* and published their results in an article in 2010. They concluded that it belonged "more in the high Apocrypha than in the Canon." Indeed, Arthur Kinney himself wrote less than fifteen years ago that "the author of Addition II shares nothing whatever *poetically* with Shakespeare" (153).

Shakespeare Co-Author?

In one chapter Craig and Kinney report the results of their tests of the claims of Sir Brian Vickers in *Shakespeare Co-Author* (2002) that four plays in the canon—*Titus Andronicus*, *Timon of Athens*, *Henry VIII*, and *The Two Noble Kinsmen*—are products of collaboration between Shakespeare and George Peele (*TA*), Thomas Middleton (*Timon*), and John Fletcher (*H8* and *TNK*). They consider these particular authorship questions "a convenient series of problems where the solution is known to a degree of certainty" (26). But they apparently tested only for the similarity in the use of function words by Shakespeare and the alleged co-author. They report the following results:

- Tests of the five longest scenes in *Titus Andronicus* indicate that Peele wrote the long opening scene, and Shakespeare the other four, as asserted by Vickers. But according to the scatter plot for these scenes, the score for the "Peele" scene is no farther from the Shakespeare centroid than the scores for several dozen text segments from undisputed Shakespeare plays. The remaining eight scenes, three of which Vickers attributed to Peele, are too short to be tested. Scholarly opinions about the percentage of *Titus* attributable to Shakespeare range from zero to 100. In the most recent Arden edition, Jonathan Bate declared that "the whole of *Titus* is by a single hand" and that hand is Shakespeare's (82-3). He based his opinion on a stylometric analysis by A. Q. Morton, who commented that the probability that Peele wrote any part of *Titus* was "less than one in ten thousand million." Although he is noted for his habit of borrowing from other writers, there is no record of Peele ever collaborating with anyone.

- Tests of the four longest scenes in *Timon of Athens* indicate that Middleton wrote the second scene, and Shakespeare the other three, as claimed by Vickers. But again, the score for the "Middleton" scene is no farther from the Shakespeare centroid than scores for some text segments from undisputed Shakespeare plays. At least one score for a Shakespeare text block (*Romeo and Juliet* I.ii.6 to I.iv.46) "placed well into Middleton territory." Here again, the evidence suggests divided authorship, but does not exclude Shakespeare's authorship of the entire play. Most modern studies of the play divide it between Shakespeare and Middleton, but both E. K. Chambers (I, 482) and Una Ellis-Fermor (271) regarded it as entirely Shakespeare's, but unfinished.

- Tests of six scenes in *Henry VIII* indicate that John Fletcher wrote III.i and V.ii, and Shakespeare the other four, as claimed by Vickers. Again, scores for the two "Fletcher" scenes were no farther from the Shakespeare centroid than scores for more than a dozen text blocks from canonical Shakespeare plays. As with *Timon* and *Titus,* the tests do not exclude Shakespeare's authorship of the entire play.

- Scores for tests of two scenes in *The Two Noble Kinsmen* attributed by Vickers to Fletcher (II.ii, III.vi), and one assigned to Shakespeare (I.i) all fell within the cluster for the author predicted. But, as before, neither of the scores for the two "Fletcher" scenes deviated as far from the Shakespeare centroid as did more than a dozen scores for blocks of genuine Shakespeare text. Nor was the score for the Shakespeare scene farther from the Fletcher centroid than numerous scores for scenes from plays by Fletcher alone.

These results are suggestive of co-authorship, but they should be considered in the context of similar tests in the undisputed portion of the canon. Using data obtained about his use of function words from the entire "core" of 27 Shakespeare plays, Craig and Kinney compared them to 62 segments of 2000 words each in six individual Shakespeare plays and 55 such segments from six other plays reliably attributed to five other authors—all twelve plays chosen at random. Of the 62 authentic Shakespeare segments tested, only 50 were correctly classified as Shakespeare's work. For instance, four of the eight segments tested in *A Midsummer Night's Dream* and three of the seven in *Love's Labour's Lost* were classified as "non-Shakespearean" (109). Of the 55 non-Shakespearean segments tested, seven were not attributed to the correct author. (See Table 5.1.) Thus, the success rate for these segments was 87%, and for the Shakespeare plays it was only 81%. A testing method that is incorrect by its own standards 13% to 19% of the time may be termed suggestive, but hardly definitive.

Table 5.1. **2000-word segments of 6 test plays by Shakespeare and 6 test plays by others classified as Shakespeare or non-Shakespeare by discriminant analysis.**

		Segments correctly classified	Segments misclassified
Shakespeare	*Coriolanus*	13	0
Shakespeare	*1 Henry VI*	10	2
Shakespeare	*King John*	8	2
Shakespeare	*Love's Labour's Lost*	7	3
Shakespeare	*A Midsummer Night's Dream*	4	4
Shakespeare	*Twelfth Night*	8	1
Shakespeare Total		50 81%	12 19%
Day	*Isle of Gulls*	8	2
Dekker	*If It Be Not Good*	9	2
Heywood	*Woman Killed With Kindness*	6	2
Middleton	*Hengist*	10	0
Middleton	*Phoenix*	9	1
Munday	*John a Kent and John a Cumber*	6	0
Non-Shakespeare Total		48 87%	7 13%
GRAND TOTAL		98 84%	19 16%

Variables are frequencies of 200 function words. The training sets are segments of 27 Shakespeare plays and 85 plays by other playwrights dated 1580 to 1619. The test plays are chosen at random from the Shakespeare and non-Shakespeare sets.

In the face of such methodological shortcomings, conflicting opinions, and dueling analyses, what is one to think? An obvious explanation is that today's orthodox scholars, including all the stylometricians here mentioned, are groping blindly in the wrong paradigm, and are thus handicapped by the confines of the conventional Shakespearean dating system. In addition, very few scholars of any period have given any consideration to the idea of a substantial corpus of Shakespearean juvenilia. We can be sure that Shakespeare did not always write like Shakespeare.

As modern research has demonstrated, Shakespeare was a meticulous and persistent reviser of virtually all his plays over the course of a long career. But the jumbled condition of his printed works, most of which exist in two or more versions, reveals a patchwork of incompletely incorporated additions and deletions, as well as numerous inconsistencies, misnamings, and misalignments. There are several instances where the original passage remains in the text alongside the revision. It is much more likely that the substandard scenes that are attributed to co-authors are Shakespeare's original versions that, by chance or by compositor's error, remained in the play after he improved and refined the rest of it. It is also possible that he may have simply abandoned his revision of some of his earliest plays for some reason or another—the manuscript eventually finding its way into a printer's hands.

Craig and Kinney and their fellow practitioners of stylistics, stylometry, etc. may have reached the limit of linguistic analysis by computer. Despite their confidence that their method can safely identify the work of an individual author, it seems clear that this type of analysis can never be more than a portion of the evidence needed to do so. External evidence, topical references, and the circumstances and personal experiences of the putative author will remain important factors in any question of authorship. The noted economist John Maynard Keynes, who was a scholarship winner in mathematics and classics at Cambridge and the author of a dissertation on probability, is said to have remarked that he was "not prepared to sacrifice realism to mathematics." We would do well to follow his example.

Bibliography

Bate, Jonathan, ed. *Titus Andronicus*. Arden Shakespeare, 3rd Series. (Routledge, 1995).

Berney, C.V. "Who wrote *The Spanish Tragedy?*" *Shakespeare Matters*. v. 4:2 (Winter 2005) p. 1.

-----. "Hidden Allusions in Oxford's *Spanish Tragedy*." *Shakespeare Matters*. v. 4:4 (Spring 2005) p. 6.

Chambers, E.K. *William Shakespeare, Facts and Problems*. (The Clarendon Press, 1930).

Clark, Eva Turner. *Hidden Allusions in Shakespeare's Plays*. (William Farquhar Payson, 1931). pp. 116-61.

Elliott, Ward E.Y. and Robert J. Valenza. "Two Tough Nuts to Crack: Did Shakespeare Write the 'Shakespeare' Portions of *Sir Thomas More* and *Edward III?*" *Literary and Linguistic Computing*. v. 25:1 (April 2010) pp. 67-83.

Ellis-Fermor, Una. "Timon of Athens, An Unfinished Play" *Review of English Studies*. v. 18 (1942) pp. 270-83.

Erne, Lucas. *Beyond the Spanish Tragedy: A Study of the Works of Thomas Kyd*. (Manchester University Press, 2001).

Hope, Jonathan. *The Authorship of Shakespeare's Plays : a socio-linguistic study*. (Cambridge University Press, 1994).

Jackson, MacDonald P. "Shakespeare and the Quarrel Scene in *Arden of Faversham*." *Shakespeare Quarterly*. v. 57:3 (Fall 2006) pp. 249-84.

Kinney, Arthur F. "Text, Context, and Authorship of *The Booke of Sir Thomas More*" in Sigrid King, ed. *Pilgrimage for Love: Essays in Early Modern Literature in Honor of Josephine A. Roberts*. (Arizona Center for Medieval and Renaissance Studies, 1999). pp. 133-160.

Lapides, Fred, ed. *The Raigne of King Edward the Third, a Critical Old Spelling Edition*. (Garland, 1980).

Merriam, Thomas. "Marlowe Versus Kyd as Author of *Edward III* I.i, III, and V" *Notes and Queries*. v. 254 (2009) pp. 549-551.

Sams, Eric., ed. *Shakespeare's Edmund Ironside, The Lost Play*. (Wildwood House Ltd., 1986).

-----, ed. *Shakespeare's Edward III*. (Yale University Press, 1996).

Ramon Jiménez

Slater, Eliot. *The Problem of the Reign of King Edward III: A Statistical Approach.* (Cambridge University Press, 1988).

Vickers, Sir Brian. *Shakespeare, Co-Author.* (Oxford University Press, 2002).

-----. "Thomas Kyd, the secret sharer – A new software program should restore Kyd to the eminence he deserves." *TLS* 19 (April 2008). p. 13.

Wentersdorf, Karl P. *The Authorship of Edward III.* Ph.D. Dissertation. (University of Cincinnati, 1960).

Appendix C:
Social Network Theory and the Claim that Shakespeare of Stratford Was the Famous Dramatist

By Donald P. Hayes, Professor of Sociology (Emeritus), Cornell University

This is an edited version of a paper by Donald P. Hayes of Cornell University, who died in 2006. The original is posted online; an edited version appeared in the *Shakespeare Oxford Society Newsletter* in 2011. Both references may be found at the end. The paper uses "network theory" to assess the implications for the authorship debate of the fact that there were no eulogies to William Shakespeare when William of Stratford died in 1616. Hayes says that "This anomaly, the 'silence of his peers,' is the single most serious threat to Stratfordianism and to its first premise. There would be no Stratfordian anomaly, no threat to the orthodox position—if even one such document were found. No such document exists." Hayes concludes that "unless a new, well-documented and far more plausible explanation can be developed for this silence of his peers, the odds that the man from Stratford grew up to become the master poet-dramatist William Shakespeare have fallen to the level of the improbable." The point is not new. What is new is that an academic expert in social network theory is saying it, and based on his own analysis.

Hayes notes in the Appendix that there is great disagreement about links among some members of the London dramatist community during the Elizabethan-Jacobean period, and especially about links to Shakespeare. He says he could have chosen an "inclusive" criterion that would accept every scholar's claim to having found a link between any two London playwrights, or an "exclusive" one omitting any claim of a relationship with Shakespeare (or any other writer) if scholars disagree among themselves. Hayes chose a middle ground between the two extremes. Whether one agrees with all of his decisions or not, it would not affect his conclusion that the lack of tributes means Shakspere was not Shakespeare. His analysis is robust, even without including Shakspere's fellow actors.

Finally, claims of finding more and more instances of "collaboration" on Shakespeare's plays in recent years greatly exacerbates the difficulty of explaining (1) the lack of any documentation of an alleged collaboration, (2) the lack of any surviving correspondence among alleged collaborators, and (3) the silence of his peers when Shakspere died. If the implication is that his collaborators must have known Shakespeare, then why the silence? The only viable explanation is that, knowing the author, they knew he didn't die in 1616. – The Editors

Orthodox biographies of the man baptized "Gulielmus Shakspere" in Stratford-on-Avon on 26 April, 1564, have generally downplayed and sometimes ignored a long-known fact which came at the end of his life. Downplaying this fact is understandable since it undermines the first premise on which Stratfordianism is based: that this man grew up to become the master poet-dramatist William Shakespeare. The troublesome fact? When Shakspere died in Strat-

Donald P. Hayes

ford in 1616, none of his London dramatist or theatrical peers wrote a tribute for him, nor did any of them do so during the ensuing seven years.

If Shakespeare's peers commonly wrote tributes to former colleagues upon their deaths, and if Shakspere became Shakespeare, then his peers should have written tributes for Shakspere—especially since he was so prominent. No such tributes exist. What makes their omission especially significant is that the month before Shakspere's death another London poet-dramatist—Francis Beaumont—died. Far from ignoring him, other dramatists celebrated Beaumont with numerous tributes, and they were active in his interment in the Poets' Corner of Westminster Abbey.

The problem is straightforward: if Shakspere was Shakespeare, why were there no tributes? Their absence implies that they were two men, not one. In this report, network theory and analysis are used to estimate the likelihood that Shakespeare's dramatist peers would (a) know Shakespeare's identity, and (b) write tributes on learning of his death.

Network Theory

Are there grounds for predicting how Shakespeare's peers would have reacted on learning that William Shakspere of Stratford had died in 1616? Modern network theory provides some basis for making such predictions. A substantial literature on social networks has developed since the 1930s, beginning with Moreno & Jennings (1938), Bavelas (1951), and Newcomb (1961). Modern forms of network analysis have become pervasive throughout the natural and social sciences as well as in engineering. In *Social Network Analysis* (CUP, 1994), Wasserman and Faust generalized about the differential resources available to the most central vs. peripheral members of social networks. Central members, for example, are more likely to be ritually celebrated than peripheral members. By implication, the expense of honoring prominent, respected members upon retirement is expected to be greater than for lesser members, and the obligation to attend a funeral is stronger for a former prominent member than for a peripheral one. For central, prominent figures in London's network of dramatists, social network theory predicts that surviving peers would have felt a strong obligation to write tributes upon their demise. But if Mr. Shakspere was not the dramatist, this theory predicts there would have been no sense of obligation; rather, to write a tribute for Shakspere would have been considered absurd.

Empirically, the network theory prediction is borne out: Marlowe, Jonson and Beaumont were widely celebrated by tributes from their peers. The "silence" of the peers on Shakspere's death puts the evidence at odds with Stratfordians' first premise. The missing tributes may yet turn up, but until then the implication is: (a) there must have been a good reason why the surviving eleven of his literary peers ignored the death of the most prominent member of their community, or (b) the man who died in 1616 was not Shakespeare. Possible explanations for his peers' silence are taken up in the Discussion.

Conditions and Relationships

The social structure of Elizabethan and Jacobean dramatists was shaped by various conditions, including two considered here: (a) the new large theaters produced a heavy demand for new or revised play scripts; and (b) relationships between the twenty major playwrights were being shaped by both internal and external forces, including their alignments with one another, the theater companies, producers and patrons.

238

Demand for Play Scripts

The large new public theaters (the Theatre, Curtain, Rose and Globe) attracted large audiences by their relatively low prices. The audience for a play was soon exhausted, which necessitated putting on several different plays a week. The demand for scripts compelled producers to look for and acquire old and new plays, to commission plays or use a playwriting corps. The demand for scripts attracted recent university graduates. New structural forms developed, including teams of dramatists working on different scenes or characters in a play—much as contemporary teams of writers do for movies and television. The dynamic character of that structure makes it difficult to assign credit for authorship, since the question becomes entangled with matters of seniority or authority. Co-authoring took several forms, including work on others' unfinished work. Not only did dramatists tinker with and revise their own scripts, so did the players and publishers. Playwrights would be curious as to what competitors were writing, what kinds of works were being commissioned, which plays were chosen, and audience reactions to plays, themes, plots and characters (e.g., a rise in the popularity of comedies; a decline in interest in revenge or history plays).

London Playwrights as a Social Network

To estimate Shakespeare's place in London's community of playwrights, a matrix was developed to estimate how twenty Elizabethan and Jacobean playwrights were linked to one another during Shakespeare's active career. Evidence for those links comes mainly from research by Elizabethan scholars on co-authorship and from evidence of literary and social relationships. These reputed relationships are subjected to quantitative network analysis, and the mathematical centrality of each dramatist in that network is estimated (cf. the accompanying matrix and graph).

The matrix and graph must be *estimates* because they are based on evidence which has survived four centuries of fires, neglect in the care of documents, and a lack of appreciation for documents' significance. Those conditions produce significant losses. For example, while there is documentary evidence for the educational backgrounds of nearly all of the others, Shakspere's education is undocumented—there are no records for the King's New School before 1700. Further, nineteenth-century discoveries of forgeries in Shakespeare-related documents, and evidence of deliberate destruction of important records, have introduced additional biases and uncertainties into his historical record. Finally, beyond the distortions attributable to deliberate and inadvertent loss are unresolved disputes among scholars over basic facts about both William Shakspere and William Shakespeare. Ongoing research may turn up evidence of relationships omitted from this matrix, and some claims of a relationship may have to be deleted. So long as modifications are minor, additions or deletions are unlikely to alter the conclusion that Shakespeare occupied a place near the center of a dense network of peer relationships.

Elizabethan Dramatists

To minimize bias in selection, all the major and several lesser dramatists from that era are included in our analysis—nineteen of Shakespeare's peers in all. Fifteen are known to have either written or received tributes (Price, 302-5). Several lesser ones are included because they had written a popular play, despite contemporary scholarly judgment that they were not important writers. Drayton is recognized mainly as a poet, but is included because he was a paid member of Henslowe's playwriting corps. While none of his plays have survived,

Nashe is included because he is known to have been linked to several early Elizabethan dramatists and poets (not always positively). Daniel is excluded because all but one of his plays fell outside the specified period. Similarly, Massinger, Shirley and Ford were omitted because they came to this theatrical scene later. Spenser, Harvey and Watson were excluded because they did not write plays. Anthony Munday, a lesser playwright, is included because he is a principal in a disputed Shakespeare play.

Matrix: Literary and Social Relationships Between English Dramatists: ~1590 – 1610

	Beaumont	Chapman	Chettle	Dekker	Drayton	Fletcher	Greene	Heywood	Jonson	Kyd	Lodge	Lyly	Marlowe	Marston	Middleton	Munday	Nashe	Peele	Webster	Shakespeare
Beaumont						X			X											
Chapman				X	X				X				X	X						
Chettle				X	X		X	X	X							X				X
Dekker		X	X		X		X	X						X	X	X			X	X
Drayton			X	X											X	X			X	
Fletcher	X	X							X					X						X
Greene		X								X	X		X				X	X		X
Heywood			X	X					X							X			X	X
Jonson	X	X	X	X		X								X	X					
Kyd							X	X					X							
Lodge							X										X	X		X
Lyly																X				
Marlowe		X								X							X	X		
Marston		X	X						X											
Middleton			X	X	X				X							X			X	X
Munday			X	X	X			X							X				X	X
Nashe							X				X		X							
Peele							X				X		X				X			X
Webster				X	X			X						X	X					
Shakespeare			X	X	X		X	X	X						X	X		X		

Graph 1: Shakespeare Network

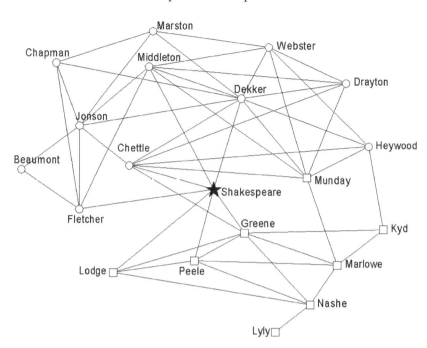

Literary and Social Relationships

The primary sources for these links are reports of co-authoring based principally on the introductions to Shakespeare's and his peers' plays in the LION database; entries in the *Dictionary of Literary Biography*; scholarly introductions to Shakespeare's plays (e.g., *Riverside*, 2nd edition, 1997); membership in a playwriting corps (e.g., as reported in Henslowe's Diary); recent text analyses (e.g., Vickers, 2002); sharing a writing room supplied by a common patron; being jailed together for writing a controversial play, on suspicion of advocating atheism, or some officially unacceptable religious or political view; and on credible reports of links in biographies, surviving private letters and manuscripts. Relationships could be brief or lengthy; positive, neutral/ambivalent or negative (e.g., Middleton vs. Munday), and could change over time (e.g., Marlowe and Kyd). Eleven of these nineteen dramatist peers were alive on the day Shakspere died—Beaumont, Chapman, Drayton, Fletcher, Heywood, Jonson, Lodge, Marston, Middleton, Munday, and Webster. Of those, Munday and Lodge came from the first half of the Shakespeare era, the others from the latter half. Aside from much missing information, the major obstacle in constructing a valid network is disagreement among Elizabethan scholars over important facts about these linkages. For whose claims for a relationship are included in this matrix, see Appendix A.

Calculating "Centrality"

The graph estimates the structure of London's dramatist network, each playwright placed in accordance with his mathematical centrality within that community; i.e., the direct and intermediary links through which news might pass about Shakspere's death. "Centrality" describes each dramatist relative to his peers. The equation is: $C(i) = n/(sum(d(i,j), j = i))$, where n is the graph size, d is the graph-distance between two persons, and the summation of distances is over all pairs of dramatists (Wasserman and Faust, 1994, cf. esp. Chapters 5, 12). This measure of a person's centrality, the C statistic, varies between 0 and 1. A person's C measure represents not only his direct but all his indirect connections to the others. A C value of .50 represents someone twice as central in the network as one with a score of .25. Table 1 supplies three sets of C estimates for these twenty dramatists: one for the first half of the Shakespeare era; one for the last half; and one for the data treated as a single network.

Table 1: Centrality

Dramatist	*First*	*Second*	*Combined*
			'Generation'
Shakespeare	0.643	0.667	0.633
Beaumont		0.462	0.365
Chapman		0.501	0.381
Chettle		0.667	0.594
Dekker		0.800	0.594
Drayton		0.571	0.463
Fletcher		0.632	0.501
Greene	0.751		0.543
Heywood	0.501	0.571	0.514
Jonson		0.706	0.501
Kyd	0.563		0.422
Lodge	0.643		0.475
Lyly	0.409		0.297
Marlowe	0.692		0.475
Marston		0.599	0.432
Middleton		0.706	0.543
Munday	0.563	0.632	0.576
Nashe	0.643		0.413
Peele	0.692		0.487
Webster		0.632	0.487

Two overlapping "generations" of dramatists are evident. The first (names represented by squares on the Graph) consists of the six Oxford and Cambridge graduates: the University Wits Marlowe, Greene, Nashe, Peele, Lodge and Lyly, plus Shakespeare, Kyd, and Munday. Four of the "Wits" and Kyd were dead by 1596, and except for Munday and Lodge, the others by 1606. These early deaths largely account for the scarcity of cross-generation ties. The central-most of the first generation were Greene (C = .75) and Peele (C = .69)—both dead by 1596. The second "generation" had as its central-most figures Dekker (C = .80), Jonson (C = .71), and Middleton (C = .71). These exceptionally high C values reflect the dense network of social relationships among those dramatists. Shakespeare was the most well-connected in the combined generations (C = .67), but not the central-most dramatist in either period. John Lyly (C = .30) was the least integrated member, in part because he had retired from writing plays early. Heywood and Chapman, while first generation in age, are included with the second generation because they began writing in the latter period.

High as these centrality values are, they underestimate the true level of relationships between these dramatists since much of the evidence, especially as it bears on their informal relation-ships, is missing. The high density of these relationships in both "generations" of dramatists ensures that each knew the other, not just by reputation, but directly—personally. That means that William Shakespeare's identity was known by all of them. If Shakspere had become William Shakespeare, all of his dramatist peers would have known who died in Stratford.

The Jonson-Shakespeare Link

There is a significant omission in the graph in what is otherwise a densely interconnected network. There is no link connecting the two most prominent members of London's dramatist community—Jonson and Shakespeare. Jonson worked with many of his colleagues, but there is no evidence that he and Shakespeare ever worked together. Nor did Jonson mention Shake-speare by name in his extensive and surviving records of works or private commentaries between 1598 and 1616.[1]

After Marlowe's reputed death in 1593, Shakespeare became the most prominent dramatist in London and remained so until the late 1590s[2] when challenged by Jonson after his successful *Every Man In His Humour*, produced by the Burbage brothers' company in 1598. Jonson had already begun working for Henslowe (receiving a £4 advance). Ever feisty, Jonson made public appraisals of his peers (e.g., he satirized Dekker and Marston's works, leading to an exchange, in kind), but as far as is known, Jonson never took on Shakespeare—in print. In both the earlier and later years, they remained distant and cool—prominent colleagues and rivals, but without documented evidence of animus. Their relationship probably affected their alignments with other dramatists, and theirs, in turn, with one another—forming small subgroups.

The relationships among those twenty dramatists were also being affected by their alignments with the rival theater companies and by their patrons. If a patron was a noble, his standing at Court would affect a dramatist's alignment with others. There were strong factions at court and, at times, bitter rivalries among noble families. In deference to his noble friends, Jonson would have avoided working with any London dramatist closely aligned with nobles who were not on good terms with the powerful Pembrokes, for example. In short, Jonson's external relationships affected his links within London's dramatist community, which, in turn, affected others with whom he was aligned.

While Shakespeare's extended association with the Lord Chamberlain/King's Men acting companies is uncontested, the identity of his patron(s) is not. Unsupported speculation has Shakespeare closely linked to the Earl of Southampton,[3] but no record confirms that Southampton was Shakespeare's patron, or that the two men ever met.

Those dramatists' alignments with theater companies, impresarios and their patrons all produced fault lines within that playwright community. The presence and absence of linkages between the members suggests some probable alignments: Beaumont, Chapman, Drayton, Marston and Middleton appear to have been aligned with Jonson; Lodge, Munday and Heywood with Shakespeare, leaving Chettle, Fletcher and Dekker in the delicate position of maintaining relations with both camps. Lyly simply withdrew from the community.

Jonson's 1623 Eulogy for Shakespeare

The relationships in the matrix and graph supply essential context for understanding Jonson's role in the 1623 First Folio, for which he wrote a lavish tribute to Shakespeare. So far as is known, Jonson never collaborated with Shakespeare, nor had he written a tribute for Shakspere on his death. In his private writings up to that time, he ignored Shakespeare. Given the absence of any indication of closeness in their relationship, it seems puzzling that Jonson was chosen to write the principal eulogy for his rival.

Can Jonson's eulogy be taken at face value? Price (2001) considers this question, noting that there has always been and continues to be debate over his eulogy. Jonsonian scholars generally agree that it is an ambiguous document. John Dryden (1631-1700) asserted that Jonson's eulogy was "an insolent, sparing and invidious panegyric." Dryden's interpretation coincides with what is known of the Jonson-Shakespeare relationship—if not hostile, it was cool and distant.

Jonson was the most prominent dramatist of his time—he became Court Poet around 1605 and England's Poet Laureate in 1616. What could have motivated him to produce the eulogy for his rival Shakespeare in the Folio? There are many speculations. Jonson may have been hired to write the eulogy as a "puff"—a public endorsement on a script designed by the promoters. Or he may have done it as a personal favor for his long-time friends and patrons, the Earl of Pembroke and his brother, to whom the Folio was dedicated. That too does not assure that his eulogy can be taken at face value. A third possibility is that despite their cool relationship Jonson admired Shakespeare and welcomed the opportunity to write an effusive tribute, even though his later appraisals of Shakespeare in his private papers were reserved, critical and ambivalent. Jonson's eulogy is an ambiguous document, particularly when read against the background of his private commentaries, others' reports of his appraisals of Shakespeare, his extended cool and distant relationship with Shakespeare, and the practice of commissioning puffs.

If Shakspere became Shakespeare, there must be some good reason for his peers' silence. If not, then they were two men: one from Stratford, born and died as Shakspere, and a second, the historical poet-playwright Shakespeare, whose identity is in dispute.

Discussion

If the silence of his peers (especially his closest co-author, Fletcher) is not to undermine the main Stratfordian premise, there must be a plausible explanation. One theory is that news of Shakspere's death in Stratford was long delayed in getting back to London—it came too late for tributes. That is implausible given the level of Shakspere's engagement with London.

Though it took days, there was regular traffic between Stratford and London. There were creditors and agents involved in Shakspere's real estate and theatrical holdings in London. A solicitor would have been required for some of his business transactions. The identity of one partner is known from his signature on the papers for the purchase of the Blackfriars gatehouse. Shakspere's London agent(s) would need to learn of his death promptly in order to negotiate the settlement on his extensive business affairs. Finally, there were his fellow shareholders in the King's Men and in the Globe and Blackfriars theaters. If not already sold, his shares and the income from them would have to be negotiated by someone acting in the interests of his family and estate.

Michael Drayton, a fellow Warwickshire native and member of the London literary community, could have spread the word. Drayton often summered with the Rainsford family, two miles from Stratford (Jiménez, 2002). Though there is no direct link between Drayton and Shakespeare in the graph, they could easily have visited one another and shared the latest literary and theatrical news. When Drayton became ill, he was treated by Shakspere's next-door neighbor and son-in-law, physician John Hall. Later, Hall made notations in his notebook about Drayton, noting his stature as a poet. His published notebook contains no mention of a remarkable coincidence: both his father-in-law and Michael Drayton shared an uncommon London occupation.

Jiménez has found another Shakspere link to London. The Stratford Corporation's solicitor and Town Clerk of Stratford for ten years was Londoner Thomas Greene. For many months he, his wife and children actually lived in Shakspere's New Place home. Greene's diary mentions Shakspere once—in connection with the Welcombe land enclosure. He refers to him as "my cosen Shakspeare." Greene was a friend of John Marston, another of Shakespeare's London dramatist peers. Greene and Marston went to school together in the mid-1590s, making it curious that Greene never mentions his Stratford host's place among London playwrights. Finally, there were people in London who had known Shakspere in his youth. One was Richard Field, publisher of *Venus and Adonis* and *Lucrece*. Another was Shakspere's brother Gilbert, a London haberdasher.

This explanation for the silence of his peers—that news of his death was long delayed in getting back to London's dramatist community—is implausible for these many reasons. Once his death became known to any one of his kin, literary, theatrical, business or legal associates, the high density of their network provided multiple channels through which the news could pass to the others, enabling them to organize some sort of tribute. Their seven-year silence after learning of his death violated their established practice, especially on the death of so prominent a member.[4]

A second proposed explanation for the silence is that Shakespeare wasn't eminent enough to warrant tributes, i.e., he was a marginal figure in their dramatist community. That may have been so in the early 1590s, but not after the two major poems appeared, followed by quartos of many of the plays. He held a central place among his peers for up to twenty years. Furthermore, his plays were often performed at Court, at Greenwich, at the Globe and Rose theaters in London, at regional theaters, at both universities, at Gray's and Lincoln Inns, at the great noble houses, and possibly in northern Europe. Meres' ranking of Shakespeare's works in *Palladis Tamia* (1598), and a quarter-century later Jonson's lavish appraisal in the First Folio, also make this explanation implausible.

In a third explanation, Kathman (2002) proposes that his peers *did* write tributes, but they were circulated privately and all have been lost. It is unlikely that this hypothesis can ever be disproved (e.g., by some new manuscript discovery). What makes the hypothesis implausible is that tributes for several dramatists, especially for the more prominent members of that community, have survived. The tributes for Jonson were so numerous that they were organized into a book. Why should tributes for the equally prominent Shakespeare not have survived? Kathman's explanation remains possible, but not plausible.

What would be a plausible explanation for his peers' silence? An obvious explanation is the one based on network theory—if his dramatist peers did not write tributes for him, then they must have known that he was not a dramatist—*William Shakspere was not William Shakespeare*. They knew him as a part-time actor, a prosperous businessman, a major shareholder in a theatrical company and theaters. Not being a dramatist, it would have been absurd for them to write tributes for him. The authorship dispute could be resolved for all time if so much as a single tribute by one of his dramatist peers had survived which honored Shakspere *as a dramatist*. It would be the first and only contemporaneous document showing that one of his peers believed Shakspere was Shakespeare. This anomaly, the "silence of his peers," is the single most serious threat to Stratfordianism and its first premise. There would be no Stratfordian anomaly, no threat to the orthodox position, if even one contemporary document were found. No such document exists.

This network analysis has established Shakespeare's central place in that small 16th and 17th century community of London dramatists. For nearly twenty years, he was near or at the center of a dense network of interpersonal relations, ensuring that all nineteen of his peers would have known Shakespeare's identity. According to network theory, if it was Shakespeare who died in Stratford in 1616, his high level of centrality would have assured many tributes from his peers. The absence of tributes undermines what is already a modest and heavily disputed evidentiary case for Shakspere being Shakespeare. The absence of their tributes encourages non-Stratfordians to seek Shakespeare's identity elsewhere. Unless a new, well-documented and far more plausible explanation can be developed for this silence of his peers, the odds that the man from Stratford grew up to become the master poet-dramatist William Shakespeare have fallen to the level of the improbable.

Appendix

Beyond who was included in the matrix of Shakespeare's literary and other social relationships, and what constituted a "link or relationship," is this question: which contested scholarly claim for a relationship should appear in this matrix and graph? Strikingly different matrices result from those contradictory claims. An *inclusive* principle would accept every Elizabethan scholar's claim to having found a link between any two of these 20 playwrights. Such claims could be based on many grounds: stylistic and metric considerations, allusions or other forms of internal or external evidence. In Shakespeare's case, Chapman has been reported to have written part of *Cymbeline*; Middleton to have written one-third of *Timon of Athens*; Kyd to have co-authored part of *Titus Andronicus* and an early version of *Hamlet*; Peele is reported to have written part of *Titus*; while still others have proposed that Nashe wrote parts of *Henry VI, Part 1*; Fletcher is reported to have collaborated with Shakespeare on *Two Noble Kinsmen*, *Pericles*, (the latter with Wilkins) and *Henry VIII*; and finally, Greene, Peele, Marlowe, Nashe, Chapman, Drayton, Kyd and Lodge have all been reported to have had a hand in the *Henry VI* plays (Baker, *Riverside Shakespeare*, 1997, p. 623). A matrix/graph based on this inclusive principle would be challenged on the grounds that some claims have not held up on further or close examination. Were such a matrix produced (not shown), Shakespeare would be directly linked with at least 14 of his 19 peers through claims of co-authorship alone. That would put Shakespeare at the very center of a dense network of social/literary relationships, but would make the silence of his peers on his death even more anomalous.

An alternative matrix could be constructed by following an exclusive principle—one which omits any claim of a relationship with Shakespeare (or any other writer) if Elizabethan scholars disagree among themselves. The First Folio is a good example of a document most accept as supporting such a matrix. By this principle, the Fletcher-Shakespeare link for *Pericles*, *Two Noble Kinsmen* and *Henry VIII* would have to be omitted as there is scholarly dispute over each. More controversial would be the links connecting Chettle, Dekker, Heywood and Munday to Shakespeare for *Sir Thomas More*. (One incongruity about that set of linkages is that all four of those dramatists worked for Henslowe, owner-producer of a competing theater company; never, so far as is known, did they work for the Lord Chamberlain's or King's Men companies.) Since the joint authoring of *Sir Thomas More* remains controversial, the exclusive principle would remove all such links from the matrix. The most controversial relationships may be those associated with *Groats-worth of Wyt*. Some scholars contend that the references to an "Upstart Crow" and other objectionable descriptions refer to Shakspere, others believe they refer to Shakespeare, still others deny that either Shakspere or Shakespeare was Greene/Chettle's target. Given the controversy on those points, those links between dramatists too would be omitted. A matrix based on the exclusive principle would show Shakespeare as having *no* links to his peers—he solo-authored every play. Given Shakespeare's stature among playwrights, at court, and with the public, the absence of any links whatsoever in what is otherwise a dense network of dramatists is implausible, though not impossible. Most contemporary Shakespearean scholars would consider such a matrix to be an invalid depiction of London's playwright community at the beginning of the 17th century.

As in the sciences, there are no courts for adjudicating scholarly disputes; consequently the data depicted here are a compromise—lying somewhere between one based on the exclusive and the inclusive principles. Three controversial works were retained in this analysis (1) *Two Noble Kinsmen*—most scholars believe it to be a Shakespeare/Fletcher collaboration; (2) the *Groats-worth* pamphlet—linking Greene to three of his playwright friends; and (3) *Sir Thomas More*, linking four Elizabethan playwrights—Chettle, Dekker, Heywood and Munday—with William Shakespeare.

References

Bavelas, Alex: "An experimental approach to organizational communication" (*Journal of the Acoustical Society of America*, 22, 1951, 271-282)

Dryden, John: *Of Dramatic Poesy and Other Critical Essays* (Edited by George Watson, 2 vols. London: J. M. Dent and Sons, 1962).

Hayes, Donald P: "Social Network Theory and the Claim that Shakespeare of Stratford Was the Famous Dramatist" (http://www.soc.cornell.edu/hayes-lexical analysis/schoolbooks/Papers/HayesSocialNetworksAndShakespeare.pdf).

_____: "The Silence of the Peers: Social Network Theory Proves Shakspere was not Shakespeare," based on the online pdf version above, edited by Michael Egan (*The Shakespeare Oxford Newsletter*, Fall 2011, 7-10, 23-28).

Jiménez, Ramon: "Camden, Drayton, Greene, Hall and Cooke: Five Eyewitnesses who saw Nothing" (*The Shakespeare Oxford Newsletter*, Fall 2002, 12-16).

Kathman, David: "Shakespeare's Eulogies" (http://shakespeareauthorship.com/eulogies.html)

Moreno, Jacob L, and Helen H. Jennings: "Statistics of social configurations" (*Sociometry*, 1938).

Newcomb, Theodore: *The Acquaintance Process* (Hold, Rinehart and Winston, New York, 1961).

Price, Diana: *Shakespeare's Unorthodox Biography* (Greenwood Press, Westport, Connecticut, 2001).

Vickers, Brian: *Shakespeare. Co-Author* (Oxford University Press, 2002).

Waith, Eugene M: *Two Noble Kinsmen* (Oxford University Press, 1989).

Wasserman, Stanley, and Katherine Faust: *Social Network Analysis* (Cambridge University Press, New York, 1994).

Endnotes

1   Jonson did, however, mention Shakespeare in his (Jonson's) collected works, published later in the same year Shakspere died (1616). He included him in the cast lists of two of his plays: *Every Man in His Humour* (1598 – eighteen years earlier), and *Sejanus* (1603 – thirteen years earlier). Oddly, he spelled the name "Shakespeare" in the first list, and "Shake-Speare" in the second list. The latter is the only instance of the hyphenated name when referring to the actor, not the author. Nothing corroborates that Shakespeare played a role in either play (or in any play for that matter). Perhaps most strangely, Jonson made no mention of Shakespeare's death earlier in the same year.

2   The claim that Shakespeare became the most prominent dramatist in London after Marlowe's death in 1593 ignores the fact that he was first identified as a dramatist in *Palladis Tamia* in 1598. By then six of his plays had been published *anonymously*, and Meres lists twelve he had written. His *plays* may have been the most popular after 1593, but he was not prominent as a playwright. As the poet of *Venus and Adonis,* and of *Lucrece*, he was prominent, but not yet as a playwright.

3   Shakespeare's first two published works, *Venus and Adonis* (1593), and *Lucrece* (1594), were dedicated to Henry Wriothesley, Third Earl of Southampton, so it is natural that scholars would speculate that they had a relationship. But the language of the second dedication, in particular, suggests otherwise; and no documentary evidence has come to light that shows they ever met.

4   Two additional reasons to doubt this theory – the silence of the three fellow actors mentioned in Shakspere's will and of publishers of editions of the works – are mentioned in the Declaration of Reasonable Doubt.

Appendix D:
Heminge and Condell Letters in First Folio

Dedicatory Epistle of Heminge and Condell to the Earls of Pembroke and Montgomery

To the most noble and incomparable pair of brethren: William Earl of Pembroke, &c., Lord Chamberlain to the King's most excellent Majesty; and Philip Earl of Montgomery, &c. Gentleman of his Majesty's Bed-Chamber—both Knights of the most noble Order of the Garter, and our singular good lords.

Right Honorable,

Whilst we study to be thankful in our particular, for the many favors we have received from your Lordships, are fallen upon the ill fortune to mingle two the most diverse things that can be: fear and rashness—rashness in the enterprise, and fear of the success. For, when we value the places your Highnesses sustain, we cannot but know their dignity greater than to descend to the reading of these trifles; and while we name them trifles, we have deprived ourselves of the defense of our dedication.

But since your Lordships have been pleased to think these trifles something, heretofore, and have prosecuted both them and their author living, with so much favor, we hope, that (they outliving him, and he not having the fate, common with some, to be executor to his own writings) you will use the like indulgence toward them, you have done unto their parent. There is a great difference whether any book choose his patrons or find them. This hath done both. For, so much were your Lordships' likings of the several parts, when they were acted, as before they were published, the volume asked to be yours. We have but collected them, and done an office to the dead, to procure his orphans guardians: without ambition either of self-profit or fame: only to keep the memory of so worthy a friend, & fellow alive, as was our SHAKESPEARE by humble offer of his plays to your most noble patronage. Wherein, as we have justly observed no man to come near your Lordships but with a kind of religious address; it hath bin the height of our care, who are the presenters, to make the present worthy of your Highnesses by the perfection.

But, there we must also crave our abilities to be considered, my Lords. We cannot go beyond our own powers: Country hands reach forth milk, cream, fruits, or what they have; and many nations, we have heard, that had not gums and incense, obtained their requests with a leavened cake. It was no fault to approach their gods, by what means they could; and the most, though meanest, of things are made more precious, when they are dedicated to temples. In that name therefore, we most humbly consecrate to your Highnesses these remains of your servant Shakespeare; that what delight is in them, may be ever your Lordships', the reputation his, and the faults ours, if any be committed by a pair so careful to show their gratitude both to the living and the dead, as is

Your Lordships' most bounden
John Heminge
Henry Condell

Appendix D

Epistle of Heminge and Condell to the readers of the First Folio.

To the great Variety of Readers.—From the most able, to him that can but spell: there you are numbered. We had rather you were weighed; especially when the fate of all books depends upon your capacities, and not of your heads alone, but of your purses. Well, it is now public, and you will stand for your privileges we know: to read, and censure. Do so, but buy it first: that doth best commend a book, the stationer says. Then, how odd soever your brains be or your wisdoms, make your license the same, and spare not. Judge your six-pen'orth, your shilling's worth, your five shillings' worth at a time, or higher, so you rise to the just rates, and welcome. But, whatever you do, buy! Censure will not drive a trade or make the jack go. And though you be a magistrate of wit, and sit on the stage at Blackfriars, or the Cockpit, to arraign plays daily, know, these plays have had their trial already and stood out all appeals; and do now come forth quitted rather by a decree of court, then any purchased letters of commendation.

It had been a thing, we confess, worthy to have been wished that the author himself had lived to have set forth, and overseen his own writings; but since it hath been ordained otherwise, and he by death departed from that right, we pray you do not envy his friends the office of their care and pain, to have collected and published them:—and so to have published them, as where before you were abused with divers stolen and surreptitious copies, maimed and deformed by the frauds and stealths of injurious impostors that exposed them, even those are now offered to your view cured and perfect of their limbs, and all the rest absolute in their numbers as he conceived them, —who, as he was a happy imitator of nature, was a most gentle expresser of it. His mind and hand went together, and what he thought he uttered with that easiness, that we have scarce received from him a blot in his papers. But it is not our province, who only gather his works and give them you, to praise him: it is yours that read him. And there, we hope, to your divers capacities, you will find enough both to draw, and hold you; for his wit can no more lie hid than it could be lost. Read him, therefore, and again and again; and if then you do not like him, surely you are in some manifest danger not to understand him, and so we leave you to other of his friends whom if you need can be your guides. If you need them not, you can lead yourselves and others, and such readers we wish him.

John Heminge.
Henrie Condell.

Recommended Reading

Most scholarly books would include a bibliography here, but since this is an edited book and most of its twelve chapters have lists of works cited, we prefer to focus the attention of general readers and Shakespeare students on the same list of highly recommended books that we have mentioned elsewhere in this book. Each of these books includes an extensive bibliography for anyone who is interested in pursuing the issue further. These are also the books we would like judges and jurors in any mock trial of the issue to read, along with the *Declaration of Reasonable Doubt About the Identity of William Shakespeare*.

Pointon, A.J.: *The Man who was Never Shakespeare: The Theft of William Shakespeare's Identity* (Parapress, Tunbridge Wells, Kent, U.K., 2011).

Price, Diana: *Shakespeare's Unorthodox Biography: New Evidence of an Authorship Problem* (paperback with corrections and additions, shakespeare-authorship.com, 2012).

Roe, Richard Paul: *The Shakespeare Guide to Italy: Retracing the Bard's Unknown Travels* (HarperPerennial, 2011).

And for good measure, for those who might enjoy a sometimes serious, sometimes satirical treatment of the issue, we recommend the e-book of comedic actor Keir Cutler, Ph.D., creator of the YouTube video "Shakespeare Authorship Question: Why Was I Never Told This?", shown on the home page of the Shakespeare Authorship Coalition at: www.DoubtAboutWill.org.

Cutler, Keir, Ph.D.: *The Shakespeare Authorship Question: A Crackpot's View* (Kindle edition, Amazon.com, 2013).

Acknowledgments

One of the great pleasures of my involvement with the authorship issue has been getting to know many of the outstanding people who care deeply about it. I'm delighted that this book will call attention to some of our best scholars. Special thanks to the other members of the team that helped to write and edit this book: Bonner Miller Cutting, Frank Davis, Ramon Jiménez, Alex McNeil, A. J. (Tony) Pointon, Thomas Regnier, John Rollett, Earl Showerman, Alexander Waugh and Richard F. Whalen. Additional thanks to my co-editor, Alexander Waugh, for his many contributions. Thanks also to Diana Price for writing *Shakespeare's Unorthodox Biography* and for the use of her Chart of Literary Paper Trails.

I wish to thank Derek Jacobi, Mark Rylance and Michael York for supporting the SAC, and I thank them and professors Ren Draya, Kristin Linklater, Felicia Hardison Londré, Don Rubin, William Rubinstein, Dean Keith Simonton, Peter Sturrock and Richard Waugaman for endorsing this book. Thanks also to those who rebutted "60 Minutes." Thanks to Michael Egan for his helpful early guidance. Thanks to Deborah Greenspan and Shari Reimann at Llumina Press for expediting the publication of this book and doing such a good job with it and to Nick Filin and Joe Skevis for the cover art and final design. The editors and publisher gratefully acknowledge the permission granted to reproduce copyrighted material in this book. Every effort has been made to trace copyright holders and obtain their permission for the use of copyrighted material. We apologize for any errors or omissions and will be happy to make corrections in future editions of this book.

– John M. Shahan

Contributors to "*Shakespeare Beyond Doubt?*"

Bonner Miller Cutting trained as a concert pianist with a Bachelor of Fine Arts degree in piano performance from Tulane University where she was a member of Phi Beta Kappa. She holds a Masters of Music degree from McNeese State University in Lake Charles, LA. Retired from a career as a teacher of piano, she continues to judge piano festivals and competitions. Turning her energies to the Shakespeare Authorship Question, she has given papers at conferences at Concordia University in Portland, OR, as well as the joint conferences of the Shakespeare Fellowship and Shakespeare Oxford Society. She serves on the Boards of the Shakespeare Fellowship and the Shakespeare Authorship Coalition.

Frank M. Davis received his undergraduate training at Emory University in Atlanta, Georgia, and his M.D. degree from Tulane University in New Orleans, Louisiana, graduating *cum laude*. He served residencies in general surgery and Neurological Surgery, the latter completed in 1968. He co-founded and practiced at the Tallahassee Neurological Clinic until his retirement in 1996. Dr. Davis was a member of the American Association of Neurological Surgeons, the American Board of Neurological Surgeons, and a Fellow of the American College of Surgeons and of the Florida Neurosurgical Society (past President). He authored or co-authored a dozen medical publications and since retirement has been involved with the Shakespeare Authorship Question. He has published and presented papers on Shakespeare's medical knowledge and on topics such as *Green's Groatsworth of Wit;* authorship of the poem *Grief of Minde;* literacy in Shakespeare's day; and research on the significance of the autographs of Shakspere and his fellow actors and writers. Dr. Davis is a past President of the Shakespeare Oxford Society (2003-2005).

Ramon Jiménez is the author of two books on Julius Caesar and the ancient Roman Republic. *Caesar Against the Celts* was a selection of the Military History Book Clubs of both the United States and the United Kingdom in 1996. The sequel, *Caesar Against Rome*, published by Praeger in 2000, was a selection of the History Book Club. In the last ten years more than a dozen of his articles and book reviews have appeared in the *Shakespeare Oxford Newsletter* and *The Oxfordian*. Jiménez has a degree in English from U.C.L.A. and lives in Berkeley, California.

Alex McNeil holds a B.A. from Yale University and a J.D., *cum laude*, from Boston College Law School. His professional career was in public service, where he served for 37 years as Court Administrator of the Massachusetts Appeals Court. He became interested in the Shakespeare authorship question in 1992. In 2001 he was one of the founding trustees of the Shakespeare Fellowship; he currently serves as its treasurer and editor of its quarterly newsletter, *Shakespeare Matters*. He also wrote a reference book on American television programming, *Total Television*, four editions of which were published by Penguin Books between 1980 and 1996.

Professor A. J. (Tony) Pointon, is a Chartered Engineer and Physicist and a former Director of Research at Portsmouth University, U.K. He was founder and national Secretary of a union for lecturers and professors in higher education, and Chairman of that union's Legal Panel, appearing for members in employment tribunals and courts of law. He was a Government-appointed member of ACAS, as well as a national-rated chess player. He has been Chairman of the International Dickens Conference, and organized the Dickens Bicentenary Conference at his (real) Birthplace, Portsmouth, in 2012. His book, *The Man Who Was Never Shakespeare*, has ruffled feathers in the Stratford pigeon loft, and his next book, with the provisional title *Great Myths of British History*—with, *inter alia*, chapters on Charles Dickens and Oliver Cromwell, may well ruffle a few more.

Thomas Regnier is an attorney based in Miami, Florida. He received his B.A. in English (Phi Beta Kappa) from Trinity College, Connecticut; his J.D., *summa cum laude*, from the University of Miami School of Law; and his LL.M. from Columbia Law School in New York, where he was a Harlan F. Stone scholar. He previously served as an appellate assistant public defender in Miami, and now practices law with Conroy Simberg in South Florida. He has been a judicial law clerk in the U.S. District Court of the Northern District of Illinois and in the Third District Court of Appeal of Florida. Tom has taught a seminar on "Shakespeare and the Law," as well as other law courses, at the University of Miami School of Law and has also taught at the John Marshall Law School in Chicago. He has presented lectures at Shakespeare conferences on such topics as "The Law in *Hamlet*," and is currently president of the Shakespeare Fellowship.

John M. Rollett studied Physics at Trinity College, Cambridge, and holds a PhD from London University. After several years as a research scientist in the semiconductor industry he joined the Research Department of what is now British Telecommunications, authoring around fifty papers and patents. In retirement he has published a number of papers on literary topics in *Notes and Queries*: an emendation of Shakespeare's sonnet 146 ("Repel These Rebel Powers," 1999) and a follow-up ("The Compositor's Reader," 2001), and more recently "William Shackspere vs. John Clayton," (2012) and "Shakespeare's Sonnet 125: Who Bore the Canopy?" scheduled for September 2013.

John M. Shahan is founder and chairman of the Shakespeare Authorship Coalition and principal author of the *Declaration of Reasonable Doubt About the Identity of William Shakespeare*. He is an independent scholar with degrees in Psychology and Public Health, both from U.C.L.A. He did masters research on the British National Health Service at the University of Bath, and he worked for the California Departments of Health and Mental Health and in exempt positions in the California Governor's Office. His main areas of interest in the authorship controversy are strategic planning, advocacy, paradigm shifts, and creativity and genius. He has co-authored four articles on flaws in stylometric research.

Earl Showerman graduated from Harvard College and the University of Michigan Medical School, and practiced emergency medicine in Oregon for over thirty years. He is past president and medical editor of Epic Software Systems, Inc., and a longtime patron of the Oregon Shakespeare Festival. Dr. Showerman has served as a trustee of the Shakespeare Fellowship and The Shakespeare Authorship Coalition, and was recently elected as an honorary trustee of the Shakespearean Authorship Trust in the U.K. In recent years he published a series of papers in peer-reviewed journals on Shakespeare's "greater Greek," a reexamination of the Greek literary sources for *Hamlet, Macbeth, The Winter's Tale, Much Ado about Nothing*, and *Timon of Athens*. Dr. Showerman is the executive producer of Mignarda's acclaimed recording, *My Lord of Oxenford's Maske*.

Alexander Waugh is General Editor of the 42-Volume scholarly edition of *Complete Works of Evelyn Waugh* for Oxford University Press. He is a book reviewer and author of several critically acclaimed works including *Time* (1999), *God* (2002), *Fathers and Sons* (2004) and *The House of Wittgenstein* (2008). He has presented documentaries on BBC television, was editor and founder of the award winning Travelman Short Story series and composed the music for the stage comedy *Bon Voyage!* which won of the 12th Vivian Ellis Award for Best New Musical. He is Senior Visiting Fellow, University of Leicester.

Richard F. Whalen, author of *Shakespeare: Who Was He?* (Greenwood-Praeger, 1994) has published dozens of research articles and book reviews on the Shakespeare authorship controversy, including articles in *Harper's Magazine* and a special issue of *The Tennessee Law Review* on the controversy. He is co-general editor with Daniel L. Wright of Concordia University, Portland, Oregon, of the Oxfordian Shakespeare Series of the most popular plays, and he co-edited *Othello* (2010) with Ren Draya of Blackburn College. His second edition of *Macbeth* was published in 2013. A graduate of Fordham College, he holds an M.A. from Yale Graduate School.

Lightning Source UK Ltd.
Milton Keynes UK
UKOW061022090713

213483UK00001B/15/P